D1601045

The CIA's
Secret War in Tibet

The CIA's
Secret War in Tibet

Kenneth Conboy and James Morrison

*This Book is full of "facts" - as is
NOT not ~~but unusable~~ in dealing
rare) with CIA "stories". So keep a lot
of salt at hand.*

UNIVERSITY PRESS OF KANSAS

Published by the University Press of Kansas (Lawrence, Kansas 66049), which was organized by the Kansas Board of Regents and is operated and funded by Emporia State University, Fort Hays State University, Kansas State University, Pittsburg State University, the University of Kansas, and Wichita State University

Library of Congress Cataloging-in-Publication Data

Conboy, Kenneth J.
    The CIA's secret war in Tibet / Kenneth Conboy and James Morrison.
        p.   cm.—"(Modern war studies)
    Includes bibliographical references and index.
    ISBN 0-7006-1159-2 (cloth : alk. paper)
        1. United States—Relations—China—Tibet.   2. Tibet
(China)—Relations—United States.   3. Espionage,
American—China—Tibet.   4. United States. Central Intelligence
Agency.   5. Subversive activities—China—Tibet.   6. United
States—Foreign relations—China.   7. China—Foreign relations—United
States.   8. United States—Foreign relations—1945–1989.   I.
Morrison, James.   II. Title.   III. Series.
    E183.8.T55   C66   2002
    327.1273'0515'09045—dc21   2001005247

British Library Cataloguing in Publication Data is available.

Printed in the United States of America

10 9 8 7 6 5 4 3 2 1

The paper used in this publication meets the minimum requirements of the American National Standard for Permanence of Paper for Printed Library Materials Z39.48-1984.

Contents

Maps and Illustrations _____

Preface

"Though a hundred Khampas die," goes a Tibetan proverb, "there are still a thousand Khampa children." While it is true that a disproportionate number of Khampa tribesmen have died in the revolts since the middle of the twentieth century, defiance against Chinese subjugation has become a defining characteristic of Tibetans from all clans and ethnic backgrounds.

The following is a story of how the U.S. government, primarily through the Central Intelligence Agency, came to harness, nurture, and encourage that defiance in one of the most remote covert campaigns of the cold war. This is not the first time that it has been told. Indeed, some of the details—such as apocryphal tales of CIA case officers chanting Tibetan Buddhist mantras to seek solace—have become cliché. Two former CIA officials have even published books on Tibet after clearing the agency's vetting process.

This take on the Tibet story is different. As much as possible, it is told on the record, through the people who managed and fought in the program: from CIA case officers to Tibetan agents to Indian intelligence officials to proprietary aircrews. Many are going public for the first time; many, too, are offering details never before revealed.

It was our intent to tell the story objectively from all angles, especially from the Tibetans' viewpoint. Through their own words and deeds, it becomes possible to cut down the inflated caricatures many Westerners have been fast to paint and thus see the Tibetans as they should be seen: as fallible mortals replete with moments of defeatism, selfishness, and brutal infighting.

Telling the story in this manner is important for several reasons. First, the Tibet saga is an important chapter in the CIA's paramilitary history. In Tibet, new kinds of equipment—aircraft and parachutes, for example—were combat tested under the most extreme conditions imaginable. New communications techniques were tried and perfected. For many of the case officers involved in this process, the Tibet campaign was a defining moment. Not only did the Tibetans win over U.S. officials with their infectious enthusiasm, but the lessons learned in Tibet were used by these officers during subsequent CIA campaigns in places like Laos and Vietnam. Tibet, therefore, became a vital cold war proving ground for CIA case officers and their spy craft.

Second, the story told in these pages is properly placed in the context of the country where most of its programs were staged: India. In past renditions of the

Tibet campaign, India's role gets barely a mention, if at all. In reality, Tibet led Washington and New Delhi to become secret partners over the course of several U.S. administrations; even when relations appeared to be particularly strained during the era of Richard Nixon, there remained a discreet undercurrent of intelligence cooperation. With an understanding of this secretive dimension to Indo-U.S. ties, American involvement in the subcontinent suddenly appears far more nuanced and pragmatic.

Finally, the CIA's secret campaign in Tibet was a vital part of contemporary Tibetan history. Though the agency's assistance was small in absolute terms—the Dalai Lama's older brother, Gyalo Thondup, has since derided it as "a provocation, not genuine help"—it proved pivotal during several key moments. Were it not for the CIA's radio agents, for example, the Dalai Lama might not have arrived safely in exile. And in his early years on Indian soil, the Dalai Lama relied on CIA assistance to get settled. Though the CIA-supported guerrilla army in Mustang proved ineffectual on the ground, the mere fact that there were Tibetan troops under arms was a significant boost to morale in the refugee community. All these factors helped carry the diaspora and its leadership through the darkest years of exile when their cause might otherwise have been forgotten. That the free Tibetan community has been able to survive and even thrive—arguably, the Tibetan issue has a higher profile today than at any time since the 1959 flight of the Dalai Lama—is owed in no small part to the secret assistance channeled by the United States.

This book is based on both written sources and extensive oral interviews. The written sources were gathered primarily from the *Foreign Relations of the United States* series, as well as releases in the Declassified Documents Reference System and relevant media transcripts recorded by the Foreign Broadcast Information Service. For oral sources, Tashi Choedak and Roger McCarthy were particularly helpful in arranging initial contacts with several key participants. Others that deserve special mention are Dale Andradé, Chue Lam, Harry Pugh, MacAlan Thompson, John Dori, and Tom Timmons. John Cross assisted with locating sources in Nepal. Frank Miller generously provided documents on the People's Liberation Army in Tibet.

As with the two other books we coauthored, the attention to detail in these pages is a reflection of James Morrison and his passion for history. Sadly, it is the last time we can appreciate his talents. Before the publication of this work, Jim passed away. With his passing, I lost a dear friend and colleague who can never be replaced. I truly hope this meets his exacting expectations, and it is in his memory that this book is lovingly dedicated.

1. Contact

Even after stripping away centuries of myth and cliché, Tibet still invites hyperbole. This is largely due to its being situated on real estate best described by superlatives. Averaging almost five kilometers above sea level and covering an area the size of the American Southwest, it is surrounded by some of the planet's highest mountain ranges: the Himalayas to the south, the Karakoram to the west, the Kunlun to the north. Within these imposing natural borders, most of northern and western Tibet—a third of the country—is a barren mountain desert of wind-blown dunes crusted with salt deposits. Life in these parts is barely present, nor welcome. In the northeast—in a zone known among Tibetans as the province of Amdo—the terrain is akin to the Mongolian steppes, with its grassy veneer sustaining a sparse population of hardy alpine animals. In the southeast quadrant—known as Kham—Tibet drops slightly in altitude, and the topography devolves into the exaggerated slopes, impossibly narrow valleys, and gnarled conifers normally associated with Chinese watercolors.

It is the central plateau, however, that has become synonymous with the landscape of Tibet. Encompassing the provinces of U and Tsang, it is a harsh, rocky land of hypnotic beauty where, because of the altitude, light seems to intensify color and detail. Here is a world where animal life copes through unique adaptations: an indigenous breed of horse with double the lung capacity of its lowland cousins, or a species of beetle containing a glycerol "antifreeze" that lets it function in the snow.[1]

The cultures of Tibet reflect these various ecosystems. In the northern and western deserts, the parched, frigid dunes have traditionally kept the region free of human habitation, save for transient trade caravans. To the northeast, the sparse population of Amdo finds little recourse on the steppes other than to eke out a living as seminomadic herdsmen—or marauding bandits that prey on the same. In the southeast, residents of Kham make the most of river valleys, using them for both pastureland and terraced agricultural plots. Tall for Asians and often lacking the Mongoloid eye fold (giving them a passing resemblance to American Indians), Khampas have earned a reputation for being clannish, courageous, and socially unpolished. This has not stopped them from making their mark as accomplished traders, plying their goods in China, India, and other parts of Tibet.[2]

Once again, it is in the central plateau where stereotypical Tibetan culture can be found. Clustered around arable meadows, inhabitants of this zone focus on animal husbandry and growing the most robust of crops, such as barley. Central Tibetans at one time also boasted a formidable martial spirit; in the late eighth century, they conquered territory as far south as the Indian plains and as far west as the Muslim lands of the Middle East. Although such prowess has since been replaced by spiritual introspection, central Tibetans have maintained a lock on the country's political power. Dominating the thin upper strata of Tibet's religious bureaucracy and lay aristocracy, they often assume a pampered, elitist air toward the more rural Khampas and Amdowas.

Despite such diversity, all the peoples of Tibet share two basic historical truths. The first is the prominent role of religion in daily life. All Tibetans are believed to have descended from nomadic tribes in the eastern part of central Asia. However, it is not their common ethnic stock but rather a shared devotion to a unique brand of Buddhism—blending metaphysical teachings from India and indigenous Bon shamanism—that has lent them a unifying identity. With its rich pantheon of demigods and demons filling a complex cosmology, Tibetan Buddhism is a superstitious and highly ritualized set of beliefs that permeates society. Traditionally, more than a quarter of Tibet's male population—usually one son in every household—chose a life of religious celibacy. Within this number, specialized monks came to serve in such diverse roles as servants and athletes. Their sprawling monasteries not only doubled as houses of worship and learning centers but also held sway over vast manorial estates that managed the bulk of national economic output. Three-quarters of the national budget, in turn, was dedicated to education for the priesthood and maintenance of religious institutions.[3]

Religion even came to replace Tibet's need for more traditional forms of diplomacy. Beginning with the Mongols in 1207—and succeeded by the Manchus in the eighteenth century—there arose an enduring priest-patron symbiosis whereby the suzerain of mainland Asia was largely held at bay in exchange for Tibetan spiritual tutelage.

The second historical truth is that geography has been Tibet's savior. Occupying a strategic crossroads at the heart of the Eurasian landmass, Tibet has been coveted for centuries by surrounding empires. As a consequence, despite its priest-patron accommodation with the suzerain, it has repeatedly suffered the humiliation of occupation by various neighbors.

Subjugation of the Tibetan population is a wholly different matter. Owing to its high altitude, invaders from the lowlands invariably weaken in Tibet's thin air. Aside from more lasting incursions onto the edge of the Amdo plains or across the Kham river valleys, foreign expeditions against the central plateau

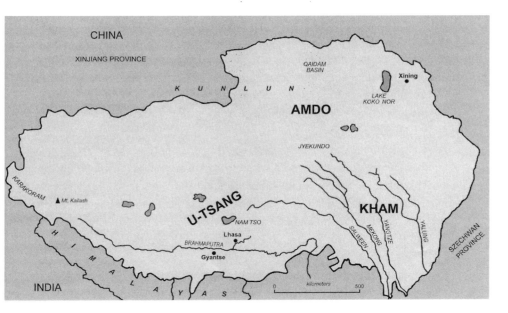

The historical divisions of Tibet

soon found the cost of sustaining a military presence prohibitive, affording the Tibetan heartland extended periods of de facto independence.

By the start of the twentieth century, however, these historical truths were under pressure. The Manchu dynasty, crumbling from within and fraying at the periphery, had its nominal control over Tibet challenged in 1904 by a British expedition staging from India (England, vying with Russia for imperial influence, wanted to extract trading privileges from the Tibetan government). Looking to salvage at least the appearance of authority, the Manchus geared up for a military drive onto the plateau and by 1910 were occupying the Tibetan capital of Lhasa.

Just as quickly, Tibet won a reprieve. In 1911, the Han Chinese—who constituted the majority of the population under Manchu domination—rebelled against their non-Han dynastic overlords. The following year, the last Manchu emperor abdicated the throne and was replaced by a provisional Chinese republican government. Almost overnight, imperial garrisons across the former empire started to revolt, enticing some of the frontier territories to proclaim independence.

This put Tibet in a fix. For centuries, Tibetans had had few qualms about their priest-patron quid pro quo with the Mongols and Manchus. But now facing a

secular republican regime, Tibetans felt no compulsion to continue this arrangement with the Han Chinese. Seizing the opportunity, they declared full autonomy and evicted the Chinese garrison in Lhasa. At the same time, Chinese troops
in Kham began deserting their posts en masse.

Unfortunately for Lhasa, it was not to be a velvet divorce. Suddenly empowered, the republicans had little intention of forfeiting the irredentist claims of
their predecessors. Briefly regrouping in neighboring Szechwan Province, the
Chinese headed back into Kham. With equal determination, they dispatched a
second task force on a southwest bearing from Amdo toward the Tibetan heartland. This latter move came easily for the republicans. Since the eighteenth century, much of Amdo had fallen under the control of local chieftains—primarily
Hiu Muslims—loyal to the Manchu empire. Now these Hiu were encouraged by
the republicans not only to directly impose their will across Amdo but also to
send troops toward central Tibet.

Facing twin threats, the Tibetans looked to fight back—not with religion, as
in the past, but by force of arms. The trouble was that Tibet had nothing
approaching a military force in the modern sense of the term. For generations,
Lhasa had seen little need for a standing army. Among the 3,000 men it retained
as a glorified border force, the weaponry was antiquated and training virtually
nil. This was especially true of the officer corps, where senior rank was doled out
as a favor to nobility.

Scrambling to bolster this paltry force, Tibet approached the British in India
and found a mildly sympathetic ear. A shipment of new rifles was rushed across
the Himalayas; despite the limited number of weapons, they proved a decisive
factor when Lhasa not only stopped China's offensive in Kham but actually
pushed it back in some sectors. A cease-fire was called in 1918, with Kham
bisected into Chinese and Tibetan sectors of influence along the Yangtze River.
Along the Amdo frontier, too, an accommodation was reached with the Hiu.

The truce was not to last. In 1928, Chiang Kai-shek's regimented Kuomintang
party took the reins of power within the republican government. Stoking Han
nationalist sentiment, the Kuomintang reemphasized the goal of a unified
China—including Tibet. To realize this goal in part, that same year it announced
plans to formally absorb Amdo and Kham as the new Chinese provinces of Tsinghai and Sikang, respectively.

In the case of Amdo, Muslim warlord Ma Pu-fang—a loyalist from the early
days of the republic—immediately complied with Kuomintang wishes and
assumed the seat as Tsinghai governor. In Kham, consolidation was more
difficult. Using Khampa clan rivalries as a pretext for intervention, the Chinese

were involved in skirmishes during 1930. After a slow start, they gained momentum and by 1932 were making headway across the zone.

Once again, the Tibetans won a reprieve. Facing an imperial Japanese invasion of Chinese Nationalist territory in Manchuria, and not wanting to be distracted by a Tibetan sideshow, the Kuomintang allowed the Kham battle lines to once again settle along the Yangtze. By the mid-1930s, most of Tibet was again enjoying de facto independence.

For the next decade, the country's isolation served it well. While most of the world was consumed in World War II, Tibet shrewdly walked a neutralist tightrope and emerged unscathed with its traditional way of life intact. It was by no means a perfect existence, however. Tibet's legions of monks were not above internecine struggles that sometimes degenerated into divisive, bloody skirmishes. The religious bureaucracy oversaw a primitive criminal code—major crimes were punishable by mutilation—and enforced economic monopolies that made for an exceedingly wide social gap. Moreover, Tibet's spiritual leaders had shunned the introduction of most Western innovations because they feared that modernity would erode their central standing in society. Tibet, as a result, was the ultimate dichotomy: a nation pushing the envelope in terms of philosophical and spiritual sophistication, yet consciously miring itself in the technology of the Middle Ages.[4]

All this changed in early 1949. To the east of Tibet, a festering civil war in China—pitting Chiang Kai-shek's Kuomintang Nationalists against communist insurgents under Mao Tse-tung—was fast coming to a head. Though better equipped, the Nationalists were riddled with corruption and petty rivalries. By that fall, their defenses were crumbling under the combined weight of ineptitude and relentless communist pressure. Looking to regroup, the Kuomintang leadership escaped with 400,000 of its troops to the island sanctuary of Taiwan.

The communists lost no time filling the void. On 1 October, a victorious Chairman Mao formally inaugurated the People's Republic of China (PRC) from a new capital in Beijing. Its grip, however, was far from consolidated. Besides facing Nationalist strongholds on Taiwan and on the tropical island of Hainan to the south, the PRC saw itself as heir to the Kuomintang claim over Tibet. Making no secret of its intentions, on 1 January 1950 communist state radio declared that the liberation of all three—Taiwan, Hainan, and Tibet—was the goal of the People's Liberation Army (PLA) for the upcoming calendar year.

Of these objectives, Hainan—separated from China by a small strait and home to only a modest Nationalist presence—was the easiest to realize. The communists placed elements of four divisions aboard junks and sailed them to the island in April 1950. With little effort, Hainan was soon occupied.

The other targets posed major challenges. To conquer Taiwan, the PLA not only had to cross a far larger strait but also had to contend with Chiang Kai-shek's concentrated defenses. Counting only limited amphibious and airborne forces in its ranks, the communists—for the time being—could do little besides verbal saber rattling.

Tibet posed a different set of difficulties. Like the Mongols, Manchus, and Nationalists before them, the PLA had to confront both distance and altitude to reach the central Tibetan plateau. With no drivable roads or airfields, trucks and transport aircraft were of little help.

Still, there were compelling reasons for the PLA to go forward with a land-grab against Tibet. For one thing, the communists had already absorbed Amdo. They had also secured a solid foothold in eastern Kham, and the communists outnumbered Tibetan troops across the Yangtze by a ratio of ten to one. For another thing, the Kham citizenry was far from united. Though intensely devout toward Tibet's religious hierarchy on a spiritual level, most Khampas were prone to interclan rivalries and were loyal to only their families, villages, or—at most—districts. A sense of binding nationalist affinity toward Lhasa was usually lacking—in no way helped by the ill-concealed chauvinism on the part of many central Tibetans. Khampas, as a result, were apt to fall behind whichever side—Lhasa or Beijing—offered the most attractive terms for absentee rule.

Nobody epitomized Khampa fence-straddling more than the wealthy Pandatsang family. Led by three brothers who had grown rich on Tibet's lucrative wool trade, the Pandatsangs were as renowned for their commercial skills as for their fiery politicking. The eldest and most orthodox sibling, Yangpel, held several senior Tibetan government titles and lived in the northeastern Indian town of Kalimpong to help run the resident Tibetan trade mission. The second brother, Ragpa, was the family ideologue who initially advocated Tibetan autonomy within republican China (which made him exceedingly unpopular in Lhasa), then tried to ingratiate himself with the advancing communists. Coming full circle, in mid-1950 he was secretly sounding out an accommodation with the Tibetan authorities west of the Yangtze. The youngest brother, Topgyay, was a charismatic firebrand and former officer in the Tibetan military who had led a failed putsch against Lhasa in 1934; he was now hedging the family's bets by offering Beijing support for any PLA invasion of western Kham.

Such waffling was not limited to the Pandatsangs or even the Khampas. Indeed, the PRC could take comfort in the fact that half measures and general confusion had characterized the Tibet policy of key foreign powers for decades. England, for one, paid lip service to "Tibetan autonomy under Chinese suzerainty" but remained cool to giving Lhasa all the aid it wanted or needed. India (which gained its independence from England in 1947) also spoke sympathetically about autonomy but had difficulty embracing Tibet with gestures more substantive than symbolic.[5]

Whereas British and Indian policy on Tibet often meandered between word and deed, it was nothing compared with the mental whiplash caused by the divergent views within the U.S. government. Not until World War II did Washington seriously explore the implications of a U.S.-Tibet relationship. Almost immediately, this resulted in a schism among policy-making bodies. On one side was the Office of Strategic Services (OSS), America's wartime spy agency, and the U.S. mission in New Delhi, both of which advocated good-faith gestures toward Lhasa. This mind-set was behind the December 1942 visit to Tibet by two OSS officers—Captain Ilya Tolstoy and Lieutenant Brooke Dolan—ostensibly to survey an Allied supply route to China through Tibetan territory. Opposing such moves were top State Department officials who, out of deference to America's Chinese allies, did not want to stray from U.S. recognition of what the Kuomintang declared was its sovereign jurisdiction.

For the duration of World War II, these two camps pursued separate and often conflicting agendas. For a brief period after the Allied victory, OSS pragmatism fully gave way to the countervailing pro-China bias. But by the summer of 1949, with Kuomintang defeat in the Chinese civil war seen as increasingly likely, the United States belatedly entertained thoughts of a policy shift. The impetus for this rethinking came from American diplomats in both India and China, who suggested that the United States weigh the advantages of courting Tibet before control was forfeited to the communists.

Back in Washington, policy makers were not swayed. Even when members of the Tibetan cabinet made a desperate plea for U.S. assistance in gaining membership in the United Nations that December, Secretary of State Dean Acheson flatly discouraged the idea, for fear that it might force Beijing's hand and result in a quick takeover. Although Washington might not have liked the idea of losing Tibet to communism, it appeared loath to do anything to stop it.[6]

None of this was lost on the PRC. By the beginning of 1950, the PLA had secretly charged its Southwest Military Command with the task of consolidating control across Kham. After massing east of the Yangtze early that spring, patrols crossed the river in late May. Apparently intent only on testing Tibetan resolve, the Chinese soon halted the probes and resumed a riverside stare-down.

Beijing had reason to pace its moves. Within a month after the May incursion into Kham, the other side of Asia grew hot as North Korean troops spilled into South Korea. For the next few months, communist columns sliced easily through the southern defenses and nearly reached the bottom of the peninsula. But after winning a United Nations mandate of support, U.S.-led reinforcements rushed to the front and by 1 October had the North Korean army reeling back toward the PRC border.

For Beijing, the turn of events in Korea was both a setback to the worldwide communist movement and a direct threat to its frontier. Throughout the month of September, statements out of the PRC grew increasingly shrill with each defeat of its North Korean ally. But with world attention now focused on East Asia, North Korea's misfortunes created an opportunity in Tibet. At the end of the first week of October, China ordered 20,000 of its troops to "realize the peaceful liberation of Tibet."[7]

In Lhasa, the Chinese incursion shook Tibet's authorities to the core. Although vastly outnumbered, the Tibetan army theoretically could have exploited Kham's rugged topography to force a protracted guerrilla campaign. Squandering this advantage, it chose instead a strategy that hinged on the conventional goal of defending the town of Chamdo. It was hardly an enlightened choice. Situated on the western bank of the Mekong headwaters, Chamdo was isolated and exposed. This allowed the PLA to traverse the Mekong at multiple points and easily cut the town's avenues of retreat. On 19 October, after a pathetic defensive showing by the local garrison, Chamdo surrendered to Chinese control. After the Tibetan commissioner-general was taken prisoner, he promptly signed over the rest of Kham to the PRC.

Though Tibet was on the ropes, the world barely took notice. This was because within a week after Chamdo fell, Beijing made good on its saber rattling and dispatched a massive intervention force to the Korean peninsula. Staggered by waves of PLA infantry, United Nations troops were forced to retreat south.

With global attention fixed on Korea, the PLA pondered its next move in Tibet. Although China could take satisfaction in how easily it had taken Kham, the Korean conflict had forced the PRC to push forward its timetable and initiate the Tibet operation before adequate preparations were complete. For example, Tibet still lacked a transportation network to support a military occupation of the central plateau. Moreover, it was late in the season, and the combination of snow and altitude would work against the PLA's lowland troops. For the interim, then, Beijing's rule hinged on co-opting Tibet's existing monastic struc-

ture. In particular, it needed to secure support from the kingdom's most powerful figure, the Dalai Lama.

If religion is the lifeblood of Tibet, the Dalai Lama is its heart. A by-product of
Tibet's priest-patron relationship with the Mongols, the title of Dalai Lama originated in the sixteenth century when a prominent monk, or lama, met ranking
Mongol chieftain Altan Khan. In an inspired exchange, the lama declared that
the Mongol was an incarnation of a great warlord from an earlier time, while he
himself was the incarnation of that warlord's spiritual adviser. By flattering the
khan in this manner, the lama was looking to win critical Mongol support for his
particular sect of Tibetan Buddhism. The khan was duly impressed and bestowed
the monk with the title *Dalai*—a partial Mongolian translation of the lama's
name—and he was thereafter known as the Dalai Lama.[8]

In naming himself an incarnation, the Dalai Lama was not breaking new theological ground. Already, the practice was entrenched among prominent Tibetan
monasteries for reasons of statecraft. By using divination to identify a child as
the reborn spirit of a recently deceased—and celibate—senior lama, the sects
could retain a sense of order in the succession process for their chief abbots. The
Dalai Lama took this a step further, posthumously naming two earlier monastic
leaders as his first and second incarnations.

When the third Dalai Lama died, a search commenced for his reborn soul.
Having already won considerable favor with the Mongols, the sect looked to
cement that support by shrewdly naming Altan Khan's great-grandson as the
fourth incarnation. The tactic worked: by the time the fifth Dalai Lama came to
power, he was able to count on firm Mongol backing to spread both his religious
and his temporal authority across Tibet.

The fifth Dalai Lama then asked his subjects to make an extraordinary leap
of faith. Besides calling himself an incarnation of previous sect leaders, he boldly
declared himself the earthly manifestation of one of Tibet's most popular divini-
ties, the Bodhisattva of Compassion. Again, this had precedent: many other Asian
rulers of the period—in Cambodia and Indonesia, for example—claimed similar celestial authority.

Coming to the fore during a golden era in Tibet's history, the fifth Dalai Lama
fit easily into the role of god-king. Subsequent Dalai Lamas, however, did not
have it so good. Several were murdered in their prime, and most retained power
for only a few short years. Most, too, oversaw only theological decisions; political control remained firmly in the hands of a powerful bureaucracy.

It was not until the turn of the twentieth century that the Dalai Lama—by then in his thirteenth incarnation—again became Tibet's undisputed religious and temporal leader. By all measures, it was a critical juncture in Tibetan history. Coming off a decade of self-imposed isolation, the country had devolved into a technological backwater. Moreover, several foreign powers—the British, Manchus, and even Russians—were all anxiously knocking at its gates.

Faced with these developments, Tibet's conservative bureaucracy had few answers. The thirteenth Dalai Lama, in contrast, met the challenge by offering a relatively warm welcome to the introduction of modern innovations. He also proved a canny survivor, twice eluding capture by fleeing abroad during a pair of short-lived foreign invasions.

By the time the thirteenth Dalai Lama died in 1933, he left behind a mixed legacy. Despite early momentum, most of his attempts at modernization were ultimately stymied by the religious elite. The country, as a result, had yet to emerge from its primeval status. Still, Tibet was arguably enjoying greater independence than at any time over the last few centuries.

It was with this benchmark fresh in Tibetan minds that religious search parties scoured the kingdom for the Dalai Lama's reborn spirit. In 1937, their quest came to an end. In a small Amdo farming village, a precocious two-year-old was identified as their ruler's fourteenth incarnation. After being brought to the capital—where he immediately became the subject of national adulation—the boy began intensive monastic schooling. Under normal circumstances, he would have continued his studies until the age of eighteen before being formally invested with secular authority. But after Beijing's invasion of Kham in October 1950, Tibet feared an imminent move against the central plateau. Desperate, the Tibetan government waived three years of preparation and on 17 November officially recognized the fifteen-year-old Dalai Lama as the kingdom's supreme ruler.

Though bright and energetic, the youthful leader was a most unlikely savior. Despite being better read than most of his cloistered predecessors, he was unversed in diplomacy and had no ready solution to counter the approaching Chinese juggernaut. Compounding his quandary was the fact that his ecclesiastical court of advisers was divided on how to deal with the PRC. Many senior lamas were inclined to negotiate away most of Lhasa's trappings of autonomy—in economic, national security, and foreign policy, for example—in exchange for a free hand in internal affairs. Such thinking was understandable, given that recent Tibetan history was rife with examples of Lhasa's muddling through unscathed from similar foreign threats.

Other Tibetan officials—led by Thupten Woyden Phala, a close assistant of the Dalai Lama, and Surkhang Shape, one of the country's few foreign envoys—were far less willing to concede their newfound freedoms. This faction had been behind the appeal for support at the United Nations in late 1949. Ignored the first time, Tibet again petitioned the world body in November 1950 to take up its case against Beijing's aggression. Once more, however, Tibet received little sympathy.

Finding deaf ears among the international community and fearful of capture if he remained in Lhasa, the Dalai Lama responded in the tradition of his immediate predecessor: he fled the capital. Disguised as a layman and escorted by an entourage of 200, he stole out of Lhasa on the night of 20 December and worked his way south toward the border town of Yatung, just twenty-four kilometers from the princely protectorate of Sikkim.

As this was taking place, American diplomats in neighboring India did what they could to monitor the Dalai Lama's movements. Perhaps none took a greater interest than the U.S. ambassador to India, Loy Henderson. Dubbed a "quintessential Cold Warrior" by one Foreign Service officer under his watch, Henderson had long harbored deep concern for Tibet, especially the threat of PRC control extending across the Himalayas. As far back as the summer of 1949 he had lobbied for a more proactive U.S. policy toward Lhasa to offset this feared Chinese advance, including sending a U.S. envoy from India to the Tibetan capital and leaving behind a small diplomatic mission.[9]

Despite the ambassador's expressed urgency, Washington dragged its feet on approving any bold moves. Frustrated, Ambassador Henderson felt that the stakes were growing too high to afford continued neglect, especially after the Dalai Lama reached Yatung in early 1951. Unless there was some immediate future indication of moral and military support from abroad, he cabled Washington on 12 January, the youthful monarch might leave his kingdom and render ineffective any future resistance to Chinese rule.[10]

But if the exile of the Dalai Lama posed problems, Henderson saw it as preferable to having him return to Lhasa. To prevent the latter, the ambassador took the initiative in March to pen a letter to the monarch. Written on Indian-made stationery and lacking a signature—thereby affording the United States plausible deniability if it was intercepted—the note implored the Tibetan leader not to move back to the capital for fear that he would be manipulated by Beijing. The letter further urged the Dalai Lama to seek refuge overseas, preferably in the predominantly Buddhist nation of Ceylon (now Sri Lanka).

Informing Washington of the note after it had been written, Henderson was in for a surprise. Finally coming around to his way of thinking, the State Department lent its approval to the scheme, with only minor editorial changes. Two copies of the anonymous appeal were eventually printed: one carried to Yatung by Heinrich Harrer, the Dalai Lama's Austrian tutor who had fled Lhasa shortly before the monarch's departure, and the second turned over to a Tibetan dignitary in Kalimpong during mid-May. Those forwarding the letter were told to discreetly convey that it came from the U.S. ambassador.

The Dalai Lama did not take long to respond. On 24 May, his personal representative sought out U.S. diplomats in Calcutta to clarify several points regarding potential exile. Among other things, the monarch wanted to know if Washington would grant him asylum in America and if the United States would extend military aid to a theoretical anti-Chinese resistance movement after his departure from Tibetan soil. He also wanted permission for his oldest brother, Thubten Norbu, to visit the United States.

Before the United States could respond, a shock came over the airwaves on 26 May. Three months earlier, the Dalai Lama had dispatched two groups of officials to China in a desperate bid to appease Beijing and keep the Kham invasion force at bay. Arriving in the Chinese capital by mid-April, neither group had been authorized by the Dalai Lama to make binding decisions on the kingdom's behalf. Despite this, several weeks of stressful talks took their toll: on 23 May, all the Tibetan emissaries lent their names to a seventeen-point agreement with China that virtually wiped out any prospect of an autonomous Tibetan identity.

When news of the pact was broadcast three days later over Chinese state radio, it was a devastating blow to the Dalai Lama. Knowing that the monarch would be under mounting pressure to formulate a response to Beijing, Henderson received approval on 2 June to grant U.S. asylum to the Dalai Lama and a 100-man entourage—provided both India and Ceylon proved unreceptive. Washington was also prepared to provide military aid if India was amenable to transshipment. Finally, Henderson was authorized to extend U.S. visas to Thubten Norbu and a single servant, though both had to pay their own expenses while in America.

Given the fast pace of events, the embassy decided to send a U.S. diplomat to Kalimpong to deal directly with Tibetan officials at their resident trade mission. These officials were shuttling to and from the Dalai Lama's redoubt at Yatung, and this offered the fastest means of negotiating with the isolated monarch. Because Kalimpong fell within the purview of the American consulate general in Calcutta, Vice Consul Nicholas Thacher was chosen for the job.[11]

There was a major stumbling block with such indirect diplomacy, however. The United States was looking to advance its Tibet policy in a third country, and that country—India—had its own national interests at heart. Despite being condemned by Beijing in 1949 as the "dregs of humanity," New Delhi was doing its best to remain on good terms with China. This precluded Indian officials from being taken into Washington's confidence. Thacher, therefore, needed to negotiate in the shadows.

With little time to concoct an elaborate charade, the American vice consul prepared for the long drive from Calcutta. Taking along his wife, young child, and nanny as cover, Thacher was to explain his Kalimpong trip as a holiday respite if questioned by Indian authorities. Before leaving, he was coached in the use of a primitive code based on the local scenery. Because his only means of communicating from Kalimpong was via telegraph—no doubt monitored by Indian intelligence—he would rely on this code to send updates to the Calcutta consulate.

Heading north, Thacher and his family drove thirteen hours to the hill station of Darjeeling. Like other British hill resorts, Darjeeling had been a summer capital for British colonial administrators looking to escape the sweltering lowlands. Like other hill stations, too, the town had earned fame as a recreation center for the social elite; its grand lodges and scenic gardens were set against the breathtaking backdrop of Kanchenjunga, the world's third tallest mountain. Darjeeling was further renowned for producing the champagne of teas; picked from Chinese bushes grown on the surrounding estates, British connoisseurs rated the local leaves as the best in the subcontinent.

Driving another fifty kilometers east, Thacher pulled into Kalimpong on 15 June. Compared with Darjeeling and its amenities, Kalimpong ranked as a minor resort. Still, the town factored prominently in the trans-Himalayan economy because for generations it had served as the final destination for mule caravans hauling products—primarily wool—from Tibet. At any given time, there was a significant community of Tibetan merchants in town, making it a logical site for that country's only overseas trade office.

After dropping off his family at an inn run by Scottish expatriates, Thacher had little trouble locating the Tibetan mission. Entering, he introduced himself in English to the ensemble of officials. Sizing up the lone youthful diplomat, they reacted with collective disappointment. "They were expecting more," he surmised.[12]

Given few specific instructions, Thacher set about explaining the U.S. offer to grant asylum and material assistance. Very quickly, the vice consul was struck by the lack of realism displayed by Lhasa's envoys. "There was a sense of the absurd," he later commented. "They were talking wistfully in terms of America providing them with tanks and aircraft." Thacher did his best to downplay expectations before taking his leave and making his way to the telegraph office to send a coded report to Calcutta. "It probably amused the Indian intelligence officers who were monitoring the transmissions," said Thacher. "They never raised the issue with us, probably because they thought it would not amount to much and was not worth the trouble of souring Indo-U.S. relations."[13]

If this was the case, the Indians were right. Hearing of the latest U.S. promises, the Tibetans found little reason for cheer. The offer of U.S. asylum, for example, was to be granted only if Asian options were exhausted, even though the Dalai Lama was adamant that he wanted exile only in America. Military aid, too, was moot, because it was contingent on Indian approval—a near impossibility, given New Delhi's desire to maintain cordial ties with China.

About the only bright spot in the U.S. proposal was the visa for the Dalai Lama's oldest brother. Twenty-nine years old, Thubten Norbu was an important Tibetan religious figure in his own right. As a child, he had been named the incarnation of a famed fifteenth-century monk. Studying at the expansive Kumbum monastery not far from his home village in Amdo, Norbu had risen to chief abbot by 1949. When Amdo was occupied by the PLA that fall, he came under intense Chinese pressure to lobby his brother on Beijing's behalf. Feigning compliance, he ventured to Lhasa in November 1950. But rather than sell the PRC, he presented a graphic report of Chinese excesses in Amdo.[14]

Because Beijing no doubt viewed Norbu's act as treachery, the Dalai Lama was anxious to see his brother leave Tibet. He succeeded up to a point, spiriting Norbu to Kalimpong by the first week of June 1951. But with Indian Prime Minister Jawaharlal Nehru doing his best to remain warm with the Chinese, there was ample reason to suspect that the Indian authorities would soon make life uncomfortable for him. The promise of a U.S. visa offered the chance for a timely exit from the subcontinent.

Just when Norbu's departure seemed secure, however, complications arose. Neither he nor his accompanying servant had passports, and they had fled Tibet with insufficient funds to pay for extended overseas travel. Thus, both of them needed to quickly secure some form of sponsorship.

At that point, the U.S. Central Intelligence Agency (CIA) stepped forward with a ready solution. By coincidence, only weeks earlier the agency had inaugurated the perfect vehicle for discreetly channeling financial support to persons like the Dalai Lama's brother. On 18 May, the San Francisco–based Committee for a Free

Asia (CFA) had been formally unveiled to the public as a means to "render effective assistance to Asians in advancing personal and national liberty throughout their homelands." The committee's charter further declared its intention to assist noncommunist travelers, refugees, and exiles in order to "strengthen Asian resistance to communism." Left unsaid was the fact that the committee was made possible by financial assistance from the CIA.[15]

The plight of Thubten Norbu meshed perfectly with the committee's goals. On 18 June, the embassy in New Delhi was informed that full sponsorship of Norbu's U.S. visit would be assumed by the CFA. If quizzed by the press, Norbu would allegedly be seeking medical treatment for rheumatism of the legs and might also use the opportunity to take English language classes at the University of California at Berkeley, near the committee's headquarters.[16]

With the sponsorship issue resolved and using temporary Indian identification papers (New Delhi, eager to avoid diplomatic embarrassment, had facilitated a quick departure), Norbu arrived in Calcutta on 24 June with plans to catch a flight to the United States within two weeks. Before leaving, he met with members of the U.S. consulate and was informed that Washington would support a third Tibetan appeal to the United Nations, provided the Dalai Lama publicly disavowed the 23 May agreement with China. Norbu assured the diplomats that his brother, despite his curious silence to date, did not approve of the May pact and was still intent on seeking overseas asylum.[17]

As scheduled, Norbu departed India on 5 July. Accompanying him was his loyal servant Jentzen Thondup. Two years Norbu's senior, Jentzen hailed from a neighboring village in Amdo and had tended to his master since the latter's schooling at Kumbum. Neither spoke much English, though they carried a guidebook written forty-two years earlier by an Indian Baptist missionary. Landing in London in transit, they reportedly answered questions at the immigration counter with such inappropriate retorts as, "There are a great many landlords under the British."[18]

From London, the pair continued to New York. Getting off the plane, they were shocked to be greeted by a white man speaking their native Amdo dialect. Their chaperone, Robert Ekvall, had a fascinating personal history. Born in 1898 on the China-Tibet border near Amdo, Ekvall had grown up speaking Chinese and Tibetan. After primary school, he worked as a missionary among the Chinese, Muslims, and Tibetans in that area. In 1944, he joined the U.S. Army as a China area expert and served in that country as a military attaché near the end of the civil war. Given his unique linguistic ability and cultural sensitivity, Ekvall was put on retainer by the CFA to assist Norbu for the duration of his stay in America.

As his first order of business, Ekvall escorted Norbu and Jentzen for a night's rest at New York's posh Waldorf-Astoria. Reporters curious about the new arrivals were fed the bromide about Norbu's rheumatism and intended study at Berkeley. In reality, the Tibetans were whisked the following day to Washington for meetings with State Department and CIA officials.

Norbu had arrived at a critical juncture. By the close of June, Thacher and his family had concluded their faux vacation and returned to Calcutta. In order to maintain coverage in Kalimpong, Thacher was to be replaced by another consulate official. Given that assignment was Robert Linn, head of the small CIA base in Calcutta.

By chance, several weeks earlier, Linn had happened across a key Tibetan contact. While exploring Calcutta by foot, he had taken note of an Asian woman and three men dressed in ornate ethnic attire who had taken up residence near the consulate. Striking up a conversation with the group, Linn received a windfall when he learned that the woman was Tsering Dolma, the elder sister of Norbu and the Dalai Lama. She had been in Calcutta since early 1950 seeking medical treatment.[19]

When Linn got orders to proceed to Kalimpong, he immediately sought out Tsering Dolma, who agreed to escort him and assist with introductions. Despite her company, however, he found the Kalimpong crowd of little help in swaying the teenage monarch and his conservative courtesans across the border at Yatung. On 11 July, Linn passed word to the Calcutta consulate that the Dalai Lama intended to return to Lhasa in ten days.[20]

With time running short, officials in Washington imposed on Norbu to translate a message for the Dalai Lama into Tibetan. This, along with two more unsigned letters prepared by the U.S. embassy in New Delhi, was quickly forwarded to Yatung. Embassy officials even flirted with fanciful plans for Heinrich Harrer, the monarch's former tutor, and George Patterson, an affable Scottish missionary who had once preached in Kham, to effectively kidnap the Dalai Lama and bundle him off to India.

All these efforts were to no avail. On 21 July, the monarch heeded advice channeled under trance by the state oracle and departed Yatung on a slow caravan back to the Tibetan capital. Still unwilling to concede defeat, American diplomats continued to smuggle unsigned messages to the Dalai Lama while he was en route. Trying a slightly more bold tack, Ambassador Henderson received approval on 10 September to write a signed note on official government letterhead. Tibetan representatives in India were allowed to briefly view the document the following week and verbally convey its contents to their leader. The United

States, read this latest message, was now prepared to publicly support Tibetan autonomy. In addition, Washington vowed to assist an anti-Chinese resistance movement with such material as may be "feasible under existing political and physical conditions."

Even if the Dalai Lama's interest was piqued by the latest round of promises, it was probably too late for him to act. He arrived in Lhasa during mid-August, and PLA troops were sighted in the capital by early the following month. On 28 September, the Tibetan national assembly convened to debate the controversial seventeen-point agreement signed the previous May. Less than one month later, confirmation was sent to Mao Tse-tung that the kingdom accepted the accord. Tibet was now officially part of the People's Republic of China.

2. Tightrope

On 13 February 1952, Thubten Norbu and his chaperone-cum-translator Robert Ekvall arrived at Foggy Bottom for a meeting with the new assistant secretary of state for Far Eastern affairs, John Allison. The reason for the tryst was the arrival of a secret letter from the Dalai Lama addressed to his eldest brother.

Messages from the Tibetan leader had come before, but nothing like this. In marked contrast to the urgency of earlier communications, the Dalai Lama was now subdued and measured. Four months after the Tibetan government had conceded on the seventeen-point agreement with Beijing, the monarch was now clearly hedging his bets. The Chinese were thus far being "correct and careful," he wrote, and he was determined to treat them in kind. As if to offset any perceived tilt toward Beijing, the letter instructed Norbu to maintain contact with U.S. officials and not allow for any "misunderstandings."

That Tibet's spiritual leader was writing in such pragmatic terms was not necessarily bad news at the upper echelons of the State Department. It had been senior department officials, after all, who had kept Ambassador Henderson at bay for so long. Now using the Dalai Lama's own sentiments as cover, Allison had no need to apologize when he assured Norbu that the United States remained sympathetic but noncommittal. Allison went further, advocating that the United States not invite undue attention to Tibet by making any public statements.[1]

Although Allison was effectively writing off Tibet, Norbu saw it otherwise. Judging from the pleasantries exchanged around the room, he logically concluded that the Americans concurred with the Dalai Lama's approach. Offering thanks to Allison, he departed.

It would be another three months before Norbu was back in contact, this time offering a decidedly different spin on events in his homeland. Allegedly tapping his own private sources, he claimed that the Dalai Lama was continuing with a long-term master plan to appear compliant with China's wishes while secretly organizing resistance against them. Tibetans in the capital, he claimed, had recently sworn oaths of allegiance to the Dalai Lama and affirmed their opposition to the Chinese.

Hearing this news, State Department officials in Washington admitted that they had little ability to verify its validity. Norbu, after all, had a vested interest in making it sound as if his brother were playing the Chinese according to a clever script, not the other way around. Still, the department's China desk thought that there was enough circumstantial evidence indicating that the Chinese in Tibet were encountering difficulties. On the pretext that the United States should allow China to make further missteps, the desk counseled continued restraint from both public statements and attempts to contact persons in Tibet who might be making the first move toward organizing an anticommunist resistance. Taking a pen to the margin of the source text, Assistant Secretary of State Allison wrote, "I agree."[2]

With those words, any residual thoughts of an activist Tibet policy by Washington entered into full remission. Plans to come to Lhasa's defense—overtly or covertly, verbally or physically—were shelved. Norbu himself lost relevance; in short order he left Washington for a brief English course at Berkeley before traveling to Japan for the 1952 conference of the Buddhist World Fellowship. While in Tokyo, both Norbu's sponsorship by the Committee for a Free Asia and his Indian identification papers expired.[3] In a telling rejection, his application for readmission to the United States was turned down, stranding the Dalai Lama's sibling in Japan as a gilded refugee.

Although Washington had no intention of coming to Tibet's assistance, it still needed to keep apprised of events in the region. In the summer of 1952, however, Tibet was more inaccessible than ever. Much as Ambassador Henderson had lamented a year earlier, most reports forwarded from the New Delhi embassy were either unreliable extracts from the Indian press or "wishfully warped" official views from the government of India.[4] One notable exception was the unique window provided by the princely state of Sikkim.

A sparsely populated cluster of mountains roughly half the size of Connecticut, Sikkim appeared to be an unlikely font of information. But squeezed among India to the south, Nepal to the west, Tibet to the north, and Bhutan to the southeast, it sat at the crossroads of the Himalayas. Sikkim also possessed several key mountain passes linking the Indian lowlands to the Tibetan plateau. These features attracted the attention of the British, who absorbed the territory in 1817 as an appendage to their vast Indian holdings.

Over the next 130 years, the British afforded Sikkim semiautonomous status and allowed its royals to remain in effective control. Since the sixteenth century, a line of chogyal, or "heavenly kings," had been both temporal and spiritual rulers of the state. Devotees of the same stylized form of Buddhism practiced in Tibet, these Sikkimese kings presided over an elite caste with its share of palace intrigue—some of it deadly. In the eighteenth century, for example, a half sister of the reigning *chogyal* helped assassinate the king by opening an artery as he rested in a hot tub; she was later strangled with a scarf for her treachery.

It was with this traditional system of leadership intact that Sikkim approached the mid-twentieth century. By 1947, however, its future was suddenly in doubt. The British were gone, and a new set of Indian authorities had come to power in New Delhi. Although the princely states were theoretically entitled to declare their independence, in reality, the Indian leadership was making every attempt to entice them into a federal republic.

Sikkim was one such case. Beginning in 1947 and continuing for the next three years, its royals scrambled to salvage some form of autonomy that would safeguard their exalted status. Unfortunately for Sikkim, its reigning monarch, Maharaja Tashi Namgyal (Britain had insisted on the change from *chogyal* to the lesser term *maharaja*, or prince, to keep Sikkim's leader on a par with other rulers across the subcontinent), was hardly in a position to negotiate. An inscrutable recluse, he frittered away most of his time painting and meditating.[5]

The job of negotiating with the Indians went to the prince's son and heir apparent, Palden Thondup. Commonly known as the *maharaja kumar*, or crown prince, he was a relative newcomer to politics. Recognized at birth as the reincarnation of his late uncle, he appeared destined for a monastic life. But after the untimely death of his elder brother during World War II, he suddenly moved up the succession ladder and was thrust into government service.

Charming and well educated—he had spent time at a British college—the crown prince quickly assumed all governing responsibilities from his father. In 1947, he ventured to New Delhi to initiate talks with the Indian government. Through force of personality, he was able to win a three-year stay on any decision about Sikkim's integration into the republic. In early 1950, he again ventured to New Delhi. If anything, his audience had grown more fickle in the interim. The previous year, the Indian government had granted generous autonomy to the neighboring kingdom of Bhutan, and it was reluctant to make concessions to yet another Himalayan territory.

Undeterred, the crown prince, then only twenty-seven years old, persisted with a convincing legal pitch that the special privileges extended by the British set Sikkim apart from the other princely states. The result was a December treaty whereby the protectorate of Sikkim was free to manage domestic matters but allowed India to regulate its foreign affairs, defense, and trade.

The Sikkimese royals saw leeway in this pact. Though prohibited from making independent foreign policy, they believed that it was still within their right to retain a degree of international personality. This held obvious appeal for the

Sikkim

United States, which appreciated Sikkim's unique perspective on Himalayan events, on account of its royals being related by blood and marriage to the elite in neighboring Bhutan and Tibet. But it also meant walking a fine diplomatic tightrope, as American contact with the Sikkimese ran the risk of agitating India.[6] In the spring of 1951, the U.S. consulate in Calcutta gingerly tested the waters. The Chinese had already invaded Kham, and Larry Dalley, a young CIA officer who had arrived in the city the previous fall under cover of vice consul, was eager to collect good intelligence on events across the border. He knew that two members of Sikkim's royal family frequented Calcutta and would be good sources of information.

The first, Pema Tseudeun, was the older sister of the crown prince. Popularly known by the name Kukula, she was the stunning, urbane archetype of a Himalayan princess. Her contact with American officials actually dated back to 1942, when she had been in Lhasa as the teenage wife of a Tibetan nobleman. OSS officers Tolstoy and Dolan had just arrived in the Tibetan capital that December and were preparing to present a gift from President Franklin Roosevelt to the young Dalai Lama. The gift was in a plain box, and the two Americans were scrambling to find suitable wrapping. "I came forward," she recalls, "and donated the bright red ribbon in my hair."[7]

For the next eight years, Kukula had it good. Married into the powerful Phunkang family (her father-in-law was a cabinet official), she now had considerable holdings in Lhasa. After the Chinese invasion of Kham, however, all was in jeopardy. Leaving many of her possessions back in Tibet, she fled to the safety of Sikkim. There she became a close adviser to the crown prince, accompanying her brother to New Delhi that December to finalize their state's treaty with India.

The second royal in Calcutta, Pema Choki, was Kukula's younger sister. Better known as Princess Kula, she was every bit as beautiful and sophisticated as her sibling. Kula was also married to a Tibetan of high status; her father-in-law, Yutok Dzaza, had been a ranking official at the trade mission in Kalimpong. Both Kukula and Kula were regulars on the Indian diplomatic circuit. "They came to many of the consulate's social functions," remembers Nicholas Thacher, "and were known for their ability to perform all of the latest dance numbers."[8]

Not all of that contact, CIA officer Dalley determined, was social. After arranging for a meeting with Princess Kukula at his apartment, he asked her if she thought the Tibetans might need anything during their current crisis. Kukula suggested that they could use ammunition and said that she would bring a sample of what they needed to their next meeting. True to her word, the princess appeared at Dalley's apartment bearing a round for a British Lee-Enfield rifle. She also mentioned that waves of Tibetan traders came to India almost quarterly to get treatment for venereal disease (a scourge in Tibet) and to pick up food shipments for import. Particularly popular at the time were tins of New Zealand fruits packed in heavy syrup.

Based on this information, Dalley devised a plan to substitute bullets for the fruit. He went as far as pouching Kukula's bullet and a sample tin label to CIA headquarters—all to no avail. "They laughed at the scheme," he recalls.[9]

Later that spring, the U.S. consulate in Calcutta again turned to the Sikkimese royals for help. At the time, the Dalai Lama was holed up in the border town of Yatung, and CIA officer Robert Linn was brainstorming ways of facilitating indirect contact with the monarch. Two of those he asked to assist in passing notes were Kukula and Kula. Although the Tibetan leader ultimately elected not to go into exile, it was not for want of trying on the part of the princesses.[10]

One year later, Sikkim's royals once more proved their willingness to help. In June 1952, Kukula approached the consulate with an oral message from the Dalai Lama. She had just returned from a visit to her in-laws in Lhasa, and although she had not personally seen the Dalai Lama, she had been given information from Kula's father-in-law, Yutok Dzaza, who had been in Lhasa at the same time, circulating among senior government circles.[11] Kukula quoted the Dalai Lama as saying that when the time was propitious for liberation, he hoped the United States would give material aid and moral support. Kukula also passed observations about food shortages in Lhasa and about the desperate conditions of the vast majority of Chinese troops in that city.[12]

To maintain the flow of such useful information, the consulate continued its discreet courtship of the Sikkimese sisters. Part of the task fell to Gary Soulen, the ranking Foreign Service officer in Calcutta. In September 1952, Soulen obtained Indian approval to visit Sikkim for a nature trek. Venturing as far as the Natu pass on the Tibetan frontier, Princess Kukula accompanied him on the trip and imparted more anecdotes about the situation in Lhasa.[13]

CIA officials, too, were looking to make inroads. Kenneth Millian, who replaced Larry Dalley in October 1952 under cover as vice consul, counted the Sikkimese as one of his primary targets. By that time, however, the Indians were doing everything in their power to obstruct contact. On one of the rare occasions when he got permission to visit the Sikkimese capital of Gangtok, for example, New Delhi leaked a false report to the press that the American vice president—not vice consul—was scheduled to make an appearance. As a result, entire villages turned out expecting to see Richard Nixon. "Discreet contact," lamented Millian, "became all but impossible."[14]

Occasional trysts with the Sikkimese were conducted by another CIA officer in Calcutta, John Turner. Born of American parents in India, Turner spent his formative years attending school in Darjeeling. He then went to college in the United States, followed by a stint in the army and induction into the agency in 1948. For his first overseas CIA assignment, he was chosen in May 1952 to succeed Robert Linn as the senior CIA officer in Calcutta. Given his cultural background and fluency in Hindi, Turner was well suited for the job. "I felt very much at home," he later commented.

The Sikkimese, Turner found, needed no prompting to maintain contact. "They offered us tidbits of intelligence to try and influence U.S. policy," he concluded.

"They were never on the payroll; they were not that sort of people." Some of the best tidbits came from the crown prince himself. "He was not the kind of person comfortable in dark alleys," quipped Turner. "He would make open, official visits to the consulate, and was the guest of honor with the consul general."[15]

As an aside to these visits, the prince would pass Turner relevant information about Tibet. One such meeting took place in the spring of 1954 immediately after the crown prince's return from a trip to Lhasa. While in the Tibetan capital, the prince had spoken with the Dalai Lama, whom he found unhappy but resigned to his fate. Even more revealing, the Chinese had feted their Sikkimese guest by showing off their new Damshung airfield north of Lhasa and had motored him along a fresh stretch of road leading into Kham. Turner found the debriefing so informative that he recorded the entire session and sent a voluminous report back to Washington.[16]

In retrospect, the crown prince had been made privy to the twin pillars behind Beijing's strategy for absorbing Tibet. Ever since it had first invaded western Kham in late 1950, the PLA knew that it could not sustain its presence without a modern logistical network. As the Chinese worked feverishly to complete this, they retained the existing monastic structure—including the Dalai Lama—and attempted to woo Tibet's lay aristocracy. They were fairly successful in winning support from the latter, especially since many aristocrats profited from the sudden influx of needy Chinese troops and administrators.[17]

This soft sell was not without its problems. In 1952, the Dalai Lama was pressured into firing his dual prime ministers over alleged anti-Chinese sentiment. There were also food shortages due to the presence of the occupying troops, as well as the affront they represented to Tibetan prestige. Various forms of nonviolent resistance—anonymous posters and sarcastic street rhymes were the preferred outlets—were already becoming commonplace in Lhasa.

Still, both the Tibetans and the Chinese had seen fit to abide by an unofficial truce. This lasted up until Beijing's transportation network was nearing completion. With the new option of rushing reinforcements to the Tibetan plateau, the PLA had the flexibility of eclipsing carrot with stick.

Beijing wasted no time driving the point home. Just weeks after the crown prince's 1954 visit, the Dalai Lama was invited to the Chinese capital, ostensibly to lead the Tibetan delegation to the inauguration ceremonies for the PRC's new constitution. Though many members of his inner circle were suspicious of Chinese intentions, the young monarch—still determined to work within the system—had little choice but to heed the call. He even made it a family affair, bringing along his mother, three siblings, and a brother-in-law.

On 11 July, the Dalai Lama and his 500-person entourage departed Lhasa. Where possible, they took stretches of the partially finished road that wove east through Kham. Once in Beijing, the visit started out well. Partial to socialist precepts, the Dalai Lama had few qualms with China's economic direction; he had already voiced support for radical land reforms at home, although the landed aristocracy and religious elite had successfully thwarted implementation. The Dalai Lama was also treated with respect by the upper echelons of China's communist hierarchy; Mao Tse-tung, in particular, doted on the teenage monarch.

But it was Mao who made a major gaff that would cloud the entire trip. Taking the Dalai Lama aside to impart a bit of fatherly wisdom, the chairman likened religion to poison. To a person who devoted his life to cultivating his spiritual side—and whose people believed that he had one foot firmly in the celestial world—this was blasphemy of the highest order.

Worse was to come. By the time the Dalai Lama headed home in the spring of 1955, the road leading from Kham to Lhasa was fully finished. A second route from Amdo to the capital was also complete. No longer feeling the need to be tolerant, the Chinese introduced atheist doctrine in Tibetan schools. The PLA also started disarming villagers in eastern Tibet prior to the implementation of harsh agrarian collectivization; as firearms were a cultural fixture in Kham and Amdo, their removal struck at a tenet of Tibetan tradition. As the Dalai Lama wove his way west, several Khampa leaders presented his entourage with petitions complaining of Beijing's heavy-handed ways.

During that same time frame, a hint of the dissatisfaction brewing in Kham reached the U.S. consulate in Calcutta via a different channel. John Turner, the CIA base chief, had been approached by George Patterson for an urgent meeting in the town of Kalimpong. Patterson, the Scottish missionary who had volunteered his services to the consulate in the past, was making the pitch on behalf of Ragpa Pandatsang, the same activist from the wealthy Kham trading family who had been alternately flirting with Lhasa and Beijing since 1950. Ragpa had done reasonably well for himself under the Chinese—he was a senior official in the town of Markham—but in a characteristic twist, he was now venturing to India to quietly sound out noncommunist options.

Based on middleman Patterson's request, Turner made his way to Kalimpong. By that time, the hill town had drawn a sizable roster of eclectic expatriates. One permanent fixture, Prince Peter of Greece and Denmark, was a physical anthropologist who spent his time measuring skulls. There was also Dennis Conan Doyle, who made a brief appearance in an unsuccessful bid to contact the spirit of his late father, Arthur. Joining them were die-hard followers of the late

Madame Helena Blavatsky, the debunked Ukrainian psychic whose nonsensical Theosophist religion had the unenviable distinction of being one of the tenets of the Nazi's Aryan master race thesis.[18]

Arriving at a house owned by the Pandatsang family, Turner waited outside. Perfectly timed, Ragpa materialized from out of the dawn mist on the back of a Tibetan pony. "He was apparently on his morning gallop," recalls Turner, "and he cut quite a figure." Dismounting, the Khampa greeted the CIA case officer. Patterson, who had befriended the Pandatsang family during his missionary days in Kham, was on hand to act as translator. After brief pleasantries, Ragpa touched lightly on the fact that the Khampas were looking for assistance in resisting the Chinese, including armaments. Without exchanging anything further of substance, he remounted the horse and melted back into the hills. Said Turner, "It was a surreal moment."[19]

Although Ragpa's approach to the CIA went nowhere (as did similar meetings he had with Indian officials and Tibetan trade representatives in Kalimpong), his hint about armed resistance proved prophetic.[20] By the close of 1955, the combination of factors simmering over the previous year—atheist indoctrination, forceful disarming of the population, rapid collectivization—sparked a wave of violence in eastern Tibet. True to their brigand reputation, nomads from the Golok region of Amdo were the first to unleash their fury on PLA garrisons across that province.[21]

Eastern Kham followed suit in early 1956. Whereas the Amdo revolt was spontaneous and unorganized, the Khampas were more deliberate. Many of their *pon* (clan chieftains) had already taken to the hills after the PLA demanded compliance with agrarian reforms. With the chieftain from the town of Lithang (also spelled Litang) taking the lead, a coordinated attack was planned for the eighteenth day of the first lunar phase of the year. Although preemptive Chinese arrests threw off that timetable by four days, some twenty-three clan leaders ultimately responded to the call and laid siege to a string of isolated Chinese posts.[22]

The PLA responded in force. That February, Beijing dispatched several of its massive Tupolev-4 bombers over the Tibetan plateau.[23] Because of their poor performance at high altitudes, the planes flew uncomfortably close to the terrain. This allowed guerrillas to fire down from ridgelines on the large, slow aircraft; one Tupolev returned to base with seventeen bullet holes.[24]

Still, thousands of Khampas and Amdowas died in the ensuing air campaign, buying time for the PLA to deploy ground reinforcements and retake lost garrisons. Particularly hard hit was Lithang; its grand monastery, home to 5,000 monks, was razed.

As this was taking place, the Dalai Lama faced mounting challenges on the political front. While in Beijing during 1955, he had been informed by Mao that a Preparatory Committee for the Autonomous Region of Tibet (PCART) would be formed to codify Tibet's status under the seventeen-point agreement. The committee was inaugurated in Lhasa during April 1956, with the Dalai Lama as chairman; the majority of PCART members, however, were either directly or indirectly named by the PRC. In this way, Beijing effectively bypassed both Tibet's cabinet and the National Assembly.

Between Beijing's PCART ploy and news filtering into the capital of Chinese brutality in the east, the Dalai Lama was fast reaching his breaking point by mid-1956. Just shy of his twenty-first birthday, he had already entertained thoughts of withdrawing from all secular life. It was at this critical juncture that his earlier foreign guest, the crown prince of Sikkim, made a return visit to Lhasa.

The crown prince was on more than a courtesy call. Back in April 1954, New Delhi had signed a landmark agreement with Beijing regarding trade with the "Tibet region of China." Building on India's desired role as arbitrator between East and West, as well as Nehru's own self-styled image as a champion for peace, New Delhi had intended the treaty as a means of blunting Chinese actions in Tibet by moral containment. But with reports of the harsh Chinese policy in eastern Tibet reaching India, the tack did not seem to be working.[25]

Disturbed by Beijing's lack of restraint, Nehru suddenly developed some backbone. By coincidence, the 2,500-year anniversary of the birth of Buddha was to be celebrated during the fourth lunar month of 1957. Special events to mark that date, known as the Buddha Jayanti, were scheduled across India beginning in late 1956. If the Dalai Lama could be enticed to travel to India for the occasion, New Delhi felt that this would symbolically underscore its interest in the well-being of Tibet and its leader. Because he already had good rapport with the Dalai Lama, and because he was president of the Indian Maha Bodhi Society (an organization that represented Buddhists across the Indian subcontinent), the crown prince was tasked by Nehru to deliver the invitation.

Upon receiving his Sikkimese guest and hearing the news, the Dalai Lama was ecstatic. For a Tibetan, a pilgrimage to India—especially one that coincided with the Buddha Jayanti—had all the connotations of a visit to the holy sites of Rome or Mecca. But more important, it would allow him to air his concerns directly to Nehru and perhaps offset Chinese influence. Perhaps, too, he could finally make good on his earlier contemplation of exile. Some of his minders, in fact, were convinced that the latter could be arranged, despite the fact that no nation, India included, had given any solid guarantee of asylum.[26]

Having delivered the invitation, the crown prince returned to India and on 28 June made his way to the U.S. consulate in Calcutta. Speaking directly with the senior diplomat, Consul General Robert Reams, he noted the apparent desire of the Dalai Lama to leave his country. The crown prince also relayed stories reaching Lhasa about horrific fighting taking place in eastern Tibet, offering Washington hearsay evidence that anti-Chinese resistance had escalated into armed rebellion. Noting the apparent lack of weapons among the insurgents, the prince astutely suggested channeling arms from East Pakistan (presumably via Sikkim) to Tibet. And in a more fanciful departure, he wondered aloud if the United States could "exfiltrate" Tibetans from Burma and Thailand—ostensibly while on religious pilgrimages—and give them artillery and antiaircraft training.[27]

The United States was clearly unprepared for this turn of events. For more than four years, Washington's Tibet policy had basically been to have no policy. Now the specter of the Dalai Lama's exile had returned. Complicating matters, the Tibetans had shifted from passive resistance to an armed struggle. For nearly four weeks, Foggy Bottom contemplated a response. When it finally came on 24 July, it was remarkable for its lack of originality. Falling back on the waffle perfected in 1951, Washington was prepared to extend a shifty promise of asylum, provided the Dalai Lama first asked India for help. No response was made to the crown prince's musings about arms and training.

It was unlikely that the U.S. offer would ever be put to the test. Hearing of the Buddha Jayanti invitation, senior Chinese authorities in Lhasa immediately threw water on the plan. Claiming that the Dalai Lama would have a tight schedule for upcoming PCART activities, they made clear their opposition to any foreign travel.

If the young monarch was frustrated, so too was India's Nehru. It was his prestige on the line following the 1954 treaty on Tibet. Moreover, with reports now beginning to circulate about the extent of the destruction in eastern Tibet, he felt the need to make a stand.[28] On 1 October, Nehru telegraphed an official invitation to the Dalai Lama to supplement the one forwarded earlier by the crown prince. Grudgingly, Beijing considered the new appeal from its treaty partner, and exactly one month later, the Chinese conceded. Tibet's young leader would be leaving his country.

3. The Prodigal Son

During the second week of September 1956, CIA officer John Hoskins arrived at Calcutta's Dum Dum Airport to a blast of late summer heat. At twenty-nine, he had already spent two years recruiting agents in Japan and another four shuttling between Washington desk assignments and vigorous tradecraft instruction.[1] Now assigned to the Calcutta consulate, his new post was an experiment of sorts. The CIA's Far East Division had just gotten permission to station its officers at any diplomatic mission where overseas Chinese were found in numbers. This meant superimposing Far East Division personnel outside of their home turf—in this case, in India of the Near East Division.[2]

In Calcutta, Hoskins could choose from a wealth of Chinese targets. Topping the list was the PRC's consulate and the People's Bank of China branch, both of which had been opened following the 1954 Sino-Indian trade agreement. In addition, some 30,000 Chinese expatriates—three-quarters of all those living in India—made their homes in and around the city.

Hoskins landed the secondary assignment of preening non-Chinese sources in the Himalayan states along the Tibetan border. Just as case officer Kenneth Millian had found out four years earlier, however, the Indians went out of their way to obstruct such efforts. "Overseas Chinese were fair game for penetration," recalls Hoskins, "but the others were considered under Indian hegemony."[3] This was driven home when Mary Hawthorne, a CIA officer assigned to Calcutta, allowed Jigme Thondup (a Bhutanese royal who later became prime minister) and his family to spend the night at her apartment. When the Indians learned of the incident, their outcry was so shrill that Hawthorne was forbidden by her superiors to attempt any similar invitations.[4]

Mindful of Indian surveillance, Hoskins made plans for an exceedingly discreet approach to establish his own ties with Princess Kukula of Sikkim. As she was known to have an affinity for equestrian events, he first considered making an overture at the Tibetan pony races held in Darjeeling. But because the crowds were small and whites were sure to attract notice, Hoskins instead opted to wait until she came to Calcutta for one of the city's thoroughbred competitions. Blending with the event's large number of Western spectators, he approached the princess. But Kukula, Hoskins found, had more reservations than in the past. "She wanted to keep contacts strictly social," he concluded. "She was not serious about getting involved."

As things turned out, the services of the Sikkimese royals would soon prove redundant. When the United States learned that the Dalai Lama had gotten permission in early November to attend the Buddha Jayanti celebrations, the CIA scrambled to bypass Sikkim and establish direct links with Tibetan sources close to the monarch.[5]

None were closer than the Dalai Lama's two brothers in exile. The eldest, Thubten Norbu, already had a history of indirect contact with the agency via the Committee for a Free Asia. After he had been unceremoniously dropped from CFA funding in 1952, both he and his servant, Jentzen Thondup, had become stateless refugees in Japan. Not until 1955, following repeated appeals channeled through Church World Services, did he and Jentzen finally get new Indian identity cards and U.S. visas. Settling in New Jersey, Norbu began to earn a modest income teaching Tibetan to a handful of students as part of a noncredited course at Columbia University.

The other brother, Gyalo Thondup, was residing in Darjeeling. Six years Norbu's junior, Gyalo was the proverbial prodigal son. The problem was, he was the figurative son to a number of fathers. He was the only one of five male siblings not directed toward a monastic life. As a teen, he had befriended members of the Chinese mission in Lhasa and yearned to study in China. Although this was not a popular decision among the more xenophobic members of his family, Gyalo got his wish in 1947 when he and a brother-in-law arrived at the Kuomintang capital of Nanking and enrolled in college.

Two years later, Gyalo, then twenty-one, veered further toward China when he married fellow student Zhu Dan. Not only was his wife ethnic Chinese, but her father, retired General Chu Shi-kuei, had been a key Kuomintang officer during the early days of the republic. Because of both his relationship to General Chu and the fact that he was the Dalai Lama's brother, Gyalo was feted in Nanking by no less than Generalissimo Chiang Kai-shek.

The good times were not to last. With the communists closing in on Nanking during the final months of China's civil war, Gyalo and his wife fled in mid-1949 to the safer climes of India. Once again because of his relationship to the Dalai Lama, he was added to the invitation list for various diplomatic events and even got an audience with Prime Minister Nehru.

That October, Gyalo briefly ventured to the Tibetan enclave at Kalimpong before settling for seven months in Calcutta. While there, his father-in-law, General Chu, attempted to make contact with the Tibetan government. With the retreat of the Kuomintang to Taiwan, Chu had astutely shifted loyalty to the People's Republic and was now tasked by Beijing to arrange a meeting between Tibetan and PRC officials at a neutral site, possibly Hong Kong.[6]

Conversant in Chinese and linked to both the Dalai Lama and General Chu, Gyalo was a logical intermediary for the Hong Kong talks. The British, however, were dragging their feet on providing visas to the Tibetan delegation. Unable to gain quick entry to the crown colony, Gyalo made what he intended to be a brief diversion to the Republic of China (ROC) on Taiwan. But Chiang Kai-shek, no doubt anxious to keep Gyalo away from General Chu and the PRC, had other plans. Smothering the royal sibling with largesse, Chiang kept Gyalo in Taipei for the next sixteen months. Only after a desperate letter to U.S. Secretary of State Dean Acheson requesting American diplomatic intervention did the ROC relent and give Gyalo an exit permit.

After arriving in Washington in September 1951, Gyalo continued to dabble in diplomacy. Within a month of his arrival, he was called to a meeting at the State Department. Significantly, Gyalo's Chinese wife was at his side during the encounter. Because of the couple's close ties to Chiang, department representatives assumed that details of their talk would quickly be passed to the Kuomintang Nationalists.[7]

Gyalo, in fact, was not a stooge of Taipei, Beijing, or, for that matter, Washington. Despite State Department efforts to secure him a scholarship at Stanford University, he hurriedly departed the United States in February 1952 for the Indian subcontinent. Leaving his wife behind, he then trekked back to Lhasa after a six-year absence.

By that time, Beijing had a secure foothold in the Tibetan capital. Upon meeting this wayward member of the royal family, the local PRC representatives were pleased. As a Chinese speaker married to one of their own, Gyalo was perceived as a natural ally. Yet again, however, he would prove a disappointment. After showing some interest in promoting a bold land reform program championed by the Dalai Lama, Gyalo once more grew restive. In late spring, he secretly met with the Indian consul in Lhasa, and after promising to refrain from politicking, he was given permission to resettle in India.[8]

Although not exactly endearing himself to anyone with his frequent moves, Gyalo was not burning bridges either. Noting his recent return to Darjeeling, the U.S. embassy in early August 1952 cautiously considered establishing contact. Calcutta's Consul General Gary Soulen saw an opportunity in early September while returning from his Sikkim trek with Princess Kukula. Pausing in Darjeeling, Soulen stayed long enough for Gyalo to pass on the latest information from his contacts within the Tibetan merchant community.[9]

Although he had promised to refrain from exile politics, Gyalo saw no conflict in courting senior Indian officials. In particular, he sought a meeting with India's spymaster Bhola Nath Mullik. As head of Indian intelligence, Mullik presided over an organization with deep colonial roots. Established in 1887 as the Central Special Branch, it had been organized by the British to keep tabs on the rising tide of Indian nationalism. Despite several redesignations before arriving at the title Intelligence Bureau, anticolonialists remained its primary target for the next sixty years.

Upon independence in 1947, Prime Minister Nehru appointed the bureau's first Indian director. Rather than suppressing nationalists, the organization now had to contend with communal violence and early problems with India's erstwhile Muslim brothers now living in the bisected nation of Pakistan.

Three years later, Mullik became the bureau's second director. A police officer since the age of twenty-two, the taciturn Mullik was known for his boundless energy (he often worked sixteen-hour days), close ties to Nehru, healthy suspicion of China, and (rare for a senior Indian official) predisposition against communism. Almost immediately, the Tibetan frontier became his top concern. This followed Beijing's invasion of Kham that October, which meant that India's military planners now had to contend with a hypothetical front besides Pakistan. Moreover, the tribal regions of northeastern India were far from integrated, and revolutionaries in those areas could now easily receive Chinese support. The previous year, in fact, the bureau had held a conference on risks associated with Chinese infiltration.[10]

Despite Mullik's concerns, Nehru was prone to downplay the potential Chinese threat. Not only did he think it ludicrous to prepare for a full-scale Chinese attack, but he saw real benefits in cultivating Beijing to offset Pakistan's emerging strategy of anticommunist cooperation with the West. "It was Nehru's idealism against hard-headed Chinese realism," said one Intelligence Bureau official. "Mullik injected healthy suspicions."

Astute enough to hedge his bets, Nehru allowed Mullik some leeway in improving security along the border and collecting intelligence on Chinese forces in Tibet. To accomplish this, Mullik expanded the number of Indian frontier posts strung across the Himalayas. In addition, he sought contact with Tibetans living in the Darjeeling and Kalimpong enclaves. Not only could these Tibetans be tapped for information, but a symbolic visit by a senior official like Mullik would lift morale at a time when their homeland was being subjugated. Such contact, moreover, could give New Delhi advance warning of any subversive activity in Tibet being staged from Indian soil.[11]

Of all the Tibetan expatriates, Mullik had his eye on Gyalo Thondup. Besides having an insider's perspective of the high offices in Lhasa, Gyalo had already passed word of his desire for a meeting. Prior to his departure for his first visit to Darjeeling in the spring of 1953, Mullik asked for—and quickly received—permission from the prime minister to include the Dalai Lama's brother on his itinerary. Their subsequent exchange of views went well, as did their tête-à-tête during Mullik's second visit to Darjeeling in 1954.[12]

Apart from such occasional contact with Indian intelligence, Gyalo spent much of the next two years removed from the tribulations in his homeland. To earn a living, he ironically began exporting Indian tea and whiskey to Chinese troops and administrators in Tibet. For leisure, he and his family were frequent guests at the Gymkhana Club. Part of an exclusive resort chain that was once a playpen for the subcontinent's colonial elite, the Gymkhana's Darjeeling branch was situated amid terraced gardens against the picturesque backdrop of Kanchenjunga. A regular on the tennis courts, the Dalai Lama's brother was the local champion.[13]

In the summer of 1956, Gyalo's respite came to an abrupt end. The senior abbot and governor from the Tibetan town of Gyantse had recently made his escape to India and in July wrote a short report about China's excesses. Gyalo repackaged the letter in English and mailed copies to the Indian media, several diplomatic missions, and selected world leaders. One of these arrived in early September at the U.S. embassy in the Pakistani capital of Karachi, and from there was disseminated to the American mission in New Delhi and consulate in Calcutta.[14]

Although the letter was less than accurate on several counts, it served two important purposes. First, it corroborated the reports of China's brutality provided by the crown prince of Sikkim in June. Second, it brought Gyalo back to the attention of Washington as a concerned activist. For the past four years, there had been virtually no contact between him and American diplomats in India. In particular, he was completely unknown among CIA officers in Calcutta.[15]

This was set to change, and quickly. Once word reached India in early November that the Dalai Lama would be attending the Buddha Jayanti, John Hoskins got an urgent cable from headquarters. Put aside your efforts against the Chinese community, he was told, and make immediate contact with Gyalo. A quick check indicated Gyalo's predilection for tennis, so Hoskins got a racket and headed north to Darjeeling. After arranging to get paired with Gyalo for a doubles match, the CIA officer wasted no time in quietly introducing himself.

First impressions are lasting ones, and Hoskins was not exactly wowed by Gyalo's persona. "There was a lot of submissiveness rather than dynamism," he noted. At their first meeting, little was discussed apart from reaching an understanding that, to avoid Indian intelligence coverage in Darjeeling, future contact would be made in Calcutta using proper countersurveillance measures.

Later that same month, the Dalai Lama and a fifty-strong delegation departed Lhasa by car. Switching to horses at the Sikkimese border, the royal entourage was met on the other side by both Gyalo and Norbu, who had rushed to India from his teaching assignment in New York. The party was whisked through Gangtok and down to the closest Indian airfield near the town of Siliguri, and by 25 November the monarch was being met by Nehru on the tarmac of New Delhi's Palam Airport.[16]

By coincidence, three days after the Dalai Lama's arrival in New Delhi, Chinese premier Zhou En-lai began a twelve-day stop in India as part of a five-country South Asian tour. Keeping with diplomatic protocol, the young Tibetan leader was on hand to greet Zhou at the airport. The two then held a private meeting, at which time the elderly Chinese statesman lectured the Dalai Lama on the necessity of returning to his homeland.

Zhou was not alone in his appeal. As eager as Nehru was to offset Chinese influence in Tibet, he, too, was against the Dalai Lama's seeking asylum—especially on Indian soil. This was partly because India wanted to maintain good relations with China. This was also because New Delhi did not want to go it alone, and not a single country to date had recognized Tibetan independence. Fearing that the monarch's brothers would have an unhealthy effect on any decision, Indian officials in the capital did all in their power to keep Gyalo and Norbu segregated from their royal sibling.[17]

The Dalai Lama hardly needed convincing from his brothers, however. During his first private session with Nehru, he openly hinted about not going back to Lhasa. He also requested that the issue of Tibetan independence be taken up by Nehru and President Dwight Eisenhower at their upcoming summit in Washington in December. Nehru was not entirely surprised by all this: Gyalo had already sought out Mullik and told the Indian intelligence chief in no uncertain terms that his brother would opt for exile.[18]

As India's leadership digested these developments, the Dalai Lama departed the capital for an exhausting schedule of Buddha Jayanti festivities. He was still in the midst of this tour when Zhou returned to New Delhi for an encore visit on 30 December. In the interim, Nehru had had his Washington meeting with Eisenhower, and the Chinese premier had scheduled the stop specifically to discuss the outcome of that summit. As it turned out, however, Tibet was a major topic of conversation. In particular, Nehru used the opportunity to press Zhou about tempering China's harsh military and agrarian policies on the Tibetan plateau.

Tibet was clearly shaping into a litmus test for Sino-Indian relations. Anxious to broker a deal that would assuage both Lhasa and Beijing, Nehru summoned the Dalai Lama from his pilgrimage and underscored to the Tibetan leader that Indian asylum was not in the cards. But if that was bitter news, Zhou had earlier proposed a sweetener. While noting that China was ready to use force to stamp out resistance, he claimed that Mao now recognized the folly of rapid collectivization and pledged to delay further revolutionary reforms in Tibet.

Zhou and his senior comrades were by now gravely concerned over permanently losing the Dalai Lama. Leaving nothing to chance, Zhou was back in New Delhi on 24 January 1957 for his third visit in as many months.

Despite Beijing's lobbying, Gyalo and Norbu were still insistent that their brother choose exile. Torn over his future, the twenty-one-year-old monarch had already departed Calcutta on 22 January for Kalimpong, which by then was home to a growing number of disaffected Tibetan elite. Once there, he did what Tibet's leaders had done countless other times when confronted with a hard decision: he consulted the state oracle. Two official soothsayers happened to be traveling with his delegation; using time-honored—if unscientific—methods, the pair went into a trance on cue and recited their sagely advice. Return to Lhasa, they channeled.[19]

As far as the Dalai Lama was concerned, the ruling of his oracles was incontrovertible, and the decision was made all the easier by the fact that nobody seemed anxious to give him refuge. Flouting the suggestions of his brothers, he declared his intention to go home. He crossed into Sikkim in early March and was compelled to remain in Gangtok until heavy snows melted from the mountain passes. There, he finalized plans to set out for Lhasa by month's end.

Prior to November 1956, Tibet had never ranged far from the bottom of the priority watch list for those in the Far East Division at CIA headquarters in Washington. The agency had no officer assigned solely to Tibetan affairs; it, along with Mongolia and other peripheral ethnic regions under PRC control, barely factored as a minor addendum to the activities of William Broe's China Branch.

But as soon as the Dalai Lama received permission to attend the Buddha Jayanti, Broe felt it prudent to show heightened interest. Looking for a junior officer to spare, he soon settled on John Reagan. Twenty-eight years old, Reagan had joined the agency upon graduation from Boston College in 1951. He was soon in Asia, where he spent the next twenty-four months working on paramilitary projects in Korea. Switching to China Branch, he served two more years in Japan as part of the CIA's penetration effort against the PRC. Returning to the United States in 1955, Reagan divided the next twelve months between Chinese language training and trips to New York City to practice tradecraft against United Nations delegates.

As the branch's new man on Tibet, Reagan initially did little more than forward instructions for John Hoskins to make contact with Gyalo. He was silent on further guidance, primarily because senior U.S. policy makers had not yet ironed out a coherent framework for dealing with Lhasa. In earlier meetings between CIA and State Department officials during the summer of 1956, there had been those who felt that the Dalai Lama should flee to another Buddhist nation to offer a rallying cry for anticommunist Buddhists across Asia. Others, primarily inside the agency, believed that he could play a more important role as a rallying symbol in Lhasa among his fellow Tibetans. This was still the CIA's operating assumption in late 1956: once the Dalai Lama was in India, the prevailing mood at agency headquarters was that he should eventually go home.[20]

Gyalo, meantime, was telling Hoskins that his brother had every intention of seeking asylum. With the Dalai Lama apparently intent on staying away from his homeland—and therefore not conforming to the agency's preferred scenario of rallying his people from Lhasa—Reagan was largely idle during most of the Dalai Lama's four-month absence from Tibet.[21]

Eventually, however, the CIA looked to hedge its bets. Since the second half of 1956, a band of twenty-seven young Khampa men—some still in their late teens—had been growing restive in the enclave of Kalimpong. Most came from relatively wealthy trading families and had been spirited to India to protect them from the instability in their native province. Full of vigor, the entire group had ventured to New Delhi shortly before the Dalai Lama's Buddha Jayanti pilgrimage to conduct street protests. Once the Dalai Lama arrived, they sought a brief audience to make an impassioned plea for Lhasa's intercession against the Chinese offensive in Kham.

To their disappointment, the Dalai Lama counseled patience. "His Holiness only said things would settle down," recalls one of the Khampas. Undaunted, the twenty-seven young men shadowed the monarch during several of the Buddha Jayanti commemorative events. By early January 1957, this took them to Bodh Gaya, the city in eastern India where the historical Buddha was said to have attained enlightenment. While there, the Dalai Lama's older brother, Thubten Norbu, approached the Khampas and asked if he could take their individual photographs as a souvenir. Although it was an odd request, they complied.[22]

For the next few weeks, nothing happened. Frustrated by the Dalai Lama's repeated rebuffs, the Khampas sulked back to Kalimpong. Several Chinese traders were in town, some of whom were rumored to have links to the Nationalist regime on Taiwan. Desperate, the Khampas sounded them out on the possibility of covert assistance from Taipei. It was at that point that Gyalo Thondup arrived and requested a meeting with all twenty-seven. For most of the young Khampas, it was the first time they had spoken with the Dalai Lama's lay brother. As they listened attentively, Gyalo lectured them to steer clear of the Kuomintang. "The United Sates," he told them cryptically, "is a better choice."[23]

Less than a week later, the Dalai Lama arrived in Kalimpong, the oracles had their channeling session, and things changed dramatically. With the monarch's return journey now imminent, John Reagan in Washington scrambled to script a program of action. At its core, the plan called for a unilateral capability to determine how much armed resistance activity really existed in Tibet; further commitments could then be weighed accordingly.

The CIA had good reason to act with prudence. It already had a long and growing list of embarrassing failures while working with resistance groups behind communist lines. Perhaps none had been more painful than its experience against the PRC. There the agency's efforts had taken two tracks. The first was a collaborative effort with the Kuomintang government on Taiwan. Clinging to its dream of reconquering the mainland, the ROC in 1950 claimed to control a million guerrillas inside the People's Republic. Although a February 1951 Pentagon study placed the figure at no more than 600,000—only half of which were thought to be nominally loyal to the ROC—Washington saw fit to support these insurgents as a means of appeasing a key Asian ally while at the same time possibly diverting Beijing's attention from the conflict on the Korean peninsula.[24]

To funnel covert American assistance to the ROC, the CIA established a shell company in Pittsburgh known as Western Enterprises (WE). In September 1951, WE's newly appointed chief, Raymond Peers, arrived on Taiwan with a planeload of advisers. A U.S. Army colonel who had earned accolades during World War II as chief of the famed OSS Detachment 101 in Burma, Peers quickly initiated a number of paramilitary efforts. A large portion of his resources was directed toward airborne operations, including retraining the ROC's 1,500-man parachute regiment. Other WE advisers, meanwhile, were tasked with putting ROC action and intelligence teams through an airborne course.[25]

To deploy these operatives, WE turned to the agency's Far East air proprietary, Civil Air Transport (CAT). By the spring of 1952, CAT planes were dropping teams and singletons on the mainland, as well as supplies to resistance groups that the ROC claimed were already active on the ground. Some of the penetrations ranged as far as Tibet's Amdo region, where the ROC alleged it had contact with Muslim insurgents.[26]

Concurrently, the agency in April 1951 initiated a unilateral third-force effort using anticommunist Chinese unaffiliated with the ROC. Allocated enough arms and ammunition for 200,000 guerrillas, the CIA recruited many of these third-force operatives from Hong Kong, trained them in Japan and Saipan, and inserted them in CAT planes via air bases in South Korea.[27]

By the spring of 1953, both the ROC program and third-force effort were in their second years. Although the Pentagon's top brass (groping for ways to pressure Beijing during Korean cease-fire negotiations) were wistfully talking in terms of "sparking a coordinated anti-communist resistance movement throughout China," those running the CIA's infiltration program could hardly have been so optimistic. "None of the Taiwan agents we dropped were successful," said one WE adviser. The third-force tally was just as bad: all its operatives were either killed or taken prisoner, and CAT lost one plane during an attempted exfiltration that resulted in the capture of two CIA officers.[28]

That summer, an armistice sent the Korean conflict into remission. This provided the CIA with convenient cover to reassess its third-force track. Although it elected to maintain a China Base at Yokosuka, Japan, this unit was to handle primarily agent penetrations and low-level destabilization efforts; support for broader unilateral resistance got the ax.

Cooperative ventures with the ROC were not so easily nixed. Although Taipei had tempered its claims somewhat, it still pegged loyal mainland guerrilla strength at 650,000 insurgents. By contrast, a November 1953 estimate by the U.S. National Security Council (NSC) put the figure closer to 50,000. Despite this huge discrepancy, the NSC still advocated continued covert assistance to the ROC in order to develop anticommunist guerrillas for resistance and intelligence. Even temporary guerrilla successes, the council reasoned, might set off waves of defections and stiffen passive resistance.[29]

Chiang Kai-shek could not have agreed more. Eager to vastly increase the scope of guerrilla support, the generalissimo in 1954 asked Washington for some 30,000 parachutes. Turned down the first time, he made further high-priority appeals over the next two years. These parachutes were needed for an ambitious plan to drop 100-man units near major PRC population centers. Hoping to set off a chain of uprisings, Chiang optimistically talked in terms of uprooting Chinese communism in as little as two years.[30]

Hearing these plans, Washington patiently counseled against the proposed airborne blitz. On a more modest level, however, the CIA's assistance program continued unabated. In this, success was more elusive than ever. Despite inserting an average of two Nationalist agents a month through the mid-1950s, the ROC operatives were still being killed or captured in short order.[31]

Reasons for the lack of success against the People's Republic were legion. First, the infiltration program took at face value some of Taipei's claims about contact with a vast network of anticommunists on the mainland. In reality, such claims were wildly exaggerated, and precious little was known about events in the PRC countryside; even top PRC leaders were prone to mysteriously disappear from public view for months on end.[32] Second, in the unlikely event such resistance existed, the logistical challenge of maintaining support to these guerrilla pockets outstripped what could realistically be staged by Taiwan and the CIA. Third, the CIA's recent experience against the Soviet Union and its satellites had shown the folly of abetting insurgents in a tightly controlled police state; Beijing's omnipresent militia and party network were no less daunting.[33] Finally, even though the PRC's ruthless experimentation in social engineering had no doubt bred detractors by the score, the corruption of the Kuomintang regime hardly endeared Taipei to any disenchanted masses on the mainland.

Although these reasons might have made covert operations against the PRC a study in frustration, Tibet appeared to be different. Unlike many of Taipei's wishful claims about other areas of the mainland, Tibet had a resistance movement corroborated by multiple, albeit dated, sources. What the CIA needed was timely data that could give a current and accurate picture of this resistance. And given the historical animosity between Tibetans and lowland Chinese, the agency needed to gather this information without resort to ROC assistance.

In February 1957, John Hoskins was ordered by Washington to immediately identify eight Tibetan candidates for external training as a pilot team that would infiltrate their homeland and assess the state of resistance. Gyalo, who had been in Kalimpong making an eleventh-hour bid to convince his brother to seek asylum, was given responsibility for screening candidates among the Tibetan refugees already in India. Although the twenty-seven Khampas did not know it, Gyalo intended to make the selection from their ranks. Using the photographs taken by Norbu at Bodh Gaya, he sought guidance from two senior Khampas in town, both of whom hailed from the extended family of Gompo Tashi Andrugtsang, a prominent trader of Tibetan wool, deer horns, and musk.

With their assistance, Gyalo soon settled on his first pick. Wangdu Gyatotsang, age twenty-seven, had been born to an affluent Khampa family from the town of Lithang. He was well connected: Gompo Tashi was his uncle, as was one of the senior Khampas helping Gyalo with the selection. Wangdu also had the

Wangdu Gyatotsang (right), leader of the Saipan-trained team dropped in Kham, with his two brothers. (Courtesy Kalsang Gyatotsang)

right disposition for the task at hand. Despite being schooled at the Lithang monastery from the age of ten, he did not exactly conform to monastic life. "He was hot tempered from childhood," recalls younger brother Kalsang.

A sampling of this temper came at age seventeen during a trip to the Tibetan town of Menling. Out of deference to the local chieftain, it was decreed that hats, firearms, and horse bells would be removed in front of the chief's residence. It was raining, however, so Wangdu continued wearing his cap. Spying this violation, the chieftain's bodyguard strode up and knocked the Khampa on the head. Without flinching, the young monk drew his pistol and shot the guard dead.[34]

On account of his family connections, Wangdu was spared punishment. In 1956, his family ties again came into play following the PLA's devastating attack on the Lithang monastery. On orders from uncle Gompo Tashi, Wangdu and his younger brother were bundled off to the safer environs of Kalimpong.

When approached by Gyalo, Wangdu immediately volunteered for the mission. Within days, five other Khampas were singled out (Washington now wanted a total of six trainees, not eight), but only Wangdu was given any hint of the impending assignment. Four were from Lithang; of these, three were Wangdu's close acquaintances, and one was his family servant. The fifth was a friend from the nearby town of Bathang (also spelled Batang). All were still on hand to attend the Dalai Lama's final open-air blessing in a Kalimpong soccer field shortly before the monarch headed back toward Tibet.

With the Dalai Lama en route to Lhasa, attention shifted in early March to smuggling the six Khampas out of India for training. This was easier said than done. Because of Nehru's determination to maintain cordial Sino-Indian ties, New Delhi's complicity remained out of the question. Moreover, the Khampas were refugees without proper identification, discounting overt travel via commercial airliner or boat. Brainstorming covert alternatives, several came to mind. "There was some talk in the Calcutta consulate about floating them off the Indian coast," said Gyalo, "then having them picked up by submarine." Consideration was also given to issuing fake Nepalese passports.[35]

A better option harkened back to a suggestion made by the crown prince of Sikkim regarding exfiltration via East Pakistan. The idea held merit: since 1954, Washington and Karachi (which governed both the East and West Pakistani territories on either side of India) had forged cordial military and diplomatic ties. A military sales pact had been signed by the United States and Pakistan that May, and both had agreed to join the Southeast Asia Treaty Organization in September; the following year, Pakistan became a member of the U.S.-supported Baghdad Pact. This was all part of a chain of alliances intended by the United States to contain the spread of communism. By 1956, Pakistan had become America's "most allied ally in Asia."[36]

In reality, Karachi had signed the treaties for reasons other than those intended by Washington. Although it was true that Pakistan had some emerging concerns about communism (China claimed some Pakistani territory on its maps, for example, and even raided border villages in 1954 to discourage grazing on its land), its main motivation was to open the spigot of American military assistance, which Karachi desperately wanted to bolster its armed forces against threats from New Delhi.

Different motivations aside, U.S.-Pakistan relations were genuinely warm, and the U.S. embassy enjoyed good access to the top echelons of government. Even before the CIA was sure that the Khampa training was going to proceed, the agency's station chief in Karachi, L. Eugene Milligan, had broached the exfiltration scheme with senior Pakistani officials. Taking his case directly to President Iskandar Mizra, Milligan asked if—hypothetically speaking—Tibetans could be allowed to cross the northern border of East Pakistan, then be discreetly transported to the abandoned Kurmitola airstrip north of Dacca.[37]

Milligan could make his pitch knowing that the CIA had particularly good relations in East Pakistan. Since mid-1954, the agency had been allowed to maintain a single case officer at the Dacca consulate. That officer, twenty-eight-year-old Walter Cox, had nurtured close links with most of East Pakistan's civilian and military authorities, helped in part when he coordinated a generous airlift of U.S. humanitarian assistance following severe floods in August 1954.[38]

Based on this spirit of cooperation, Mizra gave Milligan his consent. When Washington's final approval for the exfiltration came in February 1957, the station chief quickly assigned a Karachi-based case officer, Edward McAllister, to coordinate the operation from Dacca. Forty-three years old, McAllister was an experienced Asia hand. Schooled in China through his university years, he had gone back to the United States in 1932 and worked for nearly a decade as a fire insurance underwriter and public health inspector. Lured by the challenges of the war in Europe, he joined the British army in 1941, then transferred in 1943 to the U.S. Army.

At war's end, McAllister's linguistic skills made him a natural for what became an extended army assignment in postwar China. By 1949, he was serving as an assistant military attaché during the final months of the civil war. Leaving the armed forces in 1954 with the rank of major, McAllister signed on with the CIA. He entered the Far East Division and—like Hoskins in Calcutta—was posted to Karachi as the division's local representative assigned to penetrate the Chinese community.

Joining McAllister for the assignment in Dacca was John Reagan, who had flown in from Washington for the duration of the exfiltration. One potential hitch remained: although McAllister was fluent in Chinese (and Reagan knew the basics), neither officer shared a common language with the Khampas. They were desperate for an interpreter, but there were few qualified candidates. Gyalo himself was ineligible because he needed to run the operation from the Indian side and could not afford the diplomatic heat if he got caught on the border. Norbu could not risk the embarrassment of exposure either. While little other choice, a call was placed to Norbu's long-time servant Jentzen Thondup, who was patiently awaiting his master's return at their apartment in New Jersey.

"I got on the phone," remembers Jentzen, "with somebody who said he was from the CIA." A quiet, elderly man showed up at the house later that day, and the pair were soon winging their way to the subcontinent.[39]

It was 2:00 in the afternoon when Wangdu came to the house of twenty-seven-year-old Athar and told him they were departing that night for training in a foreign country. Like Wangdu, Athar (many Khampas go by only one name) was an alumnus of the Lithang monastery and had been one of the twenty-seven who lobbied the Dalai Lama during the Buddha Jayanti. A total of six Khampas, he was told, would be making the trip.

Athar's first reaction was shock. To maintain secrecy, none of the trainees (other than Wangdu) had been aware that preparations had reached such an advanced stage. His next reaction was disappointment. "Six was too few," he later recalled. "I thought we needed at least ten of us."[40]

With little time for debate, the six ate and changed into Indian clothes. All identification was left behind. At 9:00 that evening, they gathered on a dark road outside town. Like clockwork, Gyalo arrived at the wheel of a jeep and loaded them into the rear. In the passenger's seat was Gyalo's cook, Gelung, who was designated to escort the group across the Pakistani border. Gelung was a good choice on two counts: not only could he speak Hindi, which might come in handy if they encountered Indian authorities, but he was the only one among them who knew how to read a compass.

In silence, they drove south to the town of Siliguri, then another twenty kilometers to the East Pakistan frontier. As the road narrowed near the entrance to a tea plantation, the jeep ground to a halt and the passengers off-loaded. As Gyalo reversed direction and returned north, Gelung led the Khampas down a foot trail through the plantation. Walking until nearly dawn, they approached a large river. Studying his compass, Gelung calculated that the opposite side was Pakistani territory. In contrast to the tension along the Indo-Pakistani border in the west—where the two nations had clashed over the contested region of Kashmir—much of the 3,225-kilometer East Pakistan frontier was undefended.

The group found a suitable fording point and waded to the far shore. Moving forty-five meters inland, they came across a small road. While they waited without speaking, three soldiers materialized out of the dawn mist. Because they appeared to be armed and dressed like Indian troops, the Khampas began to panic, but Gelung rose and walked forward. Removing a flashlight from his pack, he flicked it on for a moment. Seconds later, the troops returned the signal. Gelung waved at the others to follow, and the Khampas approached the patrol and offered greetings. To their surprise, one of the soldiers was Norbu's servant Jentzen; the rest were Pakistanis. His work done, Gelung bid them farewell and retraced his steps across the river and back to India, while Jentzen, the Pakistanis, and the six Khampas walked a short distance to a covered jeep.

After riding for an hour, the group came upon an isolated cottage framed by thickets. Inside, CIA officer McAllister was waiting with hot tea and biscuits. As Jentzen attempted to translate pleasantries in halting English, they finished their refreshments and were directed to a bigger jeep. They rode for the next five hours, not stopping until they reached a railway station. Surrounded by supposed Pakistani military guards—giving them the outward appearance of a prison gang—the Tibetans were hustled aboard a train and seated alone in the first-class compartment.

Heading south, they took the train to the outskirts of Dacca. There they were off-loaded to a truck and driven to a safe house near Kurmitola. "The heat was really affecting us," remembers Athar, "so we kept the cold water running in the shower and took turns going underneath." Sweltering, they spent the next two days hidden away from prying eyes.[41]

For covert airlift needs in Asia, the CIA relied almost exclusively on its proprietary, Civil Air Transport. A handful of assignments, however, went to a special unit within the U.S. Air Force (USAF). This unit dated back to 1951, when the USAF saw the need to pluck aircrews out of the Soviet countryside after dropping nuclear ordnance and running out of fuel on the way home. Given the innocuous title of Air Resupply and Communications (ARC) wings, these recovery units were outfitted with an exotic mix of converted B-29 bombers, seaplanes, helicopters, and transports. For global coverage, three ARC wings were formed: one in the United States as reserve, one in Libya for European assignments, and one at Clark Air Base in the Philippines for Asian missions.[42]

Almost immediately, the activities of the ARC wings grew beyond their pilot recovery role. Their training was expanded to include various aerial aspects of unconventional warfare, and they became fluent in leaflet drops, agent insertions, and the resupply of guerrillas behind communist lines. The Clark-based ARC wing—which in 1954 shifted to Kadena Air Base on the U.S.-controlled island of Okinawa—was especially active, being used on psychological warfare flights over the Korean peninsula, the PRC, and French Indochina.

In September 1956, all ARC wings were formally disbanded. But electing to keep the Kadena unit intact, the USAF merely changed its name to the equally ambiguous 322nd Troop Carrier Squadron, Medium (Special). In line with the last word of this extended title, the 322nd Squadron continued to focus on unconventional contingencies; its B-29s, in particular, were kept busy performing simulated low-level parachute drops.[43]

During that time frame, CIA air operations across Asia were being run out of Tokyo. To facilitate liaison between Tokyo and the special squadron on Okinawa, two agency officers were posted to Kadena. Although the entire 322nd Squadron was qualified to fly covert operations, the most sensitive missions went to a small subset of airmen assigned to its Detachment 1. These crews flew a pair of C-54s and a lone C-118, all provided courtesy of the CIA.

Though little different from a civilian DC-6 transport on the outside, the 322nd Squadron's C-118 was an engineering marvel. "It was pieced together from so many different serial-numbered parts," recalls squadron pilot Herbert Dagg, "that it would have been untraceable if it went down." The plane also had removable tail numbers, which were sometimes changed multiple times during CIA-sponsored flights. To add to the intentional confusion, crews were required to file false flight plans and fly circuitous routes to mask points of origin and destination.[44]

Outside eyes were not the only ones the CIA was out to fool. The detachment's own aircrews were kept in the dark as to the identity of their agency passengers. All the windows were blackened, and curtains were always drawn between the cockpit and the cabin. Crews were required to use only the front door; passengers used only the rear. "I never even knew if the personnel we flew were Asians," said squadron member Justin Shires.[45]

Such was the case when the detachment got orders to fly the C-118 to Kurmitola. With perfect timing, a covered truck approached from the rear and stopped at the plane's back door. Six small figures dashed up the stairs, followed by Jentzen and John Reagan. Throttling the engines back up, the crew taxied down the runway and disappeared into the eastern skies.

4. Saipan

After a brief refueling stop in Bangkok, the Khampas were again aloft and heading over the South China Sea. Curving north, they arrived at Kadena and were taken to the small CIA compound on the air base for a three-day physical examination. Doctors found them to have well-developed chests and musculature—no surprise, given their active lifestyles at high altitude. Notable was their low, even pulse rates. A brief aptitude test showed that although none spoke any English, they exhibited good native intelligence. "Being merchants," noted one CIA case officer, "most had a certain sophistication stemming from their contact across the region."[1]

While still on Okinawa, the group was met by the Dalai Lama's brother Norbu, who joined them on the C-118 as they took to the air and veered southeast. Four hours later, they descended toward a teardrop-shaped island in the middle of the western Pacific. Though the Tibetans were never told the location—some would later speculate it was Guam—they had actually arrived at the U.S. trust territory of Saipan.[2]

Situated on the southern end of the Northern Mariana Islands chain, Saipan was of volcanic origin and had an equally violent history of human habitation. Its original population—seafarers from the Indonesian archipelago—was virtually wiped out by Spanish colonialists. Later sold to Germany and subsequently administered by Japan as part of a League of Nations mandate, the island—though no larger than the city of San Francisco—had taken on extraordinary strategic significance by the time of World War II. This was because Allied strategy in the Pacific hinged on the premise that the Japanese would not surrender until their homeland was invaded. According to Allied estimates, such an invasion would cost an estimated 1 million American lives and needed the support of a concerted air campaign. For this, Washington required a staging base where its bombers could launch and return safely; the Marianas chain, the U.S. top brass calculated, fell within the necessary range.

Before the Allies could move in, however, there remained the thorny problem of removing nearly 32,000 Japanese defenders firmly entrenched on the island. In June 1944, one week after the landings at Normandy, 535 U.S. naval vessels closed on Saipan. In what was to become one of the most hotly contested battles in the Pacific, they blasted the island from afar before putting ashore 71,000 troops.

The Japanese were not intimidated. Having already zeroed their heavy weapons on likely beachheads, they ravaged the landing columns. Some 3,100 U.S. servicemen died; another 13,100 were wounded or missing.

Despite such heavy Allied casualties, the Japanese had it worse. Overwhelmed by the size of the invasion force, some 29,500 defenders perished in the month-long battle to control the island. Of these, hundreds jumped to their deaths off the northern cliffs rather than face the shame of capture.

Once in Allied hands, the Marianas were quickly transformed into their intended role as a staging base for air strikes against Japan. It was from there, in fact, that a B-29 began its run to drop the atomic bomb on Hiroshima. Nine days later, Japan surrendered.

Following World War II, the United States remained on hand to administer the Northern Mariana Islands. In July 1947, this role was codified under a trustee-ship agreement with the new United Nations, which specifically gave the U.S. Navy responsibility for the chain. In practice, this trusteeship translated into an exceed-ingly small U.S. presence. With Japan's wartime population either dead or repa-triated, the chain boasted few settlements of any note; only Saipan hosted anything approaching the size of a town. Even its airfields—which had once been so criti-cal during the war—now fell largely dormant after being vastly overshadowed by the sprawling U.S. military bases in neighboring Guam and the Philippines.

For the CIA, however, the tranquillity of the Marianas held appeal. Looking for a discreet locale to build a Far East camp to instruct agents and commandos from friendly nations, the agency in 1950 established the Saipan Training Sta-tion. Officially known by the cover title Naval Technical Training Unit, Saipan station took up much of the island's northern peninsula and featured numerous segregated compounds where groups of Asian trainees from various nations could spend several months in isolation. "We did not even let two classes from the same country know one another," underscored one case officer.[3]

The course work offered at Saipan station ran the gamut of unconventional warfare and espionage tradecraft. By 1956, Chinese Nationalists, Koreans, Lao, and Vietnamese had passed through its gates for commando instruction; a Thai class had been coached as frogmen; and other Vietnamese had been preened to form their own version of the CIA. In some cases, classes consisted of just one or two key individuals who were going to blend into their central government structure. "There were no standard lessons," said one CIA officer. "Each cycle was custom tailored."[4]

None of the prospective trainees presented more of a challenge than the newly arrived Tibetans. The six recruits were to act as the CIA's eyes and ears back inside

Tibet, John Reagan explained to the resident instructor cadre. This necessitated that they absorb not only communications and reporting skills but also a general knowledge of guerrilla warfare techniques, as well as a limited understanding of tradecraft. Although such a broad curriculum would normally require a full year, Saipan station was told to ready the subjects in a quarter of that time.[5]

Under such strict time constraints, three different CIA training teams were assembled to begin instruction. The first team offered the Khampas an extremely rudimentary course on classic espionage tactics. The second started coaching them in Morse communications and use of the RS-1 shortwave radio and its hand-cranked generator. The final team initiated a primer on guerrilla warfare and paramilitary operations.

Very quickly, problems became apparent. Having had almost no schooling, the Khampas had trouble with such essential concepts as the twenty-four-hour clock. They also had difficulty quantifying distances and numbers. Precise reporting would be vital once they were back in the field, emphasized one agency officer, "but too often they tended to use vague descriptions such as 'many' or 'some.'"[6]

To overcome some of these challenges, the CIA instructors had to rely on visual demonstrations. "We had to physically show them," said one trainer, "not simply use a classroom." To clarify the construction of ground signals for an aerial resupply, for example, scaffolding was assembled atop the island's northern cliffs. Below, firepots were arranged on the beach so the Tibetans could visualize how they would appear from the air.[7]

Communications training proved even more difficult. The main stumbling block: Khampas traditionally received little formal language instruction. The six students, who were barely able to read or write, could hardly be expected to transmit coherent radio messages. Not realizing the seriousness of this critical deficiency until nearly halfway through the training cycle, the CIA instructors scrambled to find someone who could teach basic Tibetan grammar. Norbu, who was acting as primary interpreter for the other course work, could not be spared for double duty. Neither could Jentzen, who in any event was weak in language skills.

Enter Geshe Wangyal.

As a result of the unique symbiosis between Tibetan lamas and Mongol khans during centuries past, Tibetan Buddhism had converts spread across the Mongolian steppes of Central Asia. Some of these Mongolians, being a nomadic peo-

Geshe Wangyal, the CIA's Mongolian translator. (Courtesy Joshua Culter)

NO wonder that my son David + 2½ des Busted out in Tears when he met geshe.

ple, had wandered far with their adopted religion. By the early seventeenth century, one such band had settled in the Kalmykia region of Russia just north of the Caspian Sea.

As an ethnic and religious anomaly, the Mongolians were initially ignored by their host country. By the early twentieth century, however, their mastery of Tibetan Buddhism eventually brought them to the attention of the Russian czars. Looking

But both loved ice cream!

to outwit the British in the great game of colonial competition, the Russians sought to use a particularly gifted Mongolian monk named Agvan Dorzhiev to court favor with Lhasa.

The task proved deceptively easy. A true scholar of Tibetan Buddhism, Dorzhiev (who hailed from a displaced Mongolian clan in Siberia) not only won an introduction to the thirteenth Dalai Lama but also was retained as a palace tutor and confidant for ten years. Through this inside connection, the relationship between Tibet and Russia had the makings of a close alliance. In 1904, however, chances for this were dashed when the Dalai Lama briefly fled to Mongolia following a British incursion from India. Dorzhiev was dispatched to plead for emergency Russian support, but he returned with nothing more than moral encouragement. Having just been humiliated in the Russo-Japanese War, the czar had little time to spare for Tibet.

The Russians never had a chance to make amends. In 1917, the czar was overthrown by Bolshevik communists, and Russia became the Soviet Union. By that time, Dorzhiev had settled among his ethnic relatives in Kalmykia and opened a pair of monastic schools. Tibet never strayed far from his mind, however, and shortly after the Bolshevik revolution he personally selected several of his best pupils to continue their studies in Lhasa. Among them was a prodigy named Wangyal.[8]

Born in 1901, Wangyal had started monastic life at age six. He was known for his ability to memorize several pages of Buddhist text in a single sitting, and he regularly excelled in class. Switching briefly to medical school, he again took top honors before reverting back to religious course work following the untimely death of his professor.

After being selected to study in Lhasa, Wangyal learned that he would be part of a larger expedition with ulterior motives. As the Bolsheviks still harbored the czarist desire to court Tibet, one of his co-travelers was a communist functionary who intended to offer Lhasa weapons as a sign of good faith. Having Moscow's obvious blessing did not ease the physical challenges of journeying to the Tibetan plateau. What was expected to take four months instead took fourteen and claimed the life of one apprentice in a blinding snowstorm.

Once in Lhasa, Wangyal enrolled at the prestigious Drepung Monastic University. Located on a high ridge eight kilometers west of the capital, Drepung had once been the largest monastery in the world (its population in the seventeenth century was a staggering 10,000 monks). Setting his sights high, the newly arrived Mongolian intended to become *geshe* (doctor of divinity)—a title that can take up to thirty-five years of study to achieve.[9]

Rigorous study was not Wangyal's only challenge. He ran short of finances and was forced to leave Lhasa in 1932 to seek funds at home. Planning to return by way of China, he got as far as Beijing before hearing stories of Soviet repression back in Kalmykia. This led him to look for an alternative source of financing in Beijing, and eventually he was able to earn a good living translating Tibetan texts.

By 1935, Wangyal had amassed enough cash and headed back toward Tibet via India. Making his way to Calcutta, he had a chance meeting with Sir Charles Bell, a senior British colonial official and noted Tibetan scholar who, ironically, had earlier displaced Agvan Dorzhiev as the closest foreign confidant of the thirteenth Dalai Lama. Given his linguistic skills—Chinese, Mongolian, Tibetan, and a smattering of English—Wangyal was hired as Bell's translator during an extended tour of China and Manchuria.

Following these exhaustive travels—including a four-month visit to England—Wangyal finally made it to Lhasa. There he earned his *geshe* degree after just nine years of study. Though this was an impressive scholastic accomplishment, he found himself under a cloud of suspicion. His foreign heritage, coupled with extended time spent in China and service to the British, did not sit well among the xenophobes of the Tibetan court.

Not fully welcome in the homeland of his religion, Geshe Wangyal limited his time in Lhasa to the summer months. Winters were spent in Kalimpong, where he displayed pronounced entrepreneurial skills as a trader. Although this was financially rewarding, he yearned to open his own religious school. Stonewalled in Tibet, he instead targeted Beijing—only to cancel those plans when the communists came to power in 1949. Figuring that he would give Tibet a second chance, he again ventured to Lhasa but was forced to flee upon hearing that the PLA was approaching the Tibetan capital in late 1951.[10]

Back in Kalimpong, Geshe Wangyal grew restless. China, Tibet, Mongolia, and his native Kalmykia were all under communist occupation, but wasting away the months in tiny Kalimpong lacked both mental and spiritual stimulation.

There was one attractive alternative, however. In late 1951, the United States accepted 800 Kalmyk Mongolians who had been languishing in refugee camps since the end of World War II. These refugees were drawn from two waves that had fled the Soviet Union during the preceding decades. The first had departed Kalmykia shortly after the Bolshevik revolution; the second left in late 1943 after Joseph Stalin adopted a ruthless line against minorities and started deporting the Mongolians to Siberia aboard cattle cars. Once in the United States, the older wave of émigrés settled around Philadelphia. The newer ones—no more than seventy families—established a small but vibrant community near Freewood Acres, New Jersey.[11]

Hearing of this, Geshe Wangyal contemplated a move to the United States. His first several visa applications were rejected, and it was not until mid-1954, following introductions by a British acquaintance, that the U.S. vice consul in Calcutta processed his papers with a favorable recommendation.[12]

Arriving on American soil in February 1955, Geshe Wangyal found that word of his religious accomplishments in Tibet had already made him famous among his fellow Kalmyk Mongolians. With an instant audience, he opened a modest temple in a converted New Jersey garage.

Geshe Wangal's fame was not limited to his ethnic home crowd. As the first (and to that time, only) qualified scholar of Tibetan Buddhism in the United States, he soon came in contact with Norbu, who at the time was also living in New Jersey and teaching Tibetan at Columbia University. Out of mutual respect between *geshe* and incarnation, Norbu was given an honorary chair at the New Jersey temple.

The two cooperated in another way as well. Following Norbu's lead, Geshe Wangyal began teaching languages—first Mongolian, then Tibetan—at Columbia University in 1956. Having dissected Tibetan grammar during years of poring over Buddhist texts, he had a particularly deep appreciation for its written form. His extended time as Bell's interpreter had left him with reasonably good English skills. The U.S. government, for one, found his linguistic talents more than adequate: among his first Tibetan students at Columbia were two from the U.S. Army.[13]

Given this background, Geshe Wangyal was the perfect choice to instruct the Khampas about their own language. Having already been indirectly exposed to the U.S. government while teaching the army students—and after being informed that Norbu was already involved—the monk offered his cooperation and was soon en route to Saipan.

Beyond the serious language hurdle, the CIA staff on Saipan harbored a more fundamental concern about their Tibetan subjects. The Khampas were Buddhists, and nearly all of them had spent some time as monks. Their instructors wondered whether they would hesitate to kill a fellow human being. For Eli Popovich, chief of the seven paramilitary instructors, this was driven home during an incident early in training. A veteran of OSS operations in Burma and the Balkans, Popovich had been addressing his class when one of the Khampas came forward and pushed him. "I had been standing on an anthill," recalls Popovich, "and he didn't want me interfering with another living entity."[14]

It would take another incident—also involving ants—to put the Tibetan attitude toward life and death into better perspective. One morning, case officer
Harry Mustakos heard a commotion coming from the latrine, where trainee Tashi
(now called "Dick"; each Khampa had an American name on Saipan) was attending to cleaning duties. Beckoned by Norbu, Mustakos rushed in to find both
Tibetans hunched over a column of ants crossing from a crack in the wall toward
the urinal. "What can we do about these creatures?" Norbu pleaded.

With class set to start in minutes, Mustakos gave them a quick answer. "You
can carefully sweep them up and drop them outside," he said, "or you can continue swabbing the deck as though they weren't there."

The CIA officer left the room to let the two Tibetans discuss a solution. Dick's
voice could soon be heard reciting a Buddhist mantra as he rhythmically swung
the mop across the trespassing column. "Pragmatism prevailed," concluded
Mustakos.[15]

Indeed, the CIA was fast coming to realize that the Khampas had few reservations about taking the life of a Chinese invader. "Their ideas on what weapons
should be dropped were starting to get extravagant," remembers Mustakos.
"Machine guns for each of their friends, they said, plus artillery batteries would
be nice."[16]

Of the six Khampas, Wangdu—now known as "Walt"—led the cry for more
sophisticated weaponry. Partly, this reflected Walt's hot temper. Partly, too, it was
a face-saving gesture to compensate for his low scores in Morse training. "He
was near the bottom of the class," said fellow trainee Athar, who now went by
the name "Tom." "He began complaining that he wanted to train with bigger
guns, not waste time on radios."[17]

For the CIA, this posed a dilemma. Walt's demands for heavier firepower
conflicted with its need for skilled agents who would observe and report—not
rush to the offensive. Gingerly, the agency trainers attempted to downplay
Tibetan expectations. Said Tom, "They explained that it would be too hard to let
us carry artillery pieces into Tibet."[18]

The Khampas were not the only ones who required massaging. The two interpreters—Norbu and Jentzen—offered their own set of challenges. Like many
Asian societies, Tibet was composed of clearly defined strata, with the religious
elite and aristocracy at the top and the warrior and merchant classes well below.
On Saipan, this translated into one set of quarters for the interpreters (and, later,
Geshe Wangyal) and a different barracks for the students. For the proud Khampas, this arrangement was palatable in the case of Norbu, whose religious standing and family ties demanded reverence. Jentzen, by contrast, was viewed merely

as Norbu's servant, who was elite only by association. "His English was not too good," sniffed Tom.[19]

For his part, Norbu did not much care for the cloistered life on Saipan. Limited to a single classroom building and pair of sleeping quarters, the Tibetans were rarely allowed to leave their isolated corner of the training base. Moreover, cooks and cleaning crews were forbidden in the name of operational secrecy. As a result, all present—trainees as well as interpreters—were required to rotate chores and eat the same meals. As an incarnation and brother of the Dalai Lama, Norbu found this too much to take and at one point refused the food. The CIA cadre was not amused. "If you don't eat it," said Mustakos sternly, "the students won't eat it." Norbu eventually backed down and consumed his proletarian meal.

The Khampas, by contrast, offered no complaints about the Spartan conditions. With rare exceptions, their health rarely faltered. One scare occurred when trainee Tsawang Dorje—now going by the name "Sam"—suffered a ruptured appendix. A few weeks later, the same hapless agent accidentally shot himself in the foot with a pistol. Both incidents required emergency trips to Okinawa, and both resulted in fast recoveries.

On another occasion, Lhotse—his name now Americanized to "Lou"—caught a bad case of dysentery. By chance, CIA Director Allen Dulles was passing through Saipan during a Far East tour and had along his personal physician. From the latter, the local doctor was able to obtain a new drug and get Lou started on a course of treatment. Concerned, the CIA instructors checked with Lou daily to determine if his bowel purges continued.

"Shit today?" they asked. To this, the afflicted agent repeated the words in the affirmative. Convinced that the medication was not taking effect, the CIA instructors sent Lou and an interpreter to the hospital for closer observation. There they learned that Lou had already returned to normal and had merely been reciting the phrase to showcase his newfound command of select English words.[20]

Such medical emergencies aside, the Khampas were shaping up to be model students. "They were new to us," said Mustakos. "Culturally and psychologically, we were learning from them as much as they were learning from us." Sometimes this led to conclusions that bordered on the comical. The Tibetans, for example, saw American omnipotence in seemingly unrelated events. Each night at sundown, the CIA advisers sprayed the compound with an insecticide-dispensing unit mounted on a jeep. This awed the Tibetans, who viewed the routine as proof that the United States was a powerful country. Said case officer Mustakos, "They noted that we had devised ways of killing big things—like people—by using the weapons with which we were training, and even killing little things—like mosquitoes—with the DDT fogger."[21]

Such innocent observations only served to endear the Tibetans to their CIA instructors. One of the most impressed was Roger McCarthy. Thirty years old, the gregarious McCarthy had joined the CIA in 1952 as a communications specialist for Western Enterprises. Promoted to case officer, he arrived in Saipan in 1956 and had just completed a paramilitary training cycle for six members of the Lao intelligence service prior to the arrival of the Tibetans. "The Lao would get frightened during nighttime operations," he recalls, "and hold each other's hands." The Tibetans, by contrast, were of entirely different mettle. "They were brave and honest and strong," said McCarthy. "Basically, everything we respect in a man."[22]

Training officer Mustakos shared similar sentiments about the rugged Khampas. This was underscored during close-quarter combat instruction when he tossed a traditional short Tibetan sword to Lou and told him to attack. "I learned from that," said Mustakos, "to find out if knife fighting was native lore before trying it again."

After a month-long extension to allow Geshe Wangyal to complete his language instruction, training for the Khampas was all but finished by mid-September. To properly outfit them for their return, an urgent request had been flashed back to India for six sets of used Tibetan peasant garb, knives, and coins. Once Gyalo gathered the items, he rushed down to Calcutta and notified his case officer, John Hoskins. Smuggled into the consulate, the unwashed, reeking load was divided into half a dozen diplomatic pouches and posted to Saipan.[23]

Other preparations were well under way for insertion of the agents back into Tibet. To save time—and avoid the diplomatic and physical hazards of walking back through Indian territory—the CIA intended to drop them inside their homeland by parachute. As CIA headquarters had given the cryptonym ST CIRCUS to the emerging Tibet Task Force, this aerial portion of the project retained the same theme and was code-named ST BARNUM.[24]

Airborne infiltration posed a whole range of difficulties. First, it required a discreet staging base within range of Tibet; just as during exfiltration, East Pakistan was the optimal choice. Second, the flight would necessarily be conducted at night, which meant that the plane needed both clear weather and a full moon to negotiate its way to the drop zone. Fortunately, both weather patterns and moon phases were predictable. In East Pakistan, the annual monsoon season came to a close in October, and over Tibet, the clearest skies could be found in October and November. Factoring in a full moon, this meant that premium conditions were most likely to occur during a six-day window beginning 6 October and during another six-day window starting 5 November.[25]

An even greater challenge was determining where in Tibet the agents would be inserted. From the moment the Khampas arrived in Saipan, part of that station's mandate had been to help select drop zones. During debriefings of the trainees, each was quizzed about his hometown, where he had traveled, what routes he had taken, names of villages along the way, and people he had met. Starting from crude route tracings, the CIA instructors slowly added village names, terrain features, and distance notations.

Concurrently, CIA headquarters assigned the Far East Division's air branch to flesh out the details for ST BARNUM. Heading the task was the branch's deputy, Gar Thorsrud. No stranger to covert air support, Thorsrud had been a student at the University of Montana when first approached by a CIA recruiter in the summer of 1951. The recruiter was looking for smoke jumpers, the unique breed of firefighters employed by the U.S. Forest Service. During the dry summer months, these jumpers were on call at rural airstrips across the western half of the United States. When a forest fire flared, they donned parachutes and dropped in small teams ahead of the advancing flames. Using shovels and saws to cut firebreaks, they were responsible for saving thousands of acres of woodland.

For the CIA, smoke jumpers were attractive on a number of counts. Not only were they fit and adventurous, but the job entailed learning the basics about parachuting and air delivery techniques. Smoke jumpers, in fact, were on the leading edge with equipment such as steerable chutes and skills such as rough-terrain jumping. Moreover, many—like Thorsrud—were promising college students who volunteered for the task during summer break.

In the spring of 1951, just after his graduation, Thorsrud and another smoke jumper were asked to report early to train a pair of CIA officers in rough terrain parachuting techniques. Upon completion, both were offered CIA employment subject to a security review. By that fall, another eight were recruited and passed the review.

By year's end, the Montana smoke-jumping contingent had departed for the Far East. Once there, they were briefed by agency case officers. Indigenous teams and singleton agents were being readied for insertion into China and North Korea, they were told. Because of their parachuting background, the smoke jumpers were assigned to act as jump masters and "kickers," the descriptive term used for cargo handlers who pushed parachute-equipped supply pallets out the back of transport aircraft.

For the next two years, Taiwan-based smoke jumpers helped deliver agents and kick bundles behind communist lines. Thorsrud was involved in some of the deepest penetrations to supply Muslim guerrillas in western China. But at the end of the Korean War, nearly all the jumpers resigned from the agency for more mundane civilian assignments. Among them was Thorsrud, who joined the Air National Guard for pilot training in anticipation of a career with an airline.

It was not to be. In the summer of 1956, Thorsrud was again contacted by the agency and asked to rejoin the Far East Division's air branch. Weighed against a career as a commercial pilot, the CIA post won.

Once he was handed the Tibet assignment, one of Thorsrud's first tasks was to sort out the issue of drop zones. Although the CIA had a special office for worldwide overhead imagery, the files on Tibet were exceedingly thin. Satellites did not yet exist, and the U-2 spy plane—which had been penetrating the Soviet bloc for just a little over a year—had flown only a single Tibet overflight on 21 August 1957. Apart from this, few current photographic and cartographic resources were to be found in the agency's archives.[26]

Digging deeper, Thorsrud eventually came up with some useful, albeit dated, photographs. These came from the 1904 British military expedition that had pushed its way into Lhasa to seek a trade agreement. The best shot was a photo of the Brahmaputra River, clearly showing the dunes and extensive wash along its northern bank after flood stage. Just sixty kilometers southeast of the Tibetan capital, this sandy expanse was selected as the site for the first drop.

Based on information coming from Saipan, a second drop zone was chosen near Molha Khashar, a tiny village of two dozen families just outside Lithang. Besides being the hometown of Walt's family, Molha Khashar was reputed to be an area of armed Khampa resistance.[27]

With two drop zones selected, Thorsrud now had to decide on planes and crews. Within the agency's own Asian proprietary—Taiwan-based CAT—there was more than sufficient talent. During the Korean War, U.S. crewmen flying for CAT had conducted dozens of drop missions and intelligence-collection flights over mainland China. But after a CAT C-47 was downed over the PRC in November 1952—followed by the crash of a covert USAF flight over China in January 1953—U.S. crews were forbidden to fly agent infiltrations over the mainland.

An Asian alternative could be found within the ranks of the ROC air force. Back in 1952, five Nationalist pilots and two mechanics had been sent to Japan under CIA auspices. There they began training in low-level flights and drop techniques.

By the middle of the following year, the contingent returned home as the cadre of a new Special Mission Team. Initially supplied with a single B-26 and two B-17s on loan from Western Enterprises, the team did not see action until February 1954. That month, the B-26 dropped leaflets over Shanghai to disrupt the fourth anniversary celebrations of the Sino-Soviet Friendship Treaty. That flight was deemed a success, and the team was flying an average of one mainland infiltration per month by the time Thorsrud was planning the Tibet assignment. Its missions included not only leaflet, supply, and agent drops but also electronic-signal collection flights to gather data about the PRC's air defenses.[28]

Although there was no denying the competence of the Nationalist Chinese, their participation was ruled out. This was because the ROC still entertained the notion that Tibet was part of greater China, a position that earned them the scorn of most Tibetans. If Taipei was brought into the fold and word leaked, it would undercut the CIA's relations with the Tibetan resistance.

With Americans and Nationalist Chinese precluded, Thorsrud searched for another option. He eventually found one in an unlikely place. Back in 1949, the CIA had hired two Czech airmen when it needed a deniable crew to drop Ukrainian agents into their homeland. These Czechs had earlier distinguished themselves while flying for the British during the Battle of Britain and had remained in England after their homeland fell to communism. In a variation on this theme, the CIA and British intelligence had jointly prepared a paramilitary operation the following year to unseat the communist government in Albania. Again looking for foreign aircrews, the British had suggested tapping the large pool of Polish veterans in England who had performed brilliantly during World War II. Thus, six stateless Poles from within that community had been hired and dispatched to a staging base in Athens, Greece, for the Albanian assignment.

Pleased with the results, the CIA in 1955 again turned to stateless Poles when it needed crews for a covert operation running out of Wiesbaden, Germany. Using modified P2V Neptune antisubmarine aircraft, missions were flown along the Soviet frontier to collect electronic intelligence. Although Americans piloted many of these flights, two of the planes were flown with Polish crews and used for actual penetrations of Soviet airspace.

It was from this seasoned Polish contingent at Wiesbaden—code-named Ostiary—that the Far East Division requested the loan of two five-man crews to perform the Tibetan assignment. The first was to be headed by Captain Franciszek Czekalski, the thirty-six-year-old leader of the Wiesbaden Poles. The second was under Captain Jan Drobny, a former flying sergeant who had flown special wartime drop missions to the anti-Axis resistance movement in Poland.

After gaining agency approval to use Ostiary, Thorsrud had to decide on an infiltration plane. By 1957, the workhorse for covert China overflights from Taiwan was the B-17. The four-engined Flying Fortress had been a fixture of the European theater during World War II. For the CIA's missions over mainland China, its ROC-based bombers had been stripped of all weapons and national markings, painted black, and modified with engine mufflers to shield the exhaust. Given its range and maneuverability, it was deemed suitable for ST BARNUM.

In mid-September, the finalized plan was sent to CIA Director Dulles for his signature. Upon his consent, a Taiwan-based B-17 was flown to Clark Air Force Base in the Philippines.[29] Piloting the bomber was Robert Kleyla, one of the officers managing the CIA air fleet in the ROC. Once at Clark, he met up with the two Ostiary crews escorted by their Wiesbaden case officer, Monty Ballew. Though none of the Europeans had ever flown a B-17, they took to the bomber quickly. Acting as instructor, Kleyla gave the Polish captains what turned out to be a pro forma checkout. "They already were well qualified in four engines," he summed up.[30]

Their transition complete, the Ostiary contingent loaded into the lone bomber and ferried it to Okinawa. There they married up with the Tibetans, who had arrived to start airborne training. Much preparation and experimentation had gone into this phase of the operation. Leading the effort was James McElroy, head of the CIA's aerial resupply section at Kadena Air Base. Eighteen years old when he enlisted in 1946, McElroy had been a U.S. Army parachute rigger until seconded to the CIA in 1951. He now oversaw a section of four Americans and ninety Okinawans who were responsible for parachute delivery operations in support of CIA operations across the Far East.[31]

Just prior to the arrival of the Tibetans, McElroy had been contacted by Saipan station with two requests. First, they wanted a parachute with high maneuverability. Second, they needed a system to ensure that a large supply bundle would remain with the jumper. McElroy was told that the drop zone was at an elevation of 4,545 meters (15,000 feet) with no elaboration on the destination.

For the maneuverable parachute, McElroy took a page from the smoke jumpers. During the early 1940s, they had developed a twenty-eight-foot flat-surface chute with modified slots and tails that gave them sufficient steering ability to maneuver near the edge of firestorms. Inspired by this, McElroy back in 1953 had tried to work similar modifications into the military's standard thirty-five-foot T-10 chute. The results had been disappointing, though in hindsight, he realized that the problem was failure to compensate with sufficiently large slots for the bigger army T-10.

This time, McElroy used the same proportions as the smoke jumper prototypes. The new chutes, with bigger slots and longer tails, were tested by McElroy and Saipan training officer Roger McCarthy. After four jumps, they concluded that the modified T-10s had the required steerability.

For the second request—keeping the bundle close to the jumper—McElroy had something much more revolutionary in mind. Harkening back to the end of World War II, he recalled seeing a magazine photograph of a row of connected bundles streaming out the door of a C-47. "I wasn't sure if it was ever used in combat," he said, "but I wanted to try something similar." Sketching out his concept, McElroy envisioned a nylon line running from the chest of the jumper to the supply pallet. Static lines would deploy chutes on both the pallet and the parachutist, with a 91-meter line keeping the two connected. If one of the two chutes failed to deploy, the line was designed to break if overstressed. McElroy was confident that the system would work—at least on paper.

Once the Tibetans arrived, they were given a primer on landing techniques and then outfitted with the modified chutes. Fearless of heights after years of peering off tall canyons, they exited the plane without hesitation. Much to the case officer's delight, they even used the steerable rigs to chase one another in the air. Three jumps later, all were declared qualified.

By that time, they were into the first days of October, and optimal moon and weather conditions were set to begin over Tibet. Before leaving Kadena, the resupply section loaded bundles inside the B-17. Each of the two Tibetan teams would get a single bundle weighing no more than 114 kilos (250 pounds). Included inside was radio gear, extra crystals, and personal weapons. To get this bundle off the drop zone as fast as possible, the CIA logisticians had broken the gear down into 36-kilo (80-pound) segments and placed them inside special pouched vests similar to those used by newspaper delivery men.[32]

Once their supplies were secured on board, the Tibetans, along with a handful of CIA case officers and both Ostiary crews, took the B-17 to East Pakistan. As with their earlier C-118 exfiltration, the black, unmarked bomber was cleared to land at the unused airstrip at Kurmitola, thirteen kilometers north of Dacca. An Allied runway during World War II, the Kurmitola field was 1,060 meters long, 45 meters wide, and almost 2 meters thick—all of hand-laid brick. Adjacent to the strip was a hangar with open ends, some empty brick buildings with tin roofs in bad repair, and little else. Because East Pakistan's main north-south road had been built across the center of the runway at a right angle, soldiers from the nearby cantonment were directed to divert traffic at a discreet distance while the B-17 was present.[33]

The communications shed at Kurmitola airfield, East Pakistan; the lightning rod at right is where a CIA technician was electrocuted. (Courtesy Walter Cox)

As the bomber landed and the case officers disembarked, they were immediately hit by two bits of bad news. First, they learned that a CIA communications technician—dispatched to Kurmitola the previous week to establish a secure radio link—had been electrocuted while erecting an antenna. Second, they got word that the Soviets had just bested America and successfully launched the first satellite into Earth orbit.[34]

With little time to ponder these developments, the officers immediately set about preparing the B-17 for its drop. Captain Czekalski's five-man team was selected to crew the plane; no Americans were to be on board. To minimize exposure over Tibet, the Poles would conduct both drops on the same flight. Because the plane would need to overfly Indian territory without permission, they had to factor in the radar at Calcutta. Gar Thorsrud had already done his homework and knew that the Indian system had no compensation feature and could be defeated if the B-17 used the Himalayan massif as a radar screen. Flying north over Sikkim, the crew would go as far as the Brahmaputra for the first drop, cut east across the Tibetan plateau to Kham for the second drop, then veer southwest through Indian territory back to East Pakistan. "It would be an easy flight for the Poles," concluded Thorsrud.[35]

Inside the B-17, two supply loads were positioned near the 1.4-meter (54-

inch) hatch—known as a "joe hole"—located in the belly of the cabin. The Polish loadmaster for the flight, "Big Mac" Korczowski, reviewed with Roger McCarthy the procedure of placing each bundle over the hole and securing it with restraints.

After a one-day delay (because it was considered inauspicious according to the Tibetan calendar), all six Khampas boarded the aircraft.[36] As Kurmitola had no runway lights, flame pots framed the edges of the runway. Before the plane could take off, however, the weather closed in, and the mission was scrubbed. Three more days of overcast followed, and tension was beginning to mount as the full moon entered its final day.

With just one more chance, the weather finally proved cooperative, and the mission was given the green light. As the Tibetans filed inside the plane and their Buddhist prayers echoed through the cabin, they turned one last time to case officer Mustakos and offered up a Christian tradition. "I had taught them the sign of the cross," said Mustakos, "and now they sought a double blessing."

Lifting off from Kurmitola, Czekalski put the B-17 on a northern heading over the Sikkim corridor. With the Himalayas bathed in a celestial glow, the Ostiary crew climbed over the range and negotiated their way onto the Tibetan plateau.

Inside their homeland for the first time in over a year, the agents readied themselves for the first jump. Despite the altitude and unpressurized cabin, the Tibetans were not using oxygen bottles; a lifetime of mountain living had acclimatized them to the thin air.

As moonlight reflected off the distant Brahmaputra, two of the agents—Tom and Lou, now given the radio call signs Budwood 1 and Budwood 2—maneuvered toward the joe hole. Selected as the jumper to be connected to the bundle, Tom adjusted a short section of line near his chest; the remaining 91 meters was rolled and covered with elastic loops on the side of the supplies. "I carried a knife at my side," recalled Tom, "just in case something went wrong."

As the B-17 came over the Brahmaputra, the cockpit crew flashed a signal in the cabin. Facing forward with his feet near the hole, Tom watched as Big Mac yanked the restraints on the supplies. Once the load disappeared out the hatch, the line began to play out from the side of the bundle. A second later, Tom dropped into the void.

The sound of the bomber fast receded, followed by the sound of a dog barking. As Tom looked about to get his bearings, he eyed the bundle and its white cargo chute floating before him. The jumper–to–supply line system was working perfectly. Lou, meanwhile, used his steerable T-10 to follow in Tom's wake toward the approaching sandbank.[37]

Inside the B-17, navigator Franciszek Kot wasted no time plotting an eastern course, while Big Mac hauled the second bundle over the joe hole. When they came upon Kham, however, they found that clear skies had given way to a solid cloud bank. Without any sophisticated navigational systems aboard, the crew had little choice but to abort the second drop and head back to East Pakistan. By that time, the full moon phase had run its course; any further attempts at infiltration would have to wait until the next lunar cycle.

Back inside Tibet, Lou and Tom landed without incident on the wind-blown dunes north of the Brahmaputra. Freeing themselves from their parachute harnesses, they both unstrapped the 9mm Sten submachine guns fixed to their chests and peered into the darkness. Although there was a small settlement of three families just 364 meters (400 yards) away, they received no indication that they had been detected.

Turning their attention to the supply bundle, they broke open the load and started removing the prepacked vests. Since the area around the drop zone consisted of soft earth, they decided to dig seven holes and cache most of their supplies in the immediate vicinity. Before doing so, both changed into traditional Tibetan garb and retained one pistol and one grenade apiece. They also kept one RS-1 radio set and buried the spare.

The next morning, Tom and Lou wandered through the nearby village. Because nomads and traders are common throughout Tibet, the sudden appearance of two strangers aroused no undue suspicion. Mingling with the locals, they overheard talk about their plane passing overhead in the night. None of the villagers suspected that any parachutists had landed, so the pair felt safe waiting two days in the vicinity before taking their radio to the top of an adjacent hill. To their dismay, however, they found that the set had sustained damage in the drop. "The light on the transmitter was very faint," recalled Tom, who had graduated as best radioman among the six trainees. "I tapped a few words but had no way of knowing if it was actually sent."[38]

Leaving the malfunctioning set behind, the pair decided to follow the Brahmaputra. After trekking along its bank for a few hours, they eventually came upon a secluded riverside village near Samye. Pivotal in the history of Tibet, Samye was the site of the monastery where Buddhism was officially inaugurated as the state religion. Because it hosted a constant stream of pilgrims, the arrival of the two outsiders again aroused no attention. "I had the grenade and pistol in my pockets just in case," remembers Tom.

After purchasing horses and some food, the agents reversed direction east toward the Woka valley. Riddled with caves and hot springs, Woka was renowned for its shrines and other meditation sites. But before they could reach this area, the agents chanced upon a band of seven Khampa pilgrims heading toward the Tibetan capital. Tom and Lou were in for a shock. Two of the approaching pilgrims were friends from among their own group of young Khampas that had tailed the Dalai Lama during the Buddha Jayanti. Taking the pair aside, the agents swore them to secrecy and asked that they deliver messages to prominent Khampa trader Gompo Tashi Andrugtsang and Lou's own younger brother, both residing in Lhasa.

As the Khampa entourage continued toward the capital, Tom and Lou returned to their drop zone and unearthed the spare RS-1. Finding it in good working order, the pair tapped out several sentences, briefly outlining their activities over the past ten days.

For Irving "Frank" Holober, ten days had been a long wait. A thirty-three-year-old Harvard graduate, he had been serving as head of the Tibet Task Force since late July 1957. Like his predecessor John Reagan, Holober was a China specialist: three years at headquarters as a Chinese translator, then a tour with Western Enterprises, where he helped channel support to Muslims in Amdo. Following that had been a three-year sojourn in Indonesia before assuming Reagan's slot.

From the start, Holober had been beset with problems. Reports were coming in from Saipan that Norbu resented the harsh conditions, especially being forced to eat the same food as the students. As soon as the training cycle concluded, the incarnation and his servant promptly quit the program.

Of far greater concern was the fate of Lou and Tom. From the moment the two agents jumped from the B-17, the CIA had been straining to hear word from their pilot team. After a week had passed, there was growing fear that the pair was lost. With little to do, Geshe Wangyal had been temporarily released from service to return to his New Jersey ministry. As an emergency stopgap, Holober had arranged for help from the National Security Agency (NSA), the U.S. intelligence organization charged with communications intercepts. Based at Fort Meade, Maryland, the NSA agreed to loan the CIA its sole Tibetan linguist, Stuart Buck.[39]

Buck had his work cut out for him. While on Saipan, Geshe Wangyal had taught his Tibetan students a remedial code in which their native script was roughly adapted to the Roman alphabet. But because the six Khampas were not fluent in their own written language, spelling errors in Tibetan were compounded by an inexact Roman transliteration. This is exactly what happened when Tom's message was flashed to CIA headquarters. Trying to make sense of the poor spelling, Buck threw up his hands. "It basically says, 'I'm alive.'"

That was all Holober needed to know. "The entire Far East Division," he recalls, "was electrified."[40]

At Clark Air Base, the Ostiary crews had also been playing a waiting game. Sitting out the remainder of October while the moon ran its phases, they married up with the four remaining Tibetans and moved back to Kurmitola during the first week of November. This time the weather was fully cooperative as the B-17 made a moonlit departure for Kham.[41]

Catching sight of the Lithang River—which ran past the town of the same name—the crew dropped low over the hills. As they arrived over what they believed was the vicinity of Molha Khashar, the cockpit flashed a signal to the cabin.

Just as the agents lined up behind the joe hole, Dick hyperventilated and collapsed on the cabin floor. As the loadmaster pulled him to the side, the other three readied themselves for the jump. Repeating the procedure used in the first drop, restraints were pulled from the supply bundle, and it disappeared through the hatch. On the other end of the belly line went Sam, followed by the remaining two agents in quick succession. Reversing course, the B-17 headed back toward East Pakistan with the unconscious Dick still aboard.

Unlike Tom and Lou—who had landed on a desolate sand flat—the three Kham agents came down in a hillside of conifers. Landing without injury, they cached their supplies and ascended to the top of a nearby mountain under cover of darkness. There they heard gunfire in the distance as the PLA dueled with Khampa guerrillas.

As dawn broke, Walt took his bearings. To his dismay, he found that the plane had overshot their intended drop zone by some fourteen kilometers. Walking along the high ground into the afternoon, they spotted a lone Khampa tending to five Tibetan ponies. The herdsman was visibly apprehensive as the agents approached, though he eventually agreed to escort them to a guerrilla encampment on a neighboring hill.

By nightfall, the three agents had successfully linked up with the rebel band, which coincidentally included Walt's older brother. Together, they headed back to their cache site and retrieved their gear, and just forty-eight hours after infiltration, they radioed word of their safe arrival. ST CIRCUS was off to a good start.

5. Four Rivers, Six Ranges

On any given day for centuries past, the dusty alleys of Lhasa were crammed with monks, courtesans, pilgrims, and traders. By late 1957, however, these traditional residents were all but eclipsed by something new—the war refugee. As a result of the fierce guerrilla battles waged over the past two years, more than 10,000 displaced Khampas and Amdowas had pitched tents in the hills and plains surrounding the capital; many more had fled their villages for sanctuary in the countryside. In a vast country with just 3 million people—and with the normal population of Lhasa standing at only 10,000—this was a demographic shift of significant proportions.[1]

Lost among these refugees, Lou and Tom looked like just two more destitute Khampas making their way toward the capital when they departed Woka in November. This was not too far from the truth: on the ground for a month, they had spent nearly all the Tibetan and Chinese coins from their supply bundles.

Pausing sixty kilometers east of the capital, the agents were in for a pleasant surprise. Already awaiting them was Lou's younger brother, who had received the earlier message asking for a rendezvous. Better still, he had come with enough Chinese currency to allow Tom and Lou to buy a tent and pitch it on the outskirts of the village.

As a Lithang Khampa from a reputable family, Lou's younger brother had been living within the vast Lhasa household of Lithang's most accomplished citizen, Gompo Tashi Andrugtsang. The Khampa leader had also received a message from the agents and arrived less than a week later with a small band of assistants.

Fifty-two years old, Gompo Tashi was unique among Khampas. Though a native of Lithang, he hailed from a family of savvy businessmen who had made a profound mark in Lhasa due to their generous annual donations to Buddhist causes. Gompo Tashi had followed this example, amassing considerable wealth as a trader and continuing the family tradition of religious largesse. From a young age, he also displayed legendary bravery in confronting the bandit gangs that haunted his district.

Taken together, this put him in a category apart from his peers. Unlike Kham's conservative hereditary chieftains, Gompo Tashi was far more worldly (he had made a pilgrimage to India and Nepal in 1942) and could appreciate the benefits of modernity and the wider implications of Chinese hegemony. And unlike other successful Kham traders, such as the Pandatsang family, he was less Machiavellian and more principled when it came to support for the central government. This gave him a foot in both camps: his seniority and reputation won respect among the Khampas, while his generosity guaranteed influence within the Lhasa power structure.

There was one sore point, however. As his kinsmen were fighting and dying in Kham, Gompo Tashi rarely strayed far from his comfortable residence in the capital. He was not part of the fledgling resistance movement, nor did he field any fighters of his own. Not until December 1956, half a year after his native Lithang was struck by PLA bombers, did he begin to test the waters of armed dissent. This he did by proxy: three of his employees were dispatched to Kham, each with a letter signed by Gompo Tashi urging the disparate guerrilla bands to unite in a common struggle against the Chinese.[2]

Apart from this move, Gompo Tashi did little for the next year. Things were complicated by the fact that the Khampas themselves—despite China's shoddy treatment—were not all sour toward Beijing. In a classic display of clan rivalry, one prominent chieftain from the town of Bathang visited the capital and lectured his fellow Khampas on the benefits of cooperation with the Chinese authorities; he later made a similar pitch to influential monks in Lhasa's biggest monasteries.[3]

Having suffered some of the PLA's worst excesses, Khampas from Gompo Tashi's Lithang were less inclined to compromise. They assumed that he shared their anti-Chinese sentiment, and it was through him that they funneled multiple petitions in early 1957 seeking military assistance from Lhasa.

Despite the pitched struggle being waged in Kham, Lhasa was not listening. Instead, residents in the capital were fully preoccupied with the Dalai Lama's return from India on 1 April.[4] To affirm their collective support for his leadership, they set about preparing a special offering in the shape of a solid gold throne encrusted with gems. Given his past history of donations, Gompo Tashi was selected as a lead fund-raiser and set out for Kham to solicit contributions.

When the throne was officially presented on 4 July, the celebration was deemed a rousing success. Though this did little to help the guerrillas in eastern Tibet, Gompo Tashi's trip to Kham had given him ample opportunity to discuss resistance activities with his kinsmen. It also afforded him occasional audiences with Thupten Woyden Phala. A tall and dignified monk, Phala had long been a confidant of the Dalai Lama. His official promotion to lord chamberlain—a combination personal secretary and head of the household staff—late the previous year meant that his access to the monarch was without peer.[5]

Not only was Phala a direct conduit to the highest echelon of power; he was also known to have little tolerance for the Chinese. An ardent nationalist, he had been among the most vocal proponents lobbying for the Dalai Lama to seek exile in 1950. And during the early months of 1957, he had strongly sided with Gyalo and Norbu in trying to keep the monarch from returning to Tibet.

By the time Lou and Tom were ready to parachute to the banks of the Brahmaputra, the CIA knew enough about Phala's influence and nationalist disposition to make him a primary target for the two agents. After their rendezvous with Gompo Tashi in November, the agents sought his aid in arranging a meeting with Phala. As that would take time, the Khampa leader suggested that they wait at a location closer to Lhasa. Departing shortly thereafter, he left behind two assistants to help procure supplies.

As suggested, the agents soon moved to the village of Pempo. Twenty-six kilometers northeast of the capital, Pempo was known for its rich agriculture and cottage industry that produced glazed pots for the Lhasa markets. Resuming radio contact from there, Tom was instructed by the CIA to briefly venture farther north into the hills overlooking the Damshung airfield. Once there, he befriended some nomads, determined that the base was rarely used, and returned to Pempo to report his findings over the RS-1.[6]

By the close of 1957, the pair was again on the move. Continuing their counterclockwise trek around the capital, they reached the famed Drepung monastery, where Geshe Wangyal had studied. They stopped there for less than a week—during which time they resided inside the complex disguised as pilgrims—and then shifted to the northern city limits of Lhasa near the similarly immense Sera monastery. Pitching a tent among hundreds of others inhabited by student monks, they couriered a coded message into the capital requesting a second meeting with Gompo Tashi.

It did not take long for a response. To avoid possible Chinese surveillance, the Khampa patriarch agreed to a weekend meeting at a park inside Lhasa. Bringing along food, they lost themselves among the throngs of holidaying residents. The agents used the opportunity to again request help in arranging an audience with Phala, and Gompo Tashi promised to pursue the matter.

Their persistence eventually paid off. Two months later, Gompo Tashi sent a messenger to Sera with two sets of monk's robes. The agents were given instructions to proceed to the north gate of the Norbulingka, the walled, forty-hectare enclave on the western outskirts of Lhasa that housed the Dalai Lama's summer palace. Waiting at a cottage inside the gate was Gompo Tashi, who escorted them to Phala's residence.

Sitting in front of the Dalai Lama's confidant, the agents were immediately peppered with questions about their training. Firing back, they quizzed the lord chamberlain about what kind of help Lhasa needed or wanted. They also asked Phala to make an official request for U.S. assistance.

It would prove to be an impossible sell. Whatever Phala's personal views on the subject, the Dalai Lama was determined not to provoke Beijing. This meant restraint from offering the rebels any moral backing, much less material assistance. A die-hard pacifist, the Dalai Lama had even opposed the relatively benign *Mimang Tsongdu*—"People's Party"—an underground ensemble of Lhasa-based laymen, activist monks, and minor government officials who had been practicing civil disobedience against the Chinese. Echoing his master, Phala kept his distance from any resistance movement. "He was completely noncommittal," recalled Tom. "He also said the Chinese were playing off the Tibetan noblemen and nobody trusted each other anymore."

As they prepared to leave, the agents suggested that Phala might want to provide a written message that could be conveyed to Washington. They also asked to see the Dalai Lama at a future date, noting that his brother Norbu had suggested this during their training on Saipan. Phala promised to do his best on both counts.

Neither proved forthcoming. After two months of waiting at Sera without further contact, it became clear that Phala had gotten cold feet. "The CIA kept asking for updates," said Tom, "but there was no news to give."

Worse for the agents, they had no source of income and were constantly living off handouts from family members in Lhasa. (While in Saipan, the CIA had said that it would attempt to smuggle money to them via Phala, but the lord chamberlain truthfully professed that he had not received any such funds.)

Hungry and frustrated, the pair finally received permission for a second meeting with Phala at the Norbulingka in late March 1958. Like the first encounter, they found the lord chamberlain less than warm; he remained silent about providing any written or verbal appeals to the U.S. government. He also rebuffed their second request for a personal blessing from the Dalai Lama, noting that the monarch was surrounded by minders, and secrecy could not be assured. As consolation, he offered some religious relics purportedly from the spiritual leader.[7]

Gompo Tashi, meantime, was growing impatient with Lhasa's waffling. He was especially concerned when the Chinese authorities announced plans to perform a census around the capital and expel any Khampas or Amdowas who had lived there for less than ten years. Although he did not fall into that category, Gompo Tashi was sufficiently worried to seek advice from the influential state oracle of the Nechung monastery. This particular oracle, say Tibetans, was regularly possessed by one of the more important spirits in their cosmology, and his entranced advice held immense sway over decisions of the Lhasa government.

During his channeling session with Gompo Tashi, the oracle was unequivocal. The Khampa leader should leave Lhasa, he said, no later than the Buddha Jayanti celebrations on the seventh day of the fourth lunar month. When asked what direction Gompo should take, the oracle answered south, toward Drigu Tso lake.

With the decision made for him, Gompo Tashi quietly earmarked pack animals, employees, weapons, and a major slice of his family earnings for the guerrillas in Kham. He also urged the CIA radiomen to remain in Lhasa and stay in contact with one of Phala's assistants. But after a meeting with that assistant—who showed no more backbone than his superior—Tom and Lou elected to join Gompo Tashi in the exodus.[8]

As the date of the Buddha Jayanti approached in mid-April, the Khampa chieftain finalized his departure plans. Knowing that most of the city's residents traditionally made a brief pilgrimage to a monastery across the river from Lhasa on the day after the Buddha Jayanti, he decided to camouflage his exit among those crowds.

So, too, would the CIA's agents. Dressed as lamas and with their gear stowed on two mules, they skirted the capital on the prescribed day and waited south of the river. They were met by a band of Gompo Tashi's servants bearing extra horses—but not Gompo Tashi himself—and their small caravan headed south. A day later, the Khampa leader stylishly rendezvoused with them on a British motorcycle, which he promptly exchanged for a less flashy equestrian mount.

Continuing south, they made good time to the banks of the Brahmaputra River. They crossed the river on a wooden ferry and then pushed south in the direction of the Drigu Tso. Unfortunately, Gompo Tashi carried a poor map and was taking pains to stay clear of major trails in order to avoid PLA patrols. As a result, when they arrived at a major body of water and made inquiries with the locals, they found that they had inadvertently arrived at Lake Yamdrok—fifty-five kilometers west of their intended destination.

Pausing for the moment, Gompo Tashi sent a scout party east to reconnoiter the Drigu Tso. The scouts returned with reports that the lake was surrounded by flatland and populated by only a handful of nomads. Satisfied that the oracle had made a good choice, the Khampa leader dispatched his servants across the plateau with a request that resistance members of all Tibetan ethnic persuasions congregate at the Drigu Tso in a month's time. Meanwhile, he took Lou and Tom farther south toward the Bhutanese border to procure adequate grain supplies for the upcoming guerrilla rendezvous.

Far to the east, Walt could speak firsthand about the state of the resistance. From the moment he and his two fellow agents landed in November 1957, they were immersed in the heart of the Kham guerrilla movement. Due to district rivalries, that movement had never developed a unified province-wide command structure. Twenty-three Khampa clans, however, were fighting together under the common title of the Volunteer Army to Defend Buddhism. By early 1958, this functional name had given way to a geographic one: *Chushi Gangdruk*—"Four Rivers, Six Ranges"—a reference to the major rivers (Mekong, Salween, Yangtze, and Yalung) and mountains that ran across Kham.

In Walt's own band, 500 *Chushi Gangdruk* rebels were focused on expelling the Chinese around Lithang. Things started out well enough, including the unexpected arrival of the final Saipan-trained student, Dick. After hyperventilating in the rear of the B-17, Dick had been off-loaded in Dacca and smuggled overland back to Darjeeling. Once there, Gyalo Thondup had matched him up with another able-bodied Khampa and sent both on horseback to Tibet via Sikkim.

After making his way to Lithang, Dick presented a letter from Gyalo pledging imminent support. This was welcome news for Walt; almost from the moment he had landed, he had been sending multiple radio requests for weapons and ammunition. Now armed with Gyalo's letter, he generated considerable excitement among the insurgents and succeeded in attracting new recruits.[9]

Walt's ethnic kin were not the only ones taking notice of his recruitment activity. Due to the relatively low altitude and easy access along the new byways completed in 1956, the PLA had been able to shift 150,000 soldiers to eastern Tibet by the end of 1957. Specifically targeted against southern Kham were hordes of Hiu Muslim cavalrymen, who had already been used to devastating effect against a sister rebellion on the steppes of Amdo.

In the ensuing mismatch of numbers, the fate of *Chushi Gangdruk* was a foregone conclusion. By mid-1958, Walt's servant Thondup, known as "Dan" while on Saipan, took a bullet to the head. A month later, Sam fell victim to an ambush. Shortly thereafter, Dick was shot. With three of the four Saipan students lost, Walt and the remnants of his band had little choice but to abandon Lithang and begin a fighting withdrawal toward central Tibet.

Walt was not alone. By the summer of 1958, waves of Khampa refugees and defeated rebels were heading west toward Lhasa. Of these, some diverted south to the banks of the Drigu Tso, where on 16 June Gompo Tashi arrived to oversee the inauguration ceremony for a unified resistance movement dubbed the National Volunteer Defense Army (NVDA). With 1,500 guerrillas in attendance and Gompo Tashi named titular head by acclamation, the previous flag of the Chushi Gangdruk (a mythical snow lion on a blue background) was replaced by a new NVDA standard featuring crossed Tibetan swords on a yellow field. Tom was on hand to take photographs of the occasion; the roll of film was then couriered out to Gyalo in India.[10]

The reason for the name change was more than semantic. Although the NVDA was overwhelmingly composed of Khampas, Gompo Tashi intentionally sought to break from the regional overtones of Chushi Gangdruk and present a name and image that would appeal to all Tibetans.

As this was transpiring, Tom and Lou duly radioed updates back to the CIA. Much of their reporting consisted of requests for weapons and ammunition, both of which were in short supply. When none were forthcoming, Gompo Tashi took matters into his own hands and departed NVDA headquarters in August to lead a raid against an isolated Chinese garrison southwest of the capital. There, it was hoped, they could make off with a haul of armaments at little risk.

In the ensuing series of battles, the NVDA was less than successful. Word of its first impending attack had apparently been leaked, and the scout party walked into an ambush. Withdrawing after a three-day fight, they promptly walked into a second ambush. Continuing on a western heading, they next attempted to raid an armory of the Tibetan army.

There, the NVDA was exposed to the rude ironies of its nationalist struggle. Though it might have shared much common ground with the NVDA, the small Tibetan army, like the central government to which it answered, remained publicly opposed to the anti-Chinese resistance and took pains not to assist the resistance in any way. This was done in part to avoid angering Beijing, which was already pressuring Lhasa to take up arms against the insurgents. In part, too, it was due to lingering ethnic prejudices: the NVDA, like Chushi Gangdruk before it, could not shake the Khampa brigand stereotype held by many central Tibetans. This became painfully apparent when Gompo Tashi and his guerrillas approached the government armory. Anticipating the raid, Lhasa had secretly ordered the weapons shifted to a nearby monastery. Eventually learning of the ruse, the NVDA leaned on the local monks but found their audience to be less than receptive. Only after many days of cajoling did the religious officials reluctantly open their stores to the resistance fighters.[11]

Back in Washington, updates from their radio operators in Tibet left the CIA far from satiated. Most of the messages were being sent by Tom; although he had been the best Morse code student among the Saipan graduates, his grammatical shortcomings limited most transmissions to only a few clauses. "It was okay from an operational point of view," said Tibet Task Force chief Frank Holober, "but wanting from an intelligence standpoint."[12]

The agency was particularly reluctant to commit weaponry without a better understanding of the NVDA and where it was headed. Short of visiting Tibet, the only way to get this was to fully debrief one of the agents. For that purpose, word was sent back for Tom to make his way to India. Taking loan of a horse, the agent traveled for ten days toward the Sikkimese frontier, slipped past a PLA border ambush, and made his way to Darjeeling.[13]

Once there, Tom lost little time locating Gyalo and his personal assistant, Lhamo Tsering. Six years Gyalo's senior, Lhamo was Gyalo's distant relative from Amdo. Lhamo had fought in a Chinese youth militia unit against the Japanese, and shortly after returning to Amdo, Gyalo's mother had tasked him with chaperoning her son while the latter was studying in Nanking. Save for Gyalo's time on Taiwan and in the United States, the two had not been separated since.[14]

To assist Tom during the debriefing, Lhamo Tsering accompanied the Kham agent down to Calcutta. There they secretly rendezvoused with CIA officer John Hoskins, who had the pair lie in the back of his car as he shuttled them to a safe house. Inside was Frank Holober, who had prepared a list of detailed questions. Although Lhamo spoke passable English, he and Holober found that they shared more linguistic common ground using Mandarin. Over the ensuing week, the CIA officer translated questions into Chinese for Lhamo, who would pose them to Tom during the afternoon and present his answers the following morning.

Holober also used the opportunity to meet Gyalo. Much like the earlier assessment by Hoskins, Holober was not overly impressed by the Dalai Lama's brother. "I did the briefing," he recalls, "and Gyalo did a lot of nodding."[15]

There were other concerns as well. By that time, the team in Lithang had ceased radio transmissions and been declared missing. The apparent loss of its agents came at a critical juncture, as the CIA did not wish a repeat of the 1956 Hungarian rebellion, when ill-prepared activists proved easy fodder for Soviet cannons. "We wanted to create cells like the Communist Party," said Holober, "not a full-blown resistance that would be snuffed."[16]

But it was too late for that. Based on Tom's observations, the resistance was up and running and would continue with or without CIA support. Despite the Hungarian precedent, the agency concluded that the Tibetan rebels were one of the best things it had going behind communist lines. Accordingly, a decision was made in the late summer of 1958 to proceed with limited material support. The agency also decided in principle to train a second group of Tibetans. Unlike the first contingent—which was theoretically to act as eyes and ears—the second wave would be coached as guerrilla instructors to help the resistance multiply exponentially.

To provide material assistance to the NVDA, aerial methods were the agency's only viable option. Just as during the ST BARNUM insertions the previous year, range dictated that the plane stage from East Pakistan, and the same meteorological considerations called for the supply drop to coincide with the clear skies and full moon of mid-October.

There would also be significant differences from the earlier missions. Although the stateless Poles had performed exceptionally well during the first two Tibetan flights, they had suffered fatalities during a subsequent CIA operation in Indonesia and lobbied to permanently leave Asia for their previous posting in Germany.

With Ostiary out of the running—and Taiwan's airmen still politically unacceptable—the officers at the Far East Division's air branch saw little choice but to propose the use of Americans. The idea held more risk than ever. During the Indonesia operation in May, a CAT pilot had been downed and captured—a fiasco that helped end the agency's entire paramilitary operation in that country. The following month, a USAF C-118 had been brought down by MiG fighters along the Soviet border during an attempted reconnaissance flight, heaping yet more egg on Washington's face.

Despite these embarrassments, the ST BARNUM planners persisted and won permission to use a CAT aircrew for Tibet. Given the depth of multiengine experience in the CAT ranks, this opened up the possibility of flying a larger plane with more cargo capability than the B-17. During the Indonesia operation, CAT had used its C-54 Skymaster, the military version of the four-engine DC-4. Opting for something even bigger, ST BARNUM eyed the sanitized USAF C-118 that had been handling covert flights out of Okinawa.[17]

Once this choice was approved, the aircraft was outfitted with a set of rollers curving out its oversized rear door. This allowed for a much larger bundle than could be squeezed through the joe hole of the B-17. This also meant that the mission would need a larger complement of crewmen to disgorge the load over the drop zone. Searching for suitable candidates, the CIA soon discovered that kickers had become a rare commodity in Asia. Ever since CAT had stopped flying drops over the Chinese mainland in late 1952, nearly all the smoke jumpers on the agency's rolls had been sent packing. The situation had grown so desperate that several case officers had been pressed into service as cargo handlers during a series of covert airdrops over Indonesia in early 1958.

With time pressing, the CIA returned in the fall of 1958 to the smoke jumper community. The September rains had brought an abrupt end to the summer fire season in the western United States, and many were readily available. From Washington, Gar Thorsrud asked his brother—himself a smoke jumper in Missoula, Montana—to contact three colleagues for the sensitive assignment. In short order, Roland "Andy" Andersen, William Demmons, and Ray Schenck were in the nation's capital for a security check and briefing. "It was perfect," remembers Anderson, "because we could do Asian operations during the winter and spring, then be home for smoke jumping in the summer."[18]

As the three kickers made their way to Okinawa, the head of the CIA air operations office in Tokyo, Colonel William Weltman, was informed of the selection of a CAT aircrew. Relying heavily on Taiwan-based pilots he knew from social circles, CAT vice president Robert Rousselot had finalized picks for his so-called First Team. As pilot and copilot he named Merrill "Doc" Johnson and William Welk. Both these aviators had been among a small group of CAT aviators who had performed with distinction during deep mainland penetrations in 1952. Chosen as flight engineer was Bill Lively, the navigator slot went to James Keck, and the radioman was Bob Aubrey.

Waiting at Okinawa until the full moon phase in mid-October, Weltman personally entered the cockpit to ferry the C-118 down to Clark Air Base in the Philippines. Pausing long enough for Weltman to make a symbolic transfer to Doc Johnson—and for the kickers to get a bad sunburn scraping off all remaining markings on the plane—the First Team then proceeded toward East Pakistan.[19]

As had been the case during the B-17 flights, the First Team found that Kurmitola airfield held few amenities. "We spent the night on cots in an open hangar," recalls Thorsrud, who had arrived from Washington to oversee the mission. Several crew members sighted snakes in the rafters, and local guards repeated apocryphal tales of a man-eating tiger outside the base perimeter.

CAT-piloted C-118 at Kurmitola, East Pakistan. (Courtesy Gar Thorsrud)

All of this paled next to the dangers associated with the C-118 itself. Because it was not designed to open inward during flight, the rear door was temporarily removed at Kurmitola. The plane, as a result, would be flying unpressurized for the duration of the mission. Not only did this mean an uncomfortably cold cockpit and cabin, but the crew would need to use oxygen masks to keep from passing out in the thin air over the Tibetan plateau. Worse, the C-118's four engines barely had enough power to clear the Himalayas; if one engine shut down en route, they had little hope of getting home.

The challenges continued to mount once they got airborne the next morning. Following the same route taken during the first Ostiary mission, navigator Keck was shocked by the poor World War II–era maps they had been given. "Once over the Himalayas," he said, "the charts just showed big sections of brown and tan with no data."[20]

To compensate, Keck climbed into the plane's glass dome atop the fuselage to take a celestial reading. While he was there, disaster nearly struck. To facilitate movement, he and the rest of the crew had been outfitted with walk-around oxygen bottles. As he ascended into the dome, however, the bottle's three-meter tube was accidentally pinched. Unaware of the blockage and slowly lapsing into unconsciousness, Keck nonchalantly told the cockpit that he was going to take a nap. Only through the fast action of the flight engineer was the tube unkinked and Keck's senses restored.[21]

Once the plane approached the Drigu Tso drop zone, Keck, Aubrey, and Lively all converged in the cabin to offer assistance manhandling the loads down the rollers. As instructed by Lou (Tom was still en route from India), local guerrillas had lit a huge flaming cross on the ground. This had been done with a unique Tibetan twist: instead of wood—a precious commodity at high altitudes—the signal had been constructed from more plentiful horse and yak dung.

Sighting the fire, Johnson activated a green light in the cabin. As the plane nosed upward, this was the cue for the kickers to remove the final stops on the pallets and give them a gravity-assisted push. With static lines connected to a beam fitted to the ceiling, the supplies thundered down the conveyor and out the door. Olive canopies blossomed in the plane's wake, and the bundles floated toward the waiting guerrillas.

Converging on the pallets, the Tibetans broke them open to find two hundred .303 Lee-Enfield rifles and ammunition. A bolt-action rifle that had seen heavy action during World War I, the vintage Lee-Enfield had two advantages. First, it had been a staple of the Tibetan army since 1914. It could therefore be assumed that the Tibetans had mastered its use and maintenance. Second, it was of British origin and had been liberally supplied to regional armies such as those of India and Pakistan; the United States, as a result, was afforded plausible deniability.

Although the guerrillas had no qualms about the choice of weapon, they did question the quantities provided. Almost immediately, they leaned on Tom (who had just completed his return trek from India) to radio an appeal for a second drop.[22]

Elsewhere in the field, not all was going well for the NVDA. After strong-arming weapons from the monastery in August, Gompo Tashi and his guerrillas now wielded a mixed selection of mortars, machine guns, and rifles. Working their way clockwise around Lhasa, they eventually approached the PLA's Damshung airfield north of the capital. Despite a string of tactical wins along the way—a truck ambushed here, an outpost overrun there—the Khampa tactics were generally not working. Part of this was due to the fact that Gompo Tashi was maneuvering his rebels by the hundreds, nearly all of them on horseback. Although it might have been possible to conceal these numbers in the conifer forests of southern Kham, it was not feasible in the barren hills of central Tibet.

The Chinese, as a result, almost always knew where the NVDA was and when it would be coming. Theoretically, the guerrillas should have been able to set the pace of battle and dictate their targets; instead, they were almost always on the run and being corralled by their opponents in a very conventional manner.

Bringing spotter planes and field artillery into play, the PLA outnumbered and outgunned the main rebel concentration as it neared Damshung. Peppered with shrapnel, a wounded Gompo Tashi soon ordered a retreat to the east.

Part of the NVDA's problem was the collective cold shoulder offered by the local population. As Mao Tse-tung had preached during the Chinese civil war, revolutionary guerrillas were akin to fish thriving in the water of the community. Without water, went the metaphor, the fish could not survive. Given Tibet's sparse population, the Khampa guerrillas rarely encountered such figurative water. And when they did, central Tibetans—influenced by antirebel proclamations from Lhasa and generations of prejudice—saw them as less than brothers in arms.[23]

Facing these obstacles, Gompo Tashi in September ordered his task force on a long march out of central Tibet. By October, just as the first supply drop was landing at Drigu Tso, they arrived at the western edge of Kham. Cold and hungry after their trek through knee-deep snow, they hoped for a more friendly reception among their kin. Unfortunately for the NVDA, some of their number chose the opportunity to split from the cause and revert to banditry. Realizing that this would undercut any attempt at winning the locals' hearts and minds, Gompo Tashi had no choice but to put the anti-Chinese struggle on hold and instead spend time bringing his rogue members to justice.[24]

In southern Tibet, the NVDA was also in a state of flux. The guerrillas soon determined why so few people lived around the Drigu Tso: the winds coming off the lake were frigid during winter, and the soil did not support any agriculture. Looking for a more hospitable venue, the headquarters of the resistance shifted north to the more fertile Yarlung valley near the Brahmaputra. Lou, meanwhile, ventured with a rebel contingent to the village of Lhagyari, forty kilometers east of Yarlung. Tom briefly joined him there after his return from India, but the two soon relocated far south to an NVDA rear base at the village of Lhuntse Dzong, just forty-five kilometers from the Indian border.

While at Lhuntse Dzong, the pair got word in November that a second supply drop was in the works. Though otherwise inhospitable, the barren plains near Drigu Tso had worked perfectly as a drop zone the first time. Looking to repeat this success, the two agents agreed to take a reception committee to that area to greet the second flight.[25]

For this ST BARNUM reprise, the same C-118 and crew departed Kurmitola on an identical flight path. Without complications, olive-drab parachutes

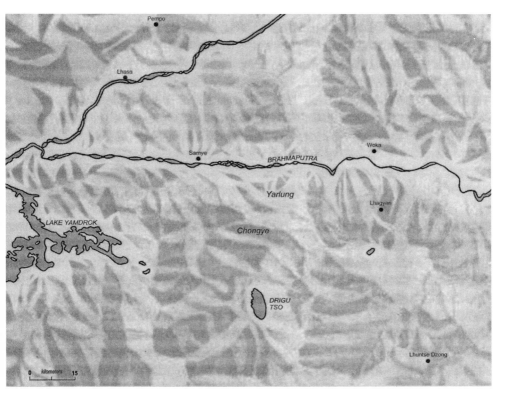

NVDA areas of operation, 1958–1959

mushroomed in the plane's wake, and the supplies floated down to the waiting rebels.

With the October and November drops, the guerrillas had now been provided with 18,000 pounds of weapons, ammunition, and communications gear. Although this should have been reason for cheer, their attention was instead fixated on a single yellow parachute used during the November shipment. Quickly appropriated by Tom and Lou, the bundle attached to this chute contained additional radios and a satchel of 300,000 Indian rupees to pay message couriers. Always game for a good conspiracy, the Tibetan rebels began bickering that the radio operators had actually received a small fortune in gold ingots—hence the color of the chute—and were not willing to share their bounty.[26]

Such destructive sniping was compounded by the arrival in December of Walt and a handful of stragglers from Lithang. He had been out of radio contact for half a year, and his sudden appearance was an intelligence windfall for the CIA. Walt, however, did not see it that way and had Tom relay his intense frustration over the radio. Infuriated with Washington's refusal to conduct a weapons drop for Lithang, the fiery Khampa reported that the resistance in that locale was crushed and his three Saipan-trained colleagues missing (only Dan was a known fatality; the fate of the other two was still unconfirmed at the time). "The CIA asked if he would return to Kham to verify their fate," recalls his brother, "but he said there was no hope and refused."

It was on that sour note—with Walt sulking at Lhuntse Dzong and Gompo Tashi wrestling with the NVDA's self-inflicted wounds—that 1958 drew to an inauspicious close.

6. Virginia

Returning from his debriefing of Tom in the late summer of 1958, Frank Holober was still far from satisfied with the Tibet Task Force's communications arrangement. Exfiltrating an agent to India had worked once, but it was hardly a practical solution. A big part of the problem was rooted in the complexity of the Tibetan language. Consisting of thirty consonants and five vowels, it had been set down in a Sanskrit script with a less than perfect arrangement. Several symbols were often used for virtually identical sounds, resulting in numerous homophones: different spellings, different meanings, same pronunciation.

Given the poor educational background of the Khampa students, homophones were just one reason they were having such difficulty composing coherent radio messages. To help overcome this, the CIA's instructors on Saipan had developed a telecode booklet listing common Tibetan words and phrases, each transliterated into the Roman alphabet and assigned a five-digit number group. For words that did not exist in Tibetan—like "bazooka"—English was used. All that remained was for the Khampa radiomen to encrypt the number groups with a one-time pad and transmit.

Although the telecode booklet was a good start, problems persisted. Not knowing how much radio traffic it would receive, the CIA had included only the most basic vocabulary. When they needed to express words not contained in the book—which was often—the agents usually picked the wrong spelling.

Each time one of the resultant garbled messages was received at the agency's communications facility on Okinawa and relayed to Washington, Holober was faced with the frustrating process of deciphering its meaning. In need of a native speaker to interpret on a phonetic basis, he frequently solicited assistance from the venerable Geshe Wangyal. "Geshe-la would take a train from New Jersey and stay at a safe house near the Zebra Restaurant off Wisconsin Avenue," said one CIA officer, using the monk's nickname. "It was stocked with beer, which he would drink to 'ward off colds.'" But even with Geshe Wangyal's linguistic skills, second-guessing the Khampa messages was a trying art. Remembers the same officer: "He would study the messages and frown in concentration: 'I think the boys are saying. . . . '"[1]

Looking ahead, Holober recognized that one way to reduce such problems in the future would be to have a telecode list with more words. To accomplish this, both he and Geshe Wangyal patiently expanded the booklet over the course of 1958. By fall, it was starting to approximate a full-fledged book.[2]

That same autumn, Holober's task force was augmented by a pair of officers. One of them, Thomas Fosmire, was a twenty-eight-year-old former sergeant in the 82nd Airborne Division who had made his CIA debut launching sabotage and agent teams from small boats during the Korean War. Although this maritime effort was successful when it came to lightning raids, Fosmire soon wrote off attempts at longer-term infiltrations. "Getting an agent into a closed society was hard enough," he said, "but sometimes it was as simple as them tracking the footprints in the snow coming off the beach."[3]

Following the Korean armistice, Fosmire served in Thailand as an adviser to the Thai border police at four different training camps stretched across the kingdom. The last of these was Hua Hin, home of the elite border police paratroopers. Following a 1957 army-led coup, however, the police paratroopers were blacklisted by the coup leaders and confined to base. Along with his troops, Fosmire idly counted the weeks.

Not until January 1958 did the situation begin to change. That month, the paratroopers requested permission to send a contingent to the Philippines to train as an air-sea recovery team. Given the unit's intended humanitarian mandate, the proposal was approved. Escorting the unit as case officer was Fosmire.

The interlude did not last long. One month after arriving in the Philippines, Fosmire got an emergency call to act as a kicker during a covert airdrop in neighboring Indonesia. Continuing on with the Indonesia assignment, he was secretly posted to the island of Sulawesi, where he advised antigovernment rebels through late spring.

When the Indonesia operation was forced to close prematurely—in large part because a CAT pilot had been shot down and captured—Fosmire was at a professional low. Emotionally tied to the Indonesian rebels, he desperately wanted to assist them in their hour of need. Headquarters was committed to divorcing itself from the effort, however, and instead sidelined him with a temporary job in Saipan as the escort officer for a Filipino counterinsurgency team in training.[4]

By the late summer of 1958, Fosmire was back in Washington and landed the slot on Holober's task force. For the first few weeks, he shuttled around the capital to elicit help in refining the Tibetan radio code. Particularly helpful was a female OSS veteran renowned in the intelligence community for her innovative approach to encryption. "I scribbled notes as she spoke," recalls Fosmire, "trying to pretend I understood what she was saying."

Not long after, the task force received a visit from the CIA's Far East Division chief, Desmond FitzGerald. Though new to the post, FitzGerald was not unfamiliar with Asia. A Harvard-trained Wall Street lawyer before World War II, he had served as liaison officer to a Nationalist Chinese battalion in the steamy jungles of Burma between 1943 and 1945. Though sometimes prone to offensive elitism commensurate with his Boston upbringing and Ivy League education, he had relished the hardships of his Burma combat experience and had come to appreciate the abilities of Asian allies when they were properly supplied and led.

FitzGerald returned to Wall Street after the war, but a pronounced idealistic streak led him to dabble in politics while investigating corruption in New York's official circles. Though he had just purchased a new brownstone and seemed ready to settle in New York City, a phone call from another former lawyer, Frank Wisner, changed his mind. An OSS veteran from the European theater, Wisner had been mandated in 1948 to run a small covert action agency innocently titled the Office of Policy Coordination (OPC). Wisner intended the OPC to take an activist role in confronting communist subversion, and he wanted FitzGerald on his team.[5]

Enthusiastic, FitzGerald readily agreed and was soon named executive officer in the OPC's Far East Division. By that time, the Korean War had started, and Wisner was groping for ways to divert Beijing's attention from the Korean peninsula. OPC's Hong Kong chief suggested harnessing the thousands of Nationalist Chinese troops that had been pushed across the Burmese border during the Chinese civil war. He believed that if properly supplied, this Kuomintang legion could be redirected against the PRC's southern underbelly.

Hearing of this scheme, FitzGerald was smitten. Sickened by tales of Chinese communist excesses, he saw merit in taking on the PRC by fomenting guerrilla uprisings. The idea also matched his somewhat romantic, British-style approach of co-opting locals—such as the Gurkhas from Nepal—as allies. Moreover, his own experiences in Burma left him with an appreciation for unconventional Chinese operations in that sector.[6]

With FitzGerald's strong hand, the Burma operation kicked off in February 1951. But despite great expectations and generous CIA supply drops through spring, the project proved an embarrassing failure. Try as they might, each Nationalist foray into Yunnan Province was immediately repelled by PLA reinforcements. Unable to keep revelations about U.S. logistical support out of the press, Washington had no choice but to pull the plug.

Although the Burma operation accomplished little, FitzGerald's career hardly suffered—quite the opposite. Forgiving superiors saw fit to approve of his tenacity and drive, regardless of the results. In 1952, with the OPC having been

absorbed into the CIA mainstream, he retained his position as deputy of the Far
East Division.

Despite his significant influence within the division (he was acting chief for
extended periods), FitzGerald yearned to make a mark in the field. He got his
wish in 1954 when he was assigned as head of the agency's China Base, located
within the U.S. naval compound in Japan's port of Yokosuka. Unfortunately for
FitzGerald, China Base was a poor vehicle for recognition. As the designated
mechanism to coordinate the CIA's regionwide efforts to penetrate and destabi-
lize the PRC, the base was mandated to conduct projects in any number of Asian
nations along China's periphery. But other station chiefs did not relish the idea of
an outside mission running operations on their turf. Worse, many of China
Base's agent sources were exposed as con artists and frauds. After a scathing
internal CIA review, China Base closed its doors in the summer of 1956.[7]

Although FitzGerald did not deserve full blame for the failings of China
Base—he had inherited an ongoing operation—its funeral occurred on his
watch. Inevitably, FitzGerald had his share of detractors. "Des was a dilettante,"
said fellow Far East hand James Lilley, "who plucked out good things to serve his
own purpose." However, he also had a strong friend and mentor in former OPC
chief and now top CIA operations officer Frank Wisner.[8]

Under Wisner's wing, FitzGerald was next assigned as head of the agency's
Psychological and Paramilitary Operations Staff. Though an impressive title, this
was actually a hollow desk slot. Not until mid-1958, following a shake-up in the
aftermath of the Indonesian debacle, did he get word that he was taking over the
Far East Division.

At the time of FitzGerald's promotion, it would have been hard not to focus
on the revolt in Tibet. In many ways, the two were a perfect match. After years of
frustrating attempts to hobble the PRC from within, FitzGerald had a verifiable
case of active and ongoing resistance. And for a man with a romantic sense of
chivalry, the rugged Khampas delivered in spades. He soon came to identify with
the Tibet project more than with any other agency operation in the Far East.
"FitzGerald personally came down to the office," remembers Tom Fosmire. "He
told us, 'We're going to do it.'"[9]

With this cryptic statement, FitzGerald was giving final authority to proceed
with training for the second Tibetan contingent. This time, however, it was
decided to offer instruction at a location more similar to their home environment
than the tropical climes of Saipan. The closest elevation to Tibet in the conti-
nental United States is in the Rocky Mountains of central Colorado. That same
state hosts the country's highest incorporated city, Leadville, at 3,162 meters

(10,430 feet). Once bloated with 40,000 residents during the silver boom of the late nineteenth century, Leadville's population in 1958 barely exceeded 4,000. While such tranquillity held appeal for the CIA, of even greater interest was the secluded valley thirty-two kilometers to its west. There, strung along a ten-kilometer stretch of the Eagle River, stood Camp Hale.

Much like Leadville, Camp Hale was a shadow of its former self. Activated in 1942, the camp at its peak had 1,022 buildings in support of 15,000 troops. On the surrounding slopes, the 10th Mountain Division learned skiing, rock climbing, and cold weather survival skills—often in temperatures that dipped to thirty degrees below zero. Their training was put to good use when the division made a daring climb up Italy's Riva Ridge in February 1945, surprising the Nazis on top. For the next two months, they pursued the Axis forces across the Alps before Germany surrendered.[10]

Despite its contribution to the war effort, Hale was destined to be a peacetime casualty. Nazi prisoners (400 of the most incorrigible members of Rommel's Afrika Korps had been confined at Hale) were assigned to dismantle the camp shortly after the war, and they nearly succeeded. Only a handful of buildings was left standing, and they were used periodically through the early 1950s to train ski troops. By the middle of the decade, however, the Pentagon saw little need to maintain specialist ski formations. The camp—what was left of it—was shuttered and abandoned.

All of this suited the CIA perfectly. In the early fall, the job of reconnoitering the Hale facilities was given to the task force's second new officer, John Greaney. A lawyer by education, Greaney had attempted to prepare himself for the Tibet assignment by perusing the CIA's files and learning what he could about the mountain kingdom. The agency, he soon concluded, knew precious little. "I tried to get permission to go to Austria and speak with Heinrich Harrer," he remembers, referring to the Dalai Lama's longtime tutor, "but the idea was rejected."[11]

As consolation, Greaney got a plane ticket to Colorado. Armed with the highest-level government permission, he received excellent cooperation from the U.S. Army officers at Fort Carson in Colorado Springs, which retained administrative control over Hale. Unfortunately for the CIA, the camp's best remaining buildings were within sight of the Denver and Rio Grande Western Railroad. From a security point of view, there was a better area further down the valley, but that would entail laying sewage and water pipes for several kilometers. Since Hale was already frozen under early snows, construction of the pipes promised to be slow. The agency, Greaney concluded, would need an alternative site for the interim.

The task of finding an alternative fell to Tom Fosmire. Shopping around for an existing facility, he took a trip in September to the CIA's expansive training base at Camp Peary near Williamsburg, Virginia—nicknamed "The Farm." He presented the camp personnel with a request for temporary use of a remote locale within the grounds.

Eyeing Fosmire's youth—and perceived lack of clout—the staff could barely conceal their boredom. Stalking out, he promised to report their lack of cooperation directly to Des FitzGerald. The threat worked. "A lanky, enthusiastic young officer caught up with me," recalls Fosmire, "and said he had a friend at Fort Eustis that could scrounge up some spare Quonset huts." Assembled in a desolate, wooded corner of Peary, the Tibet Task Force soon had its temporary training site in place.

Task accomplished, Fosmire returned to Washington and was on hand when the first C-118 supply drop was performed near the Drigu Tso. Crowded in the Zebra safe house with Geshe Wangyal, he waited patiently for the monk to make sense of the first radio message following the drop. As the Mongolian fretted for what seemed an eternity, Fosmire finally exploded and asked whether they had recovered the supplies or not. "Yes," he told the relieved case officer, "but they forgot to say 'thank you.'"

Taking leave of the capital, Fosmire next rushed to Kurmitola for the arrival of the second Tibetan contingent. Like the first group, these trainees had crossed the border with Gyalo's cook and rendezvoused with a train bound for Dacca. Also like the first group, they consisted of Lithang Khampas—ten, this time—recruited from the Kalimpong refugee community. The leader of the ten, Ngawang Phunjung, was a nephew of Gompo Tashi (as was Walt from the first group). Because the first two translators—Norbu and Jentzen—had quit the program, Gyalo dispatched his own assistant, Lhamo Tsering, to act in that capacity.[12]

As the Tibetans filed aboard the C-118, Fosmire recalls his first impressions. "Two were really just kids," he said. "They all had an earthy smell of leather and smoke."[13]

The plane was quickly on its way to Okinawa, and the flight was uneventful, save for the entire native contingent getting airsick. Once at Kadena, they were hustled aboard a bus with blackened windows and taken to a three-bedroom safe house within the CIA compound. Simple food—stew, potatoes, bread—had been prearranged on a table. "They quickly consumed all the bread," remembers Fosmire. "I made a mental note to order more for the next meal."

As evening approached, the CIA officer gathered his new subjects. Bubbling with excitement, the Tibetans ended up talking all night. Even with most of the nuances lost in Lhamo Tsering's spotty translations, Fosmire was struck by their sincerity and devotion. "They moved you in their direction," he concluded.

The next morning, all ten students began a battery of medical tests. Two of the Khampas were found to have tuberculosis and ordered to remain at the safe house. The remaining eight, plus Lhamo Tsering, reboarded the C-118 and, several refueling stops later, got off at a strip inside the confines of The Farm.

By that time, a November dusting had left Peary under a veil of snow. With the weather to their liking, the Tibetans faced a tough schedule of class and field work. Fosmire was to personally oversee the cycle. He would be assisted by a new arrival to the project, William "Billy the Kid" Smith. The nickname was apropos: the cherubic Smith was fresh out of the U.S. Army and on his first agency assignment.[14]

Together, Fosmire and Smith began teaching seven days a week. Their initial focus was on classroom drills, especially map reading. Additional specialist instructors came to the site as needed. These included several radio experts, the longest serving of whom was Ray Stark. Formerly a radio operator on merchant ships running the dangerous Murmansk gauntlet to the Soviet Union during World War II, Stark later attended Saint John's College in Maryland before joining the agency. Although he had served the previous two years in Japan, this was his first exposure to Asian students.[15]

Fosmire also received help from yet another of the Dalai Lama's older brothers, Lobsang Samten. A gentle sort, the twenty-five-year-old Lobsang had already suffered one nervous breakdown. Briefly serving as lord chamberlain in Lhasa, he had escorted the Dalai Lama to India during the Buddha Jayanti and decided not to return. Instead, he had made his way to the United States, and the CIA had arranged for him to study English at Washington's Georgetown University. When this did not prove to his liking, the agency periodically drove him down to Peary to help with translations. "He was never really in the resistance mood," said Greaney. "He preferred to come over to my house and play with the kids."

By chance, Lobsang was at The Farm when another instructor made a guest appearance. A philosophy major at Stanford University, John "Ken" Knaus, age thirty-five, had begun government service as a Chinese linguist for First Army headquarters in southern China during World War II. When the war drew to a close, he debated either a return to academia or a career as a diplomat. Hedging his bets, he passed the Foreign Service exam and then went back to Stanford. He was still there in 1951, on the verge of earning his doctorate, when the Korean War broke out and his army commission was activated. Facing the next two years in the military—probably in the Korean theater—Knaus rushed to Washington to try to reserve a slot in the Foreign Service until after his return. In response, a State Department counselor coldly told him to visit again if he made it back from Korea.

On a whim, Knaus stopped by CIA headquarters on the way to buy his army uniform. When he revealed that he was a Chinese linguist, the recruiter listened with piqued interest. Within forty-five minutes, he was hired.

Given his China credentials and academic background, Knaus was put to work on some of the agency's more cerebral Asian endeavors. Between 1954 and 1956, he was seconded to the U.S. Information Agency as a China policy officer. In this role, he helped publish in Hong Kong a small booklet entitled "What Is Communism in China?" Full of cold war rhetoric, it was intended as a primer for Asian newspaper editors.

By 1958, Knaus was back in the CIA mainstream and tasked with setting up the China segment offered at the School of International Communism in Arlington, Virginia. A CIA front, the school trained foreign cadres about the evils of socialist totalitarianism. He was still serving on its staff at year's end when the call came to lecture a class of Tibetans about the Chinese system.

Knaus jotted down some general points for a speech and made his way down to Peary. Upon seeing the Dalai Lama's own brother—and recognizing Lobsang's likely firsthand knowledge of regional events—he tore up his notes. "What I had to say to them," he later said, "was about as applicable as the Punic Wars."[16]

Self-deprecation aside, Knaus's visit was a welcome respite from a curriculum that, by early 1959, had grown more physical as tough paramilitary training eclipsed classroom activities. To help in the field, a third paramilitary officer joined Fosmire and Smith in February. That officer, Anthony "Tony Poe" Poshepny, age thirty-four, knew his material. A state-ranked college golfer at San Jose before joining the U.S. Marines, he had received a string of Purple Hearts from Iwo Jima and other Pacific battles. Leaving the corps after the war, he came to Washington in 1951 to apply for a job at the Federal Bureau of Investigation. The bureau's recruiter eyed his combat record and instead steered him across town to the CIA.

Poe was quickly added to the agency's rolls, and his paramilitary career over the ensuing seven years mirrored that of Fosmire: small boats in Korea, police training in Thailand, assisting rebels in Indonesia. After a daring submarine escape from the Indonesian island of Sumatra, he had spent the second half of 1958 giving guerrilla instruction to Chinese Nationalist teams on Taiwan and Saipan.[17]

Poe left the Far East for Peary and was on hand as the Tibetans were being readied for a series of field exercises. For one of these, the instructor cadre prevailed on the Peary staff to give permission to use a secure lake area. Wielding an assortment of British weapons ("The Tibetans loved the Bren and Lee-Enfield," recalls Fosmire), the students infiltrated by night and liberally doused the vicinity with explosive charges, accidentally damaging several boats in the process. As the camp's fire department rushed to the scene, the Tibetans raced away in the opposite direction inside a blacked-out van.[18]

By March, the exercises were over, and the training cycle was fast drawing to a close. Already, spring weather had turned parts of Peary into a swamp and unleashed hordes of mosquitoes. Work at Camp Hale had been completed, and the Tibetans warmly welcomed the news that they would soon be switching to a new, colder locale for what was supposed to be just a few weeks, according to their original schedule, before proceeding back to their homeland.

Although the Tibetans at Peary did not know it yet, their final days at Williamsburg coincided with monumental changes in Lhasa as the Tibetan government and the Chinese overlords maneuvered toward a painful showdown. The catalyst for this came in January 1959 as the NVDA reinstilled discipline in its ranks and began gearing up for renewed operations around the headwaters of the Salween in western Kham. For the previous month, Gompo Tashi had been lobbying local chieftains and was pleased with their professed support. Emboldened, he planned twin strikes on PLA strongholds sitting astride the Chinese-built road leading to Lhasa. Each assault would involve multiple prongs, including the participation of 800 horsemen from NVDA headquarters in Yarlung. Gyalo Thondup had even dispatched two Khampas from India—one was Lhamo Tsering's nephew—with a movie camera to make a propaganda film of the operation.

In planning such coordinated pincers, Gompo Tashi was expecting far too much of his guerrilla army. His own forces had no radio, limiting communications with Yarlung to the occasional message courier. And even if the Yarlung horsemen were intent on joining the battle, it entailed an extended winter trek across the heart of the Tibetan plateau.

Perhaps not surprisingly, when Gompo Tashi ultimately launched his raids, the Yarlung column never materialized. Worse from the NVDA's perspective, the PLA rushed in reinforcements along the road to both locales. Although the Chinese absorbed heavy casualties, neither site fell to the Tibetans.[19]

The NVDA had far better luck with its subsequent recruitment drives in Kham. Some 7,000 recruits joined its cause, and a personal appeal from Gompo Tashi to the local governor enabled his insurgents to walk away with nearly the entire inventory of a government armory. On a roll, 130 guerrillas headed north and laid siege to a PLA outpost near the headwaters of the Mekong. Fighting raged for a month, and it was only after Chinese airpower bloodied the rebels in late February that the NVDA was forced to withdraw and nurse its wounds.

In the immediate aftermath of this last battle, Gompo Tashi huddled with his lieutenants for a war council. Although the Tibetans had inflicted more casualties than they had received, this was not particularly problematic for the PLA, given China's enormous reservoir of manpower. Anticipating the arrival of major Chinese reinforcements come spring, the council made the strategic decision to temporarily abandon Kham and begin shifting the majority of its troops toward Yarlung.

In Lhasa, meanwhile, the PLA's top representatives were fuming. Not only was rebel activity on the rise in Kham, but when the Dalai Lama returned to his summer palace on 5 March (he had been studying in nearby monasteries since mid-1958 for an exhaustive battery of religious exams), thousands of Tibetan citizens spontaneously formed a protective cordon around the Norbulingka. They had taken this measure because word had leaked that the Chinese were insisting that the Dalai Lama attend a performance by a visiting dance troupe at their military compound in Lhasa—but without his normal contingent of bodyguards. Convinced that this was a ploy to kidnap their leader, the masses had formed a human shield around his palace.

For the twenty-three-year-old Dalai Lama, the situation had an air of the absurd. Rebels were roaming the countryside, the capital was a tinderbox, and the Chinese were irate over his nonattendance at a cultural show. Sensing that the end was drawing near, on 12 March he called for the Nechung oracle to determine whether he should stay in Lhasa. While in a trance, the medium replied in the affirmative. This was not exactly the answer the Dalai Lama wanted, so another form of divination—a roll of the dice, literally—was sought. As luck would have it, the results were the same.

Outside the palace, tempers were growing short. Over the next four days, the crowds kept their raucous vigil around the Norbulingka while the Chinese, not humored by the Dalai Lama's procrastination over the dance troupe invitation, were insisting that he commit to a date. The oracle was again summoned; apparently of a conservative bent, the entranced medium would not budge from his earlier ruling.

Not until 17 March, during the third channeling session in a week, did the oracle buckle. "Leave tonight," was his entranced message. The dice, too, cooperated, giving identical advice.[20]

The Dalai Lama hardly needed prompting. At nightfall, he stole out of Lhasa on the back of a pony while disguised as a peasant. With him were his mother, younger brother, sister, and a coterie of tutors and counsels. Just prior to this, the lord chamberlain had composed a message for the Indian consul general broaching the possibility of exile. He also dispatched a courier to Yarlung with a note for the NVDA to prepare a reception committee. Although that message had yet to reach Yarlung, Phala had arranged for a small band of rebel escorts to wait on the riverbank opposite Lhasa as the Dalai Lama's party crossed in a yak-skin coracle. Pausing briefly for a final glimpse of the lights flickering in his capital, the Tibetan leader pressed south.[21]

Back in Lhasa, neither the Chinese nor the crowds outside the Norbulingka were yet aware of the Dalai Lama's flight. His departure proved timely, for within a day after his departure, the citizenry broke into full-scale rioting. In this they were supported by the Tibetan army, which had belatedly thrown off its gloves and was attempting to seize strategic points around the capital. Responding in kind, the PLA dropped the last vestiges of restraint and on 20 March started shelling the Norbulingka. Just four days later, the resisters were in full flight from the city.

For the better part of a week, the location of the Dalai Lama and his escape party was a mystery to the outside world. The first to get a hint of his fate was the CIA; this came after the lord chamberlain's message to Yarlung was forwarded by courier on horseback to Tom and Lou at the NVDA rear base in Lhuntse Dzong.[22] Upon reading this, Tom took his radio set and, together with a small band of guerrillas, sprinted to intercept the Dalai Lama near the Chongye valley, thirty kilometers north of the Drigu Tso. Lou followed in his wake with another group hauling the bulk of the weapons received during the second weapons drop.

On 25 March, eight days after he departed Lhasa, the Dalai Lama and his followers arrived at Chongye and linked up with Tom's advance NVDA party. While there, the Tibetan leader was enlightened about the CIA supply drops and the RS-1 radio, which was kept hidden. Discreetly taking his leave, Tom returned to the radio and keyed a message to Okinawa. Tibet's god-king, he informed the agency, was alive and well.

Geshe Wangyal had been summoned from New Jersey to the capital to help the CIA stay abreast of the Dalai Lama's movements. As each of Tom's transmissions arrived via Okinawa, strings of number groups were carried over to the safe house for the sagely monk to extract meanings both stated and implied. For the next week, Tom's brief updates were at the top of Eisenhower's daily Current Intelligence Bulletin. "He was the best informed person in the world," said CIA officer John Greaney.

By 27 March, Washington time, the U.S. president knew that the Dalai Lama had already reached the NVDA rear base at Lhuntse Dzong. The monarch initially intended to wait there and negotiate his return to Lhasa, just as he had done from Yatung in 1951. But when he turned on his transistor that morning and heard that Beijing had formally dissolved the Tibetan government, chances for a temporary in-country exile began wafting away.

Defiant, the Dalai Lama gathered his entourage inside the village's hilltop fort. Repudiating the seventeen-point agreement, he cut orders for the reestablishment of the Tibetan government just disbanded by China. Though largely hollow, the move lifted spirits. Looking to celebrate with what means were at hand, Lou promptly unveiled a 57mm recoilless rifle (from the second airdrop) and fired three rounds into a nearby cliff.[23]

With his bridges figuratively burned, the Dalai Lama knew that it was only a matter of time before the PLA closed on his position. Unfortunately for him, his counselors were offering little coherent advice. During the hours after the ceremony in the fort, Phala approached the CIA agents and groped for options, including a request to have the United States dispatch a plane to Lhuntse Dzong. Remembering Phala's past indecision, the agents asked that he commit himself on paper to a single plan before radioing Okinawa.

As it turned out, Phala's hand was forced that very night. Radio reports indicated that there was heavy fighting in Lhasa, and an NVDA courier arrived at the camp with news that the PLA was massing for a push across southern Tibet. Unable to sleep, the lord chamberlain woke the agents at 2:00 the next morning, 29 March, and asked that they forward an immediate plea for Indian asylum. Returning to their set, the agents lit a butter lamp, cranked up the generator, and relayed the message. "If India refused," Tom summed up, "we were in a bad position."[24]

It was Saturday night, 28 March, when John Greaney was summoned from a downtown restaurant to the safe house on Wisconsin Avenue. He waited at Geshe Wangyal's side as the monk translated the appeal. Realizing the gravity of this development, Greaney telephoned his boss.

The Dalai Lama's move was not unexpected, and the agency already had an inkling that India would give its nod. Two days earlier, CIA Director Dulles had informed the rest of the NSC that Prime Minister Nehru had privately hinted his support of asylum for the Dalai Lama, but not for the fleeing armed rebels, for fear of provoking incursions by the PLA.[25]

At the same time, policy makers in Washington had come to the conclusion that the Dalai Lama's exile was in the United States' interest.[26] Given its radio link at the scene, the CIA was the logical intermediary to facilitate Indian approval. No time was wasted; at 1:00 in the morning on Sunday, 29 March, a message was sent from Washington to the CIA's New Delhi station asking that it relay the plea directly to Nehru.

Back in Tibet, the Dalai Lama and his entourage had not waited for an answer. Leaving Lhuntse Dzong and riding for a day, they reached a village just four hours from the Indian frontier. Huddling that night inside their tent during a torrential downpour, the CIA agents turned on their radio and learned of New Delhi's official consent via Washington.[27]

Tom and Lou waited until early the next morning for the rains to lighten and then made a dash to Phala's tent and passed on the news. For the first time, they saw the lord chamberlain break into a wide smile.

The Dalai Lama, though haggard after almost two weeks on the road and weakened by a bout of dysentery, was visibly elated. Finally granted a special audience with their leader, the two agents were given a blessing. With little on hand to give as mementos, the god-king offered each a single red coral bead and a braided necklace fashioned, ironically, out of strips of silk salvaged from parachutes from the second supply drop.[28]

The following day, 31 March, some of the fittest members of the Dalai Lama's party went forward toward the border. In one of his last acts on Tibetan soil, the monarch penned a document conveying the rank of general to Gompo Tashi. The next morning, after bidding farewell to his NVDA escorts and the CIA radiomen, he and the rest of his eighty-person entourage worked their way south over the final stretch to India's lush, steaming Assam lowlands.[29]

Watching their leader depart, Tom and Lou broke out their radio set and tapped an impassioned update. "The Dalai Lama and his officials arrived safely at the Indian border," they told their CIA handlers. "You must help us as soon as possible," they added, "and send us weapons for 30,000 men by airplane."[30]

7. Whale

For John Waller, Tibet was more than an intelligence target—it was an obsession. As a twenty-year-old fresh out of college, he had landed himself a slot with the OSS in North Africa during World War II, eventually rising to deputy Middle East theater chief for counterespionage. But it was the land farther east—above the high Himalayas—that drew his constant attention. "I was attracted to that part of Central Asia," he later commented, "precisely because few others paid much attention to it."

Joining the CIA after the war, Waller continued his private infatuation with Tibet, using his time in Washington to absorb whatever material he could find on the subject at the Library of Congress. It was only after being posted to New Delhi as the deputy station chief in January 1955 that he was forced to put aside this glorified hobby and focus on domestic Indian matters.

The following year, Tibet was back in the news, and India had front-row seats. When the Dalai Lama visited New Delhi in late 1956 and the Indian government threw a diplomatic roast in his honor, it was Waller who attended as the sole embassy representative. Perhaps appropriately, when the Tibetan leader headed home the following spring, Waller, too, took his leave of India and returned to Washington for a headquarters assignment.

Not until March 1959, after receiving word that the Dalai Lama was stealing toward the Indian border for apparent exile, did Waller receive emergency orders to rush back to the subcontinent. Once in India, he wasted no time making his way to Calcutta and linking up with fellow CIA officer John Hoskins. Together they drove to Darjeeling.

By that time, word had already leaked that Tibet's monarch was en route to the Northeast Frontier Agency (NEFA; India's euphemism for the rugged buffer it administered along the Tibetan frontier between Bhutan and Burma) and from there would presumably make his way down to the tropical lowlands of Assam state. The story had more than its share of drama, and nearly 200 representatives from the international press descended on Tezpur, a normally sleepy tea planters' town in Assam that was along the Dalai Lama's likely egress.

"It was a media circus at Tezpur," recalled Waller. The Tezpur Station Club, once a private reserve for British tea planters, had newsmen packed into its rooms, curled up on its lobby chairs, and sprawled across its billiard tables. Among them were several Waller had befriended during his New Delhi assignment. He discreetly established contact, looking to tap information without the risk of going to Assam himself. "The last thing in the world we wanted to do was go to the border and be seen with the Dalai Lama," he later explained.[2]

An even better channel was the Dalai Lama's own brother, Gyalo Thondup. From Darjeeling, Gyalo had made contact with Hoskins before racing east to intercept the monarch's entourage. On 18 April, the siblings met in a village forty-eight kilometers north of Tezpur. It was there during private conversation that the Dalai Lama laid out all that had happened in the weeks since crossing into India.

Things had started out well enough, Gyalo learned. Still weak from dysentery, Tibet's leader had taken five days to move from the ill-defined Tibetan border down to Towang. There he was given a moving reception by some 300 monks at Towang's resident monastery, the largest outside of Tibet. The group was hardly out of danger, however (the latest Chinese maps laid claim to NEFA), and a detachment from India's paramilitary Assam Rifles had deployed along the frontier in case the PLA was intent on pursuit. *NONPENCE!*

While in Towang, the Dalai Lama had his first meeting with a junior Indian political official. That official informed the monarch that he would act as escort to Bomdila, a larger town seventy kilometers farther south, where the Dalai Lama could discuss important issues with P. N. Menon, the official from the Ministry of External Affairs who had served as his liaison officer during his 1956–1957 visit to India, and A. K. Dave, a China expert from the Intelligence Bureau.

By the end of the second week of April, the Dalai Lama had reached Bomdila and made immediate contact with Menon and Dave. Just as quickly, their talks grew heated. Counseling moderation, Menon urged the monarch to refrain from any mention of an independent government in exile during his initial public statement, which he would presumably make upon confronting the mob of newsmen at Tezpur. At this, the Dalai Lama bristled. His press announcement had already been penned, he said, and he was determined to push for independence. The monarch told Menon defiantly that if New Delhi insisted that he accept the limited role of prominent religious leader, perhaps he should not accept Nehru's offer of asylum. */././*

Clearly unsatisfied, the Dalai Lama departed Bomdila by jeep on 18 April and was finally able to meet Gyalo and relay his early frustration with New Delhi. The Dalai Lama also used the opportunity to pass his brother a verbal message to the U.S. government, reaffirming his determination to support the resistance of his people and asking Washington to recognize his exiled government and supply those who were continuing the resistance.

Together, the brothers made their way down to Tezpur, where the Dalai Lama was briefly overwhelmed by the flood of journalists and the carnival atmosphere. By 23 April, Gyalo was able to quietly pass a detailed update to Hoskins and Waller, including a paraphrased account of the Dalai Lama's request.[4] /

Suddenly showing more backbone than any time in the past, the twenty-three-year-old Tibetan leader was upsetting applecarts all over. India, in particular, was in a fix. On the one hand, New Delhi hinted at its sympathy for the rebels inside Tibet. The Indians, moreover, were probably not wholly naive about Gyalo's clandestine activities over the previous years. Gossip, after all, flowed freely in the Tibetan refugee community. In addition, the Indians had a prime window into activities in Darjeeling beginning in late 1956, when Gyalo hired an Indian (a former Morse operator and government employee who had served at India's consulate in Lhasa) to give English lessons to six Tibetans he was preening as future translators and assistants. Only a fool or an innocent would believe that this tutor kept what he saw and heard from his former bosses.[5] /

On the other hand, India had long seen an advantage in its delicate dance with China vis-à-vis Tibet. As recently as 30 March 1959—just a day before the Dalai Lama crossed into India—Nehru had reaffirmed his desire for good relations with Beijing. Now that Tibet's exiled leader was speaking in terms of independence instead of autonomy—and with rumors of thousands of guerrillas fleeing for sanctuary in India—the earlier status quo was no longer viable.[6] /.

The Dalai Lama's assertive posturing also had Washington scrambling for an appropriate response. Throughout the month of April, the U.S. government took pains to ensure that it did not appear to be instigating or exploiting the revolt for cold war profit. If such a perception arose, there was fear that Nehru might lash out against both the United States and the Tibetans. This even applied to U.S. aid for Tibetan refugees; to avoid the impression that it was being offered for political rather than humanitarian reasons, no supplies were to be sent unless requested by India, and preferably for indirect distribution through the Indians themselves.[7]

Unwilling to take a lead role, Washington hinged its response on Asians themselves confronting China's aggression. To a degree, this strategy bore fruit. According to a U.S. Information Agency survey in early April, no recent communist event, including the harsh Soviet measures in Hungary during 1956, had provoked more public condemnation in South and Southeast Asia than China's actions against Tibet. By month's end, neutral Asian states were generally reacting favorably from a "free world point of view," even though India was not as forceful as Washington might have liked. President Eisenhower even talked wistfully in terms of regional archrivals India and Pakistan coming to a better understanding against a common Chinese foe.[8]

Behind the scenes, however, some U.S. policy makers were chafing to do more. Serious talk to this effect had started in late March during the final days before the Dalai Lama left Tibetan soil. Following a fast-paced exchange of memorandums between CIA Director Dulles and Eisenhower's senior NSC staffer Gordon Gray, presidential approval was extended on 1 April for continued paramilitary action in support of the Tibetan resistance. Dulles assured the president that such action fell within existing policy authorizations and that the United States was not exposing itself to an open-ended commitment.[9]

The trouble was, any commitment—much less an open-ended one—was becoming all but impossible to plan. After seeing the Dalai Lama off at the border, the CIA's pair of radio agents had headed north to seek out Gompo Tashi. They had not yet reached Lhuntse Dzong when the Khampa chieftain found them. Notified of his promotion to general, Gompo Tashi hardly had time to celebrate. With PLA forces closing for a two-pronged attack and guerrilla morale low, Tom and Lou took to the radio to relay desperate pleas for food and ammunition.[10]

Responding, the CIA loaded a C-118 with supply pallets and rushed it to Kurmitola during mid-April. By that time, however, the area around Lhuntse Dzong was on the verge of collapse. With the plane still on the tarmac, Tom and Lou broke for the border. Gompo Tashi and a band of Khampa guerrillas had preceded them by a few days, handing in their weapons to Indian guards on 29 April and crossing into the sanctuary of NEFA.[11]

With the NVDA in southern Tibet in full disarray and having lost its radio link on the scene, the CIA took two interim measures. First, it delayed plans to infiltrate the team of Lithang Khampas that had been training in the United States since the fall of 1958. As of the close of April, the team (now attrited to six members; two others had washed out because of poor mental aptitude) was on the verge of shifting to new quarters at Colorado's Camp Hale. The Khampas had originally been scheduled to parachute into their homeland by late May, but plans for the drop were now on hold, pending more information on the disposition of the resistance.

As a second measure, yet another contingent of Tibetans was to be selected by Gyalo from among the refugee community for training in the United States. The recruitment pool was now far larger than at any time in the past. By early April, the number of displaced Tibetans reaching India had grown from a trickle to a steady stream; 6,000 of the new arrivals were crowded inside hastily constructed bamboo huts near Bomdila, and another 1,000 lived in similar arrangements at a transit camp close to Sikkim. From these, eighteen young men—fifteen Khampas and three Amdowas—made the cut. Joining them as translators were three of the Tibetans Gyalo had sponsored for English lessons over the previous three years.[12]

Although Gyalo had been heavily involved in exfiltrating the two previous groups of trainees, he was now occupied with shadowing the Dalai Lama. There was no time for him to escort the third contingent along the underground railroad into East Pakistan, so the recruits were instructed to make their own way from Darjeeling to Siliguri for a rendezvous with Gyalo's cook Gelung.

As planned, the contingent linked up on the outskirts of Siliguri. Their intention was to turn south and walk the distance to the border. Unfortunately for the Tibetans, the presence of nearly two dozen Orientals marching along the roadside attracted the attention of the local Indian authorities. A police jeep drove slowly past, then returned a second time. Fearful of capture, the Tibetans slipped into the adjacent forest for a night's sleep. At daybreak they returned to the road to continue their journey and ran straight into a police roadblock.

They were placed under arrest, but Gelung, the only Hindi speaker in the bunch, came up with a plausible alibi. They were Tibetan refugees, he explained truthfully, and they had heard that there were jobs available in East Pakistan. After smoothing their story with a modest bribe (one of the Khampas was carrying a pocketful of rupees; several others were carrying Tibetan knives), they were sent back to Darjeeling with a reprimand.[13]

Several weeks later, in mid-May, the group again set out for East Pakistan. This time, Gyalo made himself available to drive some of them down to the Siliguri city limits; the remainder took the train. The group now consisted of twenty-three members: the eighteen young recruits (average age, twenty-two) and three translators, plus two older Khampas in their mid-forties. With compass in hand, Gelung successfully navigated them around Siliguri proper and across the frontier. A Pakistani officer met them on the other side, loaded them on a truck, and took them to a train car sitting on a desolate section of track. A locomotive soon arrived, hooked up with the car, and carried the group down to Dacca.

Shuttled from the train to Kurmitola aboard a bus with black curtains on the windows, the Tibetans were deposited at the rear door of the USAF's unmarked C-118. Inside to greet them was Tony Poe. "My first impression was that the Americans were so big," recalled one of the interpreters, Tashi Choedak. "I was stunned by his height."[14]

After a refueling stop at Clark Air Base, Poe took the Tibetans to Okinawa. There they were crowded inside a safe house and taken away in trios for the standard battery of physical exams and aptitude tests. Because the two older Khampas were deemed unfit to undergo the rigors of paramilitary training, they were ordered to remain behind on Okinawa. One of the younger Khampas was belatedly rejected as too frail for parachute infiltration. For the remaining twenty, Camp Hale awaited.

With two Tibetan contingents in the United States by late May, the Tibet Task Force was making headway in developing a trained cadre that would have a multiplier effect for an active resistance movement. But with the CIA's sketchy intelligence indicating that the NVDA had been soundly thrashed, there was a good chance that there might not be much resistance for them to multiply. The PLA was making a "very effective military showing," Dulles admitted during the 23 April NSC briefing, including good use of veterans from the Korean War and combat aircraft. The rebel forces, he concluded, were "pretty well knocked to pieces."[15]

China's effective showing was only half the story. Exuding little that was unconventional, the Tibetans guerrillas were consistently fighting in large concentrations, planning overly complex maneuvers, and failing to milk the advantage of their superior knowledge of the local terrain.[16]

Particularly frustrating from the U.S. perspective was the relative ease with which the PLA was overcoming the serious logistical challenges of feeding and arming thousands of Chinese infantrymen pushing across the Tibetan plateau. It took twenty-two trucks of equipment, fuel, and other essentials, the Pentagon estimated, for every one truck that reached PLA fighting forces close to the Indian border. This was an incredible logistical burden, yet it was being accomplished with virtually no harassment.[17]

The cost to Beijing, reasoned the policy makers in Washington, could be substantially increased if the supply flow was disrupted. In theory, this was not all that difficult to plan. There were only three drivable roads leading to the plateau. The first, which the Dalai Lama had used during his 1954–1955 trip to China, meandered west from Szechwan through the hills of Kham to Lhasa. A second road ran from the Tibetan capital to Xinjiang Province in a wide arc along the Indian frontier. Completed in October 1957, it had been built in secret and had portions that dipped into Indian-claimed territory; because traveling this path constituted an exhaustive trek over an excessive distance, it was not heavily used. The final road extended from the city of Xining diagonally across Amdo (officially known as Tsinghai Province) before plunging south toward Lhasa. Completed in 1955, this single-lane, graveled byway crossed swamps and long stretches of terrifying terrain, but it seemed to be a favored route for convoys supplying the PLA in Tibet.[18]

On 1 May, these roads had been the subject of discussion during a closed-door session between State Department officials and the Joint Chiefs of Staff. Questioning whether the United States was doing all it could, the USAF chief of staff, General Thomas White, broached the possibility of using airpower to deny ground access from China. That same month, Thomas S. Gates, the newly appointed deputy secretary of defense, chaired a classified Pentagon meeting on aid to Tibet. Again, the possibility of closing the roads with jet strikes was raised but rejected as too risky, given that the Eisenhower administration had no intention of going to war with Beijing over Lhasa.[19]

Instead of using jets, a more palatable solution was to have an indigenous sabotage team parachute in near the target. There were several options to consider. For one, the CIA already had the Lithang Khampas waiting patiently at Camp Hale, all of whom were versed in demolitions. However, these agents would have been ethnically out of place in the Amdo outback, and in any event, they were being held in reserve for a mission alongside the NVDA resistance.

A second option involved the considerable resources found in the Republic of China on Taiwan. For as long as Generalissimo Chiang Kai-shek had been in Taipei, he had been pleading for a chance to attack the mainland with airborne forces. By 1956, Chiang was fixated on a scheme to drop hundreds of paratroopers across the PRC, thereby sparking multiple guerrilla battles among an oppressed population supposedly desperate for liberation.

Just as during Chiang's earlier lobbying, his U.S. sponsors listened with more concern than sympathy. Washington felt that Taipei was clinging to an unduly optimistic estimate of its appeal inside the PRC, making the proposed airborne assault all but doomed to failure. Moreover, it doubted that any other Asian nation took Chiang's dream of retaking the mainland seriously, and few would be willing to voice support following a provocative attack by scores of paratroopers.[20]

Still, the United States sensed the generalissimo's growing frustration and wanted to offer him visible proof that it had not given up hope of his eventual return. To appease its ally, in October 1957 the United States approved a plan for the Pentagon to begin unconventional warfare and airborne training for a select group of 3,000 ROC troops. The catch: they could not be used against the mainland without U.S. consent.[21]

Though this was seen as a move in the right direction, Taipei was hardly satisfied. No sooner had the 3,000 commandos been officially inaugurated as the 1st Special Forces Group in January 1958 when a second group—not supported by U.S. military assistance—was unilaterally raised two months later. Chiang, in fact, was insistent on having a legion of 30,000 paratroopers and did not readily accept Washington's stipulation about bilateral consent over their use.[22]

On a parallel track, the CIA had never stopped turning out a much more modest number of airborne agents for Taiwan. Drawn from the various ethnic groups that had fled to the ROC, some of these agents were grouped on paper as the Anti-Communist National Salvation Army, a verbosely titled liberation force that Taipei claimed to be assembling for its retake of the mainland.[23] Unlike the Special Forces—whose use in an airborne blitz was almost certain to meet a U.S. veto—the salvation army was fair game for small-scale infiltrations. In mid-1958, the ROC turned to these agents when it resumed covert inserts, primarily into the PRC's southern and southeastern provinces.[24]

Just as with similar efforts in previous years, these latest infiltrations were less than successful. Between July and December, dozens of agents were dispatched by parachute, boat, or overland via Hong Kong, Macao, and (indirectly) Saigon. Most were apparently killed or captured in a matter of days, or even hours.[25]

All this must have frustrated Generalissimo Chiang, especially given the mounting evidence of genuine, even spreading, dissent on the mainland. The majority of this activity was concentrated along the PRC's periphery, where ethnic minorities were revolting against things such as economic collectivization and Beijing's campaign to have Mandarin replace local languages. Besides Tibetans, the disaffected included Mongolians, Turkic Muslims, and the Hiu.[26]

Beijing viewed the Hiu with particular concern. Unlike the Turkic minority in Xinjiang, who saw themselves as a separate people who happened to live within the PRC's borders, the Hiu thought of themselves as Chinese who happened to be Muslims. They were heavily represented across the north-central provinces; this included the eastern half of Amdo, an area of Tibet that was proving to be rich in exploitable mineral resources.[27]

Dissent among the Hiu was not exactly a new phenomenon. The community was roughly split: some had easily bent to communist rule, and their horsemen had even proved instrumental in defeating the 1956 rebellions in Amdo and Kham; others had actively resisted Beijing, launching four minor rebellions between 1950 and the summer of 1958. Particularly problematic from Beijing's perspective was Ma Chen-wu, a relatively wealthy Sufi mystic with had an enormous local following. Prone to hyperbole, the Chinese media had dubbed him "more poisonous than a viper and a scorpion" before he was arrested that October as part of a concerted campaign to "eliminate the black sheep of Islamic circles."[28]

Learning of the 1958 rebellion, the ROC had made a concerted effort to exploit the Hiu dissent by including Muslim guerrillas among the teams being trained by the CIA. There was no shortage of recruits, as many members of the more prominent Hiu clans had fled to Taiwan. Even one of former warlord Ma Pu-feng's many sons was among the novice agents. Tony Poe, later of the Tibet program, was one of their training officers. His assessment was not particularly positive: "My teams were primarily Muslims, but with Han Chinese leaders. We were jumping about five to six times a day, and exercising in the mountains of western Taiwan. It was mostly ambush training against convoys and railheads. The idea was completely unworkable because the Muslims told me they would kill the Han as soon as they landed."

Poe was not one to mince words, and his critical assessment did little to endear him to the CIA station chief in Taipei, Ray Cline. A senior OSS official during World War II, Cline had returned to Harvard for his doctorate before joining the CIA. Initially an intelligence analyst, he had been selected as Dulles's private secretary during the director's 1956 world tour. As an apparent reward for a job well done, Cline was given abbreviated agent training in late 1957 and arrived at the ROC slot early the following year.

Seeing Cline as a desk-bound academic with little appreciation for the nuances of unconventional warfare, Poe continued his haranguing of the Muslim training effort. Word of the friction eventually made it back to Des FitzGerald—by then head of the Far East Division—who transferred Poe to the Tibet training program in the United States.[29]

The Hiu agents, meanwhile, remained on Taiwan through the spring of 1959. By that time, events in Tibet were creating unforeseen opportunities in the minds of the ROC leadership. During late March, immediately after the Dalai Lama fled Lhasa, Chiang Kai-shek offered public support to his "fellow countrymen" in Tibet and called for accelerated aid to mainland revolutionary movements. Other ROC officials claimed that radios had been supplied that month at the request of the NVDA, and additional forms of assistance were reportedly being considered.[30]

In reality, the ROC's connection to the Tibetan resistance was all but non-existent. Although intelligence agents from Taiwan had been floating in and out of the refugee community in Kalimpong since at least 1956, they had been largely ineffective in winning recruits.[31] And aside from a token $15,000 in refugee assistance provided by Taipei during May, there was no paramilitary aid extended to, or requested by, the NVDA.[32]

The problem, recognized U.S. officials, was that the Tibetan revolt was not so much anticommunist as it was anti-Chinese. The Tibetans were antagonistic to all Chinese, noted U.S. Ambassador to Taipei Everett Drumright, regardless of political affiliation. Still, with Chiang's long-standing request for more action on the mainland given newfound urgency by the upsurge in Tibetan resistance, key U.S. foreign policy makers on 25 March had given the green light for exploratory discussions with the ROC regarding enhanced covert operations against the PRC. Drumright, who attended the meeting, advocated increased support to Taipei, provided there were no joint activities in Tibet.[33]

Drumright's proviso meshed perfectly with conclusions drawn earlier by the CIA. From the onset of ST CIRCUS, the agency had taken great pains to exclude the ROC from its Tibetan operations. But there was no denying a convergence of interests, especially with regard to closing the logistical corridor across Amdo. Taking exception on this single occasion, the agency in May made plans for a joint project code-named ST WHALE.

The agents for ST WHALE would be drawn from the contingent of Hiu Muslims trained earlier by Tony Poe. Four were selected as a pilot team, which was scheduled to drop near the Qaidam Basin in the central part of Amdo—within easy striking distance of the road to Lhasa. Although none of the Tibet Task Force's assets would be exposed to Taiwan, there was a hitch. The ROC's elite aviators from its Special Mission Team, which had long been handling airborne infiltrations across the mainland, had taken a beating over the previous year due to better PRC defenses strung along the coastal provinces. Its converted B-26 bombers did not have sufficient fuel for an Amdo mission and, in any event, had been eliminated from the agent-dropping role in March 1959 after taking losses. The B-26s were supposed to be replaced by the sophisticated P2V-7, but crews for this new plane had not yet graduated from the final stages of U.S. training. This left the venerable B-17, which had neither the speed nor the range to elude aerial interception and perform the round-trip from Taiwan to Amdo.

To assist, the CIA arranged to lend ST WHALE some of the aerial delivery methods it had used for ST BARNUM. Just as with the cargo drops to the NVDA, the Hiu would jump from the same CAT-piloted unmarked C-118. Significantly, that plane had recently been modified with pressurized doors, providing the crew with a quantum leap in comfort due to its now sealed cabin. As during the Tibet missions, the aircraft would stage through Kurmitola, putting it within closer range of Amdo and allowing the aircraft to circumvent the PRC's concentrated defenses along the coast.[34]

Because the team would be left to its own devices on the ground, it was important that it bring adequate supplies. The problem was turned over to the CIA's logistical guru on Okinawa, Jim McElroy. He intended to use the jumper-to-bundle system perfected during the 1957 jumps into Tibet. This time around, the lead parachutist would be connected to 5,000 pounds of supplies lashed to a plywood pallet. Inside the bundle would be everything from jerked meat to gold ingots and coral beads for trading.

To study the topography around the target area, the CIA was granted presidential approval for two U-2 overflights of Tibet and China on 12 and 14 May.[35] Shortly thereafter, the C-118 headed for Kurmitola. Most of the crew—Doc Johnson at the controls, Jim Keck as navigator, Bob Aubrey at the radio, and Bill Lively as flight mechanic—had experience on the supply drops the previous fall. In the copilot's seat was Truman "Barney" Barnes, a World War II ace with five confirmed Japanese kills in his P-38. In the rear, Richard "Paper Legs" Peterson was assigned as the kicker. One of two smoke jumpers seconded to the CIA at the close of 1958, Peterson had been sitting idle at Okinawa until ordered in April 1959 to give some additional parachute training to the Hiu team before escorting it to East Pakistan.[36]

Upon arrival at Kurmitola, the crew and agents waited at the austere base for the order to launch. Fighting off boredom, Barnes asked for permission to visit his sister-in-law, a Holy Cross sister running an orphanage in Dacca, but his request was denied by the CIA support team in the interest of secrecy. The mood was already tense, and it was not helped when Johnson and Colonel Weltman—the CIA air operations officer from Tokyo—got into an argument over stolen liquor.[37]

As soon as the weather and lunar conditions proved cooperative, the C-118 was airborne and heading northeast over NEFA, Kham, and the Amdo steppes. Upon seeing the moon reflected on the surface of Koko Nor—the largest lake in all of Tibet and China—the crew turned west for 160 kilometers. The drop zone, which had been identified in overhead imagery, proved difficult to pinpoint from the cockpit. "There were two forks in a river," recalls Barnes. "We thought we were at the right one and gave the signal."[38]

In the cabin, Peterson, Keck, and Lively were all waiting near the bundle. There had been problems earlier in the flight when they belatedly realized that the parachute harnesses did not easily fit over the padded jackets worn by the agents. Three of the Hiu eventually made the squeeze; the fourth was forced to take his jacket off. "I held on to his jacket," said Lively, "and motioned that I would throw it out the door after he jumped."[39]

There was another concern as well. As Peterson maneuvered the bundle along the rollers toward the door, one of the packing straps caught on a piece of steel. With the pallet hopelessly stuck and time pressing, he pulled out a knife and sliced off the tie. "In the back of my mind," he remembers, "I became concerned the bundle would not deploy its chute properly."

The jumper connected to the pallet, meanwhile, was also having ill-timed second thoughts. As the supplies roared out of the cabin and the cord started to play out from his chest, he stood firm. Reaching forward, Peterson grabbed the reluctant agent by the chute and heaved him out the door. "I'll never forget the look of raw terror," said Keck, "in the brief second before he disappeared into the dark."

With no further hesitation, the other three Muslims leaped from the plane. As promised, Lively stepped forward to release the jacket of the last agent into the slipstream. The plane then turned south and reached Kurmitola without incident.

Within a week, the four Hiu made brief radio contact with Taiwan. Encouraged, the same C-118 crew was summoned the next month for a repeat performance. This time around, they were to drop only supplies; McElroy had rigged almost 8,000 pounds on a single pallet.

Heading north from Kurmitola during the full moon phase, Doc Johnson came upon a ground signal and activated the green light in the cabin. Like clockwork, the bundle roared out the side, and the C-118 returned to East Pakistan. Refueling, the crew then turned east and flew for an hour before one of the engines gave a loud mechanical cough and ground to a halt. Limping along at reduced altitude, Johnson diverted to Bangkok for repairs. "If it had happened during the supply drop," said copilot Barnes, "we would have never made it back across the Himalayas."

The ST WHALE agents, it seems, were not nearly as lucky. When their handlers raised them over the radio and asked if they had received the supplies, the Hiu claimed that no cargo had come. Livid, the CIA case officers grilled the C-118 crew over the accuracy of the drop. Very quickly, however, doubt fell on the team itself. Communications intercepts later indicated that the agents had been captured early on, and the radio operator doubled. ST WHALE was quietly shelved, and no additional Hiu saboteurs were dropped inside Amdo. The PLA truck convoys to the Tibetan front remained on schedule.[40]

8. Dumra

The unmarked C-118 materialized out of the western skies and landed at Peterson Field well after nightfall. Though bustling by day—it doubled as both an air force base and the municipal airport for Colorado Springs—Peterson was sufficiently quiet after hours to allow for a discreet transfer of twenty Tibetans from their plane to a bus with covered windows. Two hundred eight kilometers later, they were at the gates of Camp Hale.

Stepping out in the predawn chill, the Tibetans were at home. Compared with the heat of East Pakistan and Okinawa, Hale was refreshingly brisk. Even in late May, the temperature dipped below freezing at night, and snow capped the surrounding mountains. "It looked and felt like Tibet," remarked interpreter Tashi Choedak.[1]

On hand to greet the new arrivals were CIA paramilitary instructors Fosmire, Poe, and Smith. Also present were the six Lithang Khampas who had shifted from Peary to Hale less than two weeks earlier. Conspicuous by his absence was the interpreter for the Lithang group, Lhamo Tsering, who—in order to maintain compartmentalization in the clandestine project—had been quietly whisked away to Peterson without a farewell.

The six Khampa holdovers were combined with the seventeen new students, and a training cycle for all twenty-three began the following day. Each Tibetan was given an American first name to ease identification. American names were also assigned to each of the three young translators: Tashi Choedak now went by "Mark"; Tamding Tsephel, a former medical student and the nephew of Gompo Tashi, became "Bill"; and the short, expressive Pema Wangdu was dubbed "Pete."

The interpreting skills of the three immediately came into play during an opening primer in radio operations. Ray Stark, one of two agency communications instructors assigned to Hale, discovered the Tibetans to be surprisingly astute. "Maybe it was the memorization and meditation associated with their Buddhist training," he later speculated. "They picked up codes fast and were a lot sharper than most people gave them credit."[2]

After two weeks, the seven best students from among the newcomers continued with an advanced radio class. For the remainder, intensive physical conditioning began. Given their mountain upbringing, the Tibetans already had tremendous lower body strength ("They could walk uphill all day," noted Tony

Poe), but their upper body strength lagged far behind. Because they would need strong arms and chests for things like pulling shroud lines to maneuver their parachutes, CIA officer Jack Wall was charged with correcting this physical shortcoming.

A former smoke jumper, Wall had been working on CIA paramilitary operations in Asia since the Korean War. Initiating a comprehensive exercise and self-defense regimen for the Tibetans, he and the other instructors found them to be a competitive bunch. During a class on pistol disarming techniques, for example, the star student from the Peary contingent—a spirited Khampa named "Donald"—took on a newly arrived Amdowa. "Donald had a certain devilment in his eyes," recalls lead instructor Fosmire, "and he began striking his opponent with the pistol butt and cut his forehead." Fosmire promptly cut the class to let tempers settle.

Weaponry training followed. Significantly, the CIA had decided that the element of plausible deniability was now less important than improved firepower. This meant that students could now be provided with the U.S.-made M1 Garand in lieu of the earlier British selection. Officially phased out of U.S. arsenals just two years earlier, the self-loading Garand was a quantum leap in sophistication over the bolt-operated Lee-Enfield. Honing their skills on a makeshift range, all the Tibetans soon became proficient shooters.

As on Saipan, the CIA officers found their trainees to be an endearing study in extremes. "They really enjoyed blowing things up during demolition class," said radio expert Stark, "but when they caught a fly in their mess hall, they would hold it in their cupped palms and let it loose outside."[3]

As on Saipan, too, the CIA instructors found that they were learning from the Tibetans as much as they were imparting. This became especially apparent when the students were taken into the snowy hills and divided into two teams: one tasked with setting up an intercepting ambush, the second group with attempting to evade. Ditching snowshoes provided by the Americans, the Tibetans instinctively marched where the sun had baked a crust on the snow. In the most powdery conditions, they used a traditional trailbreaking method whereby scouts at the head of the column would bind their legs with rags and broken branches. As they threw themselves forward, they would compress a narrow path in the snow for the others to follow. Conforming to the lay of the land, this serpentine trail was all but impossible to spot except for direct overhead observation.[4]

Particularly remarkable about the Tibetans was their lack of fear of heights. "They would nonchalantly step off the sides of a ravine with barely a thought," said Stark. On one occasion when a Khampa stumbled and came within a step

Tom Fosmire, the first training chief at Camp Hale

of falling to his death, his countrymen reacted not with horror but with shrieks of laughter over the embarrassing faux pas.[5]

Such lighthearted innocence remained the hallmark of the Tibetans through-out the weeks of tough instruction. Not once did they register anger; indeed, the students considered it humorous when the Americans displayed emotion. Con-tinued Stark, "They would intentionally leave doors open to get a rise out of me. I told them that when I visited them in a free Tibet, I was going to rip their tent flaps off. They thought this was hysterical."[6]

This rapport made an otherwise hardship assignment easier. "We were com-pletely self-contained at Hale to maintain secrecy," explained Fosmire. Besides running a full schedule of classes, the handful of instructors took turns cooking, cleaning clothes, and even driving the buses and snowplows. Only Sunday afternoons were designated as leisure time.

Theoretically, the CIA contingent could turn to Hale's parent base—Fort Carson in Colorado Springs—for support. To help with initial liaison between the training team and top brass in Carson, two U.S. Army colonels on long-term assignment to the CIA were dispatched to Colorado. The first, Gilbert Layton, had served in armored reconnaissance squadrons through 1946, then was sent on a string of agency assignments to places like Saipan and Turkey. The second, Gil Strickler, had been a logistician for General George Patton in World War II.

As it turned out, Layton and Strickler were barely needed. Soon after settling into Hale, the CIA paramilitary instructors took it upon themselves to smuggle in Brigadier General Richard Risden, the commandant from Carson, and offer him an impromptu briefing on their project. Reveling in the cloak-and-dagger nature of the program, Risden was smitten. Said Fosmire, "After that, he gave us anything we wanted."

One of the immediate results of the general's largesse was the provision of war mules. During World War II, Carson had been the processing center for hundreds of wild mules that were broken and trained in hauling field artillery. At the end of 1956, however, these beasts of burden were officially replaced by helicopters. Of

Overview of Camp Hale. (Courtesy Roger MacCarthy)

A C-130 at Kadena Air Base, Okinawa, having its USAF tail markings removed prior to an overflight of Tibet

the handful still left at the Carson stables, four were shipped to the CIA team at Hale to see if they could be adapted to carry arms for the guerrilla trainees.

Placed in charge of the resurrected mule program was Tony Poe. Very quickly, he found them to be ornery subjects. "They had been idle for years," he recalls, "and would bite and kick the Americans when we tried to tame them." By contrast, the Tibetans had no such trouble. "The Khampas talked softly to them for hours as if they were human," said Poe. "They had them domesticated in no time."

As training progressed through summer, guest instructors made an occasional appearance. Ken Knaus offered lectures on international relations and psychological warfare themes. Geshe Wangyal, who was ailing and needed bottled oxygen in Hale's thin air, coached the students in history and linguistics. He also gave the camp a native title: Dumra, Tibetan for "garden." (Hale was called "The Ranch" by the CIA trainers, a play on Camp Peary's nickname of "The Farm.")[7]

By late June, the project also got a fourth paramilitary instructor. Albert "Zeke" Zilaitis, the son of Lithuanian immigrants, had had his heart set on a career in professional football after playing for Saint Francis College in Pennsylvania. But when he did not make the cut at rookie camp for the Pittsburgh

Steelers, he opted for the CIA. The choice turned out to be a good one, as he proved himself an able adviser in Thailand alongside Fosmire and Poe.[8]

Zilaitis's arrival coincided with the start of heavy weapons instruction. Among the systems introduced to the Tibetans were bazookas, mortars, recoilless rifles, and .30-caliber light machine guns. Also making a debut at Hale was a consignment of five-inch rockets, courtesy of the U.S. Navy. Intrigued by their possible use for long-distance harassment, Zilaitis promptly loaded the rocket noses with high explosives, fitted wires to a car battery, and began firing them from a makeshift trough. Although the rocket trajectory could be slightly altered by bending the rear fins, accuracy was almost nil. Predictably, one veered off course and struck a transcontinental telegraph cable hanging across the valley, causing significant monetary loss and a flurry of angry messages from headquarters. Earning the name "Werner von Zilaitis" for the mishap, he quietly retired the remainder of the projectiles.[9]

The cable incident unnerved headquarters not so much because transcontinental cable traffic had been cut but because the operation had almost been exposed when telegraph crews arrived to make repairs. Secrecy was also threatened by crews servicing power lines through the camp, as well as by the occasional shepherd directing sheep across the valley. All these threats begged for measures to mask the camp's activities. As a first step, a platoon of military policemen was sent from Carson for perimeter patrol. Second, a cover story was concocted with the help of the Defense Atomic Support Agency (DASA) in Washington, D.C. During a 15 July news conference, Rear Admiral Edward Parker, DASA chief, claimed that his agency was carrying out a top-secret testing program at Hale. The program would not include setting off nuclear weapons, he assured the press. The following day, the *Denver Post* ran the story on its front page. As an aside, DASA informed the Public Service Company of Colorado that it needed to give a day's notice before crewmen serviced power lines near the camp.[10]

Unfortunately, the CIA's smoke screen did not extend to Carson and nearby Peterson Field. This became apparent in late summer, when the Hale instructors began the airborne phase of training. The agency had discreetly arranged to use a weather service C-47 based at Peterson to drop the students over a remote corner of Carson. The intention was to load the Tibetans into a bus with blackened windows and drive down to Colorado Springs late on Friday night, do the jump shortly after midnight, and head home before sunrise.[11]

The plan was sound, except for one crucial detail. CIA headquarters had forgotten to inform the civil aviation authorities of their impending nocturnal activity. On the night the first flight was flown, airport officials spotted a low-level aircraft on radar and assumed that it was in trouble. As this pattern continued over the next two weekends, wild rumors spread through the community; concerned and suspicious, the authorities demanded answers. In short order, phone calls were placed from Washington, and promises were made to give notification before all future night flights.[12]

By that time, the Tibetans had completed three jumps without mishap, and their training officially came to an end. For graduation, Zilaitis went to neighboring Leadville and ordered nine kegs of beer. To the surprise of the proprietors, he came back later that night with empties and asked for five more.[13]

Elsewhere within the CIA, the debate on how to return the Tibetans to their homeland had been raging for weeks. Following the earlier ST WHALE flights, the agency had firmly concluded that its DC-6 derivative, the C-118, was in need of retirement. "It might have been good for Pan Am," one CAT pilot later commented, "but it was not a war bird."[14]

Beyond this general consensus, however, there had been considerable disagreement over the C-118's replacement. George Doole, a former airline executive co-opted by the agency to oversee its aviation proprietaries, had initially decided that the DC-7C cargo plane was a good pick. At first glance, the choice appeared sound. An extended version of the DC-6 series, the DC-7C had been warmly welcomed by civilian airlines for its ability to complete nonstop Atlantic flights.

Confident in the DC-7's abilities, Doole had acquired one airframe in Miami and initiated training runs over the Atlantic. Very quickly, however, word came back that the plane was burning out engines at an alarming rate. "It was really no more reliable than the DC-6 at high altitudes," concluded CIA air branch officer Gar Thorsrud.[15]

Thorsrud, in fact, already had his eye on a better candidate. Back in 1951, the USAF had scoped the requirement for a rugged workhorse that could land in primitive conditions. The result—the C-130 Hercules—was nothing short of revolutionary. Blending propellers and jet power, it combined good speed and range and had double the payload of the C-118. Moreover, its rear ramp was specially designed for airdrops, and its reversible props allowed for quick stops on small fields. The Hercules reached USAF squadrons to rave reviews in late 1956, and the USAF almost immediately started production of a B model with an improved engine and better systems reliability.

There was one problem with the Hercules, however. In exclusive service with the USAF for less than three years, it could not be mistaken for anything other than an American military aircraft. If one were ever lost over unfriendly territory, plausible deniability would be impossible. But following the earlier decision to replace British rifles with American ones, plausible deniability for the Tibet project was now subject to exception.

Thorsrud, for one, thought that the upgrade in aircraft capability outweighed the risk of exposure. Bypassing Doole, he took his proposal directly to Des FitzGerald, who in turn placed a call to General Graves Erskine. A thirty-six-year veteran of the Marine Corps (he had led the assaults on both Iwo Jima and Guam), Erskine had been serving since 1953 in a newly formed slot as assistant secretary of defense in charge of the Office of Special Operations. An innovation of the Eisenhower administration, this post commanded great influence in allocating military support for the CIA's various cold war skirmishes. Armed with statistics supplied by Thorsrud, FitzGerald made a convincing pitch. Once Erskine gave his blessing, the Pentagon agreed to lend its new cargo carrier.[16]

The order was relayed to Sewart Air Force Base in Tennessee (which hosted one of the USAF's original Hercules squadrons), where the local wing commander, Colonel George Norman, was petitioned for loan of a single airframe and volunteer crew. The cover story: aviators were needed in Colorado Springs to give weekend joyrides to the first batch of graduates from the new Air Force Academy.

In short order, six airmen took up the offer. What was remarkable about the bunch was their lack of experience. Volunteering as aircraft commander was First Lieutenant Billie Mills, who had signed on precisely because he wanted to chalk up more hours in the Hercules. His equally green copilot, Captain Milt Chorn, had a desk assignment and merely wanted time in the cockpit to earn flight pay.[17]

Their assignment, they soon discovered, had nothing to do with an academy boondoggle. Met on the Peterson tarmac by Thorsrud, they were ordered to sign secrecy documents and given a skimpy mission brief. Palleted supply bundles were to be loaded into the back of the C-130, instructed Thorsrud, and then dropped on ground signals in the mountains around Hale.

Upon hearing their real purpose, Mills protested. His colleagues were essentially rookies, he argued, and had never performed drops in mountainous terrain. Before he put them and his plane at risk, the lieutenant requested a telephone to ask the advice of his superiors at Sewart. In the meantime, Thorsrud got on a different phone and relayed the gist of the crew's lament to Erskine's office at the Pentagon. By the time Mills got Tennessee on the line, his wing commander, Colonel Norman, was engaged in a urgent call from Washington. Though far from happy about having some of his more inexperienced men on loan to the CIA, the colonel was ordered to be cooperative. "Be careful," the colonel curtly told Mills, "and don't let them kill you."[18]

Over the following week, the Sewart aviators made flights over Colorado to boost their self-confidence. After that, the practice drops began. Jim McElroy, the agency's logistics chief from Okinawa, was temporarily deployed to Peterson to help rig loads. Once the pallets were packed inside the Hercules, the USAF crew was simply told to drop them to unknown persons setting signal fires near Hale; if they did not see the correct signal, they were to abort.[19]

After several days of this, Thorsrud eagerly lobbied to begin the next phase of Hercules trials. To confirm the suitability of the C-130 for long-distance air-drops, the agency had mapped out a circuitous route covering 2,419 kilometers (1,500 miles) of mountainous terrain leading to a small ground target at Hale. The entire flight was to be done at low level (much of it at less than 500 feet) with a full cargo load. The idea was to have the terrain mask the aircraft from radar; only if there was trouble would the crew bounce up to 606 meters (2,000 feet), above the highest terrain feature. Further, the CIA planners allowed for just a ten-second variance between flight checkpoints, and a thirty-second variance over the drop zone. As if that were not enough, the return journey was to be flown with one of the plane's four engines shut down.

Because Mills and his men had performed well during the flights to date—and because the CIA did not want to bring a second crew into confidence—the agency argued that they be retained on the project. The USAF again agreed, albeit reluctantly. Mills was also less than enthusiastic, as he knew that the CIA stipulations placed the C-130 at its performance limits. In the end, however, the flight went off without a hitch.

Now that the USAF crew had proved the concept, there remained the task of transitioning the CIA's own pilots for the actual mission. Earlier in July, the agency's Far East proprietary, Civil Air Transport, had changed its corporate identity and been renamed Air America. Despite the name change, its roster still included Doc Johnson, William Welk, and the rest of the team that had performed the initial C-118 drops over Tibet. Called to Colorado on short notice, they were turned over to the USAF crew for instruction.

Upon meeting the seasoned Air America aviators, Lieutenant Mills stood in awe. "Some of them had 20,000 hours," he recalls, "against my 1,000 hours in multiengined aircraft." Despite the mismatch, the two contingents got on well working in the cockpit. They were instructed to stage from Colorado to points west. During their low-level return trek, a mountaintop post at Nellis Air Force Base in Nevada would be actively seeking them on radar. "On the first attempt," remembers Mills, "Nellis reported spotting us for just fifteen minutes out of three hours."[20]

The next day they repeated the flight, but this time with the added challenge of having their electronic Identification Friend-Foe signaler turned on. Rising to the occasion, the Air America pilots masterfully hugged the terrain. "It was a breathtaking flight," said Mills. "Nellis tracked us for just eight minutes."

After nearly a month of Stateside training, Doc Johnson and his men were sent back to the Far East at the beginning of September. The Tibetans at Hale had also graduated, and the skies over their homeland were set to clear. Thus, the race was on to perform the first C-130 parachute infiltration as soon as the weather and lunar conditions proved cooperative. According to the CIA's original plan, the agents were supposed to link up with the NVDA and provide a multiplier training effect. But having lost its eyes inside Tibet back in April, the agency had no timely intelligence on the current location of resistance pockets, if any.

An attempt had been made to rectify this shortcoming early that summer. On his rushed return from Hale in May, Lhamo Tsering had paused briefly at the CIA's Okinawa safe house and met with a motley ensemble of seven Tibetans— all medical rejects or academic washouts from the two contingents in the United States. Of these, he selected four and escorted them back to East Pakistan, then across the border to India.[21]

Meeting up with the group in Darjeeling, Gyalo Thondup chose three to conduct an overland infiltration into Tibet to determine the disposition of the NVDA. Because the PLA was believed to be blocking most of the passes along the NEFA and Sikkim frontier, the team was to skirt west of the Kanchenjunga massif and enter Tibet via a trading route in eastern Nepal.

As it turned out, the mission did not last long. They had barely crossed the border when the agents ran headlong into a PLA patrol. Two of the three were killed instantly; the third went on the run and did not make it back to Darjeeling for several months.[22]

Still without eyes, the CIA had little recourse but to sift through the rumors circulating among Tibetan refugee camps in India. From these sources came apocryphal tales of an isolated NVDA band 190 kilometers north of Lhasa near the shores of the Nam Tso, Tibet's second largest saltwater lake. If true, the stories were dated by at least several weeks. But they reflected a certain logic: just as the lake's serenity had long made it a favorite destination for religious pilgrims, that same isolation made Nam Tso a good pick for a guerrilla redoubt.

With no better options coming to the fore, the CIA on 3 and 4 September directed its U-2 spy planes to make a pair of high-altitude passes over the Nam Tso; a third overflight was conducted on 9 September. Air America's Hercules crew was then summoned to Kadena to view the photographs and pinpoint a drop zone. Pending good weather, the mission was set for the full moon cycle during the third week of the month.[23]

Back at Hale, the CIA instructors had taken aside the original Lithang Khampas—who by that time had been training for more than ten months—and briefed them on their impending Nam Tso mission. As their number had been attrited down to six, the decision was made to augment them with a single commando from the follow-on contingent. Before departing Colorado, all were coached in the use of the "L Pill," an innocuously titled cyanide ampoule cushioned inside a small sawdust-filled box. In the event of severe injury during the parachute jump, or some other dire contingency, the agent merely had to place the pill in his mouth and bite; death was guaranteed within seconds.[24]

At the beginning of the third week of September, Fosmire loaded the seven Tibetans into Hale's shielded bus and ferried them to Colorado Springs in the dead of night. The Pentagon's Office of Special Operations had already made tentative arrangements for ten Asia-based C-130s to be set aside for what was vaguely described as a "classified general-war alert standby mission." For this initial flight, however, the decision was made to have Lieutenant Mills and his crew bring their own Hercules from Sewart.[25]

The USAF airmen and Gar Thorsrud were waiting on the Peterson tarmac as the bus pulled close to the C-130's rear ramp. All but the cockpit windows had been covered with makeshift curtains, as much to prevent prying eyes from peering in as to prevent the passengers from looking out. With the Tibetans, Fosmire, and Thorsrud taking their places in the back, the Hercules lifted off and headed west for McClelland Air Force Base near Sacramento, California. Pausing just long enough to take on more fuel, they were back in the air and en route to Hickam Air Force Base on the Hawaiian island of Oahu for another refuel.

What had been a clockwork operation to that point quickly ground to a halt as the Hercules blew an engine shortly after takeoff from Hawaii. Making an emergency return to Hickam, the crew was informed that repairs promised to be extensive and lengthy. The ST BARNUM team was now in a bind: not only would the delay make them miss their lunar window of opportunity, but it would be hard to conceal seven Asians on base for any length of time without risk of exposure.

Thinking quickly, Thorsrud relayed a call to General Erskine's Office of Special Operations. Answering on the other end was Lieutenant Colonel Leroy Fletcher Prouty, a former air transport pilot and the office's senior air force liaison. Invoking the highest national security concerns, Prouty promptly placed a call to Hickam and lit a fire under the resident top brass. In short order, one of the base's senior officers rushed out to the plane. "He was in an unmistakable deference mode," said Thorsrud. A new C-130 from Hickam's own inventory was quickly substituted for the stricken Sewart airframe, and the mission was again under way.[26]

Upon reaching Okinawa, the C-130 was joined by Doc Johnson and his Air America crew, who took their places behind the USAF aviators. Boarding, too, were smoke jumpers William Demmons, Andy Andersen, and Art Jukkala, all assigned as kickers on this maiden Hercules flight. Squeezed in among the passengers was 13,500 pounds of palleted supplies; though far short of the C-130's full potential, this was still an increase over the C-118.

Two others joined the flight as well. Baba Lekshi and Temba Tileh, both Khampas from the contingent that had exfiltrated to Hale in May, had been deemed too old to endure the stress of paramilitary training. Left behind at the Kadena safe house for the previous four months, they were now ordered to join the Nam Tso team as its eighth and ninth members.

On 18 September, the crowded Hercules proceeded southeast to Thailand and landed at Takhli Royal Thai Air Force Base, a former imperial Japanese airfield about 130 kilometers north of Bangkok. Instead of Kurmitola, the CIA intended to stage all future Tibet infiltrations from Takhli, an option made possible by the C-130's extended range. Primitive (it sported two runways—one concrete, one dirt), remote (a single nearby village numbered 300 inhabitants), and backed by a supportive government in Bangkok, Takhli had all the necessary ingredients for a discreet launch site. Moreover, Tibet flights launching from Takhli entailed a less risky overflight of remote Burma rather than India. East Pakistan's Kurmitola would still be available, but only for emergency diverts.

Shortly before midnight, Fosmire, Thorsrud, and the USAF crew stood on the Takhli runway to bid farewell. With Doc Johnson at the controls, the C-130 roared down the airstrip and disappeared into the northern sky.

Staring at the radar console, navigator Jim Keck called course corrections as the C-130 took a direct bearing up Burma's Salween valley. Leaving Burmese airspace and skirting easternmost India, the Hercules arced west toward the southern extreme of the Tibetan plateau. The flight to the drop zone promised to be a trying seven hours each way.

Though the C-130 was infinitely more comfortable than the C-118, at no point did Keck feel the tension ease. Part of this was due to the navigational challenges of the mission. Part, too, was anxiety over the ad hoc emergency precautions taken by Air America. A quick review of their on-board survival kit, for instance, found it to be stocked with items such as a life raft, dye markers, and fishhooks—all of questionable value in the mountains. Equally irrelevant was the lecture they had received by an expert nutritionist on eating herbs and bark, none of which grew at high altitude. Worse, they had been warned that a hefty white man parachuting from a disabled plane in the thin air would likely end up with broken legs. Lamented Keck, "They issued us each a silenced .22-caliber pistol and told us we were better off riding the plane in."[27]

All this was little comfort as Keck directed the plane around Lhasa and north toward the Nam Tso. Before long, the surface of the lake could be seen reflecting moonlight in the distance. Already, the nine agents had taken up positions in front of the right door, while a string of table-sized pallets was maneuvered along rollers leading out the left.

In the final minutes before the drop, the three kickers put on oxygen masks and pulled open the doors. Cold air sliced through the cabin as the airplane slowed to 120 knots with flaps down. With the plane's nose edging skyward and the green light flashing, Tibetans and cargo exited without incident. Cutting a tight circle over the Nam Tso, the Hercules was quickly on its way back to Takhli.

Remaining in Thailand, Tom Fosmire ventured down to the CIA station in Bangkok to await initial radio contact from his agents. Team leader Ngawang Phunjung, who had gone by the call sign "Nathan" while in the United States, had consistently impressed the agency instructors during training. "He had a good sense about him," opined Fosmire.[28]

But good sense or not, the days ticked by without Nathan coming on the air. After a week of fruitless waiting—and amid speculation that the team might have accidentally landed in the lake and drowned—a dejected Fosmire headed back toward the mountains of Colorado.

9. Hitting Their Stride

Nathan and his eight teammates hit the ground running—literally. The C-130 had landed them nearly a day's march from the planned drop zone and dangerously close to a PLA encampment. Frightened of detection, they immediately fled toward their intended target without pausing to recover any supply bundles, including the radio.

Over the ensuing days, their comedy of errors continued. Chancing upon some locals, Nathan learned that the resistance they sought had dispersed half a year earlier. Then when they tried to enter a village for refuge, the residents eyed their light complexions (the result of frequent classroom sessions over the previous ten months) and suspected them of being Chinese provocateurs. On the run from their own countrymen, the tired and hungry agents saw little choice but to avoid the thick PLA defenses sure to be found farther south near Lhasa and instead head west toward the Nepal border, some 500 kilometers away.[1]

None of this was known to the CIA's planners, who were busy preparing for the next round of airborne infiltrations. Once again, they had to generate a list of potential drop zones without the benefit of current intelligence inside the country. One possibility had surfaced back in early June when the head of the Tibet Task Force, Roger MacCarthy, had ventured to Darjeeling to debrief NVDA chief Gompo Tashi.

A former air force Morse operator, MacCarthy had begun his CIA career in 1952 when he answered an agency call for radio communicators. Known for his gregarious nature, he had been dispatched to Western Enterprises on Taiwan the following year and sufficiently impressed his superiors to qualify for junior officer training upon his Stateside return. Posted to Saipan after that, he was first exposed to the Tibet project while serving on the island as an instructor for the initial Khampa cadre in 1957. Deeply touched by their struggle, the thirty-two-year-old MacCarthy was quick to seize the opportunity to assume command of the Tibet Task Force from Frank Holober, who departed for an assignment in Japan just before the Dalai Lama's flight to exile in March 1959.

Arriving in Darjeeling by way of Calcutta, MacCarthy was waiting inside a safe house when Gompo Tashi arrived in formal Western attire. He offered the Tibetan two cartons of Marlboros and two bottles of Scotch to break the ice. The general readily accepted the gifts and launched into a detailed diatribe about himself and his family's background. With Lhamo Tsering (who had recently returned from Camp Hale) providing translations, the Khampa leader spoke with sincerity and passion. "He showed me his scars from battle," said McCarthy, "and recited where they occurred like a road map."[2]

Over the course of three days, the CIA officer and rebel leader reviewed details of the NVDA campaign to date. Gompo Tashi was honest about the resistance's shortcomings—including bad behavior and defeats—but overall, he thought the NVDA had done well. He was saddened, however, that he had not started organizing earlier. Apologizing for their poor guerrilla tactics, he noted his frustration in trying to convince other chieftains that a fifty-man point was excessive and could be seen from the air.

In the end, Gompo Tashi has no ready answer about the future course of the resistance. Losses were costly, he conceded, and replacements were not readily available. Given the PLA's air capabilities, it was impossible to do much more than ambushes and interdiction of convoys and perhaps some sabotage. He was optimistic about running such missions from enclaves in Nepal, but more guarded about similar strikes staged out of NEFA.

Gompo Tashi let something else slip as well. In his detailed recitation of NVDA activities, he recounted how he had operated with success along the westernmost edge of Kham in December 1958. Particularly around the town of Pembar, a supportive Khampa populace had allowed the resistance to keep the area free of Chinese. Though this information was dated, the location appealed to the CIA on another count: situated near the south bank of the Salween, Pembar was within striking distance of the drivable road the Chinese had constructed between Chamdo and Lhasa. Cutting traffic there would accomplish the same goals as the earlier stillborn effort, ST WHALE.

Brainstorming further leads, the CIA came up with two other drop zone candidates. The first of these, deeper in Kham, was chosen in order to better exploit the ethnic background of most of the Hale students. Using the same logic, a third target was selected in southern Amdo in order to milk value from the three Amdowas in the contingent. To map out the exact routes to and from these locations, a U-2 overflight was sanctioned on 4 November to cover Tibet, China, and Burma.

Back at Hale, the sixteen remaining graduates were briefed on their upcoming mission. Six would be dropped at Pembar, the CIA told them, five would land farther east in Kham, and another five would parachute inside Amdo. With the full moon falling at midmonth, the agents were rushed through Okinawa late in the second week of November on their way to Thailand. Escorting them

Roger MacCarthy, head of the Tibet Task Force. (Courtesy Roger MacCarthy)

this time was Zeke Zilaitis. Special permission had also been extended for Ray Stark to make the trip. Failure to contact the Nam Tso team, and a lingering suspicion that the agency's Thai-based communications officers might not have been sufficiently attentive to pick up a faint transmission out of Tibet, led Stark to vow to stay in Bangkok and personally "guarantee" to raise this latest group over the airwaves.

Once at Takhli, the Tibetans waited until last light on the day before the full moon. At that point, they were then given an eleventh-hour change of plans: all three teams would jump at Pembar from a single plane, the CIA had decided, rather than using three separate drop zones; the Amdo and Kham teams would travel to their final destinations from Pembar on foot. This brightened the agents considerably, as they appreciated the psychological security of infiltrating as one. Waving good-bye to Zilaitis on the tarmac, they boarded a lone C-130 and disappeared toward the Burmese frontier.

Inside the Hercules, twenty-one-year-old Donyo Pandatsang adjusted the cyanide ampoule encased in fine wire mesh that was strapped to his forearm.

Answering to the name "Bruce" while at Hale, he had spoken no English when he arrived in Colorado but showed great natural aptitude and went on to advanced radio training. He was selected as team leader for the six men designated to remain at Pembar.

Now lined up in front of the right cabin door, Bruce was petrified. "We had no idea about the fate of the Nam Tso team," he later recounted, "and none of us were natives of the Pembar area." But to his own surprise, as soon as he launched himself into the slipstream, all fear vanished. With the sound of the plane fast receding, Bruce was overwhelmed by the prospect of being home. Dangling from the risers, he could clearly see that he was heading for a valley with snowcaps glistening on either side. His one complaint: "They told us we would land in a forest, but there was nothing but rocks."[3]

Working in the moonlight, Bruce and his colleagues quickly located their supply pallets, including one that had to be fished from a river. Later that same night, they encountered locals from a small nearby village who had come to investigate the noise. Not only did the locals appear friendly, but they said that many Khampas were still living in the area.

With this positive news, Bruce assembled his radio the following morning and tapped out a short message. His handlers at the Tibet Task Force now knew that the team was alive.

Down in Bangkok, Ray Stark had taken up residence in the CIA's secure radio room inside the U.S. embassy. Though he had quiet confidence in the abilities of the agents he had trained, there was an element of anxiety about going out on a limb and guaranteeing contact.

The anxiety did not last long. When Bruce's string of Morse came over the air the morning after infiltration, the local agency radiomen were shaking with excitement. "They could barely copy the message," recalled the elated instructor.

His mission complete for the moment, Stark awarded himself two weeks' leave in Hong Kong and Tokyo on his way back to Colorado.

It did not take long for word to spread around Pembar about the arrival of the CIA-trained cadre. As would-be guerrillas flocked to the scene, the agents knew that this rousing reception was a double-edged sword. Just as when Wangdu had landed in Kham in 1957, some of the Khampas came with no weapons; others came with an assortment of rifles but no bullets. Three different calibers of ammunition were in heavy demand, and expectations were high for the CIA to deliver.

Back in Washington, the Tibet Task Force weighed the radioed requests for supplies. That a supportive public was itching to take up arms against the Chinese was a good thing, and much of the wish list emanating from Pembar (with the exception of pistol silencers) fell within reason. Approval was quickly secured for a single Hercules to be packed with pallets at Kadena and staged through Takhli during the next full moon in mid-December. Unlike the two earlier drops, the C-130's expansive rear ramp would be used instead of the smaller side doors; this would allow more supplies to be dispatched in less time.

On the ground, the Tibetan agents had assembled a veritable fleet of mules at the designated drop zone. Six enormous dung bonfires were lit in an enormous "L" shape and, like clockwork, the C-130 materialized overhead. Moments later, bundles hit earth. Inside each were stacks of cardboard boxes with four rifles apiece. As per their training at Hale, the agents had affixed ropes to the mule saddles, allowing two boxes to be quickly secured to each animal. Within two hours, the entire drop zone had been cleared.

Nearly all the 200-plus Garand rifles were disturbed to local guerrilla volunteers. Fifty rifles, however, were earmarked for a band of Khampas selected to escort the five agents destined to shift from Pembar to Amdo. As planned, those five crossed the Salween at year's end and proceeded 150 kilometers northwest. Still 80 kilometers short of Amdo's Jyekundo district, the team came upon a fertile resistance presence and decided to go no further. With this second guerrilla network running by the start of 1959, at long last the task force was beginning to hit its stride.

On the diplomatic front, too, the struggle for Tibet was heating up. Back on 23 April, the Dalai Lama had sent his oral message to the U.S. government through Gyalo Thondup, reaffirming his determination to support the resistance of his people. He made two requests of Washington at that time: recognize his soon-to-be-formed government in exile, and continue to supply the resistance. He reiterated these themes in a formal scroll, a summary of which reached the White House by 16 June. In this, the Dalai Lama further suggested that Tibetan independence be a prerequisite for Beijing's entry into the United Nations.

Pressed to compose an answer, the Department of State begged caution. The Dalai Lama should not publicly ask for recognition of a government in exile, urged one Foggy Bottom draft, unless he was assured of a warm international response. If he made an appeal to the United Nations, State Department policy makers felt that the United States should appropriately assist; if not, the United States should not take the lead in pressing Tibet's case in the international arena.

And taking a page from sweeteners offered earlier in the decade, they believed that the United States should offer a stipend and help the Dalai Lama find asylum elsewhere if India gave him the boot.

Eisenhower was of a mind to agree with such circular diplomatic niceties. When a final response was orally relayed back to the monarch on 18 June, it mouthed sympathy for the Tibetan cause with few commitments. Addressing the Dalai Lama as the "rightful leader of the Tibetan people," it even managed to dance around the earlier semantics surrounding suzerainty, sovereignty, and independence.

Not surprisingly, word quickly came back that neither the Dalai Lama nor Gyalo Thondup was pleased with Washington's limp platitudes. The monarch was especially keen to elicit stronger U.S. support, given his growing strains with Nehru (the Indian leader was insistent that the Dalai Lama work quietly for autonomy, while the Tibetan leader spent the summer threatening to make a bold declaration of independence), and Washington's less than full assurances did nothing to bolster his leverage with New Delhi.

Perhaps the only good news, from the Tibetan perspective, was the U.S. government's willingness to act as a background cheerleader for Tibet's case at the United Nations. This gained momentum on 25 July, when the International Commission of Jurists published a 208-page preliminary report entitled "The Question of Tibet and the Rule of Law." Distributed to the United Nations Secretariat and all delegations, it laid the basis for the Tibet issue to be included on the agenda for that fall's United Nations session.

Seizing this opportunity, Gyalo Thondup hired Ernest Gross, a former State Department legal adviser and alternate delegate to three United Nations General Assemblies, to represent Tibet. Unlike Lhasa's earlier flirtations with the United Nations—when it was roundly ignored at the beginning of the decade—this time the experienced Gross proved an adept lobbyist. With cosponsorship from Ireland and Malaya, a Tibet resolution was scheduled for a hearing in front of the full assembly during mid-October.

Behind the scenes, the Tibet Task Force crafted several covert efforts to support the upcoming vote. In one of these, Lowell Thomas, Jr., who had traveled with his famous father through Tibet in 1949 and become an impassioned advocate of Tibetan independence, was fed intelligence supplied by CIA guerrilla contacts. Some of this information was incorporated into his highly sympathetic book *The Silent War in Tibet*, published by Doubleday on 8 October.

Later that same week, the 12 October edition of *Life International* included an article entitled "Asia's Odd New Battlegrounds." In it were six drawings, ostensibly made by "refugees," graphically depicting Chinese excesses against Tibet. Left unsaid was the fact that the drawings had actually been made by the agent trainees at Camp Hale as part of sketching drills during a class on intelligence collection. The best of these drawings had been presented by the Hale staff to Des FitzGerald, who took them to CIA Director Dulles, who in turn phoned C. D. Jackson, the conservative *Life International* publisher (and former member of the Eisenhower election campaign), with a request that they be incorporated in a supportive article.[4]

All this culminated in passage of a United Nations resolution on 21 October deploring China's violations of human rights in Tibet. The vote was forty-five in favor, nine opposed, and twenty-six abstentions. Besides the numeric victory, there were other reasons for cheer. Though short of the declaration of independence wanted by the Dalai Lama, the vote served to keep the Tibetan case alive before the international community. Moreover, the experience had proved invaluable for Gyalo Thondup. Far from the uninspiring introvert witnessed by earlier case officers in India, a far more confident and dynamic Gyalo had emerged at the United Nations.

Gyalo could be stubborn as well. Not willing to lose momentum after the resolution, Gross immediately formulated plans for the first overseas trip by the Dalai Lama. Using the same lobbying skills that had been successful in the halls of the United Nations, he persuaded the National Council of Christians and Jews to call a conference for the spring of 1960 with the Dalai Lama as principal speaker. The venue would be the Peter Cooper Union in New York, followed by an unofficial reception hosted by Eisenhower in Washington.

All that remained was a pledge of cooperation from Gyalo and the Dalai Lama. To the shock of U.S. officials, however, both opposed the trip because it would set a precedent for an unofficial reception in the Dalai Lama's capacity as a religious leader. Though by late 1959 the monarch had temporarily shelved plans to set up a government in exile (because of ongoing opposition from India), he refused to prejudice future claims to independence in return for what he deemed was a short-term advantage. On the diplomatic front, at least, this prime opportunity ultimately wafted away.

For the agents back in Tibet, the task force was taking steps to ratchet up its resupply operations. Through December 1959, these flights had been limited to one Air America aircrew flying a single mission during each full moon phase. Since the lunar window of opportunity could not be expanded, the only other option was to increase the number of sorties flown. In anticipation of this, Air America in early December allocated additional personnel for C-130 operations. In several cases, some of its more experienced pilots were brought into the program to serve functions other than flying the plane. Captains Ron Sutphin and Harry Hudson, for example, were given quick code training in Japan before being assigned as radio operators; another pilot, Jack Stiles, was named a flight mechanic.[5]

More C-130 flights also meant the need for more kickers. Efforts to secure these personnel began in November 1959 when two Montana smoke jumpers—Miles Johnson and John Lewis—were beckoned to Washington for background security checks. John Greaney, the task force officer who had first scouted Camp Hale, reserved rooms under false names at the Roger Smith Hotel in order to conduct confidential interviews with the prospects.

The following month, half a dozen more smoke jumpers were invited to the capital. Shep Johnson, Miles's younger brother, was among them. A former marine and Korean War veteran, he had been tending cattle at a snowy Idaho ranch when he got an urgent message to come to the phone. "I thought my mother was sick," he recalls, "but it was another smoke jumper saying that I was needed in Washington. The next day I bought a sports coat and flew to D.C., where I met some of the CIA officers, including Gar [Thorsrud]. We spent ten days looking over maps. Then they gave me an advance in pay; it was the first time I had handled a $100 bill."[6]

By the full moon cycle of January 1960, nearly a dozen smoke jumpers were assembled on Okinawa. Four kickers were selected to go on that month's maiden flight: two from the new contingent, and two veterans from earlier flights. The mission took place as scheduled and without complications, prompting the ST BARNUM planners to reduce the number of kickers to two for the month's second resupply flight.

During this encore, a single Tibetan agent was scheduled to jump along with the supplies. That agent, a reserved twenty-eight-year-old Khampa monk named Kalden, had been one of the washouts from the Lithang contingent that had parachuted at Nam Tso. Kalden had been sitting idle at the Kadena safe house for the past sixteen months while the CIA debated what to do with him. That decision: drop him at Pembar.

As the Hercules made its final approach toward the drop zone, radioman Keck and flight mechanic Stiles came into the cabin to help push pallets out the rear. One of the two kickers, Andy Andersen, was positioned close to the edge of the ramp alongside the lone Tibetan. Not secured by a tether, Andersen instead wore a special small parachute set high on the shoulder to keep the waist clear and eliminate the possibility of getting snagged while pushing the cargo.[7]

When the green light went on, Kalden got a tap on his shoulder as the signal to leap off the ramp. For the first time, a Tibetan balked. Turning his back on the black void, the monk grabbed Andersen in an unwelcome embrace. All too aware of his precarious position, the kicker spun the agent around and heaved him ahead of the exiting cargo. Reaching backward in a final act of desperation, the Tibetan snatched the radio headset off Andersen's head. Trailing a thirty-foot cord in hand, he disappeared into the night sky.[8]

Down at the drop zone, Kalden landed to a reception committee of eleven fellow agents and hundreds of Khampa guerrillas. He came with orders to join the five agents meant to shift father east into Kham, though plans for that movement were now on hold. Remaining at Pembar, the twelve took stock of their growing inventory. Included in the pallets were a pair of machine guns on anti-aircraft mounts and a large stock of TNT. None of these items were rated as particularly relevant by the Tibetans, though they did go out of their way to use the explosives to down a nearby bridge. More popular were the hundreds of Garands and a carbine variant stacked inside the bundles, both of which were magnets for new recruits.

Sensing that it had arrived at a winning formula, the Tibet Task Force planned more of the same for February 1960. Helping to coordinate the ongoing resupply effort from Kadena was U.S. Air Force Major Harry "Heinie" Aderholt. No stranger to the CIA, Aderholt had been seconded to Camp Peary for three years starting in 1951 to help set up an air branch at the agency's new training facility. After a six-year interlude with the Tactical Air Command beginning in 1954, he was again detailed to the CIA in January 1960, this time as commander of the Kadena-based Detachment 2, 1045th Operational Evaluation and Training Group.

Aderholt's Detachment 2 had a long and convoluted relationship with the Tibet project. Its lineage could be traced back to the long-disbanded Asia-based ARC wing, a portion of which had been retained as the 322nd Squadron's Detachment 1. When that squadron was dissolved in late 1957, its secret cell (renamed Detachment 2 of the 313th Air Division) remained at Kadena and continued to receive orders for CIA-sanctioned flights, such as the C-118 personnel exfiltrations from Kurmitola. Its C-118 was also loaned for CAT-piloted flights into Tibet.

By the time Aderholt arrived, there had been two significant changes to the detachment. First, whereas the earlier arrangement had been a partnership

Insignia for Detachment 2 / 1045th
Operational Evaluation and Training
Group, the outfit that coordinated C-
130 support for the Tibet project.
(Courtesy Harry Aderholt)

between the agency and the air force, the CIA now fully controlled Detachment
2 in all but name. The agency went so far as to remove the Kadena unit from the
313th Air Division and place it under its own cover organization, the 1045th
Operational Evaluation and Training Group, ostensibly headquartered at Washington's Bolling Field. Second, Detachment 2 was no longer in the business of
flying classified flights on behalf of the CIA. Rather, it now acted as the CIA's on-
site management team to coordinate Air America and U.S. Air Force assets and
personnel in support of the agency's cold war ventures in Asia.

Aderholt tackled his new assignment with breathless vigor and initiated several fast changes. His immediate predecessor in command of the detachment,
Major Arthur Dittrich, was a longtime CIA hand in Asia, having helped coordinate covert flights into mainland China during the Korean War. But whereas Dittrich had preferred to err on the side of caution and limit C-130 payloads to
13,500 pounds, Aderholt elected to push the envelope by packing up to 26,000
pounds of cargo per ship.

Aderholt also took steps to upgrade the primitive conditions at Takhli Air
Base. Where once only native huts had stood, he cleared out the old imperial
Japanese living areas and erected new elevated quarters. This move was warmly
welcomed by the Air America crews, who had taken to heart Takhli's reputed
claim of being home to more king cobras than anywhere else on the planet.

By the March full moon, the C-130 crews had amassed sufficient Tibet experience to begin staging two aircraft per night. There was the occasional gaffe—
such as when Captain Harry Hudson accidentally left his survival belt atop a
pallet, resulting in a costly loss when the gold sovereigns inside went out the

rear—and periodic bouts with Murphy's Law—such as the frequent glitches with the aircraft's temperamental radar, forcing the navigator to rely on celestial fixes. But ST BARNUM was generally running on schedule.[9]

The news got even better when the Nam Tso team—on the run since September 1959—reached the Nepalese border and couriered word to Darjeeling that it wanted a resupply. Lhamo Tsering, who had been deputized by Gyalo Thondup to manage agent operations from India on a daily basis, quickly relayed the request to the Tibet Task Force. Rejecting the plea, the CIA instead ordered the team to exfiltrate via East Pakistan to Okinawa. Rearmed with carbines and recoilless rifles, Nathan and six of his men (due to failing physical health, the two older agents remained behind at Kadena) were loaded back aboard a Hercules and dropped during the March full moon to augment the five-man Amdo team that had shifted from Pembar.[10]

Not until the next month, April, did the CIA's luck finally run out. It started out well enough, with two Hercules flights set for the beginning of the lunar cycle. The first plane, with Doc Johnson as pilot and Jack Stiles serving as first officer, departed without incident at last light. The second, teaming William Welk and Al Judkins, left Takhli fifteen minutes later.

Halfway to the target, things turned sour. Hitting an unexpectedly heavy head wind, Jim Keck, one of two navigators in the lead plane, took a radar fix and determined that they were more than forty-five minutes behind schedule. Hearing this, Doc Johnson added power, and by the time they approached the drop zone, they were only four minutes late.

Head winds, however, were just part of their problem. Although April is traditionally rain free in Tibet, 1960 proved the exception to the rule. As the Hercules overflew the location where bonfires should have been, all the crew saw was a thick blanket of clouds. Circling once in frustration, Johnson made the decision to return home. As they had burned an inordinate amount of fuel to make up for lost time on the way into Tibet, his colleagues in the cockpit were keen to dump their cargo to lighten the plane for the remainder of the journey. But reasoning that the same strong head winds would provide equally strong tailwinds, Johnson insisted on keeping the payload aboard.

That decision was nearly fatal. By the time they arrived near Takhli at 5:30 the next morning, their fuel supply was almost exhausted. Worse, April is the hottest month in Thailand, coming less than two months before the summer monsoon, and farmers in the central part of the kingdom traditionally slash and burn their fields then, prior to planting a new crop. This throws into the sky a layer of haze the color and consistency of chocolate milk, which is exactly what the crew saw as they searched frantically for the lights of Takhli. Jack Stiles, who was taking his turn at the controls for the return leg, put the plane into a tight turn for a second pass. Two of the engines immediately begin to sputter, then coughed back to life as the Hercules rolled out. The engines started to die again during a third pass, prompting Stiles to order crew members in the rear to put on their parachutes and bail out. "It was probably not a bad idea," said Andy Andersen, one of two kickers on the flight, "but none of us moved."[11]

Listening from the tarmac, Heinie Aderholt acted in desperation. Locating a flare gun, he began firing red star clusters into the sky. The idea worked: spotting a red glow lighting the bottom of the haze, the crew took the plunge and emerged in clear skies near the airfield. Only one engine was still running by the time they taxied to the end of the runway. "My jaw was sore," remembers navigator Keck, "from all the sticks of gum I was chewing."[12]

Hard luck, too, plagued the second flight of the night. Captain Welk also hit a head wind and found the drop zone covered with clouds. Like Doc Johnson, he elected to return with his payload aboard. Unlike Johnson, however, he believed that the emergency facilities at Kurmitola were closer. The CIA retained a skeleton technical crew in East Pakistan for just such contingencies and had even erected a nondirectional beacon to help pilots vector toward the strip. Normally, this would have been sufficient, since April in East Pakistan is generally a month with humid temperatures but clear skies.

But in yet another exception to the rule, Kurmitola that night was hit by an unseasonably early thunderstorm. Al Judkins was at the controls, and as he dipped the Hercules for a landing, there was almost zero visibility. At the last moment, the hangar flashed in the windshield, prompting Judkins to reflexively jerk back on the controls to avoid a collision. Doing what it could to help, the CIA team rushed several jeeps out onto the tarmac, their headlights barely cutting into the pounding rain.

As Judkins nosed downward for a second attempt, kickers Miles Johnson and Richard "Paper Legs" Peterson braced for the worst. After a night of jinxes, they finally got a break. As a bolt of lightning flashed across the sky, the crew got a clear glimpse of the airstrip ahead and aligned the plane. Landing hard, they taxied to the hangar with little more than fumes left in the gas tanks.[13]

Though it had nearly lost two aircraft, ST BARNUM barely flinched. On the following night, the same Takhli crew was rescheduled to deliver its payload. Fearful of running into the same meteorological complications, the airmen brainstormed ways of carrying more fuel as an emergency reserve. Besides the internal wing tanks, they were already slinging two extra pontoon tanks, as well as a special 2,000-gallon bladder—nicknamed a Tokyo Tank—inside the cabin itself. But even with these, the crew could not fly an evasive route to the target, could not loiter, and, as the previous flights had dramatically proved, could not afford to hit a strong head wind.

Showing some lateral thinking, they came up with an offbeat solution. Reasoning that fuel is denser when chilled, the Air America crew topped its tanks on the night of the mission and circled Takhli at 9,091 meters (30,000) feet. After determining that the gas was sufficiently cold—and dense—they landed and began packing more fuel into the extra tank space. Wet burlap was draped across the wings to keep the tanks cool. Whether because of this or because the crew did not encounter another head wind, the mission made it to Tibet and back with fuel to spare.[14]

A key link in the CIA's Tibet supply program was a modest apartment just north of the Washington city limits. By that time, Geshe Wangyal had raised too many eyebrows roaming outside the original Zebra safe house in his robes. "He would go into a Chinese restaurant," recalls Tom Fosmire, "and the staff would all start bowing."[15]

To avoid uncomfortable questions from neighbors, the CIA elected to shift its elegant interpreter to a new safe house farther outside the capital. Shortly thereafter, the venerable Geshe, eager to spend more time with his Buddhist disciples, gracefully exited the program for a permanent return to New Jersey.

Though sad to see him go, the CIA had already located a willing replacement. Tsing-po Yu, a recent Chinese immigrant who had lived part of his life in Tibet and spoke the language like a native, began daily commutes to the new safe house and proved adept at squeezing meaning from the Tibet transmissions. The CIA, in turn, provided him with a salary and an occasional favor. When his wife, a waitress at a local Chinese eatery, was being seduced by a cook, the agency arranged for immigration officials to raid the establishment and deport seven illegal employees (including the problematic suitor).[16]

Because of his marital troubles and the long hours spent translating, Yu had been granted leave during April when the two Tibet overflights had their brushes with disaster. Filling in as his temporary replacement was Mark, one of the three Tibetans serving as translators at Hale. Alongside Mark was case officer John Gilhooley. Having recently come off a tour in Burma, Gilhooley was holding the headquarters job with the Tibet Task Force between field assignments.

Each morning, the young Tibetan would begin the process of converting incoming number groups into coherent messages, which Gilhooley would then convey to task force chief Roger McCarthy. Return messages would go through the same process in reverse. Mark enjoyed the work but could feel the growing sense of urgency among all those involved. There was good reason for this: the approaching May rains on the Tibetan plateau would make further resupply flights all but impossible until autumn. In order to deliver as much equipment as possible before the weather proved prohibitive, three C-130 flights were launched on two consecutive nights at the end of the April lunar cycle.[17]

In the end, even this proved insufficient. Over the previous two months, Pembar had been experiencing frequent probes by PLA infantry. Just as the April full moon was waning, Beijing got serious. Pamphlets were dropped from aircraft warning the rebels to cease contact with the foreign reactionaries. After that, groups of five aircraft began bombing runs while long-range artillery was brought forward. The guerrillas—conservatively estimated at a couple of thousand— suffered horrific casualties.

The PLA was not finished. Placing blocking forces on three sides of the guerrilla concentration, the Chinese set the forests on fire to flush out the remaining partisans. Keeping together, the twelve CIA-trained agents made an escape bid. Rather than running south toward India—as the PLA might have expected—they attempted to evade north across the Salween. "We thought it might be colder near Amdo," said Bruce, "and the Chinese would not be able to tolerate the cold."[18]

But as they approached the river, its swift waters proved too hard to ford. Complicating matters, their horses were growing weak from insufficient food and were hobbled by broken horseshoes. Abandoning their steeds, the dozen decided to reverse direction and weave their way toward the southern border on foot. After a month of harrowing encounters with the PLA, only five survivors reached Indian soil.[19]

The losses were even more horrific for the Amdo contingent. After overrunning Pembar, the PLA shifted its full attention northwest near the end of April. Under withering fire, Nathan, leader of the Amdo augmentation team, radioed frantic messages that tank-led columns were closing on their position.[20]

With few options available, the Tibet Task Force sanctioned an emergency C-130 drop for the evening of 1 May. This promised to be doubly risky: not only was the PLA massing in the area around the drop zone, but the moonless night would make navigation much more complicated. Captain Neese Hicks, who had been given a quick tutorial in codes before being assigned as a radioman for the project, was ready to board the Hercules at last light. Before he could do so,

Major Aderholt rushed over to the crew and told them that the mission was scrubbed.[21]

Aderholt did not elaborate, but the reason for the abort was a mishap in another CIA operation. That morning, a U-2 spy plane had departed from an airfield in Pakistan for an overflight of the Soviet Union. En route, Soviet air defense batteries had fired multiple surface-to-air missiles in a shotgun configuration, disabling the aircraft with one of the concussion blasts. Although the exact fate of the plane and its pilot was not yet known to the CIA (it was several days before Moscow revealed that the crewman, Francis Gary Powers, had been captured alive), Washington quickly flashed a blanket prohibition against all further aerial penetrations of the communist bloc.[22]

With its hands tied by the senior policy makers in the Eisenhower administration, the Tibet Task Force was powerless to help its Tibetans in their greatest hour of need. The radio near Amdo soon fell silent. None of the twelve agents ever reached India.[23]

10. Markham

Back on 4 February, just as the Tibet Task Force thought it had settled on a winning formula, CIA Director Dulles ventured to the White House to brief top administration officials on the agency's Tibet operation to date. He closed with an appeal for continuation of the project. His audience was complicit in its silence, with only President Eisenhower wondering aloud if the net results merited the effort involved. Might not stoking the resistance, he posed, only invite greater Chinese repression? Des FitzGerald, who had joined Dulles for the briefing, spoke directly to the president's concern. There could be no greater brutality, he assured those at the table, than that already inflicted on the Tibetans.[1]

Still playing devil's advocate, Eisenhower turned to Secretary of State Christian Herter and asked if his department held any reservations. Far from it, responded Herter. Not only could the Tibetans offer "serious harassment" of the Chinese, but a successful resistance would keep "the spark alive in the entire area." Suitably convinced, Eisenhower granted his consent for continuation of the Tibet operation.[2]/

On the heels of the president's approval, Lhamo Tsering began canvassing Darjeeling for a new batch of recruits. In short order, he assembled half a dozen suitable Khampas. Departing India on 22 March, the candidates followed the well-worn route through East Pakistan, pausing in Kadena for thorough physical exams. By 2 April, they were in Colorado, joining fifteen of their countrymen who had arrived the previous November.[3]

Hale had changed little over the previous year of training. Still in charge was Tom Fosmire. Zeke Zilaitis, back to experimenting with rockets, had been promoted to his deputy. Gil Strickler, Patton's former logistician, made irregular visits to assist with support from Fort Carson.

In the field, Tony Poe and Billy Smith remained as tactical instructors. Joining them was Don Cesare, a former marine captain with a taste for chewing tobacco. This was not Cesare's debut with the agency; he had previously served as a security officer for the U-2 spy plane program.[4]/

Other new faces included Joe Slavin and William Toler, two active-duty cooks seconded from the U.S. Army. They were warmly welcomed not only for their culinary talents but also for the fact that they freed the CIA officers from kitchen duties. A third newcomer, Harry Gordon, doubled as both project physician and medical instructor for select Tibetan students.

Making the occasional appearance was another of Roger McCarthy's logistical assistants on the Tibet Task Force, Harry Archer. A Virginia Military Institute graduate from a moneyed family, Archer had entered the Marine Corps in 1953 for a two-year stint. After switching to the CIA, he served an initial tour on Saipan with McCarthy. The two again came together on the Tibet project, where Archer earned a reputation as a "gadget man."

"Harry would go to Abercrombie & Fitch," said fellow task force member John Greaney, referring to the exclusive Manhattan outlet for pricey camping equipment, "and procure the latest in cold-weather gear, knives, and boots." Not all the purchases were appropriate. "He got us a bunch of thumb saws," recalls Fosmire, "even though there was no wood near most of our Tibet drop zones."

Given his marine background, it was Archer who lobbied for the Tibetans to be rotated from Hale to the Marine Corps School at Quantico, Virginia, for a change of pace. There was sound logic behind Archer's proposal: Quantico at the time had a special cell that trained various foreign groups in guerrilla warfare and small-unit tactics. The school also had a pack-mule course where the marine instructors could teach slinging a 75mm recoilless rifle, one of the more cumbersome weapons being dropped inside Tibet.[5]

Escorted by McCarthy, an initial group of twelve Tibetans was flown directly to the airstrip at Quantico in early 1960. There a five-man marine team—which was not privy to the students' nationality—put them through two weeks of instruction on everything from caches to camouflage. Mark and Pete were on hand to provide translations.

Near the end of the cycle, the marines planned an elaborate ambush exercise in which they would play the part of aggressors. On the night before the drill was to start, however, six inches of snow hit northern Virginia. Improvising, the aggressors grabbed white bed sheets and threw them over their ambush position. "The exercise went off perfectly," said Sergeant Willard "Sam" Poss, "and we were able to show the students the need for versatility."[6]

Impressed by the training at Quantico, McCarthy sent a request up the chain of command for the loan of two instructors. The Marine Corps was agreeable, releasing both Poss and Staff Sergeant Robert Laber that spring for temporary duty in Colorado. A Korean War veteran, Laber had been involved in the final combat actions of that conflict; he had since served as a heavy machine gun instructor before joining Quantico's special training cell.

Upon their arrival at Hale, the two marines were in awe of the base's diverse

Training officer Sam Poss stands over the burned wreck of the administration building at Camp Hale following an electrical short circuit. (Courtesy Sam Poss)

mini-armory comprising both Western and communist bloc weaponry. "We were to teach the Tibetans how to use these and maneuver in a combat situation," said Poss. "This meant overcoming their first instinct, which was to stand in a line and fire everything they had until their bullets were finished, then pick up some rocks."⁷

Initially, Poss focused on map reading. Since the Tibetans were weak in mathematics, special maps were adapted from dated World Airway charts. Printed on cloth, they were simplified for the Tibetans by making both magnetic north and true north the same.

Laber, meanwhile, spent his time at the rifle range. As both a former machine gun instructor and a mortar section leader, he focused on developing skills with both these weapons. Because Fosmire and Zilaitis insisted on keeping the training as authentic as possible, blanks were never used. This resulted in an embarrassing breach of security midway through the dry summer. As Laber watched the Tibetans blaze away one afternoon with white phosphorus rounds, one ricocheted into the tress. In minutes, an entire hillside was in flames.

The CIA staff was now in a quandary. They could not cope with the fire themselves, but inviting the Forest Service into the camp could expose the project.

There was really no choice. The Tibetans were rushed back to their quarters and quarantined before the gates were opened to allow in the fire trucks. It eventually took an entire week to bring the blaze under control. The firefighters were instructed not to ask too many questions, though they did remark that "strange inscriptions" in a foreign language had been carved into some rocks.[8]

That incident aside, the Tibetans made good progress through late summer. Groups of students were taken for overnight forays into the hills with the tactical instructors, where they would call in mountaintop resupply drops—including a leaflet printing press developed by the task force's resident scholar, Ken Knaus—and radio regular updates back to Ray Stark at base. And after word got back that the Amdo contingent had been overrun with tanks, an old Sherman was donated by Fort Carson for the students to practice both driving and disabling.[9]

As graduation approached, the Tibetans were scheduled to showcase their skills to a headquarters delegation led by Des FitzGerald. Joining him was Gyalo Thondup, who was in the United States for what was becoming an annual tour for consultations and to bolster international support at the United Nations. The Hale staff had assembled some stands for their guests and spent days rehearsing their demonstration. Recalls Fosmire: "It ended with a mad minute attack on a 'Chinese' camp. All of the weapons were used, even mortars. One camouflaged Tibetan with a Bren was hiding near the reviewing stand and surprised everyone. When the last mortar round landed, they looted the camp."

FitzGerald was delighted with the performance of what was widely recognized as his favorite project. Given his own wartime experience in Burma, he took the opportunity to quiz the Hale staff. "He was particularly interested and impressed with our cache training," remembers Cesare.[10]

Although FitzGerald might have been deeply committed to it, trouble loomed for the Tibet project. For one thing, all the airborne teams operating inside Tibet during the first quarter of 1960 were wiped out by late spring; sending more agents according to the same script no longer seemed an enlightened idea. For another thing, the Eisenhower administration was dragging its feet on lifting the prohibition against overflights put in place after the downing of the U-2 in May. Not only was Eisenhower still smarting from the diplomatic fallout from that incident, but Washington was now backdrop to a tight presidential race between Vice President Richard Nixon and Democratic Senator John Kennedy. Political prudence dictated that potentially embarrassing covert action—particularly overflights—be put on hold until after the November election.[11]

The delay came at a bad time for the Tibet Task Force. The late fall was good parachuting weather over Tibet. Moreover, there was concern that morale among the Tibetans at Hale might fray if they got stranded for an extended period. To keep them occupied, U.S. Army engineers were dispatched to build a gymnasium alongside their Quonset huts. The CIA also procured reels of television westerns and showed them every night. A favorite was *Cheyenne*, then still in the midst of its eight-year run with the hulking Clint Walker in the title role of an adventurer roaming the post–Civil War West. Said Cesare, "The Tibetans even began imitating Walker's mannerisms around camp."[12]

The CIA instructors, too, were growing bored with the tedious weeks of waiting. Billy Smith had already taken an opportunity for reassignment. A gruff Tony Poe, who was losing patience with some of his fellow officers and disappointed that many of the Tibetans had taken up the habit of cigarette smoking, left near year's end. The two marines also made plans for a return to Quantico.[13]

But the biggest blow came when Tom Fosmire elected to join McCarthy back at the task force desk in Washington. As the figurative heart of the training project since its inception, he had connected with the Tibetans more than any other CIA officer. Much of this had come about while sitting around the campfire at night swapping tales and bonding with his students. He recalls: "The Tibetans talked about going on annual trade caravans into India. There was much competition to be the first caravan of the season because their goods were in highest demand and they made the most money. This meant surviving things like avalanches and bandits. They told me that once Tibet was free, they were going to take me on the biggest caravan ever into Lhasa."

On the night before Fosmire was set to leave, he assembled all the Tibetans and made the announcement. Instantly, tears began to flow. Even when he tried to assure them that he would be working on the program from Washington, it did no good. "We were all crying like babies," said translator Mark. Choked with emotion, Fosmire took a twenty-minute walk to clear his head. "We made a note never to tell them again when one of us was leaving."[14]

With morale already low following Fosmire's departure, the project took another hit in early November. By one of the closest margins in recent presidential history, John Kennedy came out the winner. Although he had been given a pair of confidential CIA briefings by CIA Director Dulles prior to the election, Tibet had not been broached with the youthful nominee. "I'll brief Nixon," Eisenhower was rumored to have told top agency officials regarding Tibet, "but if the other guy wins, you've got to do it."[15]

When Dulles again got a chance to speak with President-elect Kennedy on 18 November, ten days after the vote, Tibet was penciled on the agenda, but it never came up in conversation. Instead, the showdown with Cuba, and the agency's plans to launch an invasion of that island, dominated their talk. Even after Kennedy was inaugurated in early January 1961, other foreign policy items grabbed the early spotlight. Besides Cuba, the deteriorating situations in Laos and South Vietnam were making headlines, relegating Tibet far down the priorities list.

Not until a snowy day in mid-February did things begin to change. Fosmire, who had been minding the quiet Tibet desk through the winter, remembers: "Bill Broe, the deputy chief of the Far East Division, stormed into the office with ice in his hair. He took off his jacket and waved a slip of paper. It was our permission to resume."[16]

That permission followed from a 14 February decision by Kennedy's top foreign policy advisers—his so-called Special Group—to continue the covert Tibet operation started under the previous administration.[17]

It had been almost a year since the last agent drop. With clear skies over Tibet, the task force moved to seize the moment. Even though the earlier airborne teams had met with only limited success—and the concept of blind drops had been a complete bust during other agency operations in places such as China, Albania, and Ukraine—plans were drawn up for yet another parachute infiltration.[18]

The CIA's Tibet officers had reason to ignore their poor airborne track record and opt for the same tired formula. One of its agent trainees at Hale, a young Khampa named Yeshi Wangyal, was easily among the most capable Tibetans to pass through its gates. Known as "Tim" during his tenure in Colorado, he hailed from the town of Markham. Located between the Mekong and Yangtze Rivers, Markham had repeatedly attracted attention during years past. Early in the twentieth century, it had been the scene of seesaw battles as Chinese and Tibetan armies wrestled for control of Kham, with the Han more often than not coming up short. Markham had still been under Lhasa's sphere of influence in 1950, but it fell as one of the initial targets of the PLA invasion. This did little to extinguish the zeal of the town's residents. Although the Kham of neighboring Lithang may have headlined the top ranks of the *Chushi Gangdruk* resistance when it formed in 1956, sons of Markham were among the budding rebellion's other prominent partisans.[19]

Markham was significant on other counts. For one thing, it sat at the terminus of a second drivable road the Chinese were building across Kham, and the CIA remained committed to disrupting Beijing's logistical flow. For another thing, not only were guerrillas around Markham still confounding the Chinese as of late 1960 (according to reports reaching India), but one of the rebel chieftains was

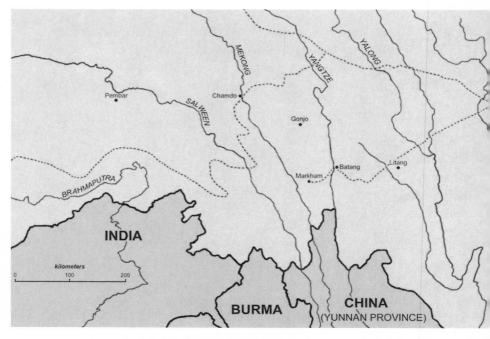

The Kham region showing the extent of Chinese highway construction, circa 1960

none other than Tim's father. Therefore, parachuting Tim back into his hometown would not exactly be a blind drop.

To increase Tim's chances of success, he was allowed to pick his own teammates from among the candidates at Hale. Selected as deputy team leader was Bhusang, a thirty-two-year-old former medical student from Lhasa who went by the call sign "Ken." Five others—Aaron, Collin, Duke, Luke, and Phillip—also made the cut.[20]

During the last week of March 1961, the seven began their long return journey from Colorado. Escorting them was translator Mark and CIA officer Zilaitis, who had been promoted to training chief following Fosmire's departure. After a three-night delay at Takhli due to unseasonably bad weather, the team boarded a C-130A as the sun set on 31 March.[21] Mark, who was the same age as Tim and had grown close to him during training, was bawling on the tarmac. Tim, his voice choked, passed on a request for Lhamo Tsering to take care of his young bride.[22]

Inside the cockpit, the Air America crew refamiliarized themselves with the controls. It had been nearly a year since they flew the last Hercules drop, and the company had few aviators to spare, given its busy flying schedule for the rapidly expanding CIA operation in nearby Laos. Smoke jumpers, too, were at a premium, with only Miles Johnson and Paper Legs Peterson assigned to Asia in early 1961; all their fellow smoke jumpers–cum–kickers were in Latin America working on the imminent CIA paramilitary invasion of Cuba.[23]

Roaring down the runway, the aircraft rose slowly on its journey toward Kham. At 2300 hours under a full moon, the green light flashed in the cabin. Seven men and cargo exited the side doors. The battle for Markham was about to heat up.

Assembling on the ground undetected, the agents had no problem locating their supplies. Though this might have been cause for celebration, Tim was far from happy. Landing among rocks, one of his teammates, Aaron, was cringing in pain with a dislocated shoulder. Worse, by sunrise he made the unwelcome discovery that the Hercules had significantly overshot the intended drop zone. Their current position, he calculated, was due west of the town of Gonjo. Like Markham, numerous skirmishes had been fought around Gonjo during the first half of the twentieth century as the Chinese and Tibetans vied for control. The difference, Tim noted with concern, was that Gonjo was more than 100 kilometers north of his hometown.

Resting through the afternoon of the second day, the team prepared for the long walk south. Given Aaron's shoulder, their supplies were divided among the six healthy members. The remaining evidence of their drop—parachutes and rigging materials—was placed atop a pyre of wood and brush. They struck a match to the tinder and then set off at dusk up the first mountain between them and Markham.[24]

By dawn on the third day, the team had reached the summit. Looking back, they could still see smoke hanging in the air from their bonfire. It was not until the next morning, after putting sufficient space between themselves and the drop zone, that the agents paused to send an initial radio message back to the Tibet Task Force, reporting the navigational error and their intended movement.

Even though the agents were tired and hungry, their journey over the first five days was trouble free. On day six, things started to change. Pausing near sunset, they spied ten PLA soldiers and a Khampa guide in the process of concealing an observation post near the crest of a nearby hill. Not knowing if this was a coincidence or if their presence was suspected, Tim ordered the team to detour into the bush and cache those supplies not deemed vital, such as a mimeograph machine and an inflatable rubber raft the CIA had provided for crossing the rivers that bracketed Markham.

Patrolling forward, Tim and Ken made a two-man reconnaissance over the next hill and detected no other Chinese. The team continued its trek under cover of darkness. After one week of slow, careful movement, they could at last see Markham in the distance. Between them was a green valley pockmarked with the black, rounded tents used by herdsmen and traders. Though their goal was almost within reach, by that point, the agents had completely exhausted their rations and were thinking of little other than their stomachs. Leaving four members behind, Tim, Aaron, and Phillip crept toward the nearest tent in a bid to procure food.

At the last moment, Tim called a halt. By sheer coincidence, he recognized the occupant as a servant of his father. Approaching cautiously, Tim offered greetings and asked the servant of his father's whereabouts. The news was heart wrenching: he had been killed during a battle with the Chinese a few months earlier. Two other local chieftains had inherited his command, said the servant, and had continued to resist near Markham until their food stocks were depleted; both were now hiding with their guerrillas in the neighboring hills. When asked, the servant admitted that locals had heard the aircraft that dropped Tim, and the Chinese had deployed patrols as a result.[25]

Tim knew that he needed to act with discretion, if not suspicion. But still without rations, he imposed on the servant to convey a request for one of the rebel leaders to rendezvous with tea bricks, yak butter, and tsampa (ground roasted barley, a Tibetan staple). This meeting took place as scheduled, and although Tim received warm embraces and the customary deference afforded the son of a martyred chieftain, there was no mistaking an undercurrent of strain.

By day ten, the team arranged for a meeting with another local chief. Again, pleasantries were tempered by palatable tension. It was fast becoming apparent that the agents were seen by some as an invitation for a Chinese crackdown. Persisting, Tim was finally taken to the forest redoubt where the remnants of his father's guerrilla band were holed up. Women and children were among the weary partisans, including Tim's sister. They were a sad sight, with food in short supply and footwear in tatters.

Tim used the opportunity to pass on statements of encouragement from the Dalai Lama, and he tried to breathe life back into his crowd by speaking about the material support he was set to receive from the United States. As proof, he sent four of his agents to the cache site to recover their hidden supplies. On the way back, they left leaflets urging all tsampa-eaters (a euphemism for Tibetans, as opposed to Han rice-eaters) to remain vigilant against Chinese attack.

Over the following week, the rebel chieftains weighed Tim's exhortation back to arms and then called an emergency meeting in his absence. Despite the promise of foreign support, more than five years of fighting had taken a heavy toll. Exile was now utmost on their minds, not ratcheting up the war against China.

Deputy team leader Ken, who was present at the meeting, tried to stem the tide. Their orders, he noted, were to exfiltrate only after exhausting all means of resistance. The rebels were hardly swayed; they were intent on heading for India.

By that time, the team had been on the ground for twenty-four days. After the conclusion of the emergency session, a radio message was sent notifying the Tibet Task Force about the impending rebel exodus from the hills around Markham. When no immediate reply was forthcoming, the agents saw little choice but to join them.

They did not get far. News of the team had invariably spread across the Markham countryside, and it was only a matter of time before local informants tipped off the PLA. Together with pro-communist Khampa militiamen, Chinese troops closed in on the guerrilla concentration just as they started to move. Nine separate engagements were fought over the course of the first day. The agents sought refuge deeper in the forest, but not before the Chinese onslaught killed Collin and Duke. Cranking up their radio, the survivors had time to tap out a brief message. Recalls Mark, who was helping with translations in Washington at the time, "It was an SOS."

Taking along fewer than two dozen guerrillas and dependents, the remaining team members slipped through the PLA cordon and for a time shook off their pursuers. Over the next three days, they attempted to rest. But again, their hunger pangs were overwhelming. After nearly running into a Chinese patrol the following morning, they left the forest to approach a lone herdsman. Upon seeing the guerrillas, the shepherd turned over a yak and hurried from the scene. Ignoring tradecraft, the famished agents butchered and cooked the animal on the spot, then ate until they were full.

The PLA was not far behind. Having corralled the rebels toward a mountain, the Chinese repeated their Pembar strategy of establishing blocking positions and flushing them out by setting the forest ablaze. With no alternatives, the agents and a handful of partisans left the protection of the trees and scurried up the bare slope in the dark. The Chinese had already circled atop the summit, allowing no escape.

As the sun rose, Ken took account of their bleak situation. "It was like a dream, unreal" he later commented. Squeezed behind boulders, Tim's sister and two other children could be heard weeping loudly. Aaron and Luke were huddled behind another rocky outcropping, Tim and Phillip behind a third. As the Chinese leapfrogged closer, they fired an occasional rifle shot and called for sur-render. "Eat shit!" the Tibetans yelled back defiantly.

By 1000 hours, the Chinese had maneuvered within a stone's throw. Surging forward, they grabbed the three bawling children. Ken fingered the cyanide ampoule hanging from a necklace around his neck. The previous night, the agents had agreed to commit suicide after firing their last shot. Seeing no move-ment from Aaron and Luke, Ken assumed that both had already taken their lives.

Craning his head toward his remaining colleagues, Ken caught a glimpse of Tim frantically motioning toward his ampoule with sign language. Uncertain if this was a call to commit suicide in unison, Ken tentatively placed the cyanide in his cheek. Seconds later, a Chinese soldier leaped from behind and planted a rifle butt on the back of his skull. Knocked unconscious before he could bite down on the ampoule, Ken was bound and led away to a prison cell in Markham. He was the only survivor of the seven and would not see freedom for another seven-teen years.

Although the CIA did not have immediate confirmation of the fate of Tim and his team, the desperate tone of their last radio message spoke volumes. It was glaringly apparent: the task force needed a new strategy.

11. Mustang

Well before the parachute drop at Markham, the seeds of a new Tibet strategy were germinating. The impetus for this had come from NVDA chief Gompo Tashi and from Lhamo Tsering, Gyalo Thondup's able lieutenant in Darjeeling, who watched with concern as thousands of able-bodied Tibetan men were siphoned from Indian refugee camps and channeled into road construction gangs to help offset mounting aid costs. Some 4,000 ended up in Sikkim alone, where they were over-seen by a special relief committee headed by Princess Kukula.[1]

Dispersing Tibetan manpower in this way put the two leaders in a quandary. Although having the refugees work on road construction was better than letting them languish in camps, employing large numbers of men as laborers sapped energy from the dream of retaking their homeland. Many of the displaced still clung to the hope of a resurgent NVDA, particularly older partisans who itched for the chance to take up arms one more time.

Although neither Gompo Tashi nor Lhamo Tsering were opposed to the idea of a reborn guerrilla army, there was a serious geopolitical hurdle to overcome. To properly refit any irregulars, they needed a secure staging area. Given Nehru's continued desire to refrain from provoking the Chinese leadership, use of India for this purpose was out of the question. Similarly, Bhutan and Sikkim were too firmly under India's thumb to consider their territory as host for a significant paramilitary endeavor.

By default, that left Nepal. A lone Hindu kingdom in the Buddhist Himalayas, Nepal was a study in selective nonalignment. For the first eight years of India's independence, Kathmandu had tempered its neutrality with a pro-Indian bias. At the same time, Nepal liked to think of Tibet (with considerable hyperbole) as a kind of vassal and not as part of China.

But in 1955, with the death of mild King Tribhuwan and the rise of bolder son Mahendra, change was in the air. In an attempt to break what he saw as overde-pendence on India and to diversify the kingdom's foreign policy, the new king established diplomatic relations with the PRC in 1956 and signed a Sino-Nepalese trade agreement that same year.

Although Kathmandu had moved a small step closer to Beijing—and now recognized the PRC's hold over Tibet—Gompo Tashi and Lhamo Tsering still had good reason to see Nepal as an attractive stepping-stone into their home-land. First, transportation difficulties and sharp ethnic differences meant that

Kathmandu's grip barely reached outside the capital. Second, Nepal was already home to a large number of recent Tibetan arrivals. Estimates placed the number of refugees at 20,000 during the first two years of the Dalai Lama's exile. Of these, many were from the western reaches of Tibet and sought sanctuary in Nepal's most remote border areas, where Kathmandu's writ was rarely heard, much less acknowledged.[2]

Third, one corner of Nepal—the enclave of Mustang—was for all intents and purposes part of Tibet. The highest kingdom in the world (with an average altitude of 3,758 feet), Mustang encompassed 1,943 square kilometers of arid gorges and cliffs centered along Nepal's northern border. Surrounded on three sides by Tibet, its population and culture were entirely Tibetan Buddhist. It had never been conquered by Nepal and, located north of the Himalayas, intuitively should have been incorporated under Lhasa's control. But after an eighteenth-century debt swap among highland royalty, Mustang passed to Nepal as a loose tributary.[3]

Nepal could be forgiven for hardly noticing its new territorial addition. Led by its own line of kings dating back to the fourteenth century, Mustang consisted of just twelve large villages and the walled capital of Lo Monthang, where a modest palace was centered in a maze of temples and homes for 800 residents. Though it had once been prosperous—thanks to its command over the salt trade into western Tibet—Mustang had degenerated into a backwater after competing principalities to the south broke that monopoly in 1890.

Despite its impoverishment, Mustang retained something more important: its autonomy. Even when Kathmandu insisted on the disbandment of other royal fiefdoms within its borders, Mustang alone was allowed to keep its king. In return for a token annual tribute of two horses and forty-five British pounds, Lo Monthang enjoyed near complete leeway in running its own affairs.[4]

Besides its quasi-independence, there were other reasons for Lhamo Tsering and Gompo Tashi to favor Mustang. First, it was there that the Lithang Khampa team had fled in late 1959 after its abortive mission to Nam Tso; in messages sent back to Darjeeling, the agents had reported that their ethnic kin were generally supportive. Second, the border between Mustang and Tibet did not have any high passes blocked by snow in winter. Third, although its climate was dry and the land largely infertile, there was a handful of valleys with enough tree cover to camouflage a guerrilla encampment during the summer. Fourth, its remote location kept it out of range of foreign visitors; only one Western interloper had ever set foot in the region as of 1960. And if that were not enough, a divination arranged by the two leaders confirmed the choice of Mustang as a good one.[5]

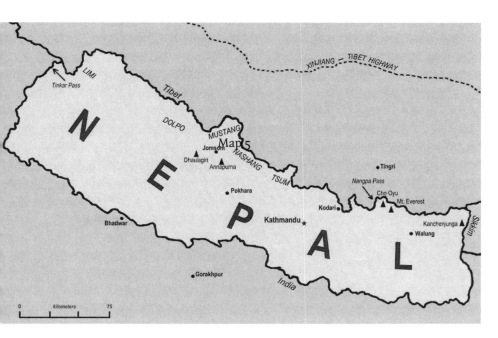

Nepal

Although Gompo Tashi and Lhamo Tsering (who, it was understood, carried Gyalo's consent) were swayed that Mustang was a sure bet for a guerrilla sanctuary, the United States had to be convinced. Traveling to Calcutta in February 1960 to meet with CIA liaison officers, the two lobbied for support of their Nepal plan. At the time, Washington's relations with Kathmandu could only be described as cool and proper. This was largely due to King Mahendra's engagement policy of playing off the major powers, milking aid from all but not endearing himself to any. Had the United States requested permission from Mahendra to use Mustang, it is unlikely that it would have been granted.[6]

But the question was never asked. Just as Gompo Tashi and Lhamo Tsering had calculated, poor transportation and communication networks severely curtailed the Nepalese government's extent of control. "Most ministers had never seen their own country," noted one American aid worker who served there in 1960."[7] Concluded Ralph Redford, the CIA station chief in Kathmandu, "The king's permission was not necessarily required."[8]

Once word of the pitch from the two Tibetans reached Washington, the CIA's task force officers quickly concurred that a modest guerrilla operation staged from Mustang had merit and would not irreparably harm U.S.-Nepal relations. Gompo Tashi was given approval in March to begin the process of identifying candidates to lead the paramilitary force.

Rushing north to Kalimpong, the ailing chieftain beckoned seven senior NVDA officers for three days of intense discussion. Informed of the pending Mustang operation, they were told to choose a field commander from among their number. Even for a people used to a challenging lifestyle, the assignment promised to be a hardship tour. Gompo Tashi, though the logical choice, was ineligible because he required too much rest and care. Similarly, six others withdrew themselves from consideration due to age or poor fitness or because they had dependents.

The only one remaining, forty-three-year-old Baba Yeshi, received their unanimous support. As suggested by his name, Baba Yeshi hailed from the central Kham town of Baba (now called Bathang). Due to its relatively low altitude, Bathang was an early target for Han colonization and had even attracted French missionaries during the early twentieth century. The locals had strongly resisted these ethnic and religious incursions. The missionaries ultimately withdrew after several priests were executed, but the Chinese battled back and held on until midcentury.

By the time of the 1956 uprising, the Khampas of Bathang were primed to explode. Among the first to revolt, they courted a harsh PLA response. Chinese aircraft rained down bombs, paying special attention to monasteries. One such destroyed temple was the home of Baba Yeshi, who had entered the priesthood at age eight and took his vows at eighteen. Though from a poor family, the monk had shown a talent for trading cloth and had amassed respectable savings. Predicting more Chinese attacks to come, he gathered his inventory and made his way to the safer climes of Kalimpong.

The respite was not to last. By mid-1958, word of the newly christened NVDA quickly filtered down to India. Prodded by other exiles, Baba Yeshi agreed to return to Tibet on the pretext of a pilgrimage. His real purpose was to help raid an armory near the Nepalese border. He attempted to do so, but the Tibetan army held firm and refused to release the weapons. Dejected, he headed toward Drigu Tso lake to link up with Gompo Tashi, only to find that the chieftain had already shifted to the north.

He remained in the vicinity of Drigu Tso, and by the fall of 1958, Baba Yeshi was elected leader of a large, albeit quiet, NVDA sector. By his own admission, they accomplished little. "I had no military background," he later recounted, "and just one in ten of my guerrillas had a weapon." Their biggest excitement

Baba Yeshi, the first commander of Mustang. (Courtesy Roger MacCarthy)

came the following spring, when they received couriered orders to secure the area north of the lake during the passage of the fleeing Dalai Lama.[9]

Not until after the Dalai Lama reached India did Baba Yeshi at long last rendezvous with Gompo Tashi. But by that time, the NVDA chief was also on his way to exile. Baba Yeshi joined him and crossed the border, where he stewed in a refugee camp for the next eight months.

Frustrated by the boredom and the heat, the monk finally saw an opportunity for action in December 1959. With Eisenhower set to make the first visit to India by a U.S. president, he and fourteen other Khampa leaders rushed down to New Delhi and stood along Eisenhower's motorcade route in an attempt to hand him a letter calling for U.S. support. Not surprisingly, the Khampas came nowhere close to getting an audience with the visiting dignitary. Dejected again, Baba Yeshi returning to the steaming refugee camp and was still there when he got the call from Gompo Tashi to come to Kalimpong.

When he learned of the impending Mustang operation—and got the unanimous support of his peers to lead it—Baba Yeshi was more than a little apprehensive. He was the first to admit that he had no formal military training. And despite his years studying Buddhist scripture, his writing skills were poor.

There was also the controversy surrounding his hometown, Bathang. Owing to its long occupation by the Chinese, Bathang was infamous for its Khampa sympathizers and informants. Bathang also hosted a large number of Muslim Hiu, many of whom had assisted Beijing in battles against the Tibetan resistance. This, plus petty rivalries with neighboring towns such as Lithang, gave Bathang residents the reputation for being antagonistic toward their countrymen.[10]

But Baba Yeshi had other qualities that offset such deficiencies. In a culture not known for oratory, he was renowned as an articulate public speaker who exuded emotion and could even bring up tears on cue. As a monk, he had no dependents. And he was also known for his keen ability to anticipate and resolve problems within his ranks. "He was nicknamed Cat," said one of his subordinates, "because he would pounce on trouble like catching a mouse."[11]

Upon confirmation of Baba Yeshi as overall leader, Gompo Tashi and Lhamo Tsering made the rounds of the various refugee camps to select another two dozen candidates to serve as a U.S.-trained officer cadre for the guerrilla force. The choice was limited to NVDA veterans without dependents and in good physical condition. To maximize clan coverage, no more than two men were chosen from each large district (such as Lithang), and only one from small districts.[12]

When the final cut was made in May, twenty-seven candidates had assembled in Darjeeling. Reflecting the composition of the NVDA, as well as the makeup of the refugee pool, only two were from Amdo; the rest were from Kham. Most were in their mid-thirties, although four were close to fifty years of age. They were told the nature of their assignment in general terms, but not the location.[13]

Before getting to Mustang, there remained the matter of training. Escorted by Lhamo Tsering to the East Pakistan frontier, the twenty-seven approached the rain-swollen river defining the border. They crossed it with difficulty and were deluged by heavy June rains for the entire bus and train ride to Dacca. Not until one week later were they were back in their element among the mountains of Colorado.[14]

As leader of the Mustang force, Baba Yeshi had a whirlwind schedule prior to departure for the front. First was a plane ride to meet CIA representatives in Calcutta, followed by a stop in Darjeeling for an audience with Gyalo Thondup. After that was a trip to Siliguri to rendezvous with two CIA-trained Tibetan radio operators.[15]

Then came the long trek into Nepal. From Siliguri, the monk and two radiomen—plus a Tibetan guide provided by Gyalo—took a train west to the Indian city of Gorakhpur, then a bus north to Kathmandu. There they rented a room near the huge Swayambhunath stupa, one of the holiest Buddhist shrines in Nepal, situated atop a hillock on the capital's western outskirts.

For two weeks, they waited near the stupa. Unknown to the Tibetans, a storm brewing within the CIA was causing delays. So as not to burden Baba Yeshi with heavy equipment during his trip into Nepal, the Tibet Task Force had intended to pass him three radio sets after his arrival in Kathmandu. Kenneth "Clay" Cathey, a CIA officer based in Calcutta, had been charged with overseeing the transfer. Helping him would be Ray Stark, the former Hale radio instructor beckoned from an assignment in Manila.[16]

Unfortunately for Cathey and Stark, the CIA station in Nepal was doing all it could to stymie the transfer plan. Backed by Near East Division colleagues in New Delhi and at headquarters, station chief Redford opposed the scheme because he did not want to risk exposure on his home turf. Only after explicit instructions from the office of Director Dulles did the Nepal embassy reluctantly cooperate.

Following this high-level directive, the three radios arrived in Kathmandu in a diplomatic pouch. To make them portable, Stark helped break them into forty smaller loads. Cathey then procured some plain burlap and, because the station chief refused to lend his men to assist, was forced to spend an extra day wrapping the equipment on his own.

By that time, Lhamo Tsering and another Tibetan radioman had arrived in Kathmandu to help with the radio delivery. Because it was too risky to have Baba Yeshi come to the embassy, they needed to bring the gear to him. The station chief, still intent on obstructing the plan, insisted on using a taxi, but Cathey eventually persevered in getting loan of an embassy jeep.

That night, Cathey, Lhamo Tsering, and the radioman drove with the disassembled communication equipment to a darkened corner of the Swayambhunath stupa. Baba Yeshi, his two radiomen, and eighteen more Khampas that had joined the party made the rendezvous. There they split in two, with a pair of the radiomen and twelve of the Khampas securing the radios on their backs and setting off on foot in the direction of Mustang.

After giving them a five-day lead, Baba Yeshi, the remaining radioman, and six other Khampas attempted to get plane tickets for Pokhara, 130 kilometers west of Kathmandu and just south of Mustang. But to Baba Yeshi's chagrin, the sales representatives for Royal Nepal Airlines were extremely suspicious, even after the monk showed Tibetan documents that "proved" they were heading to Pokhara to help fellow refugees.

Such suspicion was understandable. Tibetan exiles were doing all they could to leave Pokhara, not the other way around. There was also the matter of increased tensions along the Sino-Nepalese frontier. Beijing had recently closed its border to grazing on the Chinese side, previously a common practice among Nepalese herders. More seriously, a PLA patrol had crossed the border into Mustang during June, apparently believing that it had spotted Khampa guerrillas. In the ensuing skirmish, they killed a Nepalese soldier and took ten civilians prisoner, sending a wave of panic through Lo Monthang.[17]

Ten days later they were still without plane tickets, and Baba Yeshi and his men thought it prudent to leave the Nepalese capital. Making their way back to Gorakhpur, they took a train northeast along the border, then recrossed into Nepal from the frontier town of Bhadwar. From there, it was a five-day trek on foot to Pokhara. Fearful that the Nepalese authorities might have been alerted, they wasted no time walking another four days up narrow paths to the village of Tukuche.

In a kingdom full of breathtaking vistas, Tukuche ranked high among them. Situated in a gap in the Himalayas where the Kali Gandaki River flows through the Annapurna and Dhaulagiri Mountains, it is bracketed by canyon walls rising five kilometers on either side. By the time Baba Yeshi arrived there, the party that had departed Kathmandu on foot was already waiting in tents and had established radio contact with Darjeeling.[18]

Hearing of the successful rendezvous at Tukuche, Lhamo Tsering assembled the first group of guerrilla prospects from the Indian refugee camps. Earlier, Gompo Tashi had talked in terms of eventually building a 2,100-man force, but the CIA had approved support for only 400. Making the selection at Darjeeling, Lhamo Tsering gave each approved recruit a pair of shoes and a small rupee stipend to pay for food on the trip through Nepal. It was a relatively old crowd, with most close to forty years of age. Nearly all were Khampas.

Very quickly, word of the recruitment flashed among the refugees. What was supposed to be a clandestine shift of personnel suddenly became a very public one. On 1 August, the Indian media in Calcutta reported on the mysterious exodus of Tibetan men out of Sikkim. By early fall, Lhamo Tsering's 400 approved candidates were joined in Nepal by 200 unapproved Tibetans; several hundred others were on the way.[19]

With Tukuche fast growing crowded, Baba Yeshi sent three men north to make a ten-day reconnaissance trek for suitable locations inside Mustang. By October, they had returned with a pair of recommendations. The first was Yara, little more than a cluster of earthen huts situated in a fertile valley dotted with conifers and tucked under a massive cliff honeycombed with caves. The second, twelve kilometers southwest of Yara, was Tangya. Sited in one of the lowest valleys in Mustang, it was packed with barley fields and, like Yara, was in the shadow of an imposing cliff eroded like the flutes of an organ. Both were east of the Kali Gandaki and several days' hike from the other major villages in Mustang.[20]

Baba Yeshi started dispatching recruits to the Yara valley. In November, he himself made the shift from Tukuche to Tangya. With no weapons, a handful of tents, and little food, the prospective guerrillas and their leader settled in for the long, cold winter.[21]

On the other side of the world at Camp Hale, the Mustang leadership cadre spent the winter of 1960–1961 training alongside the agent team destined for Markham. Despite the advanced age of several in the group, the twenty-seven were put through all their paramilitary paces. No problems were encountered—with one near-fatal exception. Prior to making actual airborne jumps at Fort Carson, the Tibetans practiced in a training rig at Hale nicknamed Suspended Agony. It consisted of webbing hanging from a makeshift iron frame, and the students needed to climb a ramp to get into the parachute harness.

Suspended Agony had worked well with earlier classes, but by the time the Mustang group arrived, it was showing its age. Unfortunately for Namgyal, a forty-five-year-old Bathang native who went by the call sign "Sampson," the iron frame decided to snap while he was in it. Dropping two meters to the ground, Sampson collapsed as the metal sliced into his forehead, exposing his skull.[22]

The CIA instructors rushed to the side of the unconscious Sampson, loaded him into a station wagon, and sped him to the army hospital at Fort Carson.

There the doctors did not give him a good prognosis. "There was no way we could bring the body back to Tibet," said Sam Poss, "so talk shifted to getting lime and burying him back at Hale." But it never came to that. Showing far more resilience than the doctors thought possible, Sampson made a miraculous recovery. Returning to Hale, he eventually completed his airborne training in the spring of 1961.

By that time, his peers had graduated and been fully briefed on their impending mission to Mustang. The CIA's task force officers had been particularly impressed by Lobsang Jamba, a forty-year-old Lithang Khampa using the call sign "Sally." According to revised plans, Sally would parachute into Mustang and assume the role of field commander inside Tibet; Baba Yeshi, meanwhile, would be relegated to administrative chief at the Tangya rear base.[23]

Back in Nepal, Baba Yeshi had not yet been informed of this new leadership arrangement. His attention had been fixated on the dire food situation at his guerrilla camp. As longtime Mustang residents well knew, the infertile kingdom could not stockpile enough food to feed all its people through winter. For that reason, just 35 percent of the population of Lo Monthang (primarily the elderly) remained in town year-round; the remainder migrated for the coldest months down to Pokhara.[24]

When Baba Yeshi showed up at Tangya in November 1960, neither he nor his men at Yara had brought any food with them. They also carried little cash to purchase tsampa and other essentials. And even if they had brought money, more than 1,000 would-be guerrillas had assembled at Yara by year's end, far outstripping the amount of staples that valley could produce. Very quickly, malnutrition reached critical levels. In desperation, more than a few boiled shoe leather for a meal.[25]

Compounding matters, the CIA still did not have permission to make a supply drop, due to the prohibition against overflights following the U-2 affair. And if that were not enough, the new Kennedy administration was divided over whether the Mustang plan should even proceed. Heading the resistance was the new U.S. ambassador to India, John Kenneth Galbraith. A Canadian immigrant, Galbraith was an influential name in liberal circles. As a former Harvard professor of Keynesian economics, price czar during World War II, and editor of Fortune magazine, he had been an adviser to all Democratic presidents since Franklin Roosevelt. A prolific writer, Galbraith was renowned for his eloquent prose. He was also known for his grand ego, and as part of Kennedy's Harvard brain trust, he considered himself a logical pick for secretary of state.

But Kennedy had other ideas. It was widely known that both he and Galbraith shared a strong pro-India bias. As senator, Kennedy had spoken of India as a key to Asia. An economically strong India, went his argument, would be an essential showpiece for democracy in the Third World and a fitting challenge to Chinese communism in Asia. Although Eisenhower had stopped seeing Indian neutralism as evil by 1958, and his 1959 trip to New Delhi had been a resounding success, Kennedy felt that his predecessor had all but lost India through the misplaced goal of cultivating Pakistan.[26]

Based on this conviction, Kennedy was quick to place several well-known India supporters in important positions. Chester Bowles, a former ambassador in New Delhi, had been his foreign policy adviser during the campaign. Phillips Talbot, a scholar-journalist who specialized in things Indian, became assistant secretary of state for Near East and South Asian affairs. And on 29 March 1961, Galbraith was appointed the new ambassador to India.

Shortly before his departure for New Delhi, the ambassador-designate went to CIA headquarters for a briefing on intelligence operations in India, as well as on the fledgling guerrilla force in neighboring Nepal. Heading the briefing was Richard Bissell, chief of covert operations, who, like Galbraith, had once been an Ivy League professor of economics. Joining Bissell was Far East chief Des FitzGerald, the Tibet operation's most die-hard and senior proponent, and James Critchfield, FitzGerald's counterpart in the Near East Division.[27]

After reviewing the CIA's planned budget for throwing India's upcoming elections, Galbraith was not amused. But it was upon hearing the details of the Mustang scheme that Galbraith became livid. Pushing back his chair, he stood up and glared at the CIA officers. "This sounds like the Rover Boys at loose ends," said the soon-to-be diplomat before stalking out.[28]

Galbraith's seething opposition was apparently grounded in his belief that the Tibet operation's benefits—especially from the Mustang component—did not outweigh the risk of harm to Indo-U.S. relations. He was especially sensitive to U.S. violations of Indian airspace in the extreme northeast during resupply flights, which he felt were as potentially destructive as the U-2 affair. Galbraith further claimed that his predecessor, Ellsworth Bunker, strongly shared his opposition.[29]

The new ambassador was overstating fears, if not inventing a few. Had Ambassador Bunker indeed been opposed during his tenure, he had never protested too loudly. The Indians, too, seemed more than willing to turn a blind eye on the CIA's cavorting with the Tibetans. In 1960, B. N. Mullik, head of the Indian Intelligence Bureau, and Richard Helms, the CIA's chief of operations for the Directorate of Plans, had met discreetly during an Interpol conference in Hawaii; at that time, Mullik said that he endorsed the agency's efforts and wanted U.S. overflights to continue.[30] Galbraith's real opposition, suspected several in the CIA, was based as much on genuine diplomatic concerns as on his anti-CIA slant, especially toward an operation initiated during the previous Republican administration.[31]

But Galbraith was hardly alone. Even within the CIA, opposition to the Tibet project was evident. This had less to do with arguments over the operation's potential yield than turf battles between the agency's geographic divisions. At the level of division chief, there was little friction between the Far East's FitzGerald and the Near East's Critchfield. For his part, Critchfield was largely indifferent toward Tibet. A longtime Europe hand (he had started his agency career handling Reinhard Gehlen, the former Nazi general co-opted by the CIA for his anticommunist intelligence network), Critchfield was an Asia novice when he was picked by Dulles in late 1959 to command the Near East.[32]

By that time, the Tibet Task Force was already making regular use of India and East Pakistan. "I had zero veto power over the Tibet operation," Critchfield recalled, "even when it involved overflights of India." Only when Tibetan trainees were set to pass through Near East territory in East Pakistan was he given a courtesy alert.[33]

Although Critchfield did not find this particularly problematic, the same could not be said for others in his division. Heading that list was the CIA station chief in New Delhi, Harry Rositzke. The Harvard-educated professor and OSS alumni had been in India since May 1957. "Rositzke was strong minded, fast talking, and thought of himself as a world thinker," said one case officer who served under him. "He seemed to envision himself going back to Harvard one day, not as an agency career man."[34]

The ambitious Rositzke did not appreciate hosting part of an operation that earned him no credit in Washington but would leave him reaping bad publicity if things went sour. "The Far East Division got all the kudos," said one India case officer, "but the Near East Division risked the potential embarrassment."[35]

Rositzke's displeasure with this arrangement was focused squarely on the Far East Division's liaison officer in Calcutta, John Hoskins. Since 1956, Hoskins had been point man for dealings with Gyalo Thondup. As long as those dealings were low-key, New Delhi station had not complained too loudly. But once the Dalai Lama went into exile and the Tibet Task Force shifted into high gear, New Delhi's fear of a diplomatic incident rose accordingly. Insistent that Hoskins minimize any risk taking, the New Delhi station lobbied against his right to dispatch cables directly to headquarters. As a compromise, it was agreed that Hoskins would channel his communications through New Delhi, although Rositzke was not allowed to alter or edit the contents.

Despite striking this deal, Hoskins could not help but feel that he was under growing pressure. Even though he ultimately answered to the Far East Division, it was the Calcutta chief of base—a Near East officer—who wrote his annual performance reviews, which carried a lot of weight when it came to promotions. Fearful that his career would suffer, he approached the Near East Division in the summer of 1959 and asked if he could keep his Calcutta post but transfer under its mantle. With the request quickly approved, Hoskins continued to handle Gyalo, but now under Rositzke's complete control.

Having lost its own representative in Calcutta, the Far East Division was not about to concede in the turf war. In order to keep tabs on Hoskins, in September 1959 it insisted on assigning a Far East officer to the New Delhi embassy. That officer, Howard Bane, was senior to Hoskins and in theory would act as the primary point of contact with Gyalo. In addition, the CIA had started contributing a stipend for the Dalai Lama and his entourage—"providing them with rice and robes," said Hoskins—and Bane was in charge of the purse.[36]

Very quickly, Bane began to experience the same pressures Hoskins had endured before his transfer. Located within the same embassy as the assertive Rositzke, Bane realized that his career interests hinged on keeping the peace with the station chief. His muted cables back to the Far East Division reflected this accommodation.

Back in Washington, FitzGerald fumed over not having an aggressive division representative in India. In February 1960, he used his pull with Dulles and successfully lobbied for the stationing of yet another officer— this time to Calcutta to fill the gap left by Hoskins. Chosen for the post was Vanderbilt doctoral graduate Clay Cathey. So as not to repeat the "loss" of Bane, Cathey was briefed "up to his eyeballs" by Tibet Task Force officers McCarthy and Greaney prior to his departure the following month. "They reminded me that I worked for the Far East Division," he said, "and not to do anything just because the Near East tells me to."

As had the others before him, Cathey quickly felt the strain of the interdivision rift over Tibet. Though he remained true to his division ("He was the only one who supplied us with good information," said Greaney), Rositzke did not make the job easy. Every three months, the station chief ordered him to New Delhi for an intense grilling session. Cathey was extremely cautious about what he said, having been warned that the testy former Harvard professor would use whatever he could to shut down the project. "Rositzke did not see himself as a career man," explained Cathey, "so even if the Tibet program held favor with Dulles, he felt no need to please the director."[37]

Despite simmering opposition from the likes of Rositzke and Galbraith, President Kennedy in the second week of March 1961 approved an initial supply drop to Mustang. It was scheduled for the end of the month during the full moon phase and would total 29,000 pounds of arms and ammunition for 400 men. The bulk of the load was to consist of bolt-action Springfield rifles, plus forty Bren light machine guns and a mix of forty M1 Garands and carbines.

Also included in the drop would be seven Hale graduates. Four were from the pool of twenty-seven Mustang leaders, including field commander–designate Sally. The remaining three were radiomen, all ethnic Khampas.[38] They flew to Okinawa on the same plane as the Markham team and then waited a week on the island for weather conditions along the Nepal border to clear. Not until the last day of March did they continue on to Takhli. Sally remembers his final briefing: "The CIA said that the Chinese might have gotten to the drop zone. If so, I was to use my Sten submachine gun. If I finished those bullets, I was to use my pistol. If that was finished, I was to bite my cyanide."[39]

Back at Tangya, Baba Yeshi's radiomen had already received word of the impending drop. Eight hundred men, led by Baba Yeshi himself, shifted fifteen kilometers northeast to the border, then another ten kilometers deeper into Tibet. Given the snow and terrain, this translated into a two-day trek. As they had no beasts of burden, 600 of this number were to act as porters; the remaining 200, having borrowed a handful of antiquated rifles from local herders, were to act as a paltry security force in the event of a PLA attack.[40]

Once at the designated drop zone, the reception committee arranged piles of yak dung to serve as fuel for flame signals. Unfortunately for them, atmospheric conditions frustrated further radio contact with Takhli for two days. With the seven agents and supplies grounded in Thailand for an extra forty-eight hours, dozens among the 800 suffered frostbite.

Not until the evening of 2 April did the radio prove cooperative, and an all-clear signal was conveyed to the launch site. Due to the large size of the load, supplies had been divided between two Hercules transports. Even then, the seven agents barely had room to sit as they boarded the first aircraft. This, combined with the extreme distance, made for an exhausting albeit uneventful flight. Sighting the flame signals on the ground, the Air America crews continued deeper into Tibet, then circled around for a second pass.

In the rear, a nervous Sally was the first out the door. Landing in snow up to his waist, he worked quickly to get clear of the pallets that followed. Porters soon swarmed over the bundles, securing them on their backs before beginning the arduous journey back to Mustang.

Although the drop was a success—and the Indians had not indicated any knowledge of, much less displeasure with, the brief intrusion into their airspace—Ambassador Galbraith was more determined than ever to close the Mustang project. Traveling to Washington in May, he played on his rapport with Kennedy (who was already incensed with Dulles over the Bay of Pigs fiasco in April) to lobby the president for an end to what he saw as CIA interference. But even though the ambassador was able to stop most of the agency's covert operations inside India, he failed to put a damper on the Tibet project.[41]

Ironically, Galbraith was about to get an unlikely ally in the form of the Pakistani government. During the course of the Eisenhower presidency, the CIA had enjoyed cordial ties with Karachi. This included permission to use not only East Pakistani territory for the Tibet operation but also an airfield near the city of Peshawar as a U-2 launch site. Even when it was publicly revealed that the U-2 downed in May 1960 had originated from that airfield, Karachi hardly registered any protest over the resultant embarrassment.

But these warm ties looked set to change with the election of Kennedy and the pro-India bias he brought to office. Pakistani concerns seemed confirmed in April 1961 when Washington pledged a staggering $1 billion in economic aid for India's upcoming five-year development plan. Even more troubling for Karachi, the new administration, citing a threat from China, agreed to sell 350 tanks to New Delhi at low rates.

Pakistan wanted to retaliate, but it saw few ready options. It could not slam the door on Washington's military and economic assistance, because there were few alternative sources of aid that matched U.S. largesse. And it would do no good to withhold permission to use the Peshawar air base, because U-2 flights were still suspended. With little other choice, the Pakistanis closed their border for the Tibet project.

For the Tibet Task Force, the timing could not have been worse. Twenty-three Mustang leaders (the four others had jumped on 2 April) were still at Hale awaiting word to return. Because the onset of the monsoon season prevented further para-chute drops until late in the year, the CIA had intended to smuggle them through East Pakistan and let them enter Nepal on foot. With Karachi's change of heart, however, they were stranded in Colorado.

As it turned out, the agency saw a brief window of opportunity midway through summer. Despite his strong leanings toward India, Kennedy was unwill-ing to completely write off Pakistan. He had invited President Ayub Khan to Washington for a weeklong visit beginning 11 July. On the day of his arrival, the polished Pakistani leader and his daughter were the guests of honor at pictur-esque Mount Vernon.

Seated between Kennedy and wife Jacqueline, Khan was feted during a spec-tacular dinner. Afterward, the two leaders took a stroll on the lawns of the estate. Taking advantage of the moment, Kennedy conveyed a personal plea from CIA Director Dulles to reopen the border. Caught up in the atmospherics, Ayub relented and agreed to let ten more Tibetans pass through his territory.

Wasting little time, the CIA had the Tibetans through East Pakistan and into Mustang by August. There they found that eight companies had been formed in the Yara vicinity, each numbering less than 100 men. Half of this number were issued rifles from the first weapons drop; the remainder were designated as sup-port personnel. Eight of the Hale graduates took charge as company command-ers; the rest were to act as trainers and headquarters staff.

Despite this promising start, problems quickly ensued. First, several of the Khampas were caught stealing animals and jewelry on the Chinese side of the border; this sent a chill through the local Mustang community, which was already beginning to have second thoughts about an armed Khampa presence in its midst.[42] Second, Baba Yeshi had not responded well to the CIA's plan for him to share authority with Sally. Outmaneuvering the Hale-trained officer, he made it clear that he was in complete control of both administration and field operations.

Not that there were any field operations to command. Despite the influx of 400 weapons and couriered cash from Gyalo Thondup, allowing for the pur-chase of horses, the guerrillas stood fast inside Mustang. Not until September did seven guerrillas on horseback head northeast into Tibet. As the Chinese had declared the border area off-limits to herders, they found the region completely devoid of population. Moving over the course of four nights, they eventually came upon a small PLA outpost on the south bank of the Brahmaputra. While two tended to the horses, the remaining five guerrillas ambushed a Chinese patrol and killed several (estimates ranged between eight and thirteen) before racing back to Nepal.[43]

Upon receiving a radio message with the results of Mustang's baptism by fire, the CIA was less than impressed. No photographs had been taken as proof of the supposed ambush, and no weapons were retrieved. And as this had been the first and only operation in the six months since the weapons drop, the guerrillas were not exactly setting a breakneck pace.

Realizing that he had to do better for an encore, Baba Yeshi gathered his officers and outlined plans for a forty-man foray. Their target would be any vehicle plying the trans-Tibet road running between Lhasa and Xinjiang. Completed in 1957 and of questionable quality, it was the only route connecting PLA border garrisons along a 2,400-kilometer stretch.

Chosen to lead the incursion was thirty-five-year-old Rara, a Lithang native known by the call sign "Ross" during his stint at Hale. Since arriving via East Pakistan in August, he had assumed command of a company at Yara. For the road ambush, he assembled a composite unit by soliciting five men and five horses from each of the eight companies. They were all armed with a mix of Garands and carbines; in addition, Ross took a camera to document their foray.

Heading north from Mustang on 21 October, the guerrillas traveled for three days before crossing the frozen Brahmaputra and coming upon the Xinjiang road. Keeping their horses concealed, the Tibetans deployed in an extended line among the boulders of an adjacent hill. There they sat in the biting cold for an entire day. Not until 1400 hours on 25 October did the sound of a distant automobile break the silence. From the west, a lone olive-drab jeep came into view. Due to encroaching sand dunes, it could manage only a crawl along the clogged roadbed. Ross, who was at the closest end of the ambush, signaled the three guerrillas at his side to hold their fire until the vehicle was within range.[44]

Taking aim with his carbine, Ross initiated the attack. Bullets ripped through the windshield, the driver's head snapped back, and the jeep veered to a halt on the shoulder. Two others in the front seat—one male, one female—slumped as their bodies were riddled by gunfire. Leaving the safety of the boulders, Ross exchanged his weapon for the camera. But as he moved forward to take photographs, gunfire began to pour from the rear of the jeep. Ross dove for cover while the three other guerrillas resumed their fusillade toward the back of the vehicle. After a minute, they converged on the now silent target and removed four dead Chinese.

Putting his Hale training into practice, Ross wasted no time recovering three

Chinese-made Type 56 carbines and a machine gun. He also took a large leather case from the front seat. The bodies were laid on the ground and stripped of uniforms, shoes, socks, and watches. After setting the jeep on fire, Ross blew a whistle as the signal for the rest of the guerrillas strung along the ridgeline to rendezvous near their horses.

Three days later, the forty guerrillas were safely back in Mustang. Although photographs of the ambush were a bust (Ross had forgotten to take off the lens cap), the leather case looked promising. Baba Yeshi assigned two couriers to deliver the satchel to Lhamo Tsering in Darjeeling, who then personally carried it to Clay Cathey in Calcutta.

When the case was opened, Cathey found himself staring at 1,600 pages of documents. Once Lhamo Tsering began preliminary translations of a sampling, the CIA officer determined that most of the material was classified up to top secret. "I sent a long cable listing some of the report titles," recalls Cathey. "A day later, headquarters sent a message saying it could be a gold mine."

Once the satchel was back in Washington—Cathey had strapped it in an adjacent seat aboard a Pan Am flight—the CIA quickly realized that its initial assessment was correct. The male passenger in the front seat of the jeep, it turned out, had been a PLA regimental commander assigned to Tibet. Among the documents he was carrying were more than two dozen issues of a classified PLA journal entitled *Bulletin of Activities.* Intended for internal use among senior army cadre, the bulletins dealt frankly with problems plaguing the PLA. Some, for example, detailed food shortages and other economic problems,[45] others spoke of the lack of combat experience among junior officers, and still others reported on armed rebellions in the provinces.

From the satchel documents, the CIA also learned that the People's Militia, a paramilitary unit that reportedly totaled more than 1 million, was in reality a paper organization. Yet another document discussed the intensity of the Sino-Soviet rivalry, and others listed communication codes. In the end, more than 100 CIA reports were generated from these papers. "This single haul became the basic staple of intelligence on the Chinese army," concluded Cathey.

Better still, the Chinese did not know that the documents were missing, because the Tibetans had razed the jeep. Not until August 1963 did their existence become public knowledge after the CIA reached an agreement with scholars at Stanford University to help with the laborious translation. Although the source of the documents was not revealed, the agency threw the academics off the scent by hinting that they had been captured by the ROC navy from intercepted communist junks.[46]

The CIA was ecstatic over its intelligence windfall, but Ambassador Galbraith did not share in the celebration. Persistent in his determination to put a stop to Mustang and further supply overflights, he fired off a series of scathing cables to Washington during November 1961. To add further punch, he made special note of Kennedy's 27 May letter to all American ambassadors charging each with responsibility for operations of the entire U.S. diplomatic mission. Implicit in this was his prerogative to cancel what he deemed an objectionable CIA operation.[47]

Still, Galbraith could barely make headway. With the documents in the jeep satchel just beginning to be digested in Washington, the Tibet Task Force now had tangible proof of the operation's benefits. Armed with this, they secured final approval in early December for another pair of Hercules drops. For the guerrillas at Mustang, the omens were starting to look good.

12. Favored Son

Lyle Brown had been busy kicking cargo to guerrilla outposts in the highlands of northeastern Laos when he got the call to report to Takhli in early December. Fresh to Southeast Asia after a tour training Cuban paratroopers for the Bay of Pigs, he exemplified the rugged ideals that the CIA saw in the aerial firefighting community. "We were good under adverse conditions," he reflected. "We didn't need a martini, but would be just as happy with some C-rations and a cup of coffee around a campfire."[1]

Linking up with Tibet veterans Shep Johnson and Andy Andersen, Brown squeezed into the back of a packed Hercules piloted by Air America's Bill Welk. Behind them on the flight line was a similarly loaded C-130 with another three smoke jumpers.[2] Following the same flight path as the previous Mustang mission, the pair of aircraft skirted the Tibet-Nepal border. From several kilometers away, the pilots could see an enormous blazing "T" not far from the drop zone used seven months earlier.

On the ground, Lobsang Jamba, cyanide ampoule dangling roguishly from a cord around his neck, was among the 400-man reception party. They had arrived at the prescribed location two days earlier but had radioed an eleventh-hour delay to Thailand because the original time had coincided with nine bad omens converging on the Tibetan calendar. "The next day there fortunately were ten good omens to ward them off," he recalled.[3]

Better prepared this time than they had been in April, the Tibetans had brought along sixty mules and horses. As pallets impacted the snow, the guerrillas descended on the bundles and divided them among pack animals and porters.

By week's end, they were back in Mustang and taking inventory. Besides 600 Garands, the load included eight 60mm mortars, eight 75mm recoilless rifles, and some Bren light machine guns. "There was also a color catalog," said one Tibetan officer, "showing photos of what would come in the future."[4]

The extra weapons were sorely needed to keep pace with the fast-expanding Mustang force. Doubling on paper, it now counted sixteen light companies, nearly all commanded by Hale graduates. Between the contents of the first and second drops, half of each company was armed with rifles. Each company, too, received a single Bren and either a mortar or a recoilless rifle. Those not issued rifles or assigned to the twelve-man heavy weapons squad were given a single grenade. In that way, each guerrilla was armed in some fashion.

Although these developments gave the CIA cause for cheer, the same could not be said for the situation back in Colorado. With more than a dozen Mustang leaders still languishing at Hale, the agency had planned to whisk them back to Asia during the first week of December and appeal to Pakistan once more for permission to use its territory as a conduit.

Almost from the start, plans went awry. Late on the night of 6 December, Hale instructor Don Cesare had gotten behind the wheel of the camp's bus and loaded the remaining Tibetans. As had been done many times in the recent past, Cesare intended to get them to Peterson Field by 0600 hours the next morning and inside a waiting C-124 Globemaster well before most of Colorado Springs awoke. But snow-packed roads had conspired against him, forcing two prolonged stops en route.

By the time he pulled into the airport, he was two hours behind schedule. An early-morning crowd had already arrived for work, including the operators of a flying school that owned a hangar near the parked C-124. Afraid of public exposure, the CIA had brought along a squad of overzealous military policemen, who promptly detained sixty-five civilians at gunpoint and ordered a pair of telephone repairmen off some nearby poles.

If that were not enough to raise eyebrows, things quickly worsened. At the local police office, Sheriff Earl Sullivan received a sketchy telephoned account of the bizarre happenings at Peterson. Mindful that there had been a killing at the air base the previous fall, Sullivan issued shotguns to his two deputies and raced to the field at breakneck speed. Amazingly, they too were ordered to halt at the airport entrance by military policemen, who explained that the C-124 was being loaded with classified material.[5]

The cover story hardly held up to scrutiny. By the following day, a local radio station had it partially right when it reported that forty-five Orientals had been spotted wearing military clothes near the transport plane. That same afternoon, a front-page story in the *Colorado Springs Gazette Telegraph* entitled "Gestapo Tactics at Peterson Field Bring Apology from Army" noted that Asians in battle fatigues had disembarked from a bus with curtains over the windows.[6]

The wire services picked up the story, and it soon got the attention of the Washington bureau of the *New York Times*. When a correspondent called the Pentagon for comment, he was phoned back by a flustered official from the office of Secretary of Defense Robert McNamara. Almost without prompting, the official relayed details of the Hale operation, then pleaded with the journalist to drop the story. The gamble worked: by taking the correspondent into its confidence, the Pentagon had made it ethically difficult for the reporter to reveal the story. By the following week, the Peterson episode had been quietly forgotten.[7]

The CIA thus narrowly avoided embarrassing exposure, but for the Tibetans in the C-124, the frustration was only beginning. Cesare escorted them as far as Okinawa, where what was intended as a brief transit stop extended into days and then weeks. The reason for this was to be found at the southern end of the sub-continent, where Indian troops had invaded and annexed the small Portuguese enclave of Goa during the third week of December. Although the United States voiced criticism of this action—privately, Kennedy was amused that Nehru, a long-time proponent of peaceful coexistence, had seen fit to launch a military offen-sive—Pakistan's Ayub Khan was hardly satisfied. If Washington could refuse to help when a European ally suffered at India's hand, Khan was more doubtful than ever that the youthful U.S. president would come to Pakistan's aid in a pinch.

As U.S.-Pakistani relations plunged to a new low, use of East Pakistan for the Tibet project was well and truly out of the cards. Rather than retracing his steps back to the vacant Camp Hale, Cesare diverted his Tibetans to a remote corner of the CIA complex on the island of Saipan. With no chance for overland infiltra-tion anytime soon, he stocked up on movies and began looking for new subject matter—how to drive jeeps and trucks, for instance—to keep his students pre-occupied for the long wait ahead.[8]

Infiltration of the Mustang leaders was not the only part of the Tibet project on hold. In a concession to Ambassador Galbraith, Kennedy had given the nod to the December supply drop only on the condition that future drops would include the participation of the Indian government. Such support, knew the CIA, was a long shot. Although Indian spymaster Mullik quietly reaffirmed his tacit approval of the agency's efforts in 1961, and had earlier claimed that Nehru held similar beliefs, his influence with the aging prime minister was more than offset by India's ambitious and abrasive defense minister, Krishna Menon.[9]

Known for his frequent baiting of the West, Menon was a devout Fabian socialist whose take on nonalignment fell decidedly left of center. As India's longtime representative to the United Nations, he had gone out of his way to sab-otage Gyalo's efforts at winning votes sympathetic to Tibet. As defense minis-ter, he was openly biased toward purchases of Soviet hardware, even when his generals requested Western alternatives. And given his soft stance toward China—as well as his close links with Nehru—Indo-U.S. cooperation on the Tibet front was an impossibility as long as Menon enjoyed his pronounced clout.

Unable to meet Kennedy's requirement of Indian participation, the CIA knew that additional drops to Mustang were out of the question for the time being. The Tibet Task Force, as a result, came to reflect the resupply stand-down. With Hale vacant and no new students scheduled for arrival, all the camp's instructors had been reassigned, with the exception of Cesare at Saipan. The last two Hale-based Tibetan translators were sent to language class at Georgetown University as a reward for services rendered. Roger McCarthy had already left his seat as head of the task force in December 1961 for an assignment on Taiwan, leaving Ken Knaus to assume command over a shadow of the former program. "There was talk of even closing down the task force all together," remembers Cesare.[10]

Coincidentally, there was also a changing of the guard on the subcontinent. During May 1962, India station chief Harry Rositzke finished his tour and was replaced by David Blee. Like Rositzke, Blee was an OSS veteran with service in both the South Asian and Southeast Asian theaters. Blee, too, was a Harvard (and Stanford) graduate and had practiced law for a year before joining the agency at its inception.

Arriving along with Blee was a new deputy station chief, William Grimsley. On his second India tour (he had been posted to New Delhi between 1956 and 1958), Grimsley had found himself embroiled in the Tibet turf war even before his departure from Washington. Three months earlier, in February 1962, Richard Bissell, the head of covert operations, had belatedly fallen as the last major casualty of the Bay of Pigs fiasco. Promoted in Bissell's place was his operations officer and longtime rival, Richard Helms. Known for his instinctive caution and political acumen, Helms saw the divisional rivalries over Tibet as an internal sore that needed resolution and closure. Reflecting the realities on the ground—that paramilitary activity inside Tibet was almost nil, and liaison with the Tibetan leadership took place on Indian soil—the new covert operations chief was inclined to favor ceding more control to the Near East Division.

Following from this decision, Grimsley was called into Helms's office and given a second hat. Although a residual Tibet Task Force would remain under the Far East Division, Grimsley would take over from the departing Howard Bane as the primary Tibet case officer in India. This move effectively put Tibet operations directly under the control of the Near East, something Des FitzGerald was sure to protest. Afraid of intentional media exposure by detractors from within the Far East Division, Helms charged James Angleton, the CIA's infamous mole hunter and counterintelligence chief, with leak control. "I was personally briefed by Angleton," said Grimsley, "to report any resistance from Far East types to the conversion."[11]

Though largely emasculated, the Tibet Task Force was not yet out. In June 1962, officers from the task force traveled to Darjeeling to rendezvous with Mustang commander Baba Yeshi. To start on a good note, they congratulated the chieftain for the previous year's jeep ambush and offered an Omega chronograph in appreciation. But as talk shifted to the future, the secret tryst proved a bust. Speaking for his Tibetans, Baba Yeshi demanded a long list of supplies before his men would shift their action inside Tibet. As far as the CIA was concerned, it wanted the guerrillas to start launching reconnaissance teams north of the Brahmaputra without further preconditions. "It was basically a chicken or the egg scenario," said task force chief Knaus.

With no promises offered by either camp, the CIA men returned to Washington with little hope. "Guerrilla harassment continues," read an agency assessment prepared at month's end, "but poses no serious threat to [Beijing's] control." It even noted signs of reduced popular discontent against the Chinese.[12]

Based on this sentiment and after further consultations at the highest levels of government, the Kennedy administration in late summer decided that the entire future of the Mustang resistance—not merely supply drops—would hinge on the unlikely prospect of active, not tacit, Indian support.

Baba Yeshi, meanwhile, went back to his perch at Mustang. There his men poured their energies into improving their respective tent camps. Eight of the companies had set up quarters in a line along the eastern side of the Kali Gandaki; the remainder ran in a mirror arrangement on the opposite side of the river. Aside from this, they did little else, not launching even a single foray following the previous October's satchel snatch.[13]

For all intents and purposes, the epitaph to the Tibet project was ready to be scripted.

On the evening of Saturday, 8 September, Brigadier John Dalvi was soaking in a hot bath when the phone rang. As commander of India's 7th Infantry Brigade, he was charged with defense of the western NEFA sector, which encompassed the exfiltration route used by the Dalai Lama in 1959. That very afternoon, he had played a round of golf at the newly laid course at Tezpur, the same tea planters' town in Assam where the international media had awaited the arrival of the exiled monarch three years earlier.

Stirred from his moment of relaxation, Dalvi at first tried to ignore the incessant ringing. But having a premonition that it might be important, he wrested himself from the tub. It was a wise choice. On the other end of the phone was his deputy assistant adjutant calling from Towang, the town where the Dalai Lama had first paused after crossing from Tibet. Dalvi listened as the adjutant passed on a frantic message from a nearby outpost. Six hundred Chinese soldiers had surrounded the position earlier that day, cutting bridges and threatening the water supply. They needed help, and they needed it fast.[14]

Though Dalvi was shocked by the incursion, the Chinese maneuvers in NEFA were not wholly unexpected. Ever since the PLA had invaded Tibet, China and India had been bickering about the delineation of their common border. Basing their claims on a 1914 treaty—of which Tibet was a party—India placed its NEFA boundary generally along the Himalayan watershed. China at times appeared ready to accept this but had most recently produced maps that showed much of NEFA under its control. Complicating matters was a second area of contested territory at the westernmost extreme of the Indo-Tibet border along the desolate Ladakh Range.

For India, NEFA was of strategic concern. It was home to 800,000 primitive tribesmen, and most of NEFA's residents were ethnically and culturally closer to the Tibetans than to the people of the Indian plains. Sharing few bonds with the rest of the country, they often regarded lowlanders with suspicion. The Indian government was cognizant of this and had been trying to win their favor with comprehensive development projects, but budgetary constraints sharply limited realization of these plans. And with the poor economic situation compounded by the disruption of trade following China's closure of the Indo-Tibet border—as well as the rumor mill spinning apocryphal tales of laudable progress inside Tibet—India was correctly concerned about loyalties in this part of the country.[15]

By contrast, India's Ladakh claim—based on "historical truths," said New Delhi—was grounded more in prestige than in strategic value. Due to the high altitude (much of it over 4,850 meters) the area was home to just a handful of nomads. Moreover, land access was virtually impossible from the Indian side. The Chinese enjoyed easier access and had already constructed part of their important road link between Xinjiang and Lhasa across the disputed Ladakh zone.

Slowly at first, the two sides had resorted to arms to press their conflicting claims. The first known PLA incursion took place in September 1958 when Chinese troops arrested an Indian police patrol in Ladakh (the police were attempting to reconnoiter the true alignment of the Xinjiang-Tibet road). The following year, after the exile of the Dalai Lama, the frontier heated up after the Indians sent soldiers directly up to the Himalayan watershed; previously, they had been bivouacked well behind that line. The Chinese, in return, sent parties to both NEFA and Ladakh, including an October 1959 attack in the west that killed nine Indians.

Though the Indian military raised a cry at that time, Defense Minister Menon would hear none of it. Labeling the army chief a pro-Western alarmist, he preferred to focus attention on the threat posed by Pakistan. Intimidated by the brash defense chief, the generals took to quietly improving their readiness along the Tibet frontier. Following road and rail construction, an increase in air transport capabilities, and the deployment of more troops at key locations along the border, the top brass was increasingly confident of its ability to deal with Beijing. Reflecting this confidence, in the spring of 1962, India began deploying more patrols and establishing new forward posts in Ladakh—behind Chinese positions, but still inside Indian-claimed territory.[16]

By mid-1962, however, India's military leaders began wondering whether they were overextended. Their fears seemed justified when Dalvi's report about the Towang attack reached New Delhi. But to the shock and dismay of the field commanders in NEFA, Menon, preoccupied with preparations for the upcoming United Nations General Assembly session later in September, was keen to dismiss the incident as nothing more serious than the minor incursions of previous years.

One month later, there could be no mistaking Chinese intent. On 20 October, PLA troops rolled down from the Himalayas and smashed Indian outposts across a wide front. Better acclimated to the altitude, properly stocked from nearby roads, and outnumbering the Indians eight to one, the PLA held every key advantage and showed it. "We were flabbergasted," said one National Security Council staffer, "when the Chinese wiped the floor with the Indians."[17]

No two Indian officials felt the heat from the losses more than Defense Minister Menon and the chief of the General Staff, Lieutenant General B. M. Kaul. Both were inextricably linked: Menon had been instrumental in getting Kaul his senior post, catapulting him over better-qualified generals in the process. This was partly because Kaul was regarded as less pro-Western than many of his peers, lending him the same political mind-set as the defense minister. Menon was also well aware that Kaul shared Kashmiri roots with Nehru, who viewed the general as a protégé and trusted confidant.

Stung by the resultant whispers of nepotism, Kaul had tried to bolster his image by taking personal charge of a newly created corps set to expel the Chinese from NEFA. Not only had this fallen apart during the third week of October, but Kaul had earlier been stricken with a lung infection and sat out the bleakest days in bed in New Delhi. Humiliated and ill, the general sought out Menon to brainstorm ways of salvaging the desperate situation in the Himalayas—and their careers.

One solution, they felt, was to create a guerrilla force that could strike deep behind Chinese lines. Because the Chinese were coming from Tibet, members of that ethnic group were the logical guerrillas of choice. Finding volunteers would not be a problem; both knew that there was no shortage of Tibetans on Indian soil, and virtually all were vehemently anti-Chinese and would not hesitate to take up arms for their own patriotic reasons.

But who would lead such a force? They needed a senior Indian officer who could win the confidence of the Tibetans, embracing their independent nature and promoting a semblance of discipline without resort to a rigid army code. And he would need to have a bent for the unconventional—something that was in short supply in the Indian military, as the trench mentality in the Himalayas had dramatically proved.[18]

As they scoured the roster of available officers, one name caught their eye. Brigadier Sujan Singh Uban, until recently the commander of the 26th Artillery Brigade in Kashmir, was in New Delhi after having just processed his retirement papers. Forty-eight years old, he had been an artilleryman all his career, first under the British colonial system and then with the Indian military after independence. Normally, this would have provided little room for innovation, but Uban had spent much time with mountain units and was familiar with fighting at high altitudes. And during a stint as an artillery instructor for jungle warfare units, he had earned the nickname "Mad Sikh" for his flair and drive. That small detail was enough for Menon and Kaul, who flashed an urgent message summoning the brigadier.

On 26 October, Uban was sitting in the defense minister's office. The situation on the border—and the status of Menon and Kaul—had already reached a critical point. With the Chinese still inside Indian territory, Uban was given sketchy details of the proposed behind-the-lines guerrilla mission. Working with the Tibetans would not be easy, warned Kaul. Disciplining them, he said, would be like taming wild tigers. As a sweetener, the brigadier was promised a second star in due course. Uban was hooked; he grabbed the assignment without hesitation.[19]

Now that the guerrilla force had a leader, there remained the job of signing on Tibetan volunteers. To help, the Indians sent an emissary from the Intelligence Bureau to Darjeeling to fetch the Dalai Lama's brother, Gyalo Thondup. After years of attempting to court the Indians—who were often sympathetic but never committal—Gyalo relished the moment as he sat in front of a select group of senior intelligence and military officials in the capital. Speaking in theoretical terms, his hosts asked whether he could organize the needed volunteers. Of course, replied Gyalo. When asked how many, he conjured a robust, round figure. Five thousand, he said.[20]

Next came a key question. Would Gyalo prefer that the Intelligence Bureau or the Ministry of Defense be involved? Based on his earlier contact with Mullik and his current cooperation with the CIA (through Lhamo Tsering), the decision was easy. "Not Defense," was his indirect answer.[21]

Despite India's woes—and its newfound interest in the Tibetans—most of Washington took little notice. Half a world away in the waters around Cuba, nuclear brinkmanship was being taken to the limit as President Kennedy demanded a withdrawal of Soviet missiles from that island. Not until 28 October did the world breathe a sigh of relief when Moscow agreed to withdraw its weaponry. With that crisis over, the Sino-Indian conflict belatedly leapfrogged to the top of Washington's foreign policy agenda.

The very next day, Prime Minister Nehru made an unequivocal request for U.S. military assistance. For the tired, beaten leader, it was a humbling overture. It was an admission not only that his central belief in peaceful coexistence with the PRC was irrevocably shattered but also that his cordial relationship with the Soviet Union had proved hollow. Due to the Cuban missile crisis, the Soviets had been forced to side with China vis-à-vis India so as not to alienate a needed communist ally in their moment of danger. Not only did Moscow backpedal on its earlier promise to sell MiG-21 jets to India, but on 29 October it openly declared that it would recognize Chinese territorial claims and extend no arms at all to India.[22]

Immediately, Washington stepped into the fray and responded generously to Nehru's appeal for assistance. By 2 November, the USAF was using Europe-based Boeing 707 transports to fly eight missions into India every day for a week. Each plane was packed with basic infantry equipment to refit the soldiers streaming off the Himalayas, who in most cases were outfitted with more primitive gear than had been afforded the CIA's Tibetan guerrillas. These supplies were later ferried by USAF C-130 transports to smaller airfields near the frontier battle lines.[23]

Still, the aid did not turn the tide. On 14 November, an Indian counterattack in NEFA was soundly routed. Three days later, the entire NEFA line collapsed, giving China virtual control over 64,000 square kilometers of territory. By 19 November, leaders in New Delhi genuinely feared an attack on Calcutta, prompting Nehru to take the extraordinary step of sending two secret back-channel messages to Kennedy pleading for a pair of bomber squadrons flown by U.S. pilots.

India's infantrymen and Nehru's pride were not the only casualties of the conflict. Back on 28 October, America's bête noire, the discredited Krishna Menon, had tendered his resignation. With him out of the way and the situation on the frontier critical, Kennedy gathered some of his best and brightest on 19 November to discuss the war in the Himalayas. Among those present were Secretary of Defense McNamara, Secretary of State Dean Rusk, and Assistant Secretary of State for Far Eastern Affairs Averell Harriman. At seventy-two, Harriman was one of America's most respected diplomats and politicians. The former governor had worked closely with the Indians in the past, having appealed to Nehru the previous year to assist in formulating a negotiated end to the looming superpower rivalry in Laos. Significantly, too, throughout the summer of 1962, Harriman had been a lone senior voice in the State Department supporting the CIA's argument for ongoing paramilitary operations out of Mustang.

Discussed at the 19 November meeting was increased U.S. military assistance to India and options for a show of force in the region. Also mentioned was the possibility of using the CIA's Tibetan guerrillas. John McCone, a wealthy and opinionated Republican chosen by Kennedy to replace CIA Director Dulles after the Bay of Pigs, was on hand to brief the president on such covert matters. Joining McCone was Des FitzGerald, the Far East chief; James Critchfield, head of the Near East Division, was touring Beirut at the time.[24]

By meeting's end, it was decided that Harriman would lead a high-powered delegation to New Delhi to more fully assess India's needs. General Paul Adams, chief of the U.S. Strike Command, was to head the military component. From the CIA, Des FitzGerald won a seat on the mission, as did the head of the Tibet Task Force, Ken Knaus. Rendezvousing with them in India would be Critchfield, who received an emergency cable to depart Lebanon immediately for the subcontinent.

On 21 November, Harriman's entourage departed Andrews Air Force Base in Maryland. Although the Chinese declared a unilateral cease-fire while the group was en route, the situation was still tense when it reached New Delhi the following day. Without pause, Ambassador Galbraith ushered Harriman into the first of four meetings with Nehru. The end results of these discussions were plans for a major three-phase military aid package encompassing material support, help with domestic defense production, and possible assistance with air defenses.

As a covert aside to Harriman's talks, the CIA representatives on the delegation held their own sessions with Indian intelligence czar Mullik. This was a first, as Galbraith had previously taken great pains to downscale the agency's activities inside India to all but benign reporting functions. As recently as 5 November, he had objected to projected CIA plans due to the risk of exposure. But in a

13 November letter to Kennedy, the ambassador had a qualified change of heart, noting that Menon's departure was a turning point to begin working with the Indians on "sensitive matters."[25]

Both the CIA and the Intelligence Bureau were quick to seize the opportunity. "I went into a huddle with Mullik and Des," recalls Critchfield, "and we started coming up with all these schemes against the Chinese." Most of their ideas centered around use of the Tibetans. "The Indians were interested in the Tibet program because of its intelligence collection value," said station chief David Blee, who sat in on some of the meetings. "Mullik was particularly interested in paramilitary operations."[26] There was good reason for this: following Menon's resignation, and Gyalo Thondup's stated preference, the Intelligence Bureau had been placed in charge of the 5,000 Tibetan guerrillas forming under Brigadier Uban.

Mullik was cautious as well. Although he was well connected to the Nehru family and had the prime minister's full approval to talk with the CIA, he knew that the Indian populace was fickle, and until recently, anti-Americanism had been a popular mantra. It was perhaps only a matter of time before the barometer would swing back and make open Indo-U.S. cooperation political suicide. To offer some protection against this, Mullik and one of his close deputies, M. I. Hooja, made a special request during a session with FitzGerald and Blee. "They made us promise that our involvement," said Blee, "would remain secret forever."[27]

By the end of the Harriman mission, the CIA and Intelligence Bureau had arrived at a rough division of labor. The Indians, with CIA support from the Near East Division, would work together in developing Uban's 5,000-strong tactical guerrilla force. The CIA's Far East Division, meantime, would unilaterally create a strategic long-range resistance movement inside Tibet. The Mustang contingent would also remain under the CIA's unilateral control.

All this would depend on final approval by the highest levels of the Kennedy administration. Meanwhile, the CIA arranged for a sign of good faith. A single crew was selected from the agency's air proprietaries in Taiwan and Japan, then dispatched to Takhli aboard a DC-6 transport. Loaded with an assortment of military aid, the plane made three shuttles between Thailand and the Charbatia airfield near the city of Bhubaneswar in India's eastern state of Orissa. A relic of World War II, Charbatia had fallen into a severe state of disrepair. More remarkable than its poor condition were the precautions taken to keep the CIA's largesse a secret from the die-hard Soviet supporters among New Delhi's political elite. "We flew the last few miles just fifty feet above the ground to avoid radar," said pilot Neese Hicks. "We would land at dawn, eat a fast breakfast, and be back in the air toward Takhli."[28]

By the last week of November, the CIA representatives from the Harriman delegation were back in Washington and making their pitch before the Special Group. Though they could now count on Indian participation—which had been a prerequisite for future support to the Mustang group—they had a tough sell. CIA Director McCone, for one, was a pronounced skeptic with relatively little interest in covert paramilitary operations. Citing the example of Mustang (which had done precious little over the past year), he was dubious about the utility of developing a tactical guerrilla force that the United States could not ultimately control. And although officials in New Delhi believed that limited war with China might continue intermittently over a number of years, he questioned what would happen in the event of Sino-Indian rapprochement. Would the CIA have to cut its support to the guerrillas and the resistance in midstream?[29]

There was also sharp criticism from the Pentagon, but for a different reason. General Maxwell Taylor, the president's military adviser who had recently taken over as chairman of the Joint Chiefs of Staff, tore into Critchfield for not informing the Department of Defense about the ongoing paramilitary program at Mustang. Many upcoming contingencies might hinge on the Mustang guerrillas, chided Taylor, and the Pentagon's representatives on the Harriman mission had only belatedly found out about Mustang's existence while in India. Many suspected that Taylor's umbrage was because he had lobbied hard over the past year to have CIA paramilitary operations revert to Defense Department control, and he was livid at finding a holdout.

Despite the comments from the likes of McCone and Taylor, the chance of making significant inroads with the Indians—and giving a bigger headache to Beijing—was too good to pass up. On 13 December, the Kennedy administration approved training assistance to Uban's tactical guerrilla force. At the same time, the Tibet Task Force drew up plans to reopen Hale and school at least 125 candidates for the long-range resistance movement. Commented task force chief Knaus, "We had suddenly gone from stepchild to favored son."[30]

13. Chakrata

Jamba Kalden was a latecomer to the resistance. A successful Khampa trader from Chamdo—the first town captured by the PLA during the invasion of October 1950—he had repeatedly turned a deaf ear to early recruitment calls from the NVDA. Not until early 1959, with tension in Lhasa reaching the breaking point, did he feel compelled to visit the capital. There the sight of raucous crowds surrounding the Dalai Lama's Norbulingka summer palace proved infectious, drawing the thirty-nine-year-old businessman into the midst of the swelling anti-Chinese protests.

It was to prove a short and painful introduction to civil disobedience. On the morning of 20 March, two days after the Dalai Lama fled for the border, the PLA began shelling the palace. By that afternoon, hundreds of Tibetans lay dead or wounded. Attempting to evade the closing Chinese cordon, Jamba Kalden took a bullet to the thigh and was promptly arrested. He was confined to a small Lhasa cell while he nursed his wound, and not until summer was the injury sufficiently healed for him to be assigned to one of the prisoner gangs the Chinese had dispatched to various construction sites near the capital.

Jamba Kalden did not take well to forced labor. His once impressive physique turned gaunt from the hard work and meager rations, and he began planning his escape toward year's end. Not until 17 January 1960 did he find the opportunity to slip away from his minders. He and two fellow prisoners made their way through blinding winter snowstorms toward the southern border. In May they reached Bhutan; two months later, they crossed into India.

By that time, the Dalai Lama and his entourage had taken up residence in the town of Dharamsala. Situated 725 kilometers northwest of New Delhi in the Himalayan foothills, Dharamsala—literally, "rest house"—was once a traditional stop for Hindu pilgrims. By 1855, it had become a flourishing hill station for the British, only to see its popularity plummet after a devastating 1905 earthquake. Its last bloc of residents, a handful of Muslims, left for newly created Pakistan in 1947.

For the Indian government, Dharamsala's remote location and lack of population were now its major selling points. Since the Dalai Lama had crossed onto Indian soil, he had made his temporary quarters near another former hill station, Mussoorie. But because Mussoorie was just a short drive from New Delhi, the monarch enjoyed easy access to the media limelight. Influential leaders such as

Krishna Menon cringed at the young Tibetan's frequent and sympathetic contact with the press, leading them to propose more permanent—and distant—quarters at Dharamsala. With little choice, the Tibetan leader made the move in April 1960.

If the Indians thought that Dharamsala was the answer to stifling the Dalai Lama, they were sadly mistaken. Using its isolation to his advantage, he converted the town into his de facto capital, then made good on his threats over the past year and began creating a government in exile. Part of this involved reforming the cabinet offices that previously existed in Lhasa. It also involved preparation of a draft constitution. At the same time, a straw vote was held in each of the main refugee camps over the summer. From this rudimentary selection process, thirteen representatives were chosen: three from each province, plus one for each of the four Tibetan Buddhist sects.

Jamba Kalden arrived in Dharamsala as the thirteen delegates were convening for the first time in September 1960. In deference to his relative wealth and influential position back in Chamdo, he was anointed as a key adviser to the nascent government. He was still serving in this capacity in late October 1962 when Gyalo Thondup came looking for 5,000 volunteers to fill Brigadier Uban's tactical guerrilla force.

Gyalo's task was not particularly complicated. As with the Mustang contingent, he was partial toward recruiting Khampas. Finding willing takers was no problem, as the patriotic call to duty—and the chance for meaningful employment—held great appeal among the refugee population. With word quickly spreading, volunteers by the thousands stepped forward over the ensuing weeks.

Gyalo also sought four political leaders who could act as the force's indigenous officer cadre. Given his seniority, ethnicity, and proven aptitude in Dharamsala over the previous two years, Jamba Kalden was an easy first pick.

By early November, an initial contingent of Tibetans, led by Jamba Kalden, was dispatched to the hill town of Dehra Dun. Once popular with Indian princes because of its mild climate, it later served as a key British educational center and military base. More recently it was host to the Indian military academy, a number of regimental barracks, and several prestigious boarding schools.

Jamba Kalden had little time to appreciate Dehra Dun's climatic appeal. On hand to meet the Tibetans was Brigadier Uban and a skeleton staff of officers on loan from the army. While a transit tent camp was set up on the edge of town to process the 5,000 promised volunteers, on 14 November the Indian cadre and four political leaders shifted ninety-two kilometers northwest to the village of Chakrata.

Situated along a ridge and surrounded by forest glades, Chakrata had been chosen for good reason. Home to a thriving population of panthers and bears,

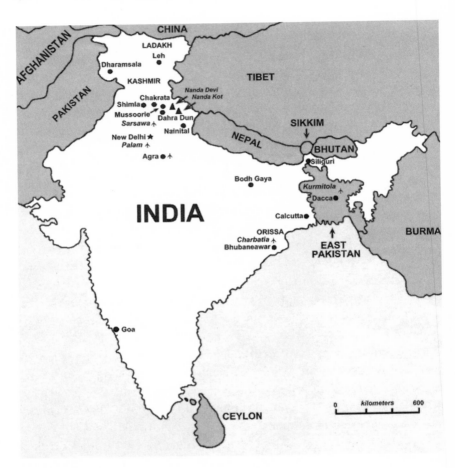

India

it had once boasted two training centers for a pair of Gurkha regiments. Since 1960, however, both regiments had relocated to more favorable climes.[1] With almost no local residents and a set of vacant cantonments, Chakrata had both the ready facilities and the seclusion needed for the covert Tibetan project. Uban and his team settled in to await the arrival of the rest of the 5,000 volunteers by year's end and began mapping out the process of molding them into effective guerrillas.

For intelligence chief Mullik, the Chakrata project signaled a new sense of militancy regarding Tibet. This was communicated in strong fashion on 29 December when Mullik—through Gyalo Thondup—told the Dalai Lama that New Delhi had now adopted a covert policy of supporting the eventual liberation of his homeland.

Although the U.S. government did not match this with a similar pledge, the CIA wasted no time making good on its promise to help with the various Tibetan paramilitary schemes. As a start, Jim McElroy—the same logistics expert who had been involved with ST CIRCUS since its inception, overseeing the air supply process from Okinawa and later helping with similar requirements at Camp Hale—was dispatched to India in early January 1963. He was escorted by Intelligence Bureau representatives to the Paratroopers Training School at Agra, just a few kilometers from the breathtaking Taj Mahal palace. Because aerial methods would be the likely method of supporting behind-the-lines operations against the PLA, McElroy began an assessment of the school's parachute inventory to fully understand India's air delivery capabilities. He also started preliminary training of some Tibetan riggers drawn from Chakrata.

McElroy's deployment paved the way for more substantial assistance. Stepping forward as liaison in the process was forty-seven-year-old Indian statesman Biju Patnaik. Everything about Patnaik, who stood over two meters tall, was larger than life. The son of a state minister from the eastern state of Orissa, he had courted adventure from a young age. At sixteen, he had bicycled across the subcontinent on a whim. Six years later, he earned his pilot's license at the Delhi Flying Club. Joining the Royal Air Force at the advent of World War II, he earned accolades after evacuating stranded British families from Burma. Other flights took him to the Soviet Union and Iran.

Patnaik also made a name for himself as an ardent nationalist. Following in his parents' footsteps—both of them were renowned patriots—he bristled under the British yoke. Sometimes his resistance methods were unorthodox. Once while flying a colonial officer from a remote post in India's western desert region, he overheard the European use a condescending tone while questioning his skills in the cockpit. Patnaik landed the plane on a desolate stretch of parched earth and let the critical Englishman walk.[2]

For actions like this, Patnaik ultimately served almost four years in prison. He was released shortly before Indian independence and looked for a way to convert his passion for flying into a business. Banding together with some fellow pilots, he purchased a dozen aging transports and founded a charter company based in Calcutta. He dubbed the venture Kalinga Air Lines, taking its name from an ancient kingdom in his native Orissa.

Almost immediately, Patnaik landed a risky contract. Revolutionaries in the Indonesian archipelago were in the midst of their independence struggle, but because of a tight Dutch blockade, they were finding it hard to smuggle in arms and other essentials. Along with several other foreign companies, Kalinga Air Lines began charter flights on their behalf. It was Patnaik himself who evaded Dutch fighters to carry Muhammad Hatta (later Indonesia's first vice president) on a diplomatic mission to drum up support in South Asia.

It was also through Kalinga Air Lines that Patnaik had his first brush with Tibet. By the mid-1950s, he was looking to expand the airline through the acquisition of a French medium-range transport, the Nord Noratlas. He intended to use this plane for shuttles between Lhasa and Calcutta, having already purchased exclusive rights to this route. Before the first flight, however, diplomatic ties between India and China soured; Patnaik's license into Lhasa was canceled, and the air route never opened.

Other ventures were more successful. Patnaik established a string of profitable industries across eastern India. And, like his father, he entered the government bureaucracy and eventually rose to chief minister—akin to governor—of his native Orissa.[3]

In November 1962—during the darkest days of the Chinese invasion of NEFA—Patnaik's patriotic zeal, taste for adventure, and brush with Tibet would all come together. As the PLA sliced through Indian lines, he rushed to New Delhi with an idea. The Chinese had overextended themselves in India, he reasoned, and therefore were vulnerable to a guerrilla resistance effort inside Assam.

Given Patnaik's stature in Orissa, he was able to take his concept directly to Nehru. The prime minister listened and liked what he heard. By reputation, Patnaik had the charisma to carry out such an effort. At the very least, having the chief minister of one state take the lead in offering assistance to another state was good press.

Patnaik was not the only one thinking along these lines. On 20 November, Mullik had notified Nehru that he wanted to quit his post as director of the Intelligence Bureau in order to focus on organizing a resistance movement in the event the Chinese pushed further into Assam. Nehru refused to accept his spymaster's resignation and instead directed him toward Patnaik, with the suggestion that they pool their talent.

Meeting later that same afternoon, the spy and the minister became quick allies. Although their resistance plans took on less urgency the next day, after Beijing announced a unilateral cease-fire, Patnaik offered critical help in other arenas. Later that month, when the CIA wanted to use its aircraft to quietly deliver three planeloads of supplies to India as a sign of good faith, it was Patnaik who arranged for the discreet use of the Charbatia airfield in Orissa. And in December, after the CIA notified New Delhi of its impending paramilitary support program, he was the one dispatched to Washington on behalf of Nehru and Mullik to negotiate details of the assistance package.

Upon his arrival in the U.S. capital, Patnaik's primary point of contact was Robert "Moose" Marrero. Thirty-two years old and of Puerto Rican ancestry, Marrero was aptly nicknamed: like Patnaik, he stood over two meters tall and weighed 102 kilos. He was also an aviator, having flown helicopters for the U.S. Marines before leaving military service in 1957 to join the CIA as an air operations specialist.

As the two pilots conversed, they recognized the need for a thorough review of the airlift requirements for warfare in the high Himalayas. They also saw the need to train and equip a covert airlift cell outside of the Indian military chain of command that could operate along the Indo-Tibetan frontier.

While Patnaik was discussing these aviation issues in Washington, the CIA's Near East Division was forging ahead with assistance for the Tibetans at Chakrata. Initially, the Pentagon also muscled its way into the act and in February 1963 penned plans to send a 106-man U.S. Army Special Forces detachment that would offer "overt, but hopefully unpublicized" training in guerrilla tactics and unconventional warfare. The CIA, meanwhile, came up with a competing plan that involved no more than eight of its advisers on a six-month temporary duty assignment. Significantly, the CIA envisioned its officers living and messing alongside the Tibetans, minimizing the need for logistical support. Given Indian sensitivities and the unlikely prospect of keeping an overt U.S. military detachment unpublicized, the CIA scheme won.[4]

Heading the CIA team would be forty-five-year-old Wayne Sanford. No stranger to CIA paramilitary operations, Sanford had achieved a stellar service record in the U.S. Marine Corps. Commissioned in 1942, he had participated in nearly all the major Pacific battles and earned two Purple Hearts in the process— one for a bullet to the shoulder at Guadalcanal, and the second for a shot to the face at Tarawa.

Remaining in the Marine Corps after the war, Sanford was preparing for combat on the Korean peninsula in 1950 when fate intervened. Before he reached the front, a presidential directive was issued stating that anyone with two Purple Hearts was exempt from combat. Coincidentally, the CIA was scouting the ranks of the military for talent to support its burgeoning paramilitary effort on Taiwan. Getting a temporary release from active duty, Sanford was whisked to the ROC under civilian cover.

For his first CIA assignment, Sanford spent the next eighteen months commanding a small agency team on Da Chen, an ROC-controlled islet far to the north of Taiwan. Part of the CIA operation at Da Chen involved eavesdropping on PRC communications. Another part involved coastal interdiction, for which they had a single PT boat. Modified with three Rolls Royce engines, self-sealing tanks, and radar, the vessel was impressive for its time. The ship's captain, Larry "Sinbad the Sailor" Sinclair, had made a name for himself by boldly attacking Japanese ships in Filipino waters during World War II; he continued the same daring act against the PRC from Da Chen.

Eventually, the Chinese took notice. In methodical fashion, the communists occupied the islets on either side of Da Chen. Then shortly before Sanford's tour was set to finish, a flotilla of armed junks surrounded the CIA bastion, and bombers spent a day dropping iron from the sky. That night, the agency radiomen intercepted instructions for the bombers to redouble their attack at sunrise. Not liking the odds, Sanford ordered his CIA officers and remaining ROC troops—thirty-seven in all—into the PT boat. Switching on the radar, Sinclair ran the junk blockade under cover of darkness and carried them safely to the northern coast of Taiwan.[5]

Returning to Washington, Sanford spent the rest of the decade on assignment at CIA headquarters. In October 1959, he ostensibly returned to active duty and was posted to the U.S. embassy in London as part of the vaguely titled Joint Planning Staff. In reality, the staff was a fusion of the CIA and the Pentagon; its members were to work on plans to counter various communist offensives across Eurasia. One such tabletop exercise involved a hypothetical Chinese invasion of South Asia.[6]

By now a marine colonel, Sanford was still in London when the Chinese attack materialized and CIA paramilitary support for India was approved in principle in December 1962. Early the following year, after the CIA received specific approval to send eight advisers to Chakrata, Sanford was selected to oversee the effort. He would do so from an office at the U.S. embassy in New Delhi while acting under the official title of special assistant to Ambassador Galbraith. As this would be an overt posting with the full knowledge of the Indian government, both he and the seven other paramilitary advisers would remain segregated from David Blee's CIA station.

Back in Washington, the rest of the team took shape. Another former marine, John Magerowski, was fast to grab a berth. So was Harry Mustakos, who had worked with the Tibetans on Saipan in 1957 and served with Sanford on Da Chen. Former smoke jumper and Intermountain Aviation (a CIA proprietary) rigger Thomas "T. J." Thompson was to replace Jim McElroy at Agra. Two other training officers were selected from the United States, and a third was diverted from an assignment in Turkey. The last slot went to former U.S. Army airborne officer Charles "Ken" Seifarth, who had been in South Vietnam conducting jump classes for agents destined to infiltrate the communist north.[7]

By mid-April, the eight had assembled in New Delhi. If they expected warm greetings from their CIA colleagues in the embassy, it did not happen. "We were neither welcomed nor wanted by the station chief," recalls Mustakos. For Sanford, this was eventually seen as a plus. "Blee gave me a free hand," he remembered, "but Galbraith wanted detailed weekly briefings on everything we did."[8]

At the outset, there was little for Sanford to report. Waiting for their gear to arrive (they had ordered plenty of cold-weather clothing), the team members spent their first days agreeing on a syllabus for the upcoming six months. One week later, their supplies arrived, and six of the advisers left Sanford in New Delhi for the chilled air of Chakrata. The last member, Thompson, alone went to Agra.

Once the CIA advisers arrived at the mountain training site, Brigadier Uban gave them a fast tour. A ridgeline ran east to west, with Chakrata occupying a saddle in the middle. Centered in the saddle was a polo field that fell off sharply to the south for 600 meters, then less sharply for another 300 meters. North of the field was a scattering of stone houses and shops, all remnants of the colonial era and now home to a handful of hill tribesmen who populated the village.

To the immediate west of the saddle was an old but sound stone Anglican church. Farther west were stone bungalows previously used by British officers and their dependents. Most of the bungalows were similar, differing only in the number of bedrooms. Each had eighteen-inch stone walls, narrow windows, fireplaces in each room, stone floors, and a solarium facing south to trap the heat on cold days and warm the rest of the drafty house. Each CIA adviser and Indian officer took a bungalow, with the largest going to Brigadier Uban.[9]

East of the saddle was a series of stone barracks built by the British a century earlier and more recently used by the two Gurkha regiments. These were now holding the Tibetan recruits. There was also a longer stone building once used as a hospital, a firing range, and a walled cemetery overgrown by cedar. The epitaphs in the cemetery read like a history of Chakrata's harsh past. The oldest grave was for a British corporal killed in 1857 while blasting on the original construction. Different regiments were represented through the years, their soldiers the victims of either sickness or various campaigns to expand or secure the borders. There was also a gut-wrenching trio of headstones dated within one month of one another, all children of a British sergeant and his wife. "Myself the father of three," said Mustakos, "I stood there heartsick at the despair that must have attended the young couple in having their family destroyed."[10]

Once fully settled, the CIA team was introduced to its guerrilla students. By that time, the Chakrata project had been given an official name. A decade earlier, Brigadier Uban had had a posting in command of the 22nd Mountain Regiment in Assam. Borrowing that number, he gave his Tibetans the ambiguous title of "Establishment 22."

In reviewing Establishment 22, the Americans were immediately struck by the age of the Tibetans. Although there was a sprinkling of younger recruits, nearly half were older than forty-five; some were even approaching sixty. Jamba Kalden, the chief political leader, was practically a child at forty-three. As had happened with the Mustang guerrillas, the older generation, itching for a final swing at the Chinese, had used its seniority to edge out younger candidates during the recruitment drive in the refugee camps.[11]

With much material to cover, the CIA advisers reviewed what the Indian staff had accomplished over the previous few months. Uban had initially focused his efforts on instilling a modicum of discipline, which he feared might be an impossible task. To his relief, this fear proved unfounded. The Tibetans immediately controlled their propensity for drinking and gambling at his behest; the brigadier encouraged dancing and chanting as preferable substitutes to fill their leisure time.[12]

The Indians had also started a strict regimen of physical exercise, including extended marches across the nearby hills. Because the weather varied widely—snow blanketed the northern slopes, but the spring sun was starting to bake the south—special care was taken to avoid pneumonia. In addition to exercise, the Indians had offered a sampling of tactical instruction. But most of it, the CIA team found, reflected a conventional mind-set. "We had to unteach quite a bit," said Mustakos.[13]

This combination—strict exercise and a crash course in guerrilla tactics—continued through the first week of May. At that point, classes were put on temporary hold in order to initiate airborne training. Plans called for nearly all members of Establishment 22 to be qualified as paratroopers. This made tactical sense: if the Tibetans were to operate behind Chinese lines, the logical means of infiltrating them to the other side of the Himalayas would be by parachute.

When told of the news, the Tibetans were extremely enthusiastic about the prospect of jumping. There was a major problem, however. Establishment 22 remained a secret not only from the general Indian public but also from the bulk of the Indian military. The only airborne training facilities in India were at Agra, where the CIA's T. J. Thompson was discreetly training a dozen Tibetan riggers. Because the Agra school ran jump training for the Indian army's airborne

T. J. Thompson with two Tibetan student riggers, Agra airbase, summer 1963. (Courtesy T. J. Thompson)

brigade, Thompson had been forced to keep the twelve well concealed. But doing the same for thousands of Tibetans would be impossible; unless careful steps were taken, the project could be exposed.

Part of the CIA's dilemma was solved by the season. The weather in the Indian lowlands during May was starting to get oppressively hot, making the dusty Agra drop zones less than popular with the airborne brigade. Most of the Tibetan jumps were intentionally scheduled around noon—the least popular time slot, because the sun was directly overhead. The Intelligence Bureau also arranged for the Tibetans to use crude barracks in a distant corner of the air base, further reducing the chance of an encounter with inquisitive paratroopers.

As an added precaution, a member of Brigadier Uban's staff went to an insignia shop and placed an order for cap badges. Each badge featured crossed kukri knife blades with the number 12 above. The reason: after independence from the British, the Indian army had inherited seven regiments of famed Gurkhas recruited from neighboring Nepal. Along with four more regiments that transferred to the British army, the regiments were numbered sequentially, with the last being the 11th Gorkha (the Indian spelling of Gurkha) Rifles. On the assumption that most lowland Indians would be unable to differentiate between the Asian features of a Gurkha and those of a Tibetan, Establishment

22 was given the fictitious cover designation "12th Gorkha Rifles" for the duration of its stay at Agra.[14]

To oversee the airborne phase of instruction, Ken Seifarth relocated to Agra. Five jumps were planned for each candidate, including one performed at night. Because of the limited size of the barracks at the air base, the Tibetans would rotate down to the lowlands in 100-man cycles. With up to three jumps conducted each day, the entire qualification process was expected to stretch through the summer.

All was going according to plan until the evening before the first contingent was scheduled to jump. At that point, a message arrived reminding Uban that the Indian military would not accept liability for anyone older than thirty-five parachuting; in the event of death or injury, the government would not pay compensation. This put Uban in a major fix. It was vital for his staff to share training hazards with their students, and he had assumed that his officers—none of whom were airborne qualified—would jump alongside the Tibetans. But although they had all completed the ground phase of instruction (which had intentionally been kept simple, such as leaping off ledges into piles of hay), his men had been under the impression that they would not have to jump from an aircraft. Their lack of enthusiasm was now reinforced by the government's denial of compensation. When Uban asked for volunteers to accompany the guerrilla trainees, not a single Indian officer stepped forward.[15]

For Uban, it was now a question of retaining the confidence of the Tibetans or relinquishing his command. Looking to get special permission for government risk coverage, he phoned Mullik that evening. The intelligence director, however, was not at home. Taking what he considered the only other option, Uban gathered his officers for an emergency session. Although he had no prior parachute training, he told his men that he intended to be the first one out of the lead aircraft. This challenge proved hard to ignore. When the brigadier again asked for volunteers, every officer stepped forward.

Uban now faced a new problem. With the first jump set for early the next morning, he had a single evening to learn the basics. He summoned a pair of CIA advisers to his room in Agra's Clarkes Shiraz Hotel. Using the limited resources at hand, they put the tea table in the middle of the room and watched as the brigadier rolled uncomfortably across the floor.

Imaging the likely result of an actual jump, Seifarth spoke his mind. At forty-seven years old, he was a generation older than his CIA teammates and just a year younger than Uban. Drawing on the close rapport they had developed over the previous weeks, he implored the brigadier to reconsider.[16]

The next morning, 11 May, a C-119 Flying Boxcar crossed the skies over Agra. As the twin-tailed transport aircraft came over the drop zone, Uban was the first out the door, Seifarth the second. Landing without incident, the brigadier belatedly received a return call from Mullik. "Don't jump," said the intelligence chief. "Too late," was the response.[17]

In the weeks that followed, the rest of Establishment 22 clamored for their opportunity to leap from an aircraft. "Even cooks and drivers demanded to go," recalled Uban. Nobody was rejected for age or health reasons, including one Tibetan who had lost an eye and another who was so small that he had to strap a sandbag to his chest to deploy the chute properly.[18]

Nehru, meanwhile, was receiving regular updates on the progress at Chakrata. During autumn, with the deployment of the eight-man CIA team almost finished, he was invited to make an inspection visit to the hill camp. The Intelligence Bureau also passed a request asking the prime minister to use the opportunity to address the guerrillas directly. Nehru was sympathetic but cautious. The thought of the prime minister addressing Tibetan combatants on Indian soil had the makings of a diplomatic disaster if word leaked. Afraid of adverse publicity, he agreed to visit the camp but refused to give a speech.

Hearing this news, Uban had the men of Establishment 22 undergo a fast lesson in parade drill. The effort paid off. Though stiff and formal when he arrived on 14 November, Nehru was visibly moved when he saw the Tibetans in formation. And knowing that the prime minister was soft for roses, Uban presented him with a brilliant red blossom plucked from a garden he had planted on the side of his stone bungalow. Nehru buckled. Asking for a microphone, the prime minister poured forth some ad hoc and heartfelt comments to the guerrillas. "He said that India backed them," said Uban, "and vowed they would one day return to an independent country."[19]

14. Oak Tree

For the eight Indians—six from the Indian air force, two from the Intelligence Bureau—even a van ride had become an abject lesson in the finer points of tradecraft. Sent to Washington in mid-March 1963, they were to be the cadre for the covert airlift cell conjured earlier by Biju Patnaik and Bob Marrero. For the first two weeks, Marrero, who was playing host, arranged for briefings at a row of CIA buildings near the Tidal Basin.

By the beginning of April, the venue was set to change. A van pulled up to their Washington hotel in the dead of night, and the eight Indians plus Marrero piled into the back. All the windows were sealed, and the Indians soon lost their bearings as the vehicle drove for an hour. When they finally stopped, the rear doors opened nearly flush against a second set of doors. Hurried through, they took seats in another windowless cabin tucked inside the belly of an aircraft.[1]

Landing at an undisclosed airfield—only years later would they learn that it was inside Camp Peary—the Indians were taken to an isolated barracks. Over the next month, a steady stream of nameless officers lectured on the full gamut of intelligence and paramilitary topics. There were surreal touches throughout: their meals were prepared by unseen cooks, and they would return to their rooms to find clothes pressed by unseen launderers.

The leader of the eight Indians, Colonel Laloo Grewal, had a solid reputation as a pioneer within the air force. A turbaned Sikh, he had been commissioned as a fighter pilot in 1943 and flew over 100 sorties during World War II in the skies over Burma. Immediately after independence in 1947, he was among the first transport pilots to arrive at the combat zone when India and Pakistan came to blows over Kashmir. And in 1952, he was in the first class of Indian aviators selected to head to the United States for transition training on the C-119 transport. When the call went out for a dynamic air force officer to manage a secret aviation unit under the auspices of the Intelligence Bureau and CIA, Grewal was the immediate choice.

Following the training stint at Peary, six of the students returned to New Delhi. The two most senior members, Grewal included, remained for several additional weeks of specialized aviation instruction. Marrero, meanwhile, made arrangements in May to head for India to conduct the comprehensive air survey broached with Biju Patnaik in their December 1962 meeting. Joining Marrero would be the same CIA air operations officer who had been involved with the earliest drops into Tibet, Gar Thorsrud.

Much had happened to Thorsrud since his last involvement with Tibet. In the spring of 1961, he was briefly involved in Latin America. Later that summer he shifted to Phoenix, Arizona, and was named president of a new CIA front, Intermountain Aviation.[2]

Among CIA air proprietaries, Intermountain was in the forefront of innovation. With its main operational base at Marana Air Park near Tucson, Arizona, the company specialized in developing new aerial support techniques. It was Intermountain, for example, that worked at perfecting the Fulton Skyhook, a recovery method that whisked agents from the ground using an aircraft with a special yoke on its nose. Intermountain experts also experimented with the Timberline parachute configuration (a resupply bundle with extra-long suspension lines to allow penetration of tall jungle canopy) and the Ground Impact system (a parachute with a retainer ring that did not blossom until the last moment, allowing for pinpoint drops on pinnacle peaks).[3]

It was this eye for innovation that Thorsrud carried with him to India. For three months, he and Marrero were escorted from the Himalayan frontier to the airborne school at Agra to the Tibetan training site at Chakrata. Much of their time was spent near the weathered airstrip at Charbatia, where they were feted by the affable Patnaik. He offered use of Charbatia as the principal site for a clandestine air support operation and immediately secured funds from the prime minister for reconstruction of the runway. Patnaik also donated steel furniture from one of his factories, cleared out his Kalinga Air Lines offices to serve as a makeshift officers' quarters, and even loaned two of his Kalinga captains. "He was Nehru's fix-it guy," said Thorsrud. "He got things done."

Returning to New Delhi after nearly three months, the two CIA men were directed to a hotel room for a meeting with a representative of the Intelligence Bureau, T. M. Subramanian. Known for his Hindu piety and strict vegetarian diet, Subramanian had been serving as the bureau's liaison officer at Agra since November, where he had been paymaster for amenities offered to the USAF crewmen rushing military gear to India. He was also one of the two intelligence officers who had been trained at Camp Peary during April.

In the ensuing discussions between the CIA aviators and Subramanian, both sides spoke in general terms about the best options for building India's covert aviation capabilities. In one area the American officers stood firm: the United States would not assist with the procurement of spare parts, either directly or indirectly, for the many Soviet aircraft in the Indian inventory.[4]

A subject not discussed was which U.S. aircraft would be the backbone for the envisioned covert unit. Earlier in the spring, this had been the subject of serious debate within the CIA. Wayne Sanford, the senior paramilitary officer in New Delhi, had initially proposed selection of the C-119. This made sense for several reasons. First, more than fifty C-119 airframes had been in the Indian inventory since 1952; it was therefore well known to the Indian pilots and mechanics. Second, beginning in November 1962, the Indians had ordered special kits to add a single turbojet atop the center wing section of half their C-119 fleet. The added thrust from this turbojet, tested in the field over the previous months, allowed converted planes to operate at high altitudes and fly heavy loads out of small fields. The United States pledged in May 1963 to send another two dozen Flying Boxcars to India from reserve USAF squadrons.[5]

Other CIA officials in Washington, however, were keen to present the Indians with the C-46 Commando. A workhorse during World War II, the C-46 had proved its ability to surmount the Himalayas while flying the famed "Hump" route between India and China. More important, other CIA operations in Asia— primarily in Laos—were making use of the C-46, and the agency had a number of airframes readily available.

There were drawbacks with the C-46, however. It was notoriously difficult to handle. Moreover, the Indians did not operate the C-46 in their fleet, which meant that the pilots and mechanics would need a period of transition. When CIA headquarters sent over a USAF officer to sing the praises of the C-46 in overly simplistic terms, Grewal cut the conversation short. Recalls Sanford, "He flatly told the U.S. officer that he had been around C-46s longer than the American had been in the air force."[6]

In the end, however, the Indians could not protest CIA largesse too loudly. When Marrero and Thorsrud had their meeting with Subramanian, selection of the C-46 was an unstated fait accompli. The next day, Subramanian returned to the two CIA officers with a verbatim copy of the hotel discussion. "Either he had a photographic memory," said Thorsrud, "or somebody was listening in and taking notes." Both Americans signed the aide-mémoire as a working basis for cooperation.[7]

As a final order of business, Marrero asked for an audience with Mullik. With the Charbatia air base—now code-named Oak Tree 1—still in the midst of reconstruction, the first aircraft deliveries would not take place until early autumn. This did not dampen Marrero's enthusiasm as he recounted the list of possible cooperative ventures over the months ahead. The aloof Mullik replied with an indifferent stare. "Bob, we will call you when we need you."[8]

Despite Mullik's lack of warmth, efforts to create the covert air unit went ahead on schedule. On 7 September 1963, the Intelligence Bureau officially created the Aviation Research Centre (ARC) as a front to coordinate aviation cooperation with the CIA. Colonel Grewal was named the first ARC operations manager at the newly completed Charbatia airfield. He was given full latitude to handpick his pilots, all of whom would take leave from the military and belong—both administratively and operationally—to the ARC for the period of their assignment.

In New Delhi, veteran intelligence officer Rameshwar Nath Kao took the helm as the first ARC director. A Kashmiri Brahman like Nehru, forty-five-year-old Kao was a spy in the classic sense. Tall and fair skinned, he was a dapper dresser with impeccable schooling; he was a Persian scholar and spoke fluent Farsi. Dignified and sophisticated, he had long impressed the officers at the CIA's New Delhi station. "I had the opportunity to drive with him from Kathmandu back to India," recalled one CIA official. "At each bridge we crossed, he would recount its technical specifications in comparison to its ability to support the heaviest tank in the Chinese inventory."[9]

To assist Kao and Grewal, the CIA dispatched Edward Rector to Charbatia in the role of air operations adviser. Qualified as a U.S. Navy dive-bomber pilot in 1940, Rector had joined Claire Chennault's famed Flying Tigers the following year. He would later score that unit's first kill of a Japanese aircraft and go on to become an ace. After switching to the U.S. Army Air Forces (later the U.S. Air Force), he retired as a colonel in January 1962.

Rector came to Oak Tree with considerable Indian experience. During his Flying Tigers days, he had transited the subcontinent. And in late 1962, following his retirement from military service, he had gone to India on a Pentagon contract to coordinate USAF C-130 flights carrying emergency assistance to the front lines during the war with China.

Now serving with the CIA, Rector was on hand for the initial four aircraft deliveries within a week of ARC's creation. First to arrive at Oak Tree was a pair of C-46D Commandos; inside each was a disassembled U-10 Helio Courier. A five-seat light aircraft, the Helio Courier had already won praise for its short takeoff and landing (STOL) ability in the paramilitary campaign the CIA was sponsoring in Laos. Without exaggeration, it could operate from primitive runways no longer than a soccer field. More aircraft deliveries followed, totaling eight C-46 transports and four Helio Couriers by early 1964.

Under Rector's watch, the CIA arranged for the loan of some of the best pilots from its Air America roster to act as instructors for the ARC crews. Heading the C-46 conversion team was Bill Welk, a veteran of the Tibet overflights. For the Helio Courier, Air America Captain James Rhyne was dispatched to Oak Tree for a four-month tour. During this same period, T. J. Thompson, who had been assisting with the Tibetans' jump training at Agra, began work on a major parachute facility—complete with dehumidifiers, drying towers, and storage space—at Charbatia. "By the time it was finished," said Thompson, "it was larger than the facilities used by the U.S. Army in Germany."[10]

Under the tutelage of the Air America pilots, the ARC aircrew contingent, including two captains on a one-year loan from Kalinga Air Lines, proved quick studies. By the close of 1963, transition training was nearly complete. For a graduation exercise, a demonstration was planned at Charbatia for 2 January 1964. Among the attendees would be Nehru himself.

Arriving on the assigned day, the prime minister took center seat in a rattan chair with a parasol shading his head. On cue, a silver C-46 (ARC planes bore only small tail numbers and Indian civil markings) materialized over Charbatia and dropped bags of rice and a paratrooper. Then a Helio Courier roared in and came to a stop in an impossibly small grassy patch in front of the reviewing stand. An "agent," hiding in nearby bushes with a bag of "documents," rushed aboard the Helio. Showcasing its STOL ability, the plane shot upward from the grass and over the stands. Nehru, at once impressed and confused, turned to the ARC and CIA officials in attendance and asked, "What was that?"[11]

While the CIA assistance at Chakrata and Charbatia was transpiring under the auspices of the Near East Division, a separate Tibet program had been taking shape since December 1962 under the Far East Division. This program called for the training and infiltration of at least 125 Tibetan agents. But whereas the Near East Division was giving support to what were essentially Indian projects, the roles were reversed for the Far East Division's project—at least as it was originally conceived: the Indians would provide some minor assistance, but the Far East Division would call the shots.

It was not long before the CIA saw the inherent weakness of this arrangement. India, after all, would be party to the recruitment of Tibetan agents on its soil and would likely be expected to provide rear bases and staging areas. This greatly bothered the Special Group (as had been the case with Uban's Chakrata force), which was leery of authorizing paramilitary assistance to a project potentially subject to an Indian veto, especially if New Delhi grew weary and withdrew its commitment following a future rapprochement with Beijing.

To allay the Special Group's concerns, the CIA worked safeguards into the Tibetan agent program. Agent training would focus on producing self-sufficient three-man radio teams that could infiltrate Tibet, find support, and build a local underground that could feed and shelter them for extended periods without having to rely on lines of supply from India.

Just as with Establishment 22, Gyalo Thondup was quick to buy into the program and went off to recruit. The CIA, meanwhile, reopened Camp Hale to handle the expected influx. Scrambling to piece together an instructor staff, it found a willing volunteer in Bruce Walker, the great-grandson of Methodist missionaries in China. Walker's moneyed parents were family friends of Frank Wisner, the CIA's influential deputy director for plans between 1952 and 1958. Joining the agency with Wisner as his mentor, Walker spent his first four years in Latin America before joining the Tibet Task Force in January 1960. Once there, he proved adept at winning choice assignments. The agency paid for him to spend almost a year at the University of Washington's newly organized Tibet program to learn that country's language and history. In March 1962, the CIA again sponsored him for language classes, this time at Sikkim's Namgyal Institute of Tibetology.[12] *See page 283.*

By the time Walker returned to the United States in the fall of 1962, he had the basics of spoken Tibetan in hand. Given its investment in his education, the CIA rushed him to Hale to prepare the camp for the first wave of Tibetans. Ken Knaus, chief of the Tibet Task Force in Washington, would again be on hand to offer occasional lectures. There was also a stream of smoke jumpers—including brothers Miles and Shep Johnson—available for parachute instruction. The USAF even provided experts to teach survival tips. Overall command of the training would be held by Robert Eschbach, an OSS veteran.

In India, meanwhile, a search had commenced for suitable translators. All but one of the previous Tibetans serving in that role were unavailable. One of the new candidates, Wangchuk Tsering, was the nephew of a former trade commissioner at Kalimpong. An English student since 1956, he had been writing for the Tibetan Freedom Press in Darjeeling when Gyalo made a recruitment pitch in December 1962. Along with forty-five agent trainees, Wangchuk immediately left for New Delhi in a bus. Unlike the earlier shadowy exfiltrations across the East Pakistan frontier, this time they departed with Indian escorts from the capital's Palam Airport.[13]

By February 1963, four groups totaling 135 Tibetans (ten more than originally planned) had arrived at Hale. Gyalo had been instructed to restrict these recruits to the younger generation, unlike the crowd of seniors at Mustang and Establishment 22. Although the Khampas were still the overwhelming majority, 5 percent were from Amdo, and another 5 percent were from central Tibet. There was even a pair of Golok tribesmen from the Amdo plains who spoke an unintelligible dialect. "We used the same written language," said interpreter Wangchuk (now going by the call sign "Arnold"), "so all instructions were given to them on paper."[14]

On the political front, Gyalo arrived in the United States during late spring and called on Michael Forrestal, then special assistant to the president. Through Forrestal, the Dalai Lama's brother was told that Kennedy offered his deepest sympathy on behalf of the American people for the plight of the Tibetans. In time-honored doublespeak, Kennedy also said that the U.S. government desired to do what it could within the limits of practical and political circumstances to improve the Tibetans' fortunes. This was the fullest statement of U.S. support to that time.

As scheduled, the Hale training concluded by June 1963. Before the Tibetans could return, however, the CIA shifted the goalposts. Although the Special Group had earlier argued that the Tibetan agents should be more self-reliant—and therefore less vulnerable to any future chill in New Delhi—the agency was suddenly taking the exact opposite tack and looking to hook New Delhi into more meaningful cooperation. Specifically, the CIA wanted to use the covert airlift unit at Charbatia for infiltration. A new operational plan now called for the dispatch of five teams by Indian aircraft and twenty-nine teams overland to the area between Lhasa and the border with Bhutan.

Notified of the revised scheme, New Delhi balked. Though not rejecting the plan outright, the Indians indicated a strong reluctance to participate in any airdrops at the present time. "They wanted us to do the drops," said paramilitary adviser Wayne Sanford, "and not incur Chinese wrath if one was downed."[15]

For the CIA instructors at Hale, India's reluctance translated into delays in returning their students to Tibet. Tibetans had been stranded in Colorado once before (when Pakistan had closed its border), but this time the problem was exacerbated by the large size of the contingent. Realizing that boredom would soon set in and morale would suffer, the staff quickly expanded the curriculum to include classes on tradecraft such as wiretapping and lectures on Marxist Leninism and the new Tibetan constitution. Walker even arranged for Dr. Terrell Wylie, who headed the Tibet program at the University of Washington and was fluent in the language, to speak to the agents on Tibetan history at a makeshift outdoor amphitheater.[16]

By early autumn, the Tibetans could absorb no more and were clearly growing impatient. One of the Khampa students, Cheme Namgyal (known by the call sign "Conrad"), was famed among his peers for having been in a rebel band that downed a Chinese bomber in 1956 with machine guns. Eager to do battle with the PLA again, he was frustrated with the delays. "We ended up playing lots and lots of volleyball," he recalls.[17]

After further negotiations, a breakthrough finally came in September 1963. Still looking to draw New Delhi into a substantial role, the CIA now had India's agreement to open a joint operations center in New Delhi that would direct the dispatch of agents into Tibet and monitor their activities. The revised plan scrapped parachute insertions in favor of overland infiltrations and called for about twenty singleton resident agents in Tibet, plus (to sweeten its appeal to New Delhi) a pair of road-watch teams "to report possible Chinese Communist build-ups" and another six "border watch communications teams" to take up positions along the frontier. Radio reports from the agents and teams would be received at a new communications center to be built at Charbatia. With the first group of forty Hale graduates scheduled to return to India in November, the secret struggle for Tibet was starting to simmer.[18]

15. The Joelikote Boys

As the CIA's covert program for Tibet regained momentum toward the end of 1963, strict compartmentalization among its component projects fell by the wayside. This had become readily apparent to Wayne Sanford, who extended his tour in October to remain as the U.S. embassy's resident CIA paramilitary adviser responsible for ongoing assistance to Establishment 22. One of his first duties after extending his tour was to escort T. M. Subramanian, the intelligence officer now working under ARC, to Camp Hale. Some of the Hale trainees, it had been decided, would be redirected from agent operations to Uban's guerrillas at Chakrata.[1]

The nuances in this were significant. Establishment 22 was an Indian operation supported by the Near East Division. The Hale agent training, however, had originally been conceived as a unilateral Far East Division project with limited Indian exposure. Now the assets from one division's program were being transferred to another—and the Indians were full partners on both.

Much the same thing had happened to the guerrilla army at Mustang. When first launched by the Far East Division, the Mustang operation had been conducted behind India's back. During the Harriman mission, however, Mullik had been fully briefed, and discussions over the best way of jointly running the guerrillas soon followed.

The CIA and Intelligence Bureau, it was discovered, held widely disparate views on Mustang, which was home to 2,030 Tibetan irregulars as of early 1963. Less than half of them had been properly equipped during the two previous CIA airdrops. Realizing that the unarmed men were a ball and chain on the rest, the agency devised a plan to parachute weapons to an additional 700 men sent to ten drop zones inside Tibet. The purpose of this was twofold. First, it would force them to leave their Mustang sanctuary and take up a string of positions inside their homeland. Second, it would go far toward rectifying the disparity between armed and unarmed volunteers.

When this plan was taken to Mullik, his reaction was poor. Just as the Indians had balked at aerial infiltration for the Hale agents, they preferred no Mustang drops by Indian aircraft (ARC was close to formation at the time), for fear of provoking the Chinese. When the CIA proposed that U.S. aircraft do the job—but insisted on Indian landing rights—New Delhi was again reticent.

Frustrated, the CIA in the early fall of 1963 hastily arranged for an airlift company to be established inside Nepal. Allocated a pair of Bell 47G helicopters and two U.S. rotary-wing pilots—one of whom was released from Air America for the job—the Kathmandu-based entity, called Air Ventures, theoretically could have solved the airdrop problem by choppering supplies to collection points near Mustang.

As it turned out, there was no need for Air Ventures to fly any covert missions. By September, at the same time agreement was reached on establishing a joint operations center in New Delhi, the CIA and Intelligence Bureau came up with a new plan for the unarmed men at Mustang to be reassigned to Establishment 22 at Chakrata. It was also agreed that nonlethal supplies for the armed portion of Mustang—which was estimated at no more than 835 guerrillas—would go overland through India and be coordinated through the New Delhi center. In addition, some of the Hale graduates would go to Mustang to assist with radio operations. Once again, distinctions between the various Tibet projects were becoming blurred.[2]

During the same month, CIA officers beckoned Mustang leader Baba Yeshi to New Delhi to gain his approval for the reassignment scheme. Unfortunately for the agency, the chieftain was not happy when he was told that his force would be more than halved. With Lhamo Tsering providing translations, talks remained deadlocked for the next week. Opting to seek the counsel of Khampa leader Gompo Tashi, they shifted the debate to Calcutta. Gompo Tashi had recently returned there after half a year in a London hospital, where he had sought relief from lingering war injuries. Still weak, he refused to take sides.[3]

Defiantly, Baba Yeshi went back to Mustang. From the perspective of a Khampa tribal leader, his reluctance to downsize Mustang was both understandable and predictable. In true chieftain fashion, he had spent the previous two years patiently padding his command. The results on several fronts were laudable. The bleak food situation, for example, had been fully rectified. With occasional funds channeled by the CIA, a small team of Khampas purchased meat, butter, and rice at Pokhara and sent the supplies north on pack animals. Baba Yeshi's Khampas also procured local barley for a tsampa mill they established in the Mustang village of Kagbeni. His men were eating; malnourishment was a thing of the past.[4]

The quality of his fighters was also improving. Unlike Mustang's first wave of aged recruits, the steady stream of trainees arriving in Mustang during 1963 were either in their late teens or young adults. Many hailed from central Tibet, providing a more representative mix than the previous Khampa-dominated ranks.

Because most of the young arrivals came with no previous guerrilla experience, the Mustang leadership had spent much of 1963 institutionalizing its training procedures. A more formal camp was set up at Tangya to offer between three and six months of drills in rock climbing, river crossing, partisan warfare, and simple tradecraft. Graduates were then posted to one of Mustang's sixteen guerrilla companies, each of which had a Hale-trained instructor for refresher courses.[5]

Baba Yeshi had made some personalized gains as well. Because his head-quarters at Tangya was uncomfortable during the coldest months, in 1963 he focused considerable energy on establishing a new winter base at the village of Kaisang. Located seven kilometers southeast of Jomsom, Kaisang was tucked at the base of the massive Annapurna. More than just a beautiful vista, the new base included a comfortable two-floor house for Baba Yeshi; it had a vegetable garden, Tibetan mastiffs chained to the front gate, and a Tibetan flag fluttering from a tall staff. Ten guards patrolled the perimeter, screening guerrilla subordinates who wished an audience with their commandant.

Sitting in Kaisang with hundreds of loyalists under arms, Baba Yeshi had few local rivals for power. The thinly spread royal Nepalese armed forces maintained almost no presence around Mustang. Even Mustang's royalty, greatly weakened by internecine fighting during 1964, was increasingly deferential toward its Tibetan guests. In a telling gesture, the crown prince of Lo Monthang (his brother, the king, had died under mysterious circumstances earlier that year) traveled by horseback to Kaisang to attend a Tibetan cultural show hosted by the Mustang guerrilla leader.[6]

Against these gains, precious little had been done to progress the war inside Tibet. In theory, the guerrillas intended to concentrate their cross-border forays during the winter, when the frozen Brahmaputra was easily fordable and the Chinese were less likely to patrol. In reality, hardly any guerrilla activities emanated from Mustang at any time of year. During all of 1963 and most of 1964, not a single truck was ambushed (land mines were occasionally laid, without any known success), and no PLA outposts were attacked.[7]

One notable exception took place in mid-1964. Two years earlier, a ten-man guerrilla team had been dispatched 130 kilometers east of Mustang to establish a lone outpost in the mountainous Nepalese border region known as Tsum. Led by a thirty-two-year-old Khampa named Tendar, they had among them a single Bren machine gun and a mix of M1 carbines and rifles. Without a radio or ready source of supplies, however, little offensive action was attempted. During their few overnight forays into Tibet, Tendar and his men had seen truck traffic only once and had never inflicted any damage.[8]

In early June 1964, their dry spell was set to end. Without warning, three white men bearing camera equipment appeared at the remote camp. The spokesman among the three was none other than George Patterson, the former missionary who had taught in Kham during the early 1950s and had since become an international advocate for the Tibetan cause. Patterson was now leading a British television team seeking footage of a guerrilla attack against the PLA. Speaking in the Kham dialect, the ex-missionary pleaded with Tendar to stage a raid for the cameras.[9]

Hearing Patterson's pitch, the guerrilla leader was torn. He would have preferred to ask permission from his guerrilla superiors at Mustang, but Tendar was handed two sealed envelopes that the missionary said were letters of support from senior Tibetan officials. Still uncertain, Tendar went to a nearby temple and cast dice. The dice were unequivocal: they told him to stage the mission.

Instructed by the fates, Tendar on 6 June began a day-long journey across the border with eight fellow guerrillas and the three foreigners. They split into four groups on a ridgeline overlooking a border road. Coincidentally, four trucks came into view that same afternoon. Tendar, in the closest group, fired his carbine at the front seat of the lead truck. After a spirited attack—which provided plenty of good camera footage—the guerrillas left behind three riddled vehicles and an estimated eight Chinese casualties. One Khampa was seriously injured in the face and shoulder but managed to get back to Tsum.[10]

It did not take long for word of the truck ambush to spread. In the mistaken belief that Baba Yeshi had invited the cameramen along to court unauthorized publicity, CIA officers in India couriered a reprimand and stopped the flow of funds for half a year. Tendar, meanwhile, was recalled to Mustang to face a round of criticism and reassignment to an administrative job. Together, these negative repercussions were ample incentive for a return to inactivity. Said one senior guerrilla, "We went on existing for the sake of existence."[11]

With Mustang relegated to a sideshow, the focus of joint Indo-U.S. cooperation shifted to the agent program. To monitor this effort, the New Delhi joint operations center—dubbed the Special Center—was formally established in November 1963. To house the site, Intelligence Bureau officers arranged to rent a modest villa in the F block of the posh Haus Khaz residential neighborhood.[12]

Ken Knaus, the first CIA representative to the Special Center, arrived in India during the final week of November. Although Knaus had the perfect background for the role—he had been heading the Tibet Task Force for almost two years— the assignment raised some eyebrows because it resurrected an earlier turf war.

When CIA assistance was still being provided without India's complicity, the Near East Division—in the form of deputy station chief Bill Grimsley—had assumed responsibility for coordinating the effort out of the U.S. embassy in New Delhi. Now a Far East Division representative—Knaus—was back on Indian soil. According to colleagues within the division, his welcome from peers at the embassy was somewhat muted.[13]

Knaus faced another opening hurdle as well. In previous years, the Tibet Task Force had counted on strong headquarters support from the Far East Division's dynamic chief, Des FitzGerald. Knaus, in fact, was one of his personal favorites. In January 1963, however, FitzGerald transferred from the Far East slot to oversee the ongoing paramilitary campaign against Cuba. His replacement, William Colby, not only was consumed by the escalating conflict in Vietnam but also was developing a pronounced aversion toward agent operations behind communist lines.[14]

Despite all this, Knaus spent his first month focusing on the center's impending operations. On 4 January 1964, he was joined by a sharp Bombay native nicknamed Rabi. A math major in college, Rabi had joined the police force upon graduation but soon switched to the Intelligence Bureau. He had been assigned to its China section and spent many years operating from remote outposts in Assam and NEFA. Now chosen as the Indian representative to the Special Center, he internally transferred to the ARC. More than merely an airlift unit, the ARC was now acting as the section of the Intelligence Bureau that would work alongside the CIA on joint efforts with the Tibet agents and guerrillas at Mustang.

In April, Knaus and Rabi were joined by a Tibetan representative, Kesang Kunga. A soft-spoken former district governor and monk, Kesang—better known as Kay-Kay—came from a landed family in central Tibet. After fleeing to India, he had risen to chief editor at the Tibetan press facilities in Darjeeling. From there he oversaw the printing of *Freedom*, a newsweekly distributed among the refugee camps. He had been personally chosen by Gyalo Thondup to represent Tibetan interests at the Special Center.

Under Kay-Kay was a small team of Tibetan assistants. Three members were former Hale translators. There was also a pool of eight Hale graduates from the 1963 training class; half provided radio assistance at the Special Center, and the other half performed similar tasks at the radio relay center being set up at Charbatia.

One of the Special Center's biggest challenges was keeping its New Delhi activities secret from the Indian public. In the midst of residential housing, the presence of foreign nationals—both the Tibetans and Knaus—was certain to draw attention. To guard against this, Knaus (who normally came to the center three times a week) was shielded in the back of a jeep until he was inside the garage. Similar precautions were taken with the Tibetans, who were ferried between a dormitory and the center in a blacked-out van. "We were not allowed to step outside," said one Tibetan officer, "until 1972."

By the time Kay-Kay got his assignment in the spring of 1964, most of the 135 agent trainees had returned to India from Hale.[15] Two dozen were diverted to Establishment 22 at Chakrata, and another eight manned the radio sets at Charbatia and the Special Center. The remainder—slightly more than 100—were taken to a holding camp outside the village of Joelikote near the popular hill station of Nainital. Built close to the shores of a mountain lake and surrounded by pine and oak forests, Joelikote once hosted Colonel Jim Corbett, the famed hunter who tracked some of the most infamous man-eating tigers and leopards on record (two were credited with killing more than 400 villagers apiece).[16]

As the agents assembled at Joelikote—where Rabi promptly dubbed them "The Joelikote Boys"—they were divided into radio teams, each designated by a letter of the alphabet. The size of the teams varied, with some numbering as few as two agents and several with as many as five; contrary to the previous year's plan to dispatch lone operatives, none would be going as singletons. As their main purpose would be to radio back social, political, economic, and military information, the CIA provided radios ranging from the durable RS-1 to the RS-48 (a high-speed-burst model originally developed for use in Southeast Asia) and a sophisticated miniature set with a burst capability and solar cells. The teams would also be charged with gauging the extent of local resistance; when appropriate, they were to spread propaganda and extend a network of sympathizers. Although they were not to engage in sabotage or other attacks, the agents would carry pistols (Canadian-made Brownings to afford the United States plausible deniability) for self-defense.

During April, the first wave of ten radio teams began moving from Joelikote to launch sites along the border. Team A, consisting of two agents, took up a position in the Sikkimese capital of Gangtok. Team B, also two men, filed into the famed colonial summer capital of Shimla. Just eighty kilometers from Establishment 22 at Chakrata, Shimla had not changed much since the days the British had ruled one-fifth of humankind from this small Himalayan settlement. Three teams—D, V, and Z—were sent to Tuting, a NEFA backwater already host to 2,000 Tibetan refugees. Two others—T and Y—crossed into easternmost Nepal and established a camp outside the village of Walung. Another two teams went to Mustang to provide Baba Yeshi's guerrillas with improved radio links to Charbatia.[17]

The tenth set of agents—two men known as Team Q—headed into the kingdom of Bhutan. The Bhutanese, though ethnic kin, harbored mixed feelings toward the Tibetans. With only a small population of its own, Bhutan had attempted to discourage further refugee arrivals after the first influx of 3,000. Then in April 1964, the country's prime minister was killed by unknown assailants. Coincidentally, this happened at the same time Team Q was crossing the border, sparking unfounded rumors that the Tibetans were attempting to overthrow the kingdom. As the rumors escalated into diplomatic protests, the two agents were quietly withdrawn, and Bhutan was never again contemplated as a launch site.[18]

Aside from the stillborn Team Q and the two others at Mustang, the other seven teams had been briefed on targets before departing Joelikote. These had been generated by the CIA and Intelligence Bureau; Knaus had access to the latest intelligence for this purpose, including satellite imagery. He and Rabi then consulted with Kay-Kay, who endorsed the missions. All involved testing the waters inside Tibet to determine whether an underground could, or did, exist.[19]

During the same month the teams headed for the border, Gyalo Thondup established a political party in India. Called *Cho Kha Sum* ("Defense of Religion by the Three Regions," a reference to Kham, Amdo, and U-Tsang), the party promoted the liberal ideals found in the Tibetan constitution that had been promulgated by the Dalai Lama the previous spring. Part of Gyalo's intent was to develop a political consciousness among the Tibetan diaspora. But even more important, the party was designed to reinforce a message of noncommunist nationalism that the agent teams would be taking to potential underground members inside Tibet. Gyalo even arranged for a party newsletter to be printed, copies of which would be carried and distributed by the teams in their homeland.

Getting the agents to actually cross the frontier was a wholly different matter. By early summer, three of the teams—in Sikkim, Shimla, and Walung—had done little more than warm their launch sites. A second set of agents in Walung, Team Y, had better luck. One of its members, a young Khampa going by the call sign "Clyde," headed alone across the Nangpa pass for a survey. He took a feeder trail north for fifty kilometers and approached the Tibetan town of Tingri. Located along the traditional route linking Kathmandu and Lhasa, Tingri was a popular resting place for an assortment of pilgrims and traders; as a result, Clyde's Kham origins attracted little attention. Better still, Tingri was surrounded by cave hermitages that offered good concealment.[20]

Returning to Walung with this information, Clyde briefed his four teammates. Three—Robert, Dennie, and team leader Reg—were fellow Khampas; the last—

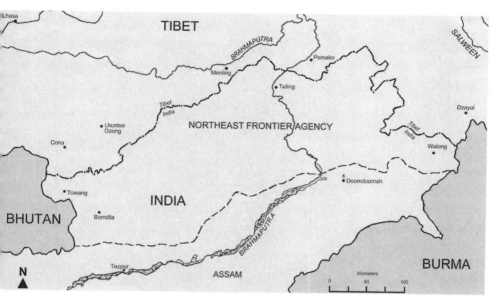

The Indian frontier

Grant—was from Amdo. Following the same route used during the survey, the five arrived at the caves and set up camp.

Tingri, they discovered, was ripe for an underground. Venturing into town to procure supplies, the team took volunteers back to its redoubt for ad hoc leadership training. They debriefed the locals for items of intelligence value and used their solar-powered burst radio to send two messages a week back to Charbatia. Settling into a routine, they prepared to wait out the approaching winter from the vantage of their cave.

Good luck was also experienced by the three teams operating from the border village of Tuting. Team D, consisting of four Khampas, arrived at its launch site with one Browning pistol apiece and a single survival rifle. Their target was the town of Pemako, eighty kilometers to the northeast. Renowned among Tibetans as a "hidden heaven" because of its mild weather and ring of surrounding mountains, this area had been the destination of many Khampas fleeing the Chinese invasion in 1950. The PLA, by contrast, had barely penetrated the vicinity because no roads could be built due to the harsh topography and abundant precipitation.[21]

That same rainfall made the trip for Team D a slog. Covering only part of the distance to their target by late in the year, most of the agents were ready to return to the relatively appealing creature comforts in Tuting. Just one member, Nolan, chose to stay for the winter. Wishing him luck, his colleagues promised to meet again in the spring of 1965.[22]

Much the same experience was recounted by the five men of Team Z. Targeted toward Pemako, they conducted a series of shallow forays to contact border villagers and collect data on PLA patrols. Finally making a deeper infiltration near year's end, they encountered some sympathizers and the makings of an underground. By that time, most of the agents were eager to return before the approaching winter. Just as with Team D, one of its members, Chris, elected to stay through spring with his embryonic partisan movement.[23]

The final group of agents from Tuting, Team V, was targeted eighty kilometers west toward the town of Menling. Located along the banks of the Brahmaputra, this low-lying region featured high rainfall and lush forests. Many locals in the area, though conversant in Tibetan, were animists, with their own unique language and style of dress.

Despite such ethnic differences, one of Team V's members, Stuart, had a number of relatives living in the vicinity. With their assistance, the team was able to contact a loose underground of resisters. Shielded by these sympathizers—who even helped them steal some PLA supplies when their cache was exhausted—the five men of Team V radioed back their intent to remain through the winter.

Reviewing their progress in November 1964, Knaus, Rabi, and Kay-Kay had some reason for cheer. Of the ten teams dispatched to date, four had at least some of their members still inside Tibet. All four, too, had identified sympathetic countrymen. Encouraged by these results, the Special Center representatives penned plans to launch a second round of nine teams the following spring, when the mountain passes would be free of snow. Slowly, the secret war for Tibet was shifting from simmer to low boil.

16. Omens

On the afternoon of 16 October 1964, the arid desert soil around Lop Nur in central Xinjiang Province rippled from the effect of a twenty-kiloton blast. "This is a major achievement of the Chinese people," read the immediate press communiqué out of Beijing, "in their struggle to oppose the U.S. imperialist policy of nuclear blackmail."[1]

The detonation had not been unexpected. For the past few months, the United States had been closely tracking China's nuclear program using everything from satellite photographs to a worldwide analysis of media statements made by Chinese diplomats. India, still smarting from the 1962 war, had supported this collection effort by allowing the CIA to use Charbatia in April to secretly stage U-2 flights over Xinjiang. By late September, there were enough indications for senior officials in Washington to publicly predict the blast three weeks prior to the event.[2]

Such forewarning did nothing to dampen anxiety in New Delhi. This resulted in a windfall of sorts for the Tibet project, with the CIA using the Indians' more permissive attitude to push for a series of covert initiatives aimed at raising Tibet's worldwide profile. The first such scheme was an effort to recruit and train a cadre of Tibetan officers for use as administrators and foreign representatives. An advisory committee of U.S. academics and retired diplomats was established to oversee this project, with Cornell University agreeing to play host and the CIA footing the bill.

In the fall of 1964, an initial group of four Tibetans arrived at the Cornell campus for nine months of course work in linguistics, comparative government, economics, and anthropology. Among the four were former Hale translators Bill and Mark; both had been at Georgetown University over the previous two years honing their English skills. A second group, totaling eight Tibetans, arrived in the fall of the following year. Included was former Hale translator Thinlay "Rocky" Paljor and Lobsang Tsultrim, the nephew of one of the Dalai Lama's bodyguards. As a teenager, Lobsang had joined the entourage that fled Tibet with the monarch in 1959. Midway through the semester, half of the class was quietly taken down to Silver Spring, Maryland, where they were kept in a CIA safe house for a month of spy-craft instruction; all eight later reassembled, completed their studies at Cornell, and went back to India together.[3]

These first dozen Cornell-trained Tibetans were put to immediate use. Three were assigned to the Special Center. Others were posted to one of the CIA-supported Tibet representative offices in New Delhi, Geneva, and New York. The New Delhi mission—officially known as the Bureau of His Holiness the Dalai Lama—was headed by a former Tibetan finance minister and charged with maintaining contact with the various embassies in the Indian capital. The Office of Tibet in Geneva, led by the Dalai Lama's older brother Lobsang Samten, focused on staging cultural programs in neutral Switzerland.[4]

The New York Office of Tibet, which included three Cornell graduates, formally opened in April 1964 following a U.S. visit by Gyalo Thondup. This office concentrated on winning support for the Tibetan cause at the United Nations, which was becoming an increasingly difficult prospect. In December 1965, Gyalo was successful in pushing a resolution on Tibet through the General Assembly for the third time, but some twenty-six nations—including Nepal and Pakistan—joined the ranks of those supporting China on the issue.[5]

During a break from lobbying at the United Nations, Gyalo had ventured down to Washington for meetings with U.S. officials. Among them was Des FitzGerald; one of the strongest advocates of the Tibet program within the CIA, he had since left his Cuba assignment and in the spring of 1965 was promoted to deputy director of plans, putting him in charge of all agency covert operations. FitzGerald used the opportunity to invite Gyalo to dinner at the elite Federalist Club. Joining them was Frank Holober, who had returned from an unpaid sabbatical in September 1965 to take over the vacant Tibet Task Force desk within the China Branch. Remembers Holober, "Des loved Gyalo, fawned over him. He would say, 'In an independent country, you would be the perfect foreign minister.'"

Gyalo proved his abilities in another CIA-supported venture. Because the Dalai Lama had long desired the creation of a central Tibetan cultural institution, the agency supplied Gyalo with secret funds to assemble a collection of wall hangings—called thankas—and other art treasures from all the major Tibetan Buddhist sects. A plot of land was secured in the heart of New Delhi, and the Tibet House—consisting of a museum, library, and emporium—was officially opened in October 1965 by the Indian minister of education and the Dalai Lama. It remains a major attraction to this day.

India's more permissive attitude allowed for increasingly sensitive Indo-U.S. intelligence operations. Some efforts were in conjunction with the Republic of China on Taiwan, which was one of the few nations that equaled—even surpassed—India and the United States in its seething opposition to Beijing. Taipei, for example, was allowed to station Chinese translators at Charbatia to monitor PRC radio traffic. ROC intelligence officers were even permitted to open remote listening outposts along the Indo-Tibetan frontier. This last effort was highly compartmentalized, even within the CIA staff in India. Wayne Sanford, the agency's paramilitary officer in New Delhi, was shocked when Indian officials escorted him to one of the border sites. He recalls, "Subramanian took me to the main listening post on October 10 [1965], which is the big Ten-Ten holiday on Taiwan. The Chinese commander saw me and asked if I had ever been on Da Chen island. I said, 'Yup.' He then asked if I had been aboard a PT evacuation boat from Da Chen. I said, 'Yup.' We then got drunk together to catch up on old times."[6]

Another sensitive project combined the CIA, the Intelligence Bureau, and the top mountain climbers from both nations. Conceived in late 1964 following the first PRC atomic test, this operation called for placement of a nuclear-powered sensor atop Kanchenjunga, the third tallest mountain bordering Sikkim and Nepal. From its vantage atop the Himalayas, the sensor would theoretically relay telemetry data from intermediate-range ballistic missiles the Chinese were developing at test sites in Xinjiang. Because Kanchenjunga was later deemed too challenging—it is one of the world's hardest peaks to scale, even without the extra weight of sensitive equipment—the target was shifted in 1965 to India's Nanda Devi. That October, a device was carried near the summit, but before the climbers had a chance to activate its generator, worsening weather forced them to secure the equipment in a crevice until they could return the following spring.[7]

Some of the most tangible Indo-U.S. cooperation was in the expansion of the ARC fleet at Charbatia. By 1964, a total of ten C-46 transports and four Helio STOL planes had been delivered to the Indians.[8] Late that year, they were augmented by two more STOL airframes that were a unique adaptation of the Helio. Known as the Twin Helio, these planes looked exactly like the single-engine version, but with two propellers placed above and forward of the wings. Developed in 1960 with the CIA's war in Laos in mind, the Twin Helio's engine placement allowed for unrestricted lateral visibility and reduced the possibility of propeller damage from debris at primitive airstrips. Only five were ever built, with one field-tested in Bolivia during the summer of 1964 and another handed over to the CIA's quasi-proprietary in Nepal, Air Ventures, in August.[9]

Of the planes delivered to the ARC, several received further modifications in India. To provide for an eavesdropping capability, CIA technicians in 1964 transformed one of the C-46 airframes into an electronic intelligence (ELINT) platform. This plane flew regular orbits along the Himalayas, recording Chinese

A Twin Helio STOL plane during USAF trials in 1961; this aircraft was later turned over to ARC. (Courtesy Harry Aderholt)

telecommunications signals from inside Tibet. For some of the nine remaining C-46 transports, ARC became a test bed during 1966 for a unique adaptation. Much like the jet packs strapped to the C-119 Flying Boxcars during 1962, four 1,000-pound rocket boosters were placed on the bottom of the C-46 fuselages to allow heavy loads to be safely carried from some of India's highest airfields.[10]

Such cooperation, however, masked tension under the surface. At the highest levels of government, problems were evident by early 1964. Following the assassination of John Kennedy the previous November, the new administration of President Lyndon Johnson withheld approval of a five-year military assistance package negotiated by his predecessor. Not helping matters was the fact that Johnson was increasingly consumed by the Vietnam War, leaving him little time to thoughtfully contemplate South Asia.

During the following year, bilateral strains were exacerbated by the Indo-Pakistan conflict that autumn. Pakistan initiated hostilities in August when it attempted to seize the contested Kashmir by infiltrating thousands of guerrillas. After that effort faltered, Karachi crossed the frontier with tanks. India responded in kind, leading to some of the bloodiest armor battles since World War II.

For the next month, the United States remained in the background as the subcontinent teetered on the edge of all-out war. Relying on the United Nations to broker a cease-fire, Washington did little apart from cut the flow of additional weapons to Pakistan. By effectively walking away from the region, the Johnson administration infuriated both sides: India was incensed because Pakistan had used U.S. weapons; Pakistan felt betrayed because the United States, a treaty partner, had not come to its assistance. Although the special U.S.-Pakistani alliance was now effectively dead, no points had been scored with India.[11]

The Soviet Union, meanwhile, was patiently working overtime to mend fences with New Delhi. In September 1964, it signed a deal not only to sell India the MiG-21 jet but also to allow mass production in Indian factories. The Soviets even impinged on areas of cooperation between the CIA and the Intelligence Bureau. During 1965, Moscow offered—and New Delhi accepted—a pair of Mi-4 helicopters for the ARC.

Nobody was more concerned about the deterioration of Indo-U.S. relations than Ambassador Chester Bowles. No stranger to the subcontinent—having served as ambassador to India a decade earlier—Bowles had replaced Galbraith in the summer of 1963. The two differed in several important ways. Galbraith, the consummate Kennedy insider, left India on a high note after winning military assistance in New Delhi's hour of need. Bowles, by contrast, was a relative outsider (he reportedly made Kennedy "uncomfortable") who arrived just as the post–November 1962 honeymoon had run its course.[12] The two also differed in their attitude toward the CIA. Initially a die-hard opponent of CIA activities on his diplomatic turf, Galbraith had reversed his position during the 1962 war to become an open—if not outspoken—proponent of the agency's activities in the subcontinent.[13]

Bowles, who inherited the CIA's cooperative ventures already in progress, was largely silent about the agency during his first two years in New Delhi. Wayne Sanford, the CIA paramilitary officer who had provided regular updates for Galbraith, had not even met Bowles for a briefing by the summer of 1965.[14]

But with Indo-U.S. tension gaining momentum, Bowles became more conscious of the damage being done to bilateral intelligence cooperation. In a bid to reverse the estrangement, he lent his support to a September 1965 CIA proposal to provide the ARC with three C-130 transports, an aircraft the Indians had been eyeing for five years. The offer came at a particularly opportune time. At Charbatia, Ed Rector had finished his tour and been replaced as air adviser by Moose Marrero, who had a long history of contact with Biju Patnaik and the original ARC cadre.

As it turned out, Marrero's past ties had only minimal effect. The C-130 deal encountered repeated delays, largely because the irate Indians did not want to remain vulnerable to a fickle U.S. spare-parts pipeline. In a telling request, they even asked Marrero to vacate Oak Tree and relocate to an office at the U.S. embassy compound in New Delhi.

Still attempting damage control, the CIA in early 1966 offered a quiet continuation of supplies for its paramilitary projects. As Washington had officially cut all arms shipments to India and Pakistan following the 1965 Kashmir fighting, this was a significant, albeit secret, exception. Four flights were scheduled, all to be conducted by a CIA-operated 727 jet transport staging between Okinawa and Charbatia.

The Indians listened to the offer and consented. But in a reprise of conditions imposed on the DC-6 flights of 1962, the government insisted that the flights into Oak Tree be made at low level to avoid radar—and to avoid any resultant publicity from the resurgent anti-American chorus in New Delhi political circles.[15]

The ARC operation at Charbatia was not the only CIA project encountering difficulties. Throughout 1964, Intelligence Bureau director Mullik had been pushing for infiltration of all the Hale-trained agents to establish an underground movement within Tibet. By year's end, the Special Center saw its limited inroads— elements of four teams operating inside their homeland—as a glass half full.

Mullik, by contrast, saw it as a glass half empty. Whereas he had once held excessive expectations of a Tibet-wide underground creating untold headaches for China, he now saw the limitations of overland infiltrations—especially by Khampa agents moving into areas where they did not have family or clan support. By the beginning of 1965, Mullik lashed out, claiming that the Tibetans were being coddled by the CIA.

Part of the problem was that Mullik himself was vulnerable and under pressure. In May 1964, ailing Prime Minister Nehru had died in his sleep, denying the fourteen-year spymaster of his powerful patron. That October, colleagues (and competitors) saw the chance to ease Mullik out of the top intelligence slot. They succeeded, but only to a degree. Although he gave up his hat as bureau director, he retained unofficial control over joint paramilitary operations with the CIA. That position—which was officially titled director general of security in February 1965— answered directly to the prime minister and oversaw the ARC base at Charbatia, the Special Center, Establishment 22, and the sensor mission on Nanda Devi.[16]

With Mullik growing impatient, the Special Center readied its agents for a second season inside Tibet. Arriving in late 1964 as the new CIA representative at the center was John Gilhooley, the same Far East Division officer who had briefly worked at the Tibet Task Force's Washington office in 1960. The Indian and Tibetan officials at the center warmed to their new American counterpart. "He was a free spirit, very good-natured," said Rabi.[17]

Cordial personal ties aside, little could spare Gilhooley from the dark news filtering in from Tibet. As soon as the snows cleared in early 1965, members of Team D had departed Tuting and headed back across the border to rendezvous with Nolan, the teammate they had left behind for the winter. Only then did they discover that he had already died of exposure. The remaining three agents returned to India and did not attempt another infiltration.[18]

Much the same was encountered by Team Z. Departing Tuting to fetch Chris, they learned that he had been rounded up during a winter PLA sweep. Radio intercepts monitored at Charbatia later revealed that Chris had refused to answer questions during an interrogation and been executed.

Team Z's bad luck did not stop there. Entering a village later that summer, the men were sheltered in a hut by seemingly sympathetic locals. While they rested, however, the residents alerted nearby Chinese militiamen. As the PLA started firing at the hut, the team broke through the rear planks and fled into the forest. One of the agents, Tex, died from a bullet wound before reaching the Indian border.[19]

Better longevity was experienced by the members of Team V, all five of whom had successfully braved the winter near Menling. By the spring of 1965, four elected to return to India, but Stuart, who had relatives in the area, stayed and was given permission to lead his own group of agents, appropriately titled Team V1. Two new members—Maurice and Terrence—were dispatched from Tuting for a linkup.

By that time, Stuart was living in his sister's house north of the Brahmaputra. During his regular crossings of the river, he used boats in order to avoid Chinese troops guarding the bridges. The new agents, however, chose the bridge option, ran into a PLA checkpoint, and panicked. Drawing their Brownings, they got into a brief firefight before being arrested. The PLA quickly isolated Maurice and forced him to send a radio message back to India claiming that he had arrived safely. This was a ploy used to good effect by the Chinese, Soviets, and North Vietnamese; by capturing radiomen and forcing them to continue sending messages, communist intelligence agencies duped the CIA and allied services into sending more agents and supplies, with both deadly and embarrassing results. In the case of North Vietnam, some turned agents continued radio play for as long as a decade.[20]

The Chinese were not as fortunate with Maurice. On his first message back, the Tibetan included a simple but effective duress code: he used his real name. This was repeated in two subsequent transmissions, after which his handlers ceased contact for fear the Chinese would triangulate the signals coming from Charbatia and expose the base to the press. A warning was then flashed to Stuart, who was able to get back to India.

Team Y, the last of the 1964 teams still inside Tibet, had a similar experience. After successfully living alongside sympathizers near Tingri through the winter, the five agents lobbied the Special Center in early 1965 for permission to rotate back to India. Agreeing to replace them in phases, the center authorized two of the veterans—Robert and Dennie—to make their way out to Walung.

At that point, the Special Center was in for a rude surprise. Due to operational compartmentalization, it was unaware that Establishment 22 had started running its own fledgling cross-border program. Using Tibetan guerrillas from Chakrata, a pilot team had been staged from Walung with a mandate to contact sympathizers near Tingri.

It came at a bad time. To great fanfare, the Chinese were preparing to inaugurate the Tibetan Autonomous Region that fall. After nine years of ruling Tibet under the PCART, the name change signified that Beijing deemed the Communist Party organs in the region fully operational. To coincide, the Chinese began a more forceful program of suppression, purging Tibetan collaborators, establishing communes, and increasing military patrols. Not only was the Establishment 22 team caught in one of these sweeps, but Robert and Dennie ran headlong into the dragnet as well.[21]

Ditching their supplies, both agents veered deeper into the hills as they evaded toward the Nangpa pass on the Nepalese border. Unfortunately for the two, the Nangpa is notoriously treacherous through late spring. Given its high elevation, it is not uncommon for entire caravans to be wiped out from slow suffocation as piercing winds blast fine powdery snow into the nose and mouth. Dennie ultimately reached Nepal; Robert did not.

Back at Tingri, the rest of Team Y faced the same Chinese patrols. Two replacement agents had already arrived by that time. In need of supplies, team leader Reg left their cave retreat to procure food. Captured upon entering a village, he was forced to lead the PLA back to the team's redoubt. In the ensuing firefight, all were killed except for the lone Amdo agent, Grant. A subsequent sweep rounded up the dozens of sympathizers they had trained over the previous year.

The news was equally bleak for the new teams launched in 1965. At Shimla, the two-man Team C endured a deadly comedy of errors during its first infiltra-

Tibet, from China's perspective

tion attempt. Looking to cross a river swollen by the spring thaw, agent Howard fell in and drowned. His partner, Irving, spent the next three days looking for a better fording point. Cold and hungry, he chanced upon an old woman and her son tending a flock. They led him to an isolated sheep enclosure, then alerted the militia. Irving was soon heading for Lhasa in shackles.[22]

Another trio of agents, Team X, was deployed to easternmost India and targeted against the town of Dzayul, renowned as an entomologist's dream because of its rare endemic butterflies. The CIA was eyeing Dzayul because the surrounding forests supposedly hosted displaced Burmese insurgents who could potentially be harnessed against the Chinese. Team X, however, found nobody of interest and came back.

More bizarre was the tale of Team U. The five-man team staged from Towang, the same border town that had factored into the Dalai Lama's 1959 escape and the 1962 war. Three members headed north from Towang toward Cona, where one of the agents had family. Upon reaching their target, they were immediately reported by the agent's own brother. Arrested and bundled off to Lhasa, they were not mistreated but instead were shown films of captured ROC agents, then photos of the captured and killed members of Team Y. After less than a month of propaganda sessions, all three were given some Chinese currency and escorted to the border. After a final warning about "reactionary India," they were allowed to cross unmolested.[23]

Sometimes the agents were their own worst enemy. The two members of Team F, which staged from Walung to Tingri, constantly quarreled with each other and with local sympathizers. After the more argumentative of the pair was replaced by a fresh agent, the two rushed to cache supplies for the coming winter.

A final pair of Tibetans, Team S, also reached Tingri during the second half of 1965. These two agents, Thad and Troy, had better rapport with the locals than did their peers in Team F. So good was their rapport, in fact, that a local sympathizer offered them shelter in his house until spring. It was with these two Tingri teams in place that the Special Center awaited its third season during the 1966 thaw.[24]

Although the Special Center's agent program had little to boast about, it looked positively dynamic compared with the paramilitary army festering in Mustang. A big part of Mustang's problem was that it was being managed from afar without any direct oversight. The Special Center had assumed handling of the program, but none of its officers had ever actually visited Mustang. The closest they got was when CIA representative Ken Knaus twice visited Pokhara in 1964 to meet Mustang officers. With no on-site presence, the agency and Intelligence Bureau had to rely on infrequent reporting by the Tibetan guerillas themselves. From what little was offered, it was readily apparent that the by-product from Mustang was practically nil.[25]

For the taciturn Mullik, disenchantment with Mustang was starting to run deep. By late 1964, he was alternating between extremes—first insisting that the guerrillas be given a major injection of airdropped supplies, later throwing up his arms and demanding that they all be brought down to India and merged with Establishment 22.

In January 1965, the pendulum swung back—with a twist. Now Mullik was proposing that Mustang be given two airdrops to equip its unarmed volunteers. These weapons would be given on the condition that the guerrillas shift inside Tibet to two operating locations. The first was astride the route between Kathmandu and Lhasa. The second was along the Chinese border road running west from Lhasa toward Xinjiang via the contested Ladakh region.

The choice of these two locations was understandable. In late 1961, the Chinese had offered to build for Nepal an all-weather road linking Kathmandu and the Nepalese border pass at Kodari, one of the few areas on the Tibet frontier not closed by winter snows. Work was continuing at a breakneck pace, with completion of the route expected by 1966. India, not surprisingly, was concerned about the road's military applications; by putting a concentration of guerrillas astride the approach from the Tibetan side, any PLA traffic could be halted. Similarly, a guerrilla pocket along the Xinjiang road would complicate Chinese efforts to reinforce Ladakh.[26]

As before, Mullik was reluctant to use the ARC to perform the supply drops. Knowing that the CIA would be equally reluctant to use its own assets—that would defeat one of the main reasons for creating the ARC in the first place—he offered two sweeteners. First, he promised that the U.S. aircraft could stage from Charbatia. Second, he would allow one ARC member to accompany the flights. This revised proposal went back to Washington and was put before the members of the 303 Committee (prior to June 1964, known as the Special Group); on 9 April, the committee lent its approval to the airdrop and Mustang redeployment scheme.

Mullik, it turned out, was a moving target. As soon as he was informed of Washington's consent, he reneged on the offer to allow an ARC crew member on the flights. The CIA fired back, insisting that the Indian member was a prerequisite for the missions to go ahead. To this, Mullik had a ready counteroffer: he would provide a cover story if the flight encountered problems.

As Mullik ducked and weaved, Ambassador Bowles urged the CIA to accept the proposal. Bowles was acutely aware that relations with New Delhi were already growing prickly on other fronts, and they were not helped when the unpredictable President Johnson unceremoniously canceled a summit that month with the Indian prime minister. Just as he would later support the stillborn C-130 deal, the ambassador felt that a compromise with Mullik was a way to keep at least intelligence cooperation on a solid footing. The CIA agreed; the flights would proceed on an all-American basis.

Now that the mission was moving forward, the agency had to decide on planes and crews. Looking over the alternatives, the CIA had only limited options. One logical source of airlift assets was Air Ventures, the Kathmandu-based company. Back in 1963, the CIA had helped establish the company; two of the airline's pilots were on loan from the agency, and its lone Twin Helio airframe had been obtained with agency approval. But once the airline began operations, the CIA station in Nepal kept its distance; Air Ventures worked almost exclusively for the U.S. Agency for International Development and the Peace Corps.[27] Moreover, the Mustang guerrillas were being handled by New Delhi; in the interest of compartmentalization, the CIA station in Kathmandu was kept wholly segregated from the operation.[28]

Another logical source of air support was the CIA's considerable airlift presence in Southeast Asia. Heading that effort was the proprietary Air America, as well as select private companies such as Bird & Son, with which the agency had special contracts. Both flew airdrops under trying conditions as a matter of course. But because CIA paramilitary operations in Laos and South Vietnam were escalating by the month, aircraft were stretched thin; the CIA managers in those theaters, as a result, tightly guarded their assets. There was also the untidy matter of the press getting whiffs of the CIA's air operations in Southeast Asia; should one of these planes be downed in Tibet, a viable cover story would be that much harder to concoct.

By process of elimination, the assignment was sent all the way to Japan. There the CIA operated planes under yet another of its air proprietaries, Southern Air Transport (SAT). Unlike Air America, which frequented jungle airstrips and braved antiaircraft fire over places like Laos, SAT flew regular routes into major international airports. Its cargo was sometimes classified, but its method of operation was overt and conventional.

In handing the task to SAT, there was some reinventing of the wheel. Four kickers were diverted from Laos and sent to Okinawa for a week of USAF instruction in high-altitude missions, including time in a pressure chamber, turns on a centrifuge, and classes on cold-weather survival. The rest of the crew came from the SAT roster in Japan; none, with the exception of the primary radio operator, had been on the earlier Tibet flights.

Taking a page from the past, SAT decided that the drop aircraft would come from its DC-6 fleet. This was the civilian version of the C-118 that had performed the Tibet missions in 1958; the only difference was a smaller cargo door in the rear. Because the smaller door meant that the supply bundles would also need to be smaller, mechanics fitted the DC-6 with a Y-shaped roller system to double the number of pallets loaded down the length of its cabin; after the first row of cargo was kicked out the door, pallets from the second row would be kicked. It was further decided to carry all the supplies aboard a single plane, rather than fly two missions as originally proposed by Mullik.

In another refrain from the previous decade, SAT made a perfunctory attempt at sterilizing its plane. External markings were painted over, but the numbers quickly bled through the thin coat. Inside the plane, most—but not all—references to SAT were removed. "The safety belts in the cockpit still had the letters 'SAT' stitched into the material," noted auxiliary radioman Henri Verbrugghen.[29]

Early on 15 May, the DC-6 departed Okinawa and made a refueling stop at Takhli. The CIA logisticians had packed the cabin to capacity, leaving little room for the kickers. Based on requirements generated by the Special Center, most of the bundles were filled with ammunition and pistols, plus a small number of M1 carbines and solar-powered radios. There was also a pair of inflatable rubber boats, to be used for crossing the wide Brahmaputra during summer. Because of the large amount of supplies involved, it was decided to make the drop inside Nepal and within a few kilometers of Tangya rather than at the more distant Tibetan drop zones used during the previous supply missions.

Once at Oak Tree, the plane was taken into an ARC hangar for servicing away from prying eyes. Wayne Sanford had arranged for the provision of fuel and support for the crew. He had also requested the Indians to temporarily suppress their radar coverage along the corridor into Nepal during the final leg of the flight.

For two days, the weather proved uncooperative. Not until the night of 17 May was the full moon unfettered by cloud cover. Not wasting the moment, the heavy DC-6 raced down the runway and lifted slowly into the northern sky.

At Tangya, Baba Yeshi had gathered his officers earlier in the week for a major speech. He was a master of delivery, his voice rising and falling with emotion as he told his men that the CIA had decided to "give them enough weapons for the next fifteen years." A massive airdrop was to take place in a valley just east of their position, he said, and each company would be responsible for lifting its share off the drop zone. Although Baba Yeshi had been informed of the quid pro quo conjured in New Delhi—weapons in exchange for a shift to positions astride the roads in Tibet—this was not mentioned in his speech.

Not surprisingly, pulses began to race as word of the impending drop flashed through the guerrilla ranks. With soaring expectations, the officers hurriedly left Tangya to assemble the necessary teams of yaks, men, and mules.[30]

As the DC-6 headed north at low altitude, Captain Eddie Sims sent regular signals back to Oak Tree. After each one, Charbatia sent a return message confirming that he should continue the mission. Sims, who was in charge of senior pilots among all the Far East proprietaries, was held in particularly high regard by the crew on this flight. This stemmed from his role in settling a salary dispute shortly before departing Japan. As a cost-cutting measure, SAT had deemed that none of the DC-6 crew members were eligible for the bonus money regularly paid to Air America crews during paramilitary missions. After several crewmen threatened to walk out, Sims successfully lobbied management to have the extra pay reinstated.

Crossing central Nepal, Sims took the plane up to 4,848 meters (16,000 feet). The rear door was then opened, allowing frigid air to whip through the cabin. Sucking from oxygen bottles, two of the kickers positioned themselves near the exit; the other two moved to the back of the first row of bundles.

Looking for one final contact with Oak Tree, Sims sent his coded signal. The radioman listened for the customary response, but none came. Again Sims sent the signal, but only static crackled over the set. After several minutes of agonizing, Sims elected to proceed without the last clearance.

Ahead, a blazing letter signal lit the drop zone in a small bowl-shaped valley. Dropping into a steep bank, the DC-6 came atop the signal and then pulled up sharply. In the rear, the four kickers worked furiously to get the loads out the small door. Only a fraction had been disgorged when they had to halt to allow Sims to make a sharp turn and realign. It would take yet another pass before the entire cabin was emptied.[31]

On the ground in Mustang, the guerrillas spent the next day collecting bundles scattered across the drop zone, in the next valley, and in the one after that. Several were never found, and rumor had it that the two rubber boats were recovered by local residents and taken to the crown prince at Lo Monthang.[32]

Even more harsh than the complaints over the wide disbursement was the disgruntlement over the content of the bundles. Taking Baba Yeshi at his word, those assembled at the drop zone had expected a lavish amount of weapons, enough to fight for fifteen years. Dozens of yaks and mules had been organized in what was envisioned to be a major logistical effort. "Just one plane came," lamented officer Gen Gyurme, "and it delivered mostly bullets and pistols."[33]

Disillusioned, the company commanders took their allotments back to their respective camps and returned to their earlier inactivity. Radio messages were placed to Baba Yeshi over the following months, calling on him to make the shift inside Tibet, but all were answered with delays and excuses. By the end of that calendar year, few cross-border forays of any note had been staged. As far as the U.S. and Indian representatives at the Special Center were concerned, Mustang was living on borrowed time.[35]

17. Revolution

The year had started on a most inauspicious note. On 10 January 1966, while in the Soviet city of Tashkent to negotiate an end to the Indo-Pakistan dispute in Kashmir, Indian Prime Minister Lal Bahadur Shastri suffered a fatal heart attack. As his body was flown home for cremation, party stalwarts in New Delhi looked to pick a second leader in as many years.

Their choice eventually fell on Nehru's daughter, Indira Gandhi. Then in her mid-forties, she had made few political ripples of her own. Looking somewhat awkward and shy in public, Mrs. Gandhi had been elevated to power precisely because party seniors thought her pliable.

President Johnson, for one, quickly found out otherwise. In March, Gandhi arrived in Washington on her first official foreign trip. Exuding both tact and charm, she earned Johnson's strong support for a major food aid package in exchange for market-oriented economic reforms.[1]

With the Washington summit a success surpassing all expectations, Indo-U.S. relations got back some of the luster lost during the previous year's Kashmir crisis. Sensing an opportunity, the CIA on 22 April asked the 303 Committee to approve a major $18 million Tibetan paramilitary package. Part of this was earmarked to maintain the Mustang force for a three-year term. The package also included two C-130 aircraft as ELINT platforms to augment the lone ARC C-46 flying in this role, as well as funding for a 5,000-man increase in Establishment 22.[2]

Most remarkable was the argument the CIA was using to justify its proposal. Moving beyond the lip service paid by Mullik in earlier years, the agency claimed that the Intelligence Bureau had drawn up plans in 1965 calling for the liberation of Tibet. Reading into this, the CIA suggested that India might be willing to commit Establishment 22 to a second front in the event circumstances in Vietnam sparked all-out hostilities between the United States and China.

In making a linkage between Tibet and Vietnam, the CIA was being politically astute. Rather than justifying the Tibetan operation solely on its own merits, the agency was now trying to loosely fix it to the coattails of Indochina policy—a topic that resonated at the top of the Johnson administration agenda.

All this smacked of geopolitical fantasy. If Mullik, just a few months earlier, had balked at making airdrops to Mustang, it was a good bet that New Delhi would not willingly invite Beijing's wrath by sponsoring a Tibet front if the United States and China went to war over Vietnam. Even Ambassador Bowles, an ardent proponent of intelligence cooperation, quickly backpedaled on the Vietnam link. There was a "strong possibility" that India would be willing to commit its guerrilla forces against Tibet, he wrote in a secret cable on 28 April, but only if Nepal, Bhutan, Sikkim, or maybe Burma were attacked by China.[3]

There was another problem with the CIA's April proposal. With few exceptions, the projects it sought to maintain had been proved ineffectual. Confirming as much was Bruce Walker, the former Camp Hale officer who had arrived that spring to replace John Gilhooley as the new CIA representative at the Special Center. In many respects, Walker was presiding over a funeral. Making a token appearance at Hauz Khas once a week, he had few remaining agents to oversee. "The radio teams were experiencing major resistance from the population inside Tibet," he recalls. "We were being pushed back to the border."[4]

A good case in point was Team S. Agents Thad and Troy had started out well, identifying a sympathetic Tingri farmer and bivouacking at his house since the onset of snow the previous winter. Thad had gotten particularly close to his host's daughter; by early spring, her abdomen was starting to show the swell of pregnancy. This sparked rumors among suspicious neighbors, who reported the case to district officials.

Alerted to the possible presence of an outsider, a Tibetan bureaucrat arrived that May to investigate. Quizzed about his daughter's mysterious suitor, the farmer folded. He brought Thad out from hiding, and they took the bureaucrat into their confidence and begged him to keep the matter a secret. Feigning compliance, the official bade them farewell—only to return that same night with a PLA squad. Thad was captured immediately; Troy, concealed in a haystack, surrendered after being prodded with a bayonet.

Giving the PLA the slip, the farmer managed to flee into the hills. Nearby was a cave inhabited by Team S1, which also consisted of two agents who had spent the winter near Tingri. Linking up, the three attempted to run south toward the Sikkimese border. Just short of the frontier, the trio encountered a PLA patrol and was felled in a hail of bullets.

That left just one pair of agents still inside their homeland. Team F, consisting of Taylor and Jerome, had occupied yet another Tingri cave since the previous year. Even though they kept contact with the locals to a minimum, word of suspicious movement in the hills eventually came to the attention of the Chinese. On 2 November 1966, the PLA moved in for an arrest. The Tibetans held them at bay with their pistols until they ran out of ammunition; both were subsequently captured and placed in a Lhasa prison.

As Team F's radio fell silent, the Special Center was at an impasse. After three seasons, the folly of attempting to infiltrate "black" radio teams (that is, teams without proper documentation or preparation to blend into the community) was evident. Earlier in the year, this growing realization had prompted the center to briefly flirt with a new kind of mission. Four agents were brought to the Indian capital from Joelikote and given instruction in the latest eavesdropping devices, with the intention of forming a special wiretap team. For practice, they climbed telephone poles around the Delhi cantonment area by night.[5]

In the end, the wiretap agents never saw service. In late November, the Special Center put team infiltrations into Tibet on hold. Aside from a handful of Hale-trained Tibetans used for translation tasks at Oak Tree, as well as the radio teams already inside Nepal, Joelikote was closed, and the remaining agents reverted back to refugee status. "I was saddened and embarrassed," said Indian representative Rabi, "to have been party to those young men getting killed."

The Special Center had also reached an impasse with its other main concern, the paramilitary force at Mustang. Despite the May 1965 arms drop, Baba Yeshi and his men had resisted all calls to relocate inside Tibet. Though frustrated, the CIA had continued financing the guerrillas for the remainder of that year. This funding flowed along a simple but effective underground railroad. Every month, a satchel of Indian rupees would be handed over by the agency representative at Hauz Khas. From there, two Tibetans and two Indian escorts would take the money to the Nepal frontier near Bhadwar. Meeting them were a pair of well-paid cyclo drivers also on the agency's payroll. They hid the cash under false seats and pedaled across the border, where they handed the money over to members of the Mustang force. The money would then go to Pokhara, where foodstuffs and textiles were purchased at the local market and shipped to the guerrillas via mule caravans.

By the time of the 303 Committee's April 1966 meeting, the CIA was still prepared to continue such funding for another three years. In addition, the agency had not ruled out more arms drops in the future. The catch: Baba Yeshi had one final chance to move his men inside Tibet.

Perhaps sensing that his financiers had run out of patience, the Mustang chieftain was jarred from complacency. Employing vintage theatrics, he gathered his headquarters staff in late spring and announced that he would personally lead a 400-man foray against the PLA. "We begged him not to do anything rash," said training officer Gen Gyurme. "Tears were flowing as he began his march out of Kaisang."[6]

Traveling north to Tangya, the chieftain and thirty of his loyalists canvassed the nearby guerrilla camps for more participants. Another thirty signed on, including one company commander. Though far short of the promised 400, sixty armed Tibetans on horseback cut an impressive sight as they steered their mounts toward the border. Once the posse reached the frontier, however, the operation began to fall apart. A fifteen-man reconnaissance party was sent forward to locate a suitable ambush site, and the rest of the guerrillas argued for two days over whether Baba Yeshi should actually lead the raid across the border. After his men pleaded with him to reconsider, the chieftain finally relented in a flourish. Armed with information from the reconnaissance team, thirty-five Tibetans eventually remounted and galloped into Tibet.

What ensued was a defining moment for the guerrilla force. Apparently alerted to the upcoming foray through their informant network, Chinese soldiers were waiting in ambush. Pinned in a valley, six Tibetans were shot dead, including the company commander. In addition, eight horses were killed and seven rifles lost. In its six years of existence, this was the greatest number of casualties suffered by the project.[7]

As word of the failed foray filtered back to New Delhi, the Special Center finally acknowledged the limitations of Mustang. On the pretext of not provoking a PLA cross-border strike into Nepal, the guerrillas were "enjoined from offensive action which might invite Chinese retaliation." Any activity in their homeland, they were told, would be limited to passive intelligence collection. The guerrilla leadership, never really enthusiastic about conducting aggressive raids, offered no resistance to their restricted mandate.[8]

By process of elimination, the only remaining Tibetan program with a modicum of promise was Establishment 22. Not only did this project have India's strong support, but it was the linchpin in the CIA's April pitch to the 303 Committee about a second front against China.[9] Even before the committee had time to respond, the agency was bringing in a new team of advisers to boost its level of assistance to Chakrata. Replacing Wayne Sanford in the U.S. embassy was Woodson "Woody" Johnson, a Colorado native who had served in a variety of intelligence and paramilitary assignments since joining the CIA in 1951. Working up-country alongside Establishment 22 was Zeke Zilaitis, the former Hale trainer with a taste for rockets, and Ken Seifarth, the airborne specialist on his encore tour with Brigadier Uban's guerrillas.[10]

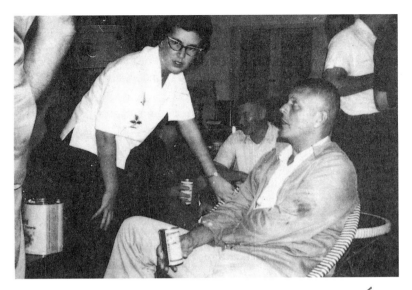

Tucker Gougelmann, the CIA's senior paramilitary adviser in India

Boosting its representation a step further, the CIA that summer introduced forty-nine-year-old Tucker Gougelmann as the senior adviser for all paramilitary projects in India. A Columbia graduate, Gougelmann had gone from college to the Marine Corps back in 1940. A major by the summer of 1943, he was serving as intelligence officer for the marine airborne regiment before being seconded to a raider battalion during an amphibious landing at Vangunu Island in the Pacific. That transfer nearly sealed Gougelmann's fate. Just one day after landing, a sniper's bullet struck his upper left leg from the rear, ripping through nerve and bone. The wound was gangrenous by the time he was evacuated to a field clinic. Arriving in San Diego during late August, he was in and out of hospitals for the next three years.[11]

By June 1946, the doctors had done all they could for Gougelmann's stricken limb. He retired from the marines that month with a permanent limp and a new wife from a moneyed family in Oakland. Her father, owner of a racetrack and a fruit-canning company, wanted his son-in-law to inherit part of the business. Gougelmann, however, had his heart set on overseas travel. Leaving his spouse behind, he joined the foreign relief organization CARE (Cooperative for American Remittances to Europe) as its Romanian representative. He would spend the next seventeen months in that country, the last being detained by Romania's newly empowered communist authorities.[12]

Released from jail after an international outcry, Gougelmann returned home to find that his wife had had their marriage annulled in his absence. Repeating the same formula, he married again—this time a New York girl—before leaving her behind to work for an aid organization in China. Again he was chased out by advancing communists, and he came home to a second divorce.

Given his passion for foreign adventure, Gougelmann joined the CIA in the fall of 1950. His first assignment was somewhat cloistered. Posted to a safe house on the outskirts of Munich, he served as an administrator for James Critchfield, then a case officer handling ex-Nazi spymaster Gehlen. "Tucker came with two pairs of highly polished paratrooper boots in a footlocker," recalled Critchfield, "and little else."[13]

Though competent in the office, Gougelmann longed for the field. He transferred to Korea in the midst of the conflict on that peninsula and served as a maritime case officer and later as chief of operations at a training base that turned out road-watching teams. "His leg did not stop him," said fellow adviser Don Stephens. "He was still able to climb the rugged mountains with his students."[14]

After returning from Korea with a refugee as his adopted daughter, Gougelmann served a stint as instructor at Camp Peary. Not until the summer of 1959 was he again overseas, this time posted as chief of station in Afghanistan. The assignment hardly suited the gruff former major. Arriving with his infamous footlocker and ready to do battle, he was instead channeled toward the cocktail circuit to keep tabs on the Soviets in a more classic espionage duel. "Tucker was devoid of any social graces," said fellow Afghan officer Alan Wolfe, "and ill at ease in such diplomatic settings."[15]

By the time his Kabul tour finished in the summer of 1962, Gougelmann was yearning for a return to paramilitary action. The Vietnam conflict was fast escalating at that time, and a choice slot had opened up in the coastal city of Da Nang. To put pressure on the communist government in Hanoi, the CIA was mandated to begin a maritime raiding campaign using an exotic mix of Swift boats, Norwegian mercenary skippers, and Vietnamese frogmen. For the next three years, Gougelmann led this effort, often with more flair than success.[16]

Gougelmann remained in Vietnam for another year, and it was then that he made his mark. While advising the South Vietnamese Special Branch—a police-cum-intelligence organization focused on the communist infrastructure—he organized a string of provincial interrogation centers. Despite his unpolished demeanor and proclivity for salty language, Gougelmann displayed a sharp, calculating mind in this role. "He could walk to an empty blackboard," said one fellow officer, "and start diagramming the local communist party . . . from memory."[17]

By the time Gougelmann got his India assignment in mid-1966, he had a full plate. Part of his time was devoted to managing the mountaineering expeditions aimed at placing a nuclear-powered sensor atop the Nanda Devi summit.[18] Even more of Gougelmann's time was spent arranging assistance for the guerrillas at Chakrata. The Indians were eager to double the number of Tibetans at Establishment 22 and were even calling for the recruitment of Gurkhas into the unit. Reflecting bureaucratic creep, Director General of Security Mullik had come up with a new, more formal name for the outfit—the Special Frontier Force, or SFF—and had given Uban an office in New Delhi.

The SFF had matured considerably since its humble start. One hundred twenty-two guerrillas made up each of its companies, with five or six companies grouped into battalions commanded by Tibetan political leaders.

Though expanding the size of the SFF would be easy in one sense—with thousands of idle refugees eager for meaningful employment—there were problems. Most of the training was being handled by Uban's seasoned cadre; aside from perfunctory oversight provided by Seifarth and Zilaitis, the CIA was relegated to funding and bringing in the occasional instructor from Camp Peary for brief specialist courses. One such instructor, Henry "Hank" Booth, was dispatched in 1967 to offer a class in sniping. The six-week program went well, with the Tibetans proving themselves able shots with the 1903 Springfield rifle. For graduation, Uban held a small ceremony, during which Booth awarded his students a copy of the 1944 U.S. Army field manual for snipers.

What came next was a telling indictment of the relationship between the Tibetans and their Indian hosts. Late that same evening, a fellow CIA officer took Booth to a hill overlooking the SFF cantonment. Below were lights burning bright at five separate camps. The Tibetans were in the process of translating the field manual into Tibetan, with each camp doing a section of the manual. Multiple copies were being made—including hand-drawn reproductions of the diagrams—and exchanged by runners. By sunrise, as Booth departed for New Delhi, each unit had a complete copy of the book, and the Indians moved in to confiscate the manual.[19]

Not helping the relationship between the Indians and the Tibetans was the decision to add Gurkhas to their ranks. The Indians saw this as a means of expanding the mandate and abilities of the force beyond things Tibetan. The Tibetans, however, bristled at the ethnic dilution of their unit. Brigadier Uban

Hank Booth with the top SFF marksmen at his sniper course, December 1967.
Standing at center is Jamba Kalden, the SFF's senior political leader.

recognized the delicacy of juggling two different cultures. "The Tibetans were more ferocious," he reflected, "but the Gurkhas were more disciplined."[20]

Wayne Sanford, who had returned to India for another CIA tour in New Delhi, was less generous in his assessment of the Gurkhas. "We would kill off their leaders during training exercises," he said. "The Tibetans were natural fighters and would move the next best guy into the leader's slot and keep on operating; the Gurkhas were clueless without leadership."[21]

To keep peace within the force, a cap was set at no more than 700 Gurkhas. In addition, the two ethnicities would not be mixed; the Gurkhas would be segregated into their own "G Group" at Chakrata. Though given the same paramilitary training as in the previous SFF cycles, G Group was relegated primarily to base security and administration.[22]

The Tibetan majority, meanwhile, was being rotated along the Ladakh and NEFA border in company-size elements. Several ARC air bases were established specifically to support these SFF operations. In the northeast, the ARC staged from a primitive airstrip at Doomdoomah in Assam. For northwestern operations and airborne training, it used a larger air base built at Sarsawa, 132 kilometers south of Chakrata.[23]

To feed the remote SFF outposts along the border, the CIA had enlisted the Kellogg Company to help develop a special *tsampa* loaded with vitamins and other nutrients. Not only did this appeal to Tibetan tastes, but it allowed for healthy daily rations to be concentrated in small packages that could be airdropped from ARC planes.[24]

Not all the SFF missions were within India's frontier. Back in 1964, an Establishment 22 team had staged a brief but deadly foray from Nepal toward Tingri. In 1966, the force inherited the wiretap mandate originally conjured for the special team selected from Joelikote. There was good reason to target China's phones. Nearly all the communications between China and Tibet used overground lines supported by concrete or improvised wooden poles. The CIA, moreover, had already started a successful wiretap program in southern China using agent teams staging from Laos.

Placing the taps posed serious challenges. The lines paralleled the roads built across Tibet, most of which were a fair hike from the border. Once a tap was placed at the top of a pole, a wire needed to run to a concealed cassette recorder. Because the recording time on each cassette was limited, an agent had to remain nearby to change tapes and then bring them back to India for CIA analysis.

The SFF proved up to the task. In a project code-named GEMINI, it began infiltrating from NEFA with recording gear during mid-1966. To supply the guerrillas while they filled the tapes, an ARC C-46 was dispatched to an airfield near Siliguri. Taking off during predawn hours, the plane would overfly the Sikkimese corridor and be at the team's position by daybreak. Flying with the rear door open, the kickers briefly took leave of their oxygen bottles and shawls to push the cargo into the slipstream. On the way home, they would hang a bag of soft drinks out the door in order to have chilled refreshments by the time they returned to base.[25]

The results of GEMINI were mixed. Although the SFF guerrillas were able to exfiltrate without loss of life, the project was put on hold near year's end after a Calcutta newspaper reported the mysterious flights over Sikkim. "We got miles of tapes," recalled New Delhi officer Angus Thuermer, "but much of it was useless, like Chinese talking about their families back home." Deputy chief of station Bill Grimsley was more upbeat in his assessment: "One never knows where the intelligence will lead in these matters."[26]

The 303 Committee apparently agreed. On 25 November, after repeated failed attempts during the first three quarters of the year, the CIA put a small portion of its $18 million Tibet package before the committee for endorsement. It totaled just $650,000, most of it going to pay for Mustang. This time, the policy makers offered their approval for the paramilitary program to proceed.

The Chinese, however, were not taking notice. In mid-1966, Beijing had reached a turning point. Its Great Leap campaign toward rapid industrialization and full-scale communism, launched by Chairman Mao with much fanfare late the previous decade, had been such a failure that its third Five-Year Plan had to be delayed three years. The country had also suffered a series of foreign policy setbacks, including the annihilation of the Communist Party in Indonesia—which included some of China's closest political allies in Asia—following an abortive September 1965 coup. And with Mao both aging and ailing, there were questions about who would succeed him.

Reacting against all this, Mao formally proclaimed a Great Proletarian Cultural Revolution in August 1966. In what was part ideological purge, part power struggle, part policy dispute, Mao steered the nation toward a destructive campaign of sophomoric Marxism and paranoid suspicion, ostensibly to "cleanse its rotten core." Leading the charge was disaffected youth gathered into a mass organization dubbed the Red Guard. These teenagers joined with the army and attacked allegedly anti-Mao elements in the Communist Party, then hit the party machine as a whole.

Three months before the Cultural Revolution was proclaimed, Red Guards had already started arriving in Lhasa from Beijing. As the revolution's goal was to wipe out divergent habits and cultures in order to make all of Chinese society conform to a communist ideal, minorities were a prime target. Tibetans, predictably, suffered tremendously. Thousands were jailed by marauding Red Guard gangs. Monasteries were emptied, monks publicly humiliated, scriptures burned, and priceless art treasures destroyed.

Belatedly realizing that he had lost control, Mao in January 1967 attempted to soften his rhetoric and asked the military to intervene. This had little effect in Tibet, where the empowered Red Guard took on the army in street battles across Lhasa through the spring and summer.

As China descended into this orgy of violence, India watched with understandable concern. With nobody in clear control of Beijing (Mao was prone to prolonged absences from the capital, apparently for fear of his life), the Chinese were more dangerous neighbors than ever. Making matters worse, they had successfully tested a nuclear-tipped medium-range ballistic missile in October 1966.

In years past, such conditions might have made India's covert Tibetan assets appear all the more relevant as both a border force and a potential tool to exploit China's turmoil. By the spring of 1967, however, New Delhi had irreversibly soured toward most of its joint paramilitary projects. After all, the black radio teams inside Tibet had already been canceled, and the Mustang force hardly inspired confidence.

The Indians were also nervous about media revelations concerning the CIA. In March 1967, *Ramparts*, a liberal U.S. magazine critical of the government, published an exposé on covert CIA support for various private organizations, including the Asia Foundation (originally known as the Committee for a Free Asia). Because numerous U.S. educational and voluntary groups were active in India, this sparked an anti-CIA furor in the Indian parliament.[27]

Never openly embraced, the CIA now had few advocates on the subcontinent. Mullik, who had chaperoned the Tibet projects since the beginning of Indian involvement, had already given up his seat as director general of security in mid-1966. His replacement, Balbir Singh, had an independent and forceful personality but only limited clout with the prime minister. For her part, Mrs. Gandhi showed little appreciation for the agency or its assistance. "We became a tolerated annoyance," summed up Woody Johnson.[28]

If any tears were being shed at the CIA, they were of the crocodile variety. Back in June 1966, the director's slot had been filled by Richard Helms. Coming to the office with extensive experience managing clandestine intelligence collection, Helms was known to be highly skeptical of covert action like that attempted in Tibet. However, he was being counseled otherwise by Des FitzGerald, his deputy for operations and longtime proponent of activism in Tibet. Unfortunately, FitzGerald dropped dead while playing tennis in July 1967. "When Des died," said Near East chief James Critchfield, "the 'oomph' for the program quickly dissipated."[29]

Even before FitzGerald's death, the agency had taken measured steps to disengage itself from Tibet. In the wake of the March *Ramparts* revelations, President Johnson had approved a special committee headed by Undersecretary of State Nicholas Katzenbach to study U.S. relationships with private organizations. Katzenbach's findings, released later that month, recommended against covert assistance to any American educational or private voluntary organization.[30]

Following this finding, the CIA terminated funding for the third cycle of eight Tibetans undergoing training at Cornell University. They were repatriated to

Dharamsala in July, and no further students were accepted. Though the agency contemplated a continuation of the program on a smaller scale at a foreign university, this never came to fruition.[31]

Other changes came in rapid succession. In Washington, the Tibet desk, which had been under the Far East Division's China Branch ever since its establishment in 1956, was transferred to the Near East Division. John Rickard, one of four brothers born to missionary parents in Burma (three of whom went to work for the CIA), headed the desk during this period and changed his divisional affiliation to reflect the shift. More than just semantics, the change underscored the fact that the remaining Tibetan paramilitary assets, with rare exception, would probably not be leaving Indian soil. Apart from a single representative at the Special Center, the Far East Division had been completely excised from the Tibet program.[32]

The CIA also reduced its links to the ARC. Although attrition was starting to take a toll on the planes delivered during 1963 and 1964—the latest casualty, a Twin Helio, crashed in 1967—no replacements were budgeted. More telling, after the CIA removed the C-130 from the limited proposal passed by the 303 Committee the previous November, the Indians opted in 1967 to add the Soviet An-12 transport as the new centerpiece for its ARC fleet.[33]

For the Tibetans, the biggest blow took place in the spring of 1967. Ever since arriving on Indian soil, the CIA had secretly channeled a stipend to the Dalai Lama and his entourage. Totaling $180,000 per fiscal year, the money was appreciated but not critical. Most of it was collected in the Charitable Trust of His Holiness the Dalai Lama, which in turn was used for investments, donations, and relief work. To their credit, the Tibetans had worked hard to wean themselves off such handouts. "Financially underpinning the Dalai Lama's refugee programs was no longer warranted," said Grimsley.[34]

Gyalo did not see it that way. Sullen, he made the assumption that all money would soon be drying up. He was not wrong.

18. Civil War

Signs of dissent against Baba Yeshi were not new. Trouble dated back to 1962, when the Mustang chieftain reduced food stipends issued directly to individual guerrillas. He then turned a blind eye to—even condoned—the rustling of yaks and goats on the Tibetan side of the frontier as a ready, and free, source of protein. This rubbed many of the Hale-trained cadre wrong, who claimed that their commander was still charging the CIA for the meat and pocketing the difference.[1]

During 1967, with the guerrillas sulking and spent, their demand for an audit of Baba Yeshi's finances grew more shrill. Leading the call were six idealistic Hale graduates, including Rara, who had commanded the 1961 jeep ambush. All six later trekked to Darjeeling, where they made their demands known to Gyalo's longtime assistant, Lhamo Tsering.

When word of the complaints got back to Mustang, Baba Yeshi was, predictably, less than receptive. With little appreciation for standardized accounting procedures, he had few recorded finances to audit. Even if he did have books to open, his assumed prerogative as a Khampa chieftain left him with a perceived sense of immunity toward questioning by subordinates.

In years past, Baba Yeshi's aloof stance would have carried the day. But following the end of the Dalai Lama's stipend and the curtailing of offensive action from Mustang, Gyalo and Lhamo Tsering feared that an open scandal in Nepal would provide a ready excuse for the CIA to target funding. Scrambling for a face-saving solution that would ease tensions at Mustang, they determined that Baba Yeshi should get a competent, respected, and untainted assistant. The trouble was, there were few Tibetans who fit that bill. Many of the proven warriors from the NVDA generation were past their prime. And although there were plenty of younger candidates, they had yet to amass the seniority and respect to lead effectively.

One exception was Wangdu, the feisty Khampa trained on Saipan in 1957. After fleeing Tibet for India in January 1959, he had turned his back on the resistance. Bitter, he had refused an earlier offer to join Establishment 22; instead, he had closed himself off at Dajreeling and frittered away the years reading and studying English. "I would stop to meet him whenever I went to Darjeeling," recalled Gyalo. "He still talked with disgust about the small amount of U.S. assistance."[2]

Despite such negativity, Wangdu had all the right attributes to serve as Baba Yeshi's understudy. Still physically fit at thirty-eight years old, he evoked memories of his charismatic call to arms in Kham. In a society where tribal lineage counts for much, he could draw on the respect accorded to his uncle, the late Gompo Tashi. He was relatively educated and, though somewhat of a womanizer, had officially remained a monk and had no dependents.

In early 1968, Gyalo called Wangdu down from Darjeeling to his New Delhi house. It took repeated appeals, but the Khampa finally relented. After nearly a decade, he would be rejoining the cause.

Baba Yeshi took the arrival of his uninvited deputy relatively well. "Gyalo sent a message emphasizing that Wangdu was there to help and assist," said Kay-Kay, the senior Tibetan representative at the Special Center, "not to replace."[3] Although no warm welcome was offered, neither was there any animosity.

A division of responsibility between the two came easily. With Baba Yeshi spending much of his time at Kaisang—usually absorbed in prayer—Wangdu headed for Tangya. Low-level intelligence was still being collected by the network of radio agents posted to frontier outposts at Dolpo, Limi, Nashang, and Tsum, so Wangdu had the rest of the guerrillas focus on training for the remainder of the year. Some improvements were soon evident. Besides arranging for the delivery of extra uniforms and shoes, Wangdu increased monthly food allowances from 30 to 150 Indian rupees; rustling was no longer permitted.[4]

At the beginning of 1969, Lhamo Tsering decided to inspect the guerrillas himself. His findings were heartening. After working together for a year, Baba Yeshi and Wangdu were apparently getting along and in good spirits. Though Wangdu expressed some reservations in private, the threat of a schism within the ranks appeared slim.

Very quickly, the atmosphere soured. The precipitating factor: To commemorate the tenth anniversary of the insurrection in Lhasa, a series of events was being planned for Dharamsala in March. Baba Yeshi was invited to attend the Dharamsala memorial services after a stop in New Delhi. Wangdu would be taking his annual home leave at the same time, with Lhamo Tsering left in temporary command.[5]

Baba Yeshi smelled a putsch in the making but could hardly turn down the invitation from the highest quarters of the Tibetan government in exile. When he arrived in the Indian capital, his fears were confirmed. He was greeted with the news that he would be receiving a permanent transfer to Dharamsala. Wangdu, his deputy, would be in charge of the Nepal project. This was hardly a slap in the face: Baba Yeshi was fifty-one years old and had spent eight years in the often inhospitable climes of Mustang; the relative luxuries in Dharamsala

Mustang officers (left to right) Gen Dawa, Gen Gyurme, Rara, unknown, 1968.
(Courtesy Lhamo Tsering)

could be considered a reward for good service. As a further sweetener, he would be assuming the prestigious post of deputy to the security minister in the Dalai Lama's own cabinet.

Baba Yeshi wanted none of it. Resistant to the transfer after almost a month of negotiations in New Delhi, he retired to the quarters of Tashi Choedak, the former Hale interpreter now serving as the deputy Tibetan representative at the Special Center. "I came home to find his rosary and tea cup," said Tashi, "but Baba Yeshi was gone."[6]

A week later, the irate chieftain was spotted in Darjeeling. A few weeks after that, Lhamo Tsering woke to find him at Kaisang. The situation quickly teetered on the edge of confrontation. Baba Yeshi, supported by loyalists among the headquarters staff, demanded his right to properly turn over command to Wangdu before returning to India. As a compromise, Lhamo Tsering gave him two weeks to sort out his affairs.

After the allotted time, the chieftain departed Kaisang with two dozen bodyguards. But instead of going to his promised seat in Dharamsala, he got as far

Lhamo Tsering (center) at Mustang, 1968. (Courtesy Lhamo Tsering)

as Pokhara and stopped. In letters smuggled back to Mustang, he implored his men to rally to his side. A civil war was about to begin.

At the same time trouble was brewing in Mustang, Indo-U.S. intelligence cooperation experienced major changes in structure and personalities. In June 1968, David Blee departed as the New Delhi station chief after more than six years in the post. Replacing him the following month was John Waller, the former deputy station chief in India between 1955 and 1957. A consummate blend of scholar and spy, Waller had spent the intervening years pursuing his passion for Tibetan history. In 1967, he had published an authoritative book on Sino-Indian relations, much of it devoted to Tibetan issues. That same year, he had written an article for *Foreign Service Journal* about U.S. diplomacy and the thirteenth Dalai Lama. He had also completed a draft of a book about exploration in Tibet.[7]

Once in New Delhi, Waller had little time to pursue his glorified research hobby. Within two months after his arrival, he was confronted with a new counterpart organization. Intentionally patterned after the CIA, the Research and Analysis Wing (RAW) was officially unveiled on 2 September. Both the foreign intelligence desk of the Intelligence Bureau (now downgraded to domestic activities) and the paramilitary projects of the director general of security would fall under RAW's control.[8]

Selected as the first RAW director was R. N. Kao. Previously head of the ARC, the debonair Kao had a long history of close cooperation with U.S. officials. Despite this warm past, Kao was faced with Indo-U.S. relations that were again on a downward spiral. In November, Richard Nixon won the U.S. presidential election. Like his predecessor Johnson, Nixon was fixated on bringing the unpopular war in Vietnam to an end. Not only was South Asia far from Nixon's mind, but many Indians recalled his pronounced slant toward Pakistan when he was Eisenhower's vice president.

Mrs. Gandhi was showing a tilt of her own. Backed into a political corner by

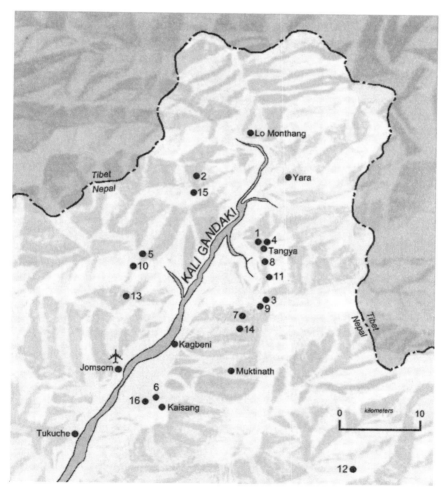

The location of the sixteen guerrilla companies in Mustang, circa 1968

Mustang guerrillas practice with a recoilless rifle, circa 1968. (Courtesy Lhamo Tsering)

1969, she shrewdly began courting the populist left at home and the Soviet Union abroad. This, combined with the perceived hostility from Nixon, led to outward relations between New Delhi and Washington sinking to their lowest depth in over a decade.

Behind the scenes, intelligence cooperation toward Tibet remained only a shadow of its former self. Arriving in June 1968 as the new CIA representative at the Special Center was John Bellingham. Much like Bruce Walker had presided over a funeral, Bellingham was there for the same extended wake. He arrived at the center each Friday afternoon, but there was little for him to do aside from delivering the monthly payments for Mustang.

On two occasions during Bellingham's watch, the Special Center looked to break from its freefall. The first concerned a program to infiltrate singleton resident agents into Tibet. This had been proposed back in 1967 as the long-range replacement for the canceled radio teams. There was a significant difference between the two: the teams had gone in black; the resident singletons, by contrast, would merge directly into society.

The two programs required different kinds of people. The teams had been composed of men versed in paramilitary skills and expected to live in concealment under rugged conditions. Singletons required the intelligence and wit to operate as classic spies. Doing so was complicated by the Cultural Revolution; deep paranoia and suspicion had taken root across Tibetan society.

Although finding a suitable singleton candidate would be difficult, one possibility had been identified back in 1967. That year, an uninvited visitor in his early thirties had arrived at Mustang. Amdo Tsering claimed to be a Muslim from the Amdo city of Sining. He had fled his hometown and supposedly escaped to Nepal via an extended trek through Xinjiang and western Tibet.

Incredulous, Baba Yeshi's men sized up the interloper. Because he looked Chinese and spoke some Xinjiang dialects, they began to suspect that he was a plant dangled by Beijing. Gearing up for a rather unpleasant interrogation, they suddenly found themselves on the receiving end of a verbal flogging from the spirited Amdowa. Uncertain what to do, Mustang flashed a message down to the Special Center. Equally uncertain, the center sent back orders for Amdo Tsering to be escorted to New Delhi. There he languished for over a year; not until the spring of 1969 was it decided to use him as the first in the proposed resident singleton program.

Code-named "Red Stone," Amdo Tsering was given extensive training in secret writing techniques. The CIA also forged a set of Chinese travel documents showing that he worked in westernmost Tibet but was going to Xinjiang on holiday. Once in Xinjiang, he was to head for Lop Nur and attempt to collect dirt samples. Lop Nur was the location of China's primary nuclear testing facility, and the dirt would be analyzed to determine levels of radioactivity.

Mustang guerrillas in training, circa 1968.

In September 1969, Red Stone took a train to Siliguri. Escorting him was Tashi Choedak and the senior Indian representative at the Special Center. Heading north through Sikkim, they came to the Tibetan frontier and watched Red Stone gallop across the border. The two Special Center representatives returned to New Delhi to await news of his progress. They did not have to wait long. After just a couple of days, they received word that a nervous Red Stone had attracted attention and been arrested before boarding a bus at Shigatse, the town midway between Tingri and Lhasa. The singleton program subsequently went into remission.

The second project initiated by the Special Center was the activation of special refugee debriefing teams. For years, the radio agents posted along the Nepalese frontier had been collecting low-level intelligence from pilgrims and traders. Building on this theme, in late 1968 the center dispatched a five-man team to Kathmandu to debrief cross-border travelers. The Nepalese capital was a fertile recruiting ground for several reasons. First, Nepal was the only nation still allowed to maintain a trade mission and consulate general in Lhasa. Second, there was a substantial community of ethnic Tibetans who had opted for Nepalese citizenship after 1959, and China had decreed that these Nepalese passport holders were allowed to visit their families or conduct business in Tibet once a year.[9]

In locating sources, the Kathmandu debriefing team had competition from an unlikely source: the Republic of China on Taiwan. Until that time, Taipei had never had much success recruiting a network of Tibetan supporters, mainly because the Kuomintang firmly agreed with the PRC about China's right to rule Lhasa. Efforts to sign up agents from Kalimpong late the previous decade had fallen flat. So, too, had a brief attempt to fund intelligence-gathering forays by Nepal-based Tibetans beginning in 1962.[10]

In 1968, Taipei tried again. This time, it was looking to exploit the chaos of the Cultural Revolution. There were also indications in February that the ROC leadership might be prepared to endorse Lhasa's independence, a shift that would have made its support more palatable to Tibetan patriots.[11]

Late that year, Taipei dispatched a pair of Hiu Muslim recruiters to Kathmandu in its latest bid to seek Tibetan sources. The recruiters, both former residents of Kalimpong, dangled financial incentives and the chance for scholarships on Taiwan. The Special Center's team, meanwhile, sought volunteers through nationalistic appeals. "We only had a little money to cover operational expenses," said team leader Arnold, a former Hale translator and Cornell graduate, "so we looked for good Buddhists who respected the Dalai Lama."[12]

By 1969, Arnold and his men were claiming some success. Despite numerous attempts, they were never able to recruit a Tibetan staff member working at the Nepalese consulate in Lhasa. They were, however, able to network among dozens of Nepalese passport holders returning from their annual leave in Tibet. The team debriefed the travelers in Kathmandu and dispatched frequent reports to the Special Center via the mail or messengers.[13]

Although the information from the Kathmandu team was welcome, John Bellingham's main focus was on managing the denouement of Mustang. Earlier in 1969, the Indians had made it apparent that their contingency plans no longer involved any participation by Tibetan guerrillas in Nepal. The CIA was of a similar mindset. When it came time for the 303 Committee to review Tibet operations on 30 September, it endorsed a provision to scale back Mustang to a token force.

The Tibetans learned of this pivotal decision indirectly. In early October, Bellingham arrived at the Special Center with the monthly funds for Nepal. As was customary, Kay-Kay and Tashi Choedak came to witness the transfer. Turning to the Indians as he left, the CIA representative offered a comment in passing: "I guess this is one of the last."

Kay-Kay froze. "It was my darkest moment," he later said. No matter how poorly it had fared in the field, the Tibetan leadership had looked on Mustang as the symbolic paramilitary arm of its government in exile.[14]

A Royal Nepal Airlines flight took Kay-Kay and two junior officers from the Special Center to Pokhara, where they mounted horses and went to bring the news directly to the guerrilla leadership. They arrived at Kaisang in driving rains and found Wangdu in his office. After explaining the decision, Kay-Kay paused for comments, but Wangdu offered only a silent gaze.

Reduced funding was only part of Mustang's troubles. After spending the summer and fall stewing at Pokhara, Baba Yeshi had enticed a company of loyalists to move east to Nashang. Tempers were starting to flare between the two factions, leading to the death of two Baba Yeshi followers and five horses. Vowing to expel dissidents, Wangdu placed Baba Yeshi's sympathetic assistant, a hulking Andowa and Hale graduate named Abe, in detention. Abe, in turn, got possession of a razor and committed suicide by slicing open the vein in his neck. Incensed, Baba Yeshi retreated to a house in Kathmandu and began plotting his revenge.

In 1970, Lhamo Tsering returned to New Delhi after his prolonged deployment to Nepal. Waiting for him at the Special Center was John Bellingham, who was anxious to finalize a formal demobilization plan for Mustang. Until that point, the CIA was still funding 2,100 guerrillas at a cost of $500,000 a year. Pressed for time, Lhamo Tsering outlined a schedule whereby the force would be cut by a third over each of the next three calendar years. Without delay, Bellingham approved the scheme.[15]

Part of the demobilization plan involved a rehabilitation program for the guerrillas, to ensure that they would be able to support themselves. Members of the Special Center were immediately deployed to Kathmandu and Pokhara to oversee this program. Their purpose was to ensure that rehabilitation funds would be wisely invested in self-generating enterprises. Although the demobilized guerrillas had few marketable skills, existing Kathmandu-based projects funded by the Dalai Lama and foreign aid groups demonstrated that Tibetan handicraft and carpet factories were profitable ventures.

Drawing on this precedent, the first third of the rehabilitation funds was channeled into two carpet factories in Pokhara. Part of the money was also used to break ground for a thirty-room budget hotel in the same town. With a third of the guerrillas dutifully filing out of the mountains to take up employment at these sites, demobilization appeared to be progressing according to plan.

At Tangya, not everybody was embracing the conversion to civilian life. Wangdu, for one, was game for alternative forms of funding that would allow him to maintain some of his men under arms. In early 1971, he received word that interest was being expressed by an unexpected source—the Soviet Union.

This was not the first time Moscow had flirted with the Tibetan resistance. In 1966, Soviet intelligence officers had approached Gyalo in New Delhi with a proposal to assume support for Tibetan paramilitary operations. During the course of eight meetings over the next three years, the Soviets spoke fancifully of establishing a joint operation in Tashkent; from there, they promised, Tibetan agents could be parachuted back to their homeland.

Intrigued but noncommittal, Gyalo requested that Moscow, as a sign of good faith, first raise the Tibet issue at the United Nations. Do not make preconditions, the Soviets sniffed, and ultimately ceased contact.[16]

In 1970, Moscow showed renewed interest in Tibet. This followed the Soviets' brief border war with the PRC in 1969, prompting them to reexplore paramilitary options against China in the event of renewed hostilities. Rather than approaching Gyalo—who in any event had moved to Hong Kong and washed his hands of resistance operations—this time they looked toward Nepal.

Leading the effort was Colonel Anatoli Logonov, the defense attaché at the

Soviet embassy in Kathmandu. Named a Hero of the Soviet Union in 1944 while an armor commander, Logonov had already been expelled from Canada for espionage activities and reprimanded by the Nepalese government for bribing a military officer. Undaunted, the brash Logonov approached the U.S. defense attaché, William Stites, at a diplomatic function. Sauntering up to the American colonel, he left little doubt about his focus of interest. "What do you have on Tibet?" he asked. Stites was not amused by the bold pitch; nor was he pleased to hear that the colonel had invited his assistant to dinner and asked the same question.[17]

Though he came up short with the American officers, Logonov had better luck with the Tibetans themselves. Cornering a Khampa shopkeeper in Kathmandu, he conveyed word that he sought contact with the Mustang leadership. As news of this reached the Tibetans at the Special Center, Tashi Choedak quietly rushed to Nepal, linked up with Wangdu, and rendezvoused with the Soviet colonel in the Nepalese capital. Matching his direct personality, Logonov's house was functional and unsophisticated. "It had no carpets," said Tashi, "but plenty of Johnny Walker and a refrigerator stocked with boiled cabbage."[18]

Coming to the point, the Soviet colonel asked for information on the size of the Mustang force. Over the course of three subsequent meetings, the Tibetans brought photograph albums (created for accounting purposes during the phased demobilization) that contained a portrait of each guerrilla still under arms. Logonov took copies of the albums and promised to quiz Moscow about assuming financing for the force.

One month later, Logonov returned with an answer. Although funding for Mustang was not feasible at that time, he offered payment for specific items of information, such as the location of PLA border posts and the deployment of aircraft at Tibetan airfields. Accepting this limited offer, the Tibetans prepared a sampling of intelligence for the Soviet officer. In return, Logonov paid the equivalent of $1,800. Convinced that this sum was hardly worth the effort, Wangdu unilaterally terminated further contact.

Ironically, the CIA did not necessarily see Soviet inroads into the subcontinent as a bad thing. "By keeping the Soviets onboard in India," said CIA New Delhi chief David Blee, "they were a counterweight to the Chinese."[19]

Such realpolitik led to previously unthinkable levels of cooperation regarding support to the ARC. With an aging C-46 fleet ("We squeezed as much life from them as possible," said one ARC officer[20]) and no C-130 ELINT platforms forthcoming, the ARC inventory by 1967 was dominated by the Soviet-made Mi-4 chopper and

An-12 transport. Whereas this transformation might have had the CIA howling in earlier years, the agency was now perfectly willing to assist the Indians with their new Soviet hardware. In 1968, for example, agency technicians installed oxygen consoles in the unpressurized An-12 cabins for use during SFF parachute training. Because this aircraft had an extremely fast cruising speed—more than double that of the C-46—a CIA airborne adviser was dispatched to India that spring to train an ARC cadre in high-speed exit techniques. Two years later, CIA technicians were back in India to modify an ARC An-12 with ELINT gear.[21]

CIA support for the SFF, meanwhile, was declining fast. One of the last CIA-sanctioned operations took place in 1969, when four SFF commandos were trained in the use of sophisticated "impulse probe" wiretaps. Buried underneath a telephone line, the tap transmitted conversations to a solar-powered relay station established on a border mountaintop in NEFA, which in turn relayed data to a rear base farther south. Although several taps were installed successfully, two SFF members disappeared on a 1970 foray, and further infiltrations were halted. By the following year, the PLA detected the extent of the tampering and started rerouting its lines away from the border.[22]

By early 1971, direct CIA contact with the SFF was almost nonexistent.[23] This came as tension between India and Pakistan was once again on the rise. The reason was the humanitarian disaster unfolding inside East Pakistan, where a heavy-handed campaign to suppress secessionists (who wanted independence from the western half of the bifurcated nation) had led to a deluge of refugees into India.

The situation had New Delhi's full attention not only because of the humanitarian ramifications but also because it presented a chance to cripple its archrival. During previous wars with Pakistan, fighting had focused on the western front. Now the Pakistani government not only had to keep that flank protected but also had to rush reinforcements to the eastern side of the subcontinent. Logistically challenged, the Pakistanis were getting whipsawed in the process.

Compounding Pakistan's woes, the Indian government was quietly supporting scores of resistance fighters from East Pakistan. Playing a major role in this was Major General Uban (he had finally gotten his promised second star), who was now considered one of India's most seasoned unconventional warfare specialists on account of the nine years he had spent with the SFF. Taking temporary leave of his Tibetans, the general was placed in charge of a guerrilla training program for 10,000 East Pakistani—soon to be called Bangladeshi—insurgents.[24]

Uban made room at Chakrata for a training site for the Bangladeshis. By that time, the SFF had grown to sixty-four Tibetan companies; most were divided into eight battalions of six companies apiece, with the remainder going into support units. Despite this increase, the force had not seen any serious combat since its inception. Worse, Uban learned that seven companies were being misused for traffic control in Ladakh.

Protesting this abuse of his elite unit, Uban lobbied to incorporate his men into contingencies against East Pakistan. By fall, the Indians were already well on their way to completing plans for a major combined arms campaign—one of the largest since World War II—to liberate that territory. Though Uban made a strong case for the SFF's inclusion—his men could act as guerrillas with plausible deniability, he argued—such a decision would be controversial. Until that point, there had been an unwritten rule that the SFF would not be used for anything other than its intended purpose against China. There were also Tibetan attitudes to consider. Tibet, noted several members of the force, had no quarrel with Pakistan. Rather, Tibet had benefited from assistance offered by the East Pakistani authorities, recalled ranking political leader Jamba Kalden.

As word flashed to Dharamsala, senior Tibetan officials were in a quandary. If they did not agree with Uban's proposal, they feared that the Indians would see them as ungrateful; with CIA support largely dissipated, they could ill afford to alienate their primary benefactor. Although some in the Dalai Lama's inner circle felt that they should demand a quid pro quo—participation against East Pakistan in exchange for Indian recognition of their exiled government—the idea was not pushed. Quietly, Dharamsala offered its approval.

By late October, an ARC An-12 airlift began shuttling nearly 3,000 Tibetans to the Indian border adjacent to East Pakistan's Chittagong Hill tracts. To reinforce their deniable status, the guerrillas were hurriedly given a shipment of Bulgarian-made AK-47 assault rifles.

At the border, they assembled at Demagiri. Normally a quiet frontier backwater, Demagiri by that time was overflowing with refugees. As the Tibetans turned it into a proper military encampment, they made plans to divide into three columns and initiate operations. Their exact mission had been the subject of prior debate. India's military staff had wanted them to perform surgical strikes, such as destroying the key Kaptai Dam. Uban, in contrast, saw them doing something "more worthy," such as joining forces with his Chakrata-trained Bangladeshi insurgents and seizing Chittagong port. This was vetoed by the top brass because neither the SFF nor the Bangladeshis had integral heavy weapons support. After further discussion, it was decided that the SFF would be charged with staging guerrilla raids across the Chittagong Hill tracts, known for their thick jungles, humid weather, and leech-infested marshes. This promised to be a difficult mission for the mountain-faring Tibetans.[25]

SFF members during the Bangladesh
campaign, 1971

The hills held another, more deadly, challenge. Based along the tracts was a
Pakistani composite brigade, including part of a battalion of elite commandos,
the Special Service Group. Not only did this brigade threaten the flank of one of
the Indian corps massing to move against Dacca, but it could conceivably open
an escape route to nearby Burma.

At the beginning of the second week of November, the SFF began Operation
EAGLE. Taking leave of Demagiri, the guerrillas used nineteen canoes to shuttle
across the Karnaphuli River and steal into East Pakistan. Coming upon an outpost that night, the Tibetans overran the position while the Pakistanis were eating. Boosted by their swift victory, they made plans to hit the next post the
following morning.

Listening over the radio, General Uban was anxious. As he moved into Demagiri to coordinate both the SFF and his Bangladeshi force, he had few qualms
about the Bangladeshis—they were native boys and could live off the land—but
he knew that the Tibetans were untested under battle conditions and careless in
open march.

Very quickly, his fears were confirmed. On 14 November, the lead element of
Tibetans came running back toward the Indian border. Dhondup Gyatotsang,
Uban learned, had been shot dead. The cousin of Mustang commander Wangdu

and a Hale graduate, Dhondup had been one of the most senior political leaders in the force. Realizing that he could lose momentum, Uban got on the radio and barked at the Tibetans to resume their advance. "I told them not to come back until the position was taken," he said.[26]

The strong words had an effect. Reversing course, the SFF split into small teams and curled behind the Pakistanis in classic guerrilla fashion. Using both their Bulgarian assault rifles and native knives, they smashed through the outpost. "After that," remembers Uban, "they were unstoppable."[27]

By the time all-out war was officially declared early the following month, the SFF had been inside East Pakistan for three weeks. Multiple Indian corps blitzed from all directions on 3 December, forcing Pakistani capitulation within two weeks; Bangladesh's independence would soon follow.[28]

At the time of the cease-fire, the Tibetans were within forty kilometers of Chittagong port and had successfully pinned down the Pakistani brigade in the border hills. Taking leave of their normal anonymity, the SFF paraded through Chittagong to ecstatic Bangladeshi masses. A total of twenty-three Indian officers and forty-five Tibetans would be awarded for their gallantry; 580 Tibetans received cash bonuses. Their victory had had a cost, however. Forty-nine Tibetans had paid with their lives for the birth of a nation not their own.

19. A Pass Too Far

Fallout from the Bangladeshi operation was swift. The CIA lodged a protest against the RAW over the use of the Tibetans in Operation EAGLE. Director Kao hardly lost any sleep over the matter; with U.S. financial and advisory support to the SFF all but evaporated, the agency's leverage was nil. Bolstering his indifference was the diplomatic furor over deployment of the U.S. aircraft carrier *Enterprise* to the Bay of Bengal during the brief war. Although Washington claimed that the vessel was there for the potential evacuation of U.S. citizens from Dacca, New Delhi suspected that it had been sent as a show of support for the Pakistanis. Bilateral ties, never good during the Nixon presidency, ebbed even lower.

More serious were the protests against Operation EAGLE from within the Tibetan refugee community. In this instance, it was Dharamsala that was under fire, not the RAW. Facing mounting criticism for having approved the deployment, the Dalai Lama made a secret journey to Chakrata on 3 June 1972. After three days of blessings, most ill feelings had wafted away.

As this was taking place, John Bellingham was approaching the end of his tour at the Special Center. He had just delivered the second installment of rehabilitation funds, which arrived in Nepal without complication. With this money, two Pokhara carpet factories had been established, and construction of a hotel in the same town was progressing according to plan. Another carpet factory was operating in Kathmandu, as was a taxi and trucking company.

By the summer of 1973, with one-third of the funds still to be distributed, the CIA opted not to deploy a new representative to the Special Center. Because Bellingham had moved next door as the CIA's chief of station in Kathmandu, and because he was already intimately familiar with the demobilization program, it was decided to send him the Indian rupees in a diplomatic pouch for direct handover to designated Tibetans in Nepal. Although this violated the agency's previous taboo against involving the Kathmandu station, an exception was deemed suitable in this case, given the humanitarian nature of the project.

The money was well spent. That November, ex-guerrillas formally opened their Pokhara hotel, the Annapurna Guest House. Bellingham and his wife were among its first patrons.[1]

* * *

The Dalai Lama and Major General Uban, the inspector general of the SFF, review the SFF at Chakrata, June 1972

Although all the promised funds had been distributed, the CIA was not celebrating. Wangdu had dipped into extra money saved over previous years, defied orders to completely close the project, and retained six companies—600 men—spread across Mustang. Worst of all, not a single weapon had been handed back.

All this was happening as a new set of geopolitical realities was conspiring against the Tibetans. President Nixon, besides having frosty relations with India, was dedicated to normalizing ties with the PRC. In February 1972, he traveled to Beijing and discussed this possibility with Chinese leaders, who were slowly distancing themselves from the self-inflicted wounds of their Cultural Revolution. Although the phaseout of Mustang was not directly linked to this visit—as many Tibetans have incorrectly speculated—it is equally true that Washington had little patience for a continued Mustang sideshow, given the massive stakes involved with Sino-U.S. rapprochement.

The royal Nepalese government, too, was getting a dose of realpolitik. In January 1972, King Mahendra suddenly died and was succeeded by his son, Birendra Bir Bikram Shah Dev. Looking around the subcontinent, Birendra had reason for concern. Pakistan had been dismembered only a month earlier, and the Indians had signed a cooperation treaty with the Soviet Union the previous August.

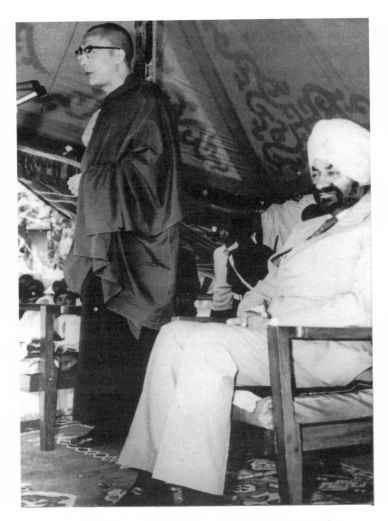

The Dalai Lama addresses the SFF, June 1972. To his right is Major
General Uban.

Although Nepal's security rested in astutely maintaining the nonaligned foreign
policy championed by his father, the new monarch believed that it was in his kingdom's interest to offset a stronger India by fostering goodwill with Beijing. In
November 1972, he dispatched his prime minister to the Chinese capital; in
December 1973, Birendra himself made the trip.

Following these diplomatic developments, Wangdu's residual force at Mustang counted no allies of note by the beginning of 1974. Even the local Nepalese

population had turned against them. Almost since the time the guerrillas began operations, the residents of Lo Monthang had been leery of their armed Khampa neighbors. This was compounded by petty jealousy. The swaggering guerrilla bachelors, with their relatively generous food stipends, were seen as prize catches for Mustang girls. Though the men of Lo Monthang were fast to charge the Khampas with rape, their womenfolk proved more than willing to marry the guerrillas.[2]

Between apocryphal tales of rape and an eagerness to demonstrate good intentions toward Beijing, the royal Nepalese government was eager to move forcefully against the long-standing affront to its sovereignty in Mustang. Playing a supporting role in this was deposed chieftain Baba Yeshi. Ever since retreating to Kathmandu in early 1970, he had been in intermittent contact with a small band of loyalists in Nashang. He had also been in touch with the Nepalese authorities and offered them assistance in confronting his rival, Wangdu. Though eager to do so, the Nepalese military, as yet untested in combat, was biding its time until conditions were right.

In the spring of 1974, there arose just such conditions. As he had done in previous years, Lhamo Tsering traveled overland to Pokhara to inspect ongoing rehabilitation projects in that town. Although his trips had not been controversial in

The Annapurna Guest House, Pokhara, built with CIA rehabilitation funds. (Courtesy Kenneth Conboy)

the past—he had kept the Nepalese Home Ministry fully apprised of the guerrilla demobilization—this time, Kathmandu saw him as a useful pawn. On 19 April, he was arrested at the Annapurna Guest House and taken to the town's police station.

With Lhamo Tsering in detention, the Royal Nepalese Army dispatched a lieutenant colonel to Jomsom to initiate a dialogue with Wangdu. At the time, the Nepalese maintained only a single infantry company at Jomsom; not only was it outnumbered and outgunned by the guerrillas, but the Tibetans held the strategic high ground at Kaisang. But with Lhamo Tsering behind bars, Wangdu was in a conciliatory mood. Venturing down from Kaisang with a coterie of bodyguards, he offered to turn in 100 weapons in exchange for Lhamo Tsering's release. The Nepalese, suddenly emboldened, rejected the offer. With bad feelings all around, Wangdu retreated to his headquarters.

Realizing that they needed more muscle, the Nepalese began mobilizing military reinforcements from around the kingdom. During June, an infantry brigade massed at Pokhara, then began walking north in driving rains to join the company already at Jomsom. Making the same hike was an artillery group consisting of a howitzer, a field gun, and a mortar.

Although the Nepalese were slowly starting to develop critical mass, all their troops were green. The ranking officer at Jomsom, Brigadier Singha, had absolutely no combat experience. "None of us did," added company commander Gyanu Babu Adhikari.[3]

Despite this, the government troops had sufficient confidence to deliver an ultimatum to Wangdu. His guerrillas had until 26 July (later extended by five days) to hand in their weapons; after that, the army vowed to forcibly disarm them. To add emphasis, a team of Baba Yeshi loyalists, working alongside the Nepalese, sent surrender leaflets to Kaisang. "You can not push the sky with your finger," read one.[4]

Almost until the eleventh hour, the saber rattling had little effect. But upon hearing of the impending confrontation, the Tibetan authorities in Dharamsala intervened. The Dalai Lama recorded a personal plea, and a senior Tibetan minister rushed the tape to Mustang and played it in front of the guerrilla audience.

Hearing their leader implore them to disarm, the warriors broke down. Four of the six companies came out of the mountains and did as instructed. At Kaisang, one Khampa officer shot himself in the head rather than turn over his rifle. Two other guerrillas leaped to their deaths in the swift waters of the Kali Gandaki.[5]

Still at large was Wangdu, backed by a pair of companies commanded by deputies Rara and Gen Gyurme. The surrender deadline had expired, and the

Nepalese were contemplating their next move. Still looking to employ carrot over stick, they couriered appeals to Kaisang during early August, promising a festive celebration at Jomsom if Wangdu bowed out gracefully. When that failed, they began moving against the guerrilla headquarters.

Undaunted, the Tibetans at Kaisang unpacked a recoilless rifle. They had never used this weapon inside Tibet during all the preceding years, but they now sent a round impacting into a nearby hillside. Intimidated, the Nepalese scurried back to Jomsom. "The Khampas had better weapons than we did," said Major Gyanu, "and better terrain."[6]

Wangdu, meanwhile, had beckoned Rara and Gen Gyurme for what was to be their final meeting. He would make a dash west toward India with forty followers, he told them. His two deputies were to delay the Nepalese for eight days to allow him sufficient time to escape.[7]

By that time, the Nepalese were gearing up for a second foray against Kaisang. Advancing at night, they surrounded the headquarters at 0300 hours. When they made a final push after sunup, however, they found only a handful of Tibetans present; Wangdu was not among them.

Determined to get serious, the army made plans for a major sweep north across Mustang. The Nepalese had initially intended it as a helicopter operation— the first in their history. Since early that year, a British squadron leader had been posted to Kathmandu to teach them such airmobile tactics. But with only four available helicopters and three inexperienced aircrews (one of the choppers was flown by a French civilian pilot), they opted instead for a long slog from Jomsom on foot.[8]

Marching along the east bank of the Kali Gandaki, a single Nepalese battalion eventually reached Tangya by the end of August. In an anticlimax, the remaining guerrillas surrendered without a fight. Searching the camp, the government troops found few weapons; the rest had been cached, they presumed. At the same time, the smaller pro–Baba Yeshi faction at Nashang turned in its arms. There were no firefights at that location either. Apart from two Nepalese who succumbed to altitude sickness, nobody died during the operation.

Wangdu, however, was still at large. Correctly assuming that the last two company commanders were coconspirators in his escape, the Nepalese invited Rara and Gen Gyurme to Pokhara to review the status of the rehabilitation projects. After three nights at the Annapurna Guest House, they were taken away in chains to join Lhamo Tsering.

Though they had yet to capture the Mustang leader, the Nepalese authorities had a pretty good idea where he was heading. During the march north from

Jomsom, the government battalion had spotted a band of horsemen riding west. Assuming that Wangdu might be destined for India, Kathmandu alerted its 4th Brigade posted along the northwestern border of the kingdom. Because there were only a limited number of passes along the frontier with India, the troops were especially vigilant at those locales.

Their calculations proved correct. During the second week of September, a line of horsemen was seen approaching the 5,394-meter Tinkar Pass separating Nepal and India. Only meters from the Indian border, a Nepalese sergeant took the column under fire. Two were killed and one severely wounded; the rest escaped across the frontier. Uncertain as to the identity of the corpses, the Nepalese flew in Baba Yeshi. He positively identified Wangdu, and the traitorous chieftain had the bodies buried on the spot.

Back in Kathmandu, the conclusion of the Mustang operation was celebrated with pomp. On 16 October, King Birendra handed out sixty-nine awards, including a promotion for the sergeant who had shot Wangdu.[9] Coinciding with this, a tent display was unveiled near the capital's center. In it were Buddhist scriptures and idols captured at Kaisang. Other tables held rifles, rocket launchers, ammunition, and "ultra modern miniature communication equipment powered by solar batteries."[10]

Lured by the spectacle, Tibetan agents Arnold and Rocky, both still in the Nepalese capital to oversee the rehabilitation projects, filed past the display. As a macabre centerpiece, the authorities had arranged Wangdu's pistol, binoculars, watch, and silver amulet given to him by the Dalai Lama. Attitudes in Kathmandu, the two discovered, had turned decidedly hostile. To accompany the tent display, government-owned newspapers were trumpeting claims that the Mustang Khampas had conducted a twenty-six-day spree of raping and looting. "Tibetans were forced to temporarily close their shops," recalls Arnold. "It was very tense for two months."[11]

At Pokhara, the last Mustang guerrillas were directed to temporary resettlement centers while the Nepalese authorities debated their future. Half ultimately left for India; of these, nearly 100 joined the SFF. For the remainder, favoritism was shown toward Baba Yeshi's followers formerly at Nashang; a camp was built for them near Kathmandu, with funds from the United Nations. Those loyal to Wangdu, by contrast, were given barren plots near Pokhara and, due to government intransigence, had no access to United Nations funding.[12]

That was still far better than the prison cells holding Lhamo Tsering, Rara, and Gen Gyurme. Four other unrepentant guerrillas soon joined them, including the wounded member from Wangdu's escape party and a Hale-trained radioman named Sandy. They were taken to Kathmandu for trial, where the authorities were deaf to pleas for leniency. All received life sentences.

At the Special Center in New Delhi, the Tibetan and Indian representatives had been monitoring Mustang's death throes as best they could. Until the final days of July, the radio teams at Kaisang, Tsum, Dolpo, and Limi had been sending back regular updates. Once those fell silent, gloom set in among the operatives at Hauz Khas.

With a whimper, their secret war in Tibet had come to an end.

Epilogue

For many of the CIA officers involved in the Tibet operation, cold war battles in Southeast Asia loomed. Roger McCarthy, the long-serving head of the Tibet Task Force, went on to serve in South Vietnam and then in Laos just as its royalist government fell to communism in 1975. Smitten by Tibet, he visited Lhasa for the first time in 1996. Said McCarthy, "I could see the sandbank where Tom and Lou jumped all those years ago."

Tom Fosmire, the Hale instructor beloved by his Tibetan students, spent many years with the CIA's paramilitary campaign in Laos, which in terms of budget and duration was the largest in the agency's history. He was later in South Vietnam until its fall to communism.

Another Hale trainer, Tony Poe, served brilliantly in the highlands of Laos for nearly a decade. Eventually succumbing to the pressure and isolation, he took to alcohol and was sidelined to training centers in Thailand by embarrassed superiors.

Among the CIA advisers who served in India, Harry Mustakos and T. J. Thompson both had tours in Laos. Thompson would later become a world-renowned parachute designer. In 1981, he returned to Charbatia on a CIA-sanctioned trip to inspect the state of the ARC rigging facility he had helped establish two decades earlier. "Not only was the facility in great shape," he said, "but there were still some of the Tibetan riggers I trained in 1963."

Ken Seifarth, who spent two tours at Chakrata, served several years at a Thai base training guerrillas headed for the war in Laos.

Jim Rhyne, the Air America pilot who qualified ARC aircrews in the Helio and Twin Helio, flew for the CIA in Laos until an 85mm antiaircraft round struck his plane in January 1972 and took off his leg. Unfazed, he was flying in Laos six months later with a prosthetic limb. In 1980, still working for the agency, Rhyne flew into the Iranian desert to take soil samples at the makeshift runway later used during the ill-fated hostage rescue mission. In April 2001, he died when his biplane crashed near his home in North Carolina.

Tucker Gougelmann, the senior paramilitary adviser in India, went directly to Vietnam for a final CIA tour as a key official with Phoenix, the campaign aimed at neutralizing the communist infrastructure. Retiring in Southeast Asia, he ventured to Saigon during its final months to explore business opportunities, then to evacuate his common-law Vietnamese wife and their children as communist

tanks closed in during April 1975. Unable to escape, he was arrested; once his cap-
tors uncovered his earlier Phoenix involvement, he was killed in detention that
June. His remains, bearing the hallmarks of torture, were returned to the United
States in September 1977. David Blee, the former station chief in New Delhi, made
the arrangements for Gougelmann's interment at Arlington National Cemetery.

Among the Indian veterans of the Tibet project, RAW director R. N. Kao rode
Indira Gandhi's skirt to great influence. In the wake of the successful Bangladesh
operation, as well as the assistance RAW lent Mrs. Gandhi during her 1969 political struggles against party stalwarts, Kao was elevated to the additional post of
cabinet secretary (security). When Gandhi briefly fell from power in 1977, her
intelligence supremo was shunted aside, only to return as national security
adviser when she regained power three years later. Although the Tibet operation
was downgraded during his watch and with his concurrence, Kao would later
disingenuously lay blame solely on the United States. "The Tibetans were looking for somebody to hold their finger," he later commented, "and the Americans
dropped them like a hot potato."[1]

Laloo Grewal, the first ARC manager at Charbatia, went on to become vice
chief of staff of the Indian air force.

Major General S. S. Uban retired as inspector general of the SFF in January
1973.[2] A deeply religious man, Uban delved into various beliefs. More than anything, he became a devotee of Baba Onkarnath, a popular Bengali mystic whose
prophecies, say followers, are invariably accurate. During one sitting with Onkarnath, Uban claims that his guru predicted the Bangladesh war a year in advance.
On another occasion, Uban was present when the seer was asked whether Tibet
would become free. Yes, said Onkarnath confidently, Tibet would gain its independence. His audience, eager for details, pressed the Bengali for details as to
when liberation would take place. To this, the prophet offered no insights.

Among the Tibetan members of the CIA's covert projects, those assigned to
the Special Center in Hauz Khas continued working alongside their Indian coun-
terparts after the departure of John Bellingham. In 1975, they attempted to deploy
a singleton agent without U.S. participation. Code-named "Yak," he was a native
of Yatung near the Sikkimese border. On three occasions over the next year, he
was dispatched back to his hometown to collect intelligence from family members. Suspected of embellishing his tales, Yak was dropped from the Special Center's payroll. Apart from this brief flirtation with running a bona fide agent, the
center spent most of its time tasking and debriefing Tibetan refugees going on
pilgrimages or visiting family members. This continued until late 1992, at which

Tibetan paratroopers during the first SFF freefall course, 1976

time the Hauz Khas villa was closed after almost three decades and Tibet operations began running out of RAW headquarters.

Within the SFF, Jamba Kalden retired as its senior political leader in 1977.
Much had happened to his force since the Bangladesh operation. Looking to
patch over its earlier protests regarding Operation EAGLE, the CIA deployed two
airborne advisers to Chakrata in the spring of 1975 to instruct the Tibetans in
jumping at high altitudes. Drop zones in Ladakh, some as high as 4,848 meters
above sea level, were used for these exercises. Two years later, one of the same
advisers, Alex MacPherson, returned to India to test a special high-altitude chute
specially designed for SFF missions.[3]

Though exposed to such expanded training, the SFF was seeing less action
in the field. In 1974, the unit had been guarding the border near Nepal to stem
an influx of Chinese-trained insurgents. Following Kathmandu's suppression of
Mustang, however, it was feared that the SFF might stage reprisal forays against
the Nepalese. To prevent this, India pulled its Tibetan commandos away from
the border.

The following year, a second ruling prohibited the SFF from being posted
within ten kilometers of the Tibet frontier. This came after a series of unauthorized incursions and cross-border shootings, including a four-hour firefight in
Ladakh during 1971 that resulted in two SFF fatalities.

By the late 1970s, the future of the SFF was no longer certain. With Indo-Chinese tensions easing somewhat, there was criticism that maintenance of a Tibetan commando force was an unnecessary expense. However, the SFF was soon given a new mission: counterterrorism. Because the Tibetans were foreigners, and therefore did not have a direct stake in Indian communal politics, they were seen as an ideal, objective counterterrorist force. In 1977, RAW director Kao (who wore an additional hat as director general of security) deployed 500 SFF commandos to Sarsawa for possible action against rioters during national elections. After the elections, which went off without major incident, only sixty Tibetans were retained at Sarsawa for counterterrorist duties.

Three years later, when Indira Gandhi (and Kao) returned to power, the SFF's war against terrorism received a major boost. Over 500 trainees were sent to Sarsawa for counterterrorist instruction. Upon graduation, they formed the SFF's new Special Group. Significantly, no Tibetans were incorporated into this new group within the force.

The Special Group would soon see action across India. In June 1984, one of its companies was used during an abortive attack against Sikh extremists holed up in the Golden Temple in the Punjab. The temple was subsequently retaken in a bloody army operation, leading Indira Gandhi's Sikh bodyguards to assassinate the prime minister later that year.[4]

The Tibetan mainstream of the SFF, meanwhile, continued to see action closer to the border. Companies from its eight battalions under the control of the director general of security rotated along the entire frontier. In 1978, three additional Tibetan battalions were raised at Chakrata; under the operational control of the Indian army, these three battalions were posted to Ladakh, Sikkim, and Doomdoomah air base in Assam. Seventeen members of the Ladakh battalion were killed while fighting Pakistani troops on the Siachen Glacier in 1986; as after the Bangladesh operation, there were protests against Dharamsala for taking losses outside of the battle to liberate the Tibetan homeland.

Among the veterans of the Mustang force in Nepal, there were few winners. Baba Yeshi, the original chief, rarely strays from his house in Kathmandu. Though he sought audiences with the Dalai Lama in 1991 and 1994—and allegedly received forgiveness for his actions against Wangdu—the former commander is still seen as a duplicitous traitor by the refugee community at large.

Toward the other members of Mustang, the royal Nepalese government maintained a tense relationship for a decade. Continuing with its smear campaign, Kathmandu in early 1976 released reports that it had uncovered an eighteen-hole golf course and badminton courts at one of the Khampa bases. The following year, the Nepalese accused the former Tibetan warriors of continued looting and hashish smuggling.[5]

Suffering the most from Kathmandu's wrath were the seven prisoners given life sentences. Not until late December 1981, with a birthday and the tenth anniversary of his coronation looming, did the king of Nepal release six from jail; the last, Lhamo Tsering, was set free five month later. All were declared persona non grata and sent to India. This put Rara, the leader of the October 1961 jeep ambush, at a loss. Having lived in Nepal for the past two decades, he preferred that kingdom over India. After stealing back across the border, he was rearrested by Nepalese authorities for violating the conditions of his release; he later died in prison.

Equally harsh treatment was meted out to the Tibetan agents captured by Chinese authorities. In prison for almost two decades—much of it in solitary confinement—they were offered unexpected freedom in November 1978 as part of Beijing's slight softening in policy toward Tibet. The years had taken a toll. From Team S, agent Thad was still alive; his teammate Troy had been executed for bad behavior. From Team F, Taylor was released, but his partner, Jerome, had died in detention from a prolonged illness. Team Vi's Terrence had his freedom, but teammate Maurice had been executed for provoking fights in jail. Irving, the agent from Team C turned in by the old lady and her son, survived his incarceration. So did Choni Yeshi, the sole survivor of the team parachuted into Amdo, and Bhusang, the only living member of the team dropped at Markham in 1961.

Two others remained in detention. Amdo Tsering, the restive Muslim singleton who was supposed to collect dirt at Lop Nur, stayed behind bars because of an unrepentant attitude. Grant, the lone survivor of Team Y, was sickly and opted to stay in prison voluntarily. Not until 1996 did both finally leave their cells.

Overseas, Geshe Wangyal, the Mongolian who had served as translator for the Tibet project, died in 1983 while still teaching at his New Jersey monastery.

Gyalo Thondup, the key link with the CIA, had stayed away from the resistance since 1969. Not until late 1978, with the Chinese government apparently loosening its constraints on Tibet, did he rejoin the cause and lead a negotiating team to Beijing; results from this trip ultimately proved scant. Gyalo currently shuttles between residences in New Delhi and Hong Kong.

The Dalai Lama has gone from strength to strength, winning the 1989 Nobel Prize for Peace and earning an enormous international audience that includes Hollywood celebrities, rock musicians, New Agers, and scores of other Westerners looking for answers in the East. His Tibet, however, has yet to be set free.

Notes

1. Contact

1. Donald S. Lopez, Jr., *Prisoners of Shangri-La* (Chicago: University of Chicago Press, 1998), p. 140; Jeff Long, "Going After Wangdu," *Rocky Mountain Magazine*, July–August 1981, p. 36; "Pack Animal of Tibetan Valley May Be Horse of a Different Era," *Washington Post*, 8 January 1996, p. A3.

2. About 90 percent of lowland Chinese have at least a partial epicanthic eye fold, although only about half of all Khampas show this trait. More than 44 percent of all Chinese have a complete eye fold, but this is found among only 8 percent of those from eastern Tibet. Warren W. Smith, Jr., *Tibetan Nation, a History of Tibetan Nationalism and Sino-Tibetan Relations* (Boulder, Colo.: Westview Press, 1996), p. 10.

3. Melvyn C. Goldstein, *A History of Modern Tibet, 1913–1951* (Berkeley: University of California Press, 1989), p. 21.

4. Both the Allied and the Axis powers attempted to win Lhasa's favor during World War II. The British and Americans, for instance, sought permission to supply their besieged ally in China via a Tibetan mule route. Germany was interested in Tibet as a potential staging ground for attacks against British India and because the Nazi's ethnic pseudoscience credited Tibet with being the "pure" cradle of the Aryan race. For a good account of the attempted Nazi inroads, see Karl E. Meyer and Shareen Blair Brysac, *Tournament of Shadows* (Washington, D.C.: Counterpoint, 1999), pp. 509–528.

5. Goldstein, *History of Modern Tibet*, p. 619; "Memo to the Chief of the Division of Chinese Affairs," 12 April 1949, in *Foreign Relations of the United States*, 1949, (Washington, D.C.: U.S. Government Printing Office, 1974), 9:1067 (hereafter cited as FRUS, with the applicable years and volumes).

6. Even before January 1949, the U.S. embassy in New Delhi had recommended a review of America's Tibet policy. These initial dispatches were so wrought with qualifiers and counterarguments, however, that it was all but impossible to determine what policy shift, if any, was being advocated. Not until July 1949 did the embassies in both India and China advocate a more proactive approach toward Lhasa. See FRUS, 1949, 9:1065; "The Ambassador in China to the Secretary of State," 8 July 1949, ibid., p. 1078; "The Secretary of State to the Ambassador in India," 21 December 1949, ibid., p. 1096.

7. Mei Siyi and Zhu Bian, eds., *Zhong Guo Ren Min Jie Fang Jun Da Shi Dian* [Encyclopedia of the Chinese People's Liberation Army], vol. 2 (Beijing: Tian Jin People's Publishing House, 1992), p. 1101. The 20,000 troops targeted against Kham comprised six regiments divided into a northern and a southern task force. The northern task force, which moved south from Amdo to block the retreat of the main Tibetan garrison at Chamdo, was drawn primarily from the 52nd Division of the 18th Army/Southwest Military Command; it was also supported by a Hiu cavalry detachment from the Northwest Military Command. The southern task force, which staged from the city of Chengdu

toward Chamdo, was composed of the 53rd Division of the 18th Army and a regiment of the 42nd Division.

8. A double entendre of sorts, *Dalai Lama* is also Mongolian for "broad ocean," which could be interpreted as a teacher whose knowledge is as expansive as the open seas.

9. Interview with Nicholas Thacher, 28 September 1999; "The Secretary of State to the Ambassador in India," 28 July 1949, in FRUS, 1949, 9:1078.

10. "The Ambassador in India to the Secretary of State," 12 January 1951, in FRUS, 1951, 7:1507.

11. The first contact between U.S. and Tibetan officials at Kalimpong had taken place in mid-May 1951 when Fraser Wilkins, first secretary of the U.S. embassy in New Delhi, ventured to that town to deliver a copy of Henderson's unsigned letter.

12. Thacher interview.

13. Ibid.

14. In recognition of his status as an incarnation, Norbu was also known as the twenty-fourth *Taktser Rinpoche* ("incarnation from Taktser"). Taktser is the town in Amdo where Norbu spent his youth; his late uncle, also from that town, was the twenty-third Taktser Rinpoche. U.S. diplomatic cables over the ensuing years variously (and incorrectly) referred to Norbu as "Takster" and "Tak Tser."

15. Although the CIA connection was repeatedly denied over the years, there were public suspicions from the start. On 27 June 1951, Alfred Kohlberg, a prominent U.S. importer of Chinese textiles, sent a letter to CFA president George Greene accusing the organization of being a government front. In his letter, Kohlberg astutely noted that the Committee for a Free Europe, a sister entity created the previous year, was correctly suspected of having CIA links. Letter on file at the Hoover Institution Archives, A. Kohlberg Collection, Box 37, "Committee for a Free Asia" folder (hereafter Kohlberg Collection).

16. During the same month, the Committee for a Free Asia factored in another aspect of America's Tibet policy. On 22 June, Secretary of State Acheson handed the Thai ambassador to the United States a copy of a letter written on CFA stationery. The note, which was addressed to the secretary, claimed that the committee would underwrite the expenses of the Dalai Lama if he were granted asylum in Thailand. The idea of Thai asylum—and related CFA sponsorship—was apparently not pursued.

17. "Consul General at Calcutta to the Secretary of State," 26 June 1951, in FRUS, 1951, 7:1718.

18. Kohlberg Collection, "Press Comments."

19. Interview with Robert Linn, 29 September 1999.

20. Ibid.; "Consul General at Calcutta to the Secretary of State," 12 July 1951, in FRUS, 1951, 7:1747.

2. Tightrope

1. "Memorandum of the Substance of a Conversation," 13 February 1952, in FRUS, 1952–1954, 14:8–9.

2. "Memorandum by the Acting Director of the Office of Chinese Affairs to the Assistant

Secretary of State for Far Eastern Affairs," 14 May 1952, in ibid., pp. 51–52. This same memorandum noted several reports in the Indian press concerning increased Tibetan hardening against Chinese occupation; these reports were similar to the information relayed by Norbu.

3. Although the CFA's direct sponsorship of Norbu expired, the committee extended financial support to produce "World Buddhist Brotherhood," a thirty-minute documentary about the 1952 Buddhist World Fellowship conference that Norbu attended in Tokyo. See Kohlberg Collection, "Background Information," p. 4.

4. "The Ambassador in India to the Secretary of State," 12 January 1951, in FRUS, 1951, 7:1507.

5. According to one CIA officer who forged contact with the Sikkimese royals, the prince was a closet alcoholic. Interview with Kenneth Millian, 13 November 1999.

6. U.S. government officials had dealt with Sikkim's royals on at least one occasion before the December 1950 treaty with India. In September 1949, the widening civil war in China had forced Washington to abandon its consulate in the far reaches of Xinjiang Province. Cut off from the east, the party was forced to trek south through Tibet toward India. Upon reaching Tibet's frontier in late April 1950, Tibetan border guards (apparently intent on robbing the party) shot dead CIA officer Douglas MacKiernan. As word of the attack was relayed to New Delhi, the U.S. embassy made arrangements to recover the body and receive the survivors, who by June had arrived in Lhasa. Because one of its own had been killed, the CIA was eager to participate in the retrieval. This job went to Frederick Latrash, a junior case officer assigned to the consulate in Calcutta. Dispatched north to Sikkim, he stopped briefly to speak with Sikkimese officials in the capital of Gangtok before proceeding twenty-eight kilometers northeast to meet the Xinjiang stragglers as they crossed the Tibetan border. MacKiernan's body was left where it fell and was never recovered.

7. Interview with Princess Kukula, 4 November 1999. During his stay in Lhasa, OSS officer Dolan befriended Kukula's sister-in-law and fathered her child. See Meyer and Brysac, Tournament of Shadows, p. 544.

8. Thacher interview.

9. Interview with Lawrence Dalley, 2 April 2000.

10. Linn interview.

11. Back in September 1951, Yutok Dzaza, a former official at the Tibetan trade office in Kalimpong, had been brought down to the consulate in Calcutta and shown Ambassador Henderson's last-ditch appeal to the Dalai Lama written on U.S. embassy letterhead. Yutok took notes from the letter and then went to Lhasa, where he met several senior government officials. He also met with one of the Dalai Lama's older brothers, Lobsang Samten. It was the information gathered from these sources that he passed to Princess Kukula.

12. Editorial Note No. 35, in FRUS, 1952–1954, 14:73; Kukula interview.

13. "The Consul at Calcutta to the Department of State," 11 September 1952, in FRUS, 1952–1954, 14:96.

14. Millian interview.

15. Interview with John Turner, 5 August 1998.

16. Ibid.

17. China's strategy also involved the cultivation of the pliable Panchen Lama, the second

most influential incarnation in Tibet, as a counterweight to the Dalai Lama. Beginning in 1954, Beijing insisted on treating the two as virtual equals.

18. George N. Patterson, *Patterson of Tibet* (San Diego, Calif.: ProMotion Publishing, 1998), p. 303. In contrast to the rational grounding of his literary masterpiece Sherlock Holmes, Arthur Conan Doyle put great credence in the spirit mediums of his time.

19. Turner interview.

20. There were several reasons for Ragpa's lack of success. First, the history of waffling by the Pandatsang clan gave India and the United States good reason for pause. Second, his hint of armed insurrection in Tibet ran counter to the hopes of India's leaders, who in April 1954 had signed a trade treaty with China. Among other things, that treaty granted the PRC control over Tibet's trade office in Kalimpong, which explains the latter's rebuff of Ragpa.

21. Nomads in Amdo had initially resisted PRC rule during the early 1950s, though a lull had settled over the province by 1952. The resumption of fighting in late 1955 was tied to the imposition of Beijing's heavy-handed "democratic reforms." Robert Barnett and Shirin Akiner, eds., *Resistance and Reform in Tibet* (London: Hurst and Company, 1994), pp. 191–192.

22. Ibid., pp. 192–193.

23. The Tu-4 was a near exact Soviet copy of the U.S. B-29 Superfortress that had devastated Japan during World War II. Three of these long-range bombers had been forced to ditch in Siberia during the war, providing Soviet designers with an opportunity to reverse-engineer a communist clone. They were mass-produced as the Tupolev-4, and Stalin presented ten airframes to Mao as a birthday gift in 1953.

24. *Chung-kuo chih i* [Chinese Air Force in Action, series 3] (Taipei: Yun Hao, 1990), p. 212.

25. John Rowland, *A History of Sino-Indian Relations: Hostile Co-existence* (Princeton, N.J.: D. Van Nostrand, 1967), pp. ix, 81. As part of the 1954 trade agreement, India was allowed to maintain trade agents in three Tibetan towns. These agents, in addition to the Indian consul in Lhasa, would have been able to keep New Delhi abreast of rumored events in eastern Tibet.

26. John Kenneth Knaus, *Orphans of the Cold War* (New York: Public Affairs, 1999), p. 132. In his memoirs, the Dalai Lama does not mention his desire to seek exile during the crown prince's 1956 visit to Lhasa. See Tenzin Gyatso, *Freedom in Exile: The Autobiography of the Dalai Lama* (New York: HarperCollins, 1990), p. 112.

27. Knaus, *Orphans*, p. 132.

28. There were other reasons for Nehru to register concern. Over the past two years, there had been several minor PLA violations along the Indo-Tibetan border. In addition, on 20 September 1956, China signed a trade agreement with Nepal. Coupled with its military presence in Tibet, this was seen as further Chinese encroachment into the Himalayas at the expense of Indian influence.

3. The Prodigal Son

1. Assigned to the CIA's China Base located within the U.S. naval compound at the Japanese port city of Yokosuka, Hoskins was tasked with poring over interrogation reports

of prisoners released from Soviet labor camps after World War II and repatriated to Japan. From these reports, Hoskins identified, recruited, and trained four ethnic Mongolians. When a plan to parachute the four agents back into Mongolia was nixed at the eleventh hour as too risky, they were dropped from the agency's rolls and allowed to resettle in Japan and Taiwan.

2. William Broe, chief of the China Branch between 1955 and 1957, initiated the worldwide program of assigning Far East Division officers to any station where there was a substantial expatriate Chinese community. This followed the example set by the CIA's Soviet–East European Division, which since the late 1940s had been assigning its officers to any country with a sizable expatriate Russian community. Interview with William Broe, 6 June 2000.

3. Interview with John Hoskins, 9 December 1999.

4. Interview with Mary Hawthorne, 18 February 2000.

5. Once the CIA decided to bypass the Sikkimese in late 1956, the royals grew somewhat annoyed. The crown prince, in particular, sniped at Gyalo Thondup and gradually came to oppose the idea of armed resistance against the Chinese. "He felt angry and used," said one of his closest confidants, "and thought the U.S. had only been toying with the Tibetans." Correspondence with Sikkimese source, 22 March 2000.

6. Goldstein, *History of Modern Tibet*, p. 644.

7. Knaus, *Orphans*, p. 341 n. 45.

8. The monthly report from the Indian consul in Lhasa clearly notes Gyalo's assurance that he would "scrupulously avoid involvement in politics." Gyalo denies in contemporary interviews that this promise was given. See Knaus, *Orphans*, p. 344 n. 31.

9. "The Consul at Calcutta to the Department of State," 10 September 1952, in FRUS, 1952–1954, 14:96.

10. Bhashyam Kasturi, *Intelligence Services* (New Delhi: Lancer Publishers, 1995), p. 31; B. N. Mullik, *The Chinese Betrayal: My Years with Nehru* (Bombay: Allied Publishers, 1971), p. 105.

11. Mullik, *Chinese Betrayal*, p. 181.

12. Ibid., p. 180. Gyalo later put a wholly different spin on his foreign contacts during this time. According to several contemporary interviews (including one with the author), he claims to have written letters in August 1952 to President Dwight Eisenhower and Chiang Kai-shek requesting assistance for Tibet. There is no evidence that such a letter was ever received in Washington; in fact, Eisenhower was not elected president until November. Gyalo further claims that the Indians, tipped off by the Americans, sent a senior political officer to Darjeeling in August to insist that Gyalo refrain from his letter-writing campaign. However, when Consul General Soulen met Gyalo the following month, the latter made no mention of the letters or associated Indian complaints. Gyalo also claims that Mullik specifically requested the 1953 Darjeeling meeting to offer his apologies for the letter incident; Mullik makes no mention of any letters and more plausibly describes his Darjeeling travels as part of a tour of the Tibetan expatriate community. See Mary Craig, *Kundun* (London: HarperCollins, 1997), p. 177; interview with Gyalo Thondup, 2 February 1998.

A close Gyalo associate, Lhamo Tsering, gives a slightly different version of events in a 1992 memoir. He claims that Gyalo sent telegrams to Dean Acheson and Chiang in

November 1952 asking for assistance, including foreign training for Tibetan guerrillas. See Knaus, *Orphans*, p. 119. Again, there is no evidence that such a telegram was ever received in Washington. It also stretches credibility to credit Gyalo with proposing foreign guerrilla training in 1952—three years before serious armed resistance in Tibet even existed.

13. Gyalo Thondup interview; interview with George Patterson, 30 August 1999; Craig, *Kundun*, p. 197. In contemporary interviews, Gyalo claims to have formed an umbrella organization of key Tibetan expatriates and sympathizers to spread propaganda leaflets inside Tibet and start an embryonic underground resistance. He contends that profits from his exports to Chinese troops were really part of a clever effort to gain funds for these covert ventures; he further alleges that his whiskey exporters got an extra dig at the Chinese by diluting the alcohol with urine (Knaus, *Orphans*, p. 123). Little of this can be corroborated, and it is probably an effort to recast cross-border profiting in a positive light. Princess Kukula, whom Gyalo claims was part of his umbrella organization, scoffs at the idea that she belonged to any such network (Kukula interview).

14. Smith, *Tibetan Nation*, p. 411 n.

15. Millian interview; Turner interview; Hoskins interview.

16. To make the Dalai Lama's visit more palatable to Beijing, Nehru had asked that the Panchen Lama—Tibet's second most prominent incarnation, who was feverishly being preened by the PRC—make the trip as well. Although the Chinese insisted that the Panchen Lama be given equal billing with the Dalai Lama during the Buddha Jayanti, Indian, Tibetan, and diplomatic audiences focused their attention squarely on the latter during the entire pilgrimage.

17. Smith, *Tibetan Nation*, p. 461 n. Gyalo claims that Nehru initially promised comfortable asylum to the Dalai Lama—"he could live in any of the Maharajahs' palaces"—if he attended the Buddha Jayanti, then hypocritically retracted the offer (see Craig, *Kundun*, p. 205). The Dalai Lama has never claimed that Nehru either directly or indirectly suggested that he seek exile during the Buddha Jayanti.

18. Mullik, *Chinese Betrayal*, p. 160; interview with CIA source, 26 March 2000. The issue of Tibetan independence was not taken up during the talks between Eisenhower and Nehru in Washington.

19. Foreign Broadcast Information Service (hereafter FBIS), Near East edition, 23 January 1957, p. 13.

20. As further indication of the low priority afforded to Tibet, the CIA station chief in India, Walter "Jack" Kaufman, received no background briefing on Tibet prior to his assignment to New Delhi in September 1954; nor did his predecessor, Henry "Robbie" Robertson, pass on any information about Tibet during their transition briefing. For the first two years of his tour, Kaufman recalls no involvement in any covert plans for Tibet. Interview with Walter Kaufman, 16 February 2000.

21. Interview with John Reagan, 18 June 1998. Hoskins was not privy to the debates over whether the Dalai Lama should seek exile or return home. "I was never informed of what Washington was thinking," he said, "so I could not and did not steer Gyalo one way or the other" (Hoskins interview).

22. Interview with Athar, 17 June 2000. Like many Khampas, Athar goes by only one name.

23. Ibid.

24. William M. Leary, *Perilous Missions* (University: University of Alabama Press, 1984), p. 132.

25. Interview with Pat Dailey, 9 August 1998. Dailey was one of three Western Enterprises advisers assigned to give jump training to ROC action teams during this period.

26. According to a June 1952 U.S. intelligence report, the Chinese air force was already dropping supplies to alleged pockets of mainland guerrillas. See "Special National Intelligence Estimate," June 1952, Declassified Documents Reference System (hereafter DDRS), #3015-1986. In fact, these supply drops were being conducted by CAT; the Chinese air force did not start flying covert drop operations until 1954. Interview with Irving "Frank" Holober, 29 July 1999. Holober was a WE adviser assigned to the Amdo guerrilla project.

27. Evan Thomas, *The Very Best Men* (New York: Simon and Schuster, 1995), p. 360 n.

28. "Joint Chief of Staff memorandum, subj.: Future Course of Action in Connection with Situation in Korea," 28 March 1953, DDRS, #165A-1981; Dailey interview.

29. "The Chargé in the Republic of China to the Department of State," 18 June 1953, in FRUS, 1952–1954, 14:209; "Statement of Policy by the NSC," 6 November 1953, ibid., p. 323.

30. "Memorandum of Conversation," 1 August 1956, in FRUS, 1955–1957, 3:415.

31. Thomas, *Very Best Men*, p. 155. One five-man Nationalist team was parachuted into Kwangtung Province in October 1956; four members were immediately killed, and the fifth commando was sentenced to death. See FBIS, East Asia edition, 1 August 1958, p. AAA3, and 4 September 1958, p. AAA12.

32. During an August 1956 NSC meeting, CIA director Allen Dulles noted that the top leaders of the PRC had been out of public view for the past seven weeks. See "NSC Memorandum, subj.: Discussion at the 417th Meeting of the NSC," 26 August 1956, DDRS, #2181-1997.

33. The agency, for example, had supported a failed anti-Soviet uprising among Ukrainian nationalists between 1949 and 1952. More embarrassing was its assistance to Polish insurgents beginning in 1950, which was revealed in December 1952 to have been turned from the start. During the same period, the CIA fell victim to another Soviet-orchestrated resistance sting in Albania.

34. Interview with Kalsang Gyatotsang, 31 January 1998.

35. Gyalo Thondup interview; Kalsang Gyatotsang interview.

36. Rekha Datta, *Why Alliances Endure: The United States–Pakistan Alliance* (New Delhi: South Asian Publishers, 1994), p. 58. In mid-1956, Pakistan again factored into U.S. strategic planning when aviation experts testifying at Senate hearings noted that the Soviet Union appeared on the verge of making an intercontinental ballistic missile. Pakistan, the Pentagon subsequently surmised, could be used both as the staging ground for bomber attacks and for surveillance activities.

37. Karachi was Milligan's first South Asia assignment. Earlier, he had won kudos in the Far East Division when he exposed a stream of PRC documents emanating from Hong Kong as part of a paper-mill scam run by fraudulent Chinese agents.

38. Correspondence with Walter Cox, 21 May 2000.

39. Reagan interview; interview with Jentzen Thondup, 18 November 1998.

40. Athar interview.

41. Ibid.

42. The Stateside ARC wing was intended for eventual deployment to England. Plans for a fourth ARC wing never came to fruition. "Department of Defense memorandum, subj.: Presentation for Delivery to the President's Committee on International Information Activities," undated, DDRS, #2479-1999.

43. "Initial Historical Report for 322 Troop Carrier Squadron, Medium (Special), 18 Sep 56–31 Dec 56," prepared by Captain Lewis M. Jolls (on file at Maxwell Air Force Base).

44. Interview with Herbert Dagg, 22 March 1998.

45. Interview with Justin Shires, 21 March 1998.

4. Saipan

1. Athar interview; interview with Harry Mustakos, 28 August 1998.

2. Athar interview; Chris Mullin, "Tibetan Conspiracy," *Far Eastern Economic Review*, 5 September 1975, p. 32.

3. Interview with Eli Popovich, 21 March 1998.

4. Interview with Jack Shirley, 7 August 1995; interview with Thomas Fosmire, 14 March 1995; interview with David Zogbaum, 9 June 1997.

5. Mustakos interview; Popovich interview.

6. Mustakos interview.

7. Popovich interview.

8. Geshe Wangyal, *The Door of Liberation* (Boston: Wisdom Publications, 1995), p. xvi.

9. Geshe Wangyal, *The Jewelled Staircase* (Ithaca, N.Y.: Snow Lion Publications, 1986), p. 19.

10. Knaus claims that Geshe Wangyal was dispatched from Tibet to Calcutta in the spring of 1951 by the Dalai Lama's mother for the purpose of contacting the U.S. consulate to seek assistance in having her son flee Tibet (see Knaus, *Orphans*, p. 87). Several CIA and State Department officials who were in Calcutta at the time have no knowledge of the Mongolian monk, and Norbu insists that Geshe Wangyal played no intermediary role between his family and the U.S. government. Correspondence with Thubten Norbu, 13 November 1998 (via Mary Pattison); Turner interview; Thacher interview; Dalley interview.

11. The Freewood Acres land was donated to the Mongolians by Countess Tolstoy, descendant of both the famed writer and the OSS officer who visited Tibet during World War II. Correspondence with Ted Jacobs, 22 May 2000; interview with David Urubshurow, 2 December 1999.

12. Interview with David Regg, 19 January 2000.

13. Interview with George Zournas, 24 January 2000. Zournas studied under Geshe Wangyal at Columbia.

14. Popovich interview.

15. Mustakos interview.

16. Ibid.

17. There have been contemporary claims among the Tibetan expatriate community that Wangdu rebelled while on Saipan and, as a result, was placed in isolation by the CIA staff.

Mustakos denies any such disciplinary problems: "There were only three small buildings in our compound. We could not have isolated anybody if we wanted to; there was simply no room" (Mustakos interview).

18. Athar interview.

19. Ibid.

20. Mustakos interview.

21. Ibid.

22. Interview with Roger McCarthy, 16 May 1997.

23. "Indian surveillance no doubt spotted all this unusual behavior," speculates Hoskins. "They weren't stupid" (Hoskins interview).

24. The "ST" prefix denotes an operation under the Far East Division's China Branch.

25. After a B-17 was downed by a communist MiG-17 in June 1956, further mainland penetrations staged from Taiwan were forbidden during the moonlit phase. But because the PLA radar network and interceptor fleet were concentrated along the coast facing Taiwan—and Tibet was relatively barren of air defenses—moonlit infiltrations in the Tibet sector were not considered unduly risky.

26. "Memorandum from Dulles to Brigadier General Andrew J. Goodpaster, subj.: U-2 Overflights of Soviet Bloc," 18 August 1960, DDRS, #0022-2000.

27. Kalsang Gyatotsang interview.

28. In the summer of 1955, a second special air unit had briefly taken shape on Taiwan. Flying at the behest of the USAF, three Chinese crews used converted PB4Y subchasers on electronic-collection flights over the mainland in what was known as Operation FOX TERRIER. After fourteen successful infiltrations through the spring of 1956, FOX TERRIER was terminated, and the electronics missions were assumed by the B-17s of the Special Mission Team.

29. Interview with Gar Thorsrud, 3 December 1999.

30. Interview with Robert Kleyla, 19 June 1998.

31. Interview with James McElroy, 15 September 1997.

32. Each of the team bundles included two sets of radios, backup signal plans, Tibetan boots and attire, ground barley (tsampa, a Tibetan staple) and jerked beef, Tibetan and Indian currency, a pamphlet message of encouragement from the Dalai Lama, waterproof maps, a compass, small cooking pots, binoculars, a shovel, Tibetan knives, shielded flashlights with extra batteries, signal mirrors, a first-aid kit, flares, matches in waterproof containers, writing materials, ponchos, a .303 rifle for each member, and ammunition. In addition, each member jumped with a Sten submachine gun, extra magazines, and some canned rations in a small bag attached by D-rings to the individual. The main radio operator designated for each team carried the primary signal plans for the radio. Roger E. McCarthy, *Tears of the Lotus* (Jefferson, N.C.: McFarland, 1997), p. 241.

33. Interview with Walter Cox, 6 July 2000.

34. The CIA had brought in a generator to provide electricity at Kurmitola, but the cable leading from the generator to the radio shed had frayed and come in contact with the shed's tin roof. When the technician attempted to erect an antenna atop the shed, he grounded himself and absorbed the charge (Cox interview).

35. Thorsrud interview.

36. The Tibetans follow a lunar calendar that generally lags four to six weeks behind the Western solar-based calendar.

37. Athar interview.

38. Ibid.

39. The sons of Lutheran missionaries in Japan, Stuart Buck and his brother Frank spoke Japanese like natives. With an ear for Asian languages, Stuart went on to learn Tibetan, while Frank (who worked for a time at the CIA's Foreign Broadcast Information Service in Japan) became fluent in Mongolian. Holober interview; Hisao Kimura, *Japanese Agent in Tibet* (London: Serindia Publications, 1990), p. 213.

40. Holober interview.

41. Interview with Stanislaw Putko, 19 October 1998.

5. Four Rivers, Six Ranges

1. Estimates of Tibet's population vary widely. Goldstein (*History of Modern Tibet*, p. 611 n) places the figure at a little more than 1 million in 1945. Mullik (*Chinese Betrayal*, p. 3), the Indian spymaster, put it at 3 million in 1950. An official 1953 census gave an estimated figure of "over" 3 million ethnic Tibetans. The Dalai Lama claimed 6 million countrymen as of 1958 (Tenzin Gyatso, *Freedom in Exile*, p. 129). The 3-million figure used in this chapter is the mean of these estimates.

2. Gompo Tashi Andrugtsang, *Four Rivers, Six Ranges* (Dharamsala, India: Information and Publicity Office of H. H. The Dalai Lama, 1973), p. 42

3. Ibid., p. 48.

4. Officials in Lhasa had another reason to profess indifference to the revolt in the east: both Kham and Amdo had already been officially detached from Tibet and absorbed as provinces of the PRC.

5. Yet another of the Dalai Lama's older brothers, Lobsang Samten, had briefly served as lord chamberlain in 1955 before being named a member of the PCART security department. Phala succeeded Lobsang as lord chamberlain.

6. Damshung was designed to accommodate Il-28 transports, but after the first Il-28 landed and failed to take off, the runway fell into disuse. It was subsequently converted into a horse racetrack and trade fairground every autumn by nomadic herdsmen. Tibetan exiles later claimed that the chief engineer was the son of rich parents who had been killed in a communist purge; in retaliation, he intentionally sited Damshung on poor soil. Tashi Chutter, *Confidential Study on Deployment of Chinese Occupational Force in Tibet* (New Delhi, 1998), p. 84.

7. Athar interview.

8. Journalist Chris Mullin ("Tibetan Conspiracy," p. 32) claims that the CIA was furious with its radiomen for leaving their Lhasa perch and following Gompo Tashi. Athar says that the agency fully approved of their move (Athar interview).

9. Kalsang Gyatotsang interview.

10. Estimates of the number of guerrillas in attendance vary between 1,500 and 5,000. The larger figure probably includes rebel pockets assumed to be in other parts of Tibet. Knaus, *Orphans*, p. 350 n. 30.

11. Gompo Tashi, *Four Rivers*, pp. 72–74.

12. Holober interview.

13. Athar interview.

14. Gyalo Thondup interview; interview with Lhamo Tsering, 7 February 1998.

15. Holober interview.

16. Ibid.

17. By that time, the parent unit of the sanitized C-118 had ceased to exist. In November 1957, the 322nd Squadron had fallen victim to the sharp budget-cutting knives of the second Eisenhower administration. But even though the USAF had elected to dissolve the squadron, the CIA believed that the 322nd's special cell at Kadena filled a vital airlift niche, supplementing the capabilities of its own air proprietaries. To satisfy the CIA's requirements, the former squadron's Detachment 1 was retained intact under the new designation Detachment 2, 313th Air Division. As before, Detachment 2 received assignments from the CIA air operations office in Tokyo. "Historical Report for 322 Troop Carrier Squadron, Medium (Special), period 1 Jul to 8 Dec 57, prepared by Cpt. Lewis M. Jolls" (on file at Maxwell Air Force Base).

18. Interview with Roland Andersen, 10 September 1997.

19. Thorsrud interview; Andersen interview.

20. Interview with James Keck, 12 February 1997.

21. Ibid.

22. During his first attempt to return to Tibet, Tom's party was ambushed by PLA border guards. Taking casualties, the Tibetans recrossed into Sikkim. Tom located Gyalo Thondup and procured a fake Bhutanese identity card and successfully infiltrated via Bhutan.

23. During a September 1958 interview, the Dalai Lama claimed that the troubles in Tibet were being "instigated by a handful of reactionaries." See FBIS, East Asia edition, 17 September 1958, p. AAA4.

24. Gompo Tashi, *Four Rivers*, p. 89.

25. Knaus, citing Lhamo Tsering, claims that the second supply drop took place on 22 February 1959. Athar, as well as several crew members on the C-118, distinctly recalls that the second drop was conducted in November 1958 (Athar interview; Andersen interview; interview with William Demmons, 5 August 1998; interview with Bill Lively, 3 February 1998; McElroy interview).

26. Four decades later, this "yellow parachute" controversy was still being debated within the Tibetan exile community in India (Athar interview; interview with Donyo Jagotsang, 5 February 1998).

6. Virginia

1. Interview with John Greaney, 8 May 1997.

2. Holober interview. After one trip to Washington, Geshe Wangyal returned to Freewood Acres with badly broken ribs from an apparent mugging. "He said he had fallen against the corner of a desk," remembers one of his students, "but I was shocked one day shortly after, as he was convalescing, to see a sharp butcher's knife under his pillow" (correspondence with Ted Jacobs).

3. Interview with Thomas Fosmire, 22 June 1997.

4. A detailed account of Fosmire's Indonesian experiences can be found in Kenneth Conboy and James Morrison, *Feet to the Fire* (Annapolis, Md.: Naval Institute Press, 1999).

5. Thomas, *Very Best Men*, p. 50.

6. Ibid., p. 55.

7. In 1955, China Base shifted from Yokosuka to Subic Bay in the Philippines. Ibid., p. 157.

8. Telephone conversation with James Lilley, 10 July 1998.

9. Fosmire interview. Although both Frank Wisner and Des FitzGerald were eager proponents of the Tibetan resistance, the previous Far East Division chief, Al Ulmer, never shared their enthusiasm. "I didn't want it," says Ulmer of the Tibet program during his watch (correspondence with Al Ulmer, 15 May 2000, via Marguerite Ulmer).

10. David Wise, *The Politics of Lying* (New York: Random House, 1973), p. 183; Kristin Kenney Williams, "Camp Hale's Top Secret," *Vail Trail*, 3 July 1998, p. 8.

11. Greaney interview.

12. Lhamo Tsering interview.

13. Fosmire interview.

14. Interview with William Smith, 30 October 1997.

15. Interview with Ray Stark, 1 March 1999; Knaus, *Orphans*, p. 218.

16. Interview with John Kenneth Knaus, 17 June 1998.

17. Interview with Anthony Poshepny (Poe), 2 October 1997. A full account of Poe's participation in the Indonesian operation can be found in Conboy and Morrison, *Feet to the Fire*.

18. Fosmire interview.

19. Gompo Tashi, *Four Rivers*, p. 91.

20. In October 1997, an American journalist—citing an anonymous source allegedly in the CIA—claimed that the agency had secretly scripted the oracle's instructions to the Dalai Lama, including a detailed escape route from Lhasa. See John B. Roberts II, "The Dalai Lama's Great Escape," *George*, October 1997, p. 132. This is false, says Tibet Task Force officer Holober. "The CIA never had any plans for evacuating the Dalai Lama; we did not have that kind of contact" (Holober interview).

21. Thirty-six years later, an article in *China Youth Daily*, an official government publication, implausibly claimed that PLA troops had had the Dalai Lama's escape party in their gun sights but allowed him to escape Lhasa because Mao Tse-tung wanted to divide the Tibetan upper class and see who supported Beijing. See "Mao Let the Dalai Lama Escape," *International Herald Tribune*, 11 July 1995.

22. The CIA agents had an understanding with NVDA headquarters that regular updates would be forwarded to Lhuntse Dzong. Athar interview.

23. Ibid. The Dalai Lama remembers the recoilless rifle being fired but notes that it was "not an impressive performance" (Tenzin Gyatso, *Freedom in Exile*, p. 140).

24. Athar interview.

25. "Discussion of the 400th Meeting of the NSC," 26 March 1959, DDRS, #2240-1997.

26. Written evidence of this sentiment can be found in a 31 March 1959 CIA memorandum written by the agency's representative on the Operations Coordinating Board (OCB).

With an OCB lunch discussion scheduled for the following day, the representative wrote that "it is in U.S. interests to assist in the establishment of a Tibetan Government in Exile, and specifically to do all we can to help the Dalai Lama escape." Established in 1953, the OCB was Eisenhower's preferred instrument for coordinating sensitive foreign operations approved by the president. "CIA Memorandum for Mr. Karl G. Harr, Jr. and Mr. Bromley Smith, subj.: Exploitation of Tibetan Revolt," DDRS, #618-1997.

27. The two-man film team, which had been dispatched by Gyalo Thondup earlier in the year to get movie footage of the NVDA's exploits, had stopped short of the front and instead went to Lhuntse Dzong to record the Dalai Lama's escape.

28. In his autobiography, the Dalai Lama fails to mention that news of approval for his asylum came from the CIA radiomen; instead, he claims that members of his escape party went forward to the border and received the approval.

29. When leaving Lhasa, the Dalai Lama's party had taken a satchel of Tibetan paper currency, which was all but worthless in India. Before crossing the border, Tom and Lou gave the entourage 200,000 Indian rupees they had received in the second weapons drop. The two agents retained 40,000 rupees for their future operations; the other 60,000 rupees had already been used to pay couriers to deliver rolls of film and sketches to Gyalo Thondup and to offset travel costs for prospective agent recruits destined for Kalimpong.

30. Untitled Department of State message dated 2 April 1959, DDRS, #1620-1985.

7. Whale

1. Interview with John Waller, 17 June 1998.

2. Ibid.

3. John Waller, writing under the pen name John Rowland, notes that the PRC was the first country to announce the Dalai Lama's entry into India, a scoop attributed to the efficiency of Beijing's spy network. See Rowland, History of Sino-Indian Relations, p. 112.

4. The paraphrased message from the Dalai Lama eventually reached the desk of President Eisenhower a week later on 30 April. It was subsequently restated in a formal scroll written in Tibetan script, with full seals attached.

5. Interview with Tashi Choedak, 2 February 1998. Choedak was one of the students who received English lessons between late 1956 and the spring of 1959.

6. White House message, "Synopsis of State and Intelligence material reported to the President, March 31, 1959, " DDRS, #2061-1991; Rowland, History of Sino-Indian Relations, p. 113; White House message, "Synopsis of Intelligence material reported to the President, May 2, 1959," DDRS, #2756-1991.

7. Editorial Note (intelligence briefing notes for 1 April 1959), in FRUS, 1958–1960, 19:753.

8. "White House Staff Notes #56," 8 April 1959, DDRS, #1370-1985; Department of State memorandum, "Memorandum for the President from Acting Secretary Douglas Dillon, subj: Message from the Dalai Lama," 30 April 1959, in FRUS, 1958–1960, 19:764; "NSC memorandum, subj: Discussion at 404th Meeting of the NSC," 30 April 1959, DDRS, #1640-1997.

9. "Memorandum from Director of Central Intelligence Dulles to the President's Special Assistant for National Security Affairs," 31 March 1959, in FRUS, 1958–1960, 19:554–555; "Memorandum for President Eisenhower's Files," 6 April 1959, ibid., pp. 555–557.

10. "Memorandum Prepared by the Central Intelligence Agency," undated (circa 25 April 1959), in FRUS, 1958–1960, pp. 758–759; Athar interview.

11. FBIS, East Asia edition, 8 May 1959, p. BBB1; Athar interview; Demmons interview; Gompo Tashi, Four Rivers, p. 106.

12. Bureau of H. H. the Dalai Lama, Tibetans in Exile, 1959–1969 (New Delhi: Gutenberg Printing Press, 1969), pp. 1–2; Tashi Choedak interview; Donyo Jagotsang interview; interview with Pema Wangdu, 15 July 1998.

13. Pema Wangdu interview; Donyo Jagotsang interview.

14. Tashi Choedak interview.

15. Editorial Note (memorandum of discussion, 403rd meeting of the NSC, 23 April 1959), in FRUS, 1958–1960, 19:755. According to the official PLA history, China's armed forces attacked the "heart of the Tibet uprising" on 21 April, killing more than 2,000 rebels. Siyi and Bian, Zhong, p. 1408.

16. The rebels had initially made the mistake of fighting in large groups, said Dulles at a 30 April NSC briefing, and would probably discover that the essence of guerrilla warfare consists of fighting in small bands. "NSC Memorandum, subj: Discussion at 404th Meeting of the NSC," 30 April 1959, DDRS, #1640-1997.

17. L. Fletcher Prouty, "Colorado to Koko Nor," Sunday Empire (Denver Post magazine), 6 February 1972, p. 12. Beijing recognized the vulnerability of its road network. According to the official PLA history, as of mid-1959, the equivalent of four divisions were used to keep the roads into eastern Tibet secure and open. Siyi and Bian, Zhong, p. 1408.

18. Smith, Tibetan Nation, pp. 422, 489; Lowell Thomas, Jr., The Silent War in Tibet (New York: Doubleday, 1959), p. 128.

19. "Memorandum on the Substance of Discussion at a Department of State–Joint Chiefs of Staff Meeting," 1 May 1959, in FRUS, 1958–1960, 19:561; Prouty, "Colorado to Koko Nor," p. 12. Prouty, a USAF lieutenant colonel who served as liaison between the USAF and the CIA during part of ST BARNUM, mistakenly claims that the Koko Nor team was composed of Tibetans trained at Camp Hale.

20. "White House message, subj: President Eisenhower's Far Eastern Trip," 6 June 1960, DDRS, #000489-1987.

21. "Discussion of the 338th Meeting of the NSC," 2 October 1957, DDRS, #33750-1991.

22. In a move not supported by the United States, the ROC in April 1958 instructed its Airborne Regiment (a unit separate from the Special Forces) to qualify an additional 10,000 soldiers for airborne duty; Taipei intended this number to eventually triple. "Despatch from the Embassy in the Republic of China to the Department of State," 3 April 1958, in FRUS, 1958–1960, 19:13; "Letter from the Assistant Secretary of State for Far Eastern Affairs to the Ambassador to the Republic of China," 29 April 1958, ibid., pp. 19–20.

23. The Anti-Communist National Salvation Army was the name originally attributed to the pro-ROC units that staged from Burma into Yunnan Province during the early 1950s.

This was later adopted as an umbrella title for virtually all ROC agents and raiding units infiltrating the mainland during the 1960s.

24. These infiltrations appear to have picked up during the Taiwan Strait crisis in the summer of 1958 and may have been partially used for their diversionary effect.

25. For a sampling of the many reported captures, see FBIS, East Asia edition, 31 July 1958, p. AAA13; 5 September 1958, p. AAA12; 23 September 1958, p. CCC1; 29 September 1958, p. BBB1; 7 October 1958, p. BBB10.

26. Rowland, *History of Sino-Indian Relations*, p. 162; Smith, *Tibetan Nation*, p. 428; "Telegram from the Ambassador in the Republic of Korea to the Department of State," 16 September 1957, in FRUS, 1955–1957, 3:604. There are indications that the Soviets may have stoked the Xinjiang uprising.

27. In 1957, China opened the first lead and zinc mines in northern Amdo. One year later, copper mining started in the province, followed by coal in 1959. Exploitation of numerous other resources, such as uranium and borax, did not begin until the early 1960s. Research and Analysis Centre, *Tibet, a Land of Snows* (Dharamsala: Department of Security of H. H. the Dalai Lama, 1991), pp. 9, 12, 21.

28. FBIS, Far East edition, 17 October 1958, p. BBB1; 20 October 1958, p. BBB1; interview with Jonathan Lipman, 13 November 1958.

29. Poe interview.

30. FBIS, East Asia edition, 24 March 1959, p. DDD1; 26 March 1959, p. DDD2; 30 March 1959, pp. DDD2–3; 7 May 1959, p. DDD1; 8 May 1959, p. DDD1.

31. Among the ROC recruiters was Tsepah Dorje, a pilot and an ethnic Amdowa who fled to Taiwan in 1950 and joined the ROC's Office for Tibetan and Mongolian Affairs. In 1957, he arrived in Kalimpong to recruit Tibetan agents on behalf of Taipei. Rebuffed the first time around, he returned in late May 1959 and remained in Kalimpong for nearly two months. During that time, he scored the ROC's only recruitment success when he lured six Lithang Khampas and some elderly Amdowas to Taiwan for radio training. After they completed their instruction, however, plans to infiltrate the team were canceled, and all the trainees resettled in the ROC (Athar interview; Kalsang Gyatotsang interview). Taipei unconvincingly claimed that 3,000 Tibetans entered Yunnan Province in May 1959 and joined forces with pro-ROC rebels in that area. See FBIS, East Asia edition, 15 June 1959, p. DDD1.

32. FBIS, East Asia edition, 27 May 1959, p. DDD2.

33. "Discussion at the 400th Meeting of the NSC," 26 March 1959, DDRS, #2240-1997; "Memorandum for President Eisenhower's Files," 6 April 1959, in FRUS, 1958–1960, 19:557.

34. Demmons interview; McElroy interview.

35. Office of the Director, "Memorandum for General Andrew J. Goodpaster, subj.: U-2 Overflights of Soviet Bloc," 18 August 1960, DDRS, #0022-2000.

36. Interview with Truman Barnes, 19 September 1997; interview with Richard Peterson, 8 September 1997.

37. Ibid.

38. Given the similarity of these flight profiles with those of the earlier ST BARNUM

drops, several of the C-118 crew members incorrectly assumed that the ST WHALE agents were ethnic Tibetans from ST CIRCUS. In fact, they were two separate programs.

39. Lively interview.

40. McElroy interview; Keck interview; Peterson interview.

8. Dumra

1. Tashi Choedak interview. The nearby town of Leadville recorded a minimum average temperature of twenty-six degrees Fahrenheit during the month of May 1959.

2. Stark interview.

3. Fosmire interview; Stark interview.

4. Poe interview; Fosmire interview.

5. Stark interview.

6. Ibid.

7. Tashi Choedak interview; Greaney interview.

8. Interview with Sioux Zilaitis, 31 October 1997; Fosmire interview.

9. Poe interview; Fosmire interview; Greaney interview; Stark interview. Some case officers recall a rocket hitting the electrical lines running into the Climax Molybdenum mine near Leadville. Steve Voynick, a Colorado historian who spent years researching the mining company's records, found no evidence of a rocket incident affecting Climax Molybdenum. Correspondence with Nancy Manly, 8 July 1998.

10. Wise, *Politics of Lying*, p. 185; Robert Byers, "Atom Unit Making Tests Near Leadville," *Denver Post*, 16 July 1959, p. 1.

11. Interview with Jack Wall, 4 September 1997; Fosmire interview.

12. Poe interview.

13. Greaney interview.

14. Interview with Billie Mills, 20 October 1997.

15. Thorsrud interview.

16. Knaus (*Orphans*, p. 155) claims that permission to use the C-130 followed from a call by CIA Deputy Director Charles Cabell to USAF Deputy Chief of Staff Curtis LeMay. This is disputed by CIA air branch officer Gar Thorsrud (Thorsrud interview).

17. Mills interview.

18. Ibid.

19. McElroy interview.

20. Mills interview.

21. Of the four, two were from the Lithang Khampa group that had earlier been diagnosed with tuberculosis, another was a Lithang member deemed academically unfit, and the last was a medical washout from the twenty-man contingent that arrived in May 1959. Lhamo Tsering interview.

22. Ibid.

23. Thorsrud interview; CIA memorandum for General Goodpaster, 18 August 1960.

24. Greaney interview; Fosmire interview.

25. In the summer of 1959, ten of the USAF's fifty Asia-based C-130s were assigned to a

classified general-war alert standby mission. Those ten were no longer available for intratheater airlift operations. Robert L. Kerby, "American Military Airlift During the Laotian Civil War, 1958–1963," *Aerospace Historian* 24, no. 1 (March 1977): 4; Fosmire interview; Mills interview.

26. Thorsrud interview; Mills interview.

27. Keck interview.

28. Fosmire interview.

9. Hitting Their Stride

1. Lhamo Tsering interview; Fosmire interview.

2. Correspondence with Roger McCarthy, 17 March 2000.

3. Interview with Donyo Pandatsang, 5 February 1998.

4. *Life International*, 12 October 1959, p. 18.

5. Lively interview; interview with Ron Sutphin, 3 August 1998; interview with Jack Stiles, 6 September 1997.

6. Interview with Shep Johnson, 30 August 1997.

7. Interview with Ed Beasley, 18 September 1997.

8. Keck interview; Stiles interview.

9. Hudson had removed the survival belt when he went to change into cold-weather gear, a routine for all crew members prior to reaching the frigid skies above Tibet. CIA officers gave Hudson a polygraph test upon his return from the mission before concluding that the coins had indeed been lost and not stolen. Interview with Tom Sailor, 3 September 1997; interview with Doug Price, 25 April 1998.

10. Lhamo Tsering interview; Athar interview; Tashi Choedak interview.

11. Andersen interview; Stiles interview; interview with Neese Hicks, 10 September 1997.

12. Keck interview; Price interview; William M. Leary, "Secret Mission to Tibet," *Air and Space*, January 1998, p. 70.

13. Interview with Miles Johnson, 7 August 1995; Peterson interview.

14. Hicks interview; Keck interview.

15. Fosmire interview.

16. Greaney interview.

17. To allow more payload per plane, Tom Fosmire had lobbied hard to save the considerable weight of rigging and have the aircraft actually land on Tibetan soil and unload the supplies. He went so far as to send a message to Pembar for the agents to begin looking for a suitable landing strip. Fosmire interview; Tashi Choedak interview.

18. Donyo Pandatsang interview.

19. Ibid.

20. Athar interview. Two of the original Saipan students, Athar and Lhotse (Tom and Lou) were exfiltrated to Camp Hale in November 1959 to serve as interpreters. While in Colorado, Athar reviewed the radio traffic from Nathan and the Amdo team.

21. Hicks interview; Shep Johnson interview.

22. The prohibition against communist-bloc overflights was extended to include missions

into China flown by ROC crews in U.S.-supplied aircraft. This resulted in cancellation of a critical resupply flight for an ROC team dropped in Anhui Province during April. Monitoring the hapless agents from Taiwan, CIA case officer Jack Shirley could offer no help as the team radioed frantic pleas before being overrun by communist troops. Interview with Jack Shirley, 25 July 1995.

23. Of the five agents who originally moved from Pembar toward Amdo, all were killed. Of the seven agents in Nathan's augmentation team, six were killed. The one exception was Choni Yeshi, a Lithang Khampa whose family members were servants of Gompo Tashi. He was captured and kept in prison until November 1978. While in detention, he was coerced into making a complete confession, which was used by Chinese propagandists in an attempt to win over the local population. Upon his release, Yeshi did not leave for India but elected to remain near Lhasa, where he worked as a motorcycle mechanic.

10. Markham

1. Des FitzGerald would later earn a reputation for being cavalier with the lives of indigenous agents on some of his Asian operations. Not so, insists Tibet Task Force chief Roger McCarthy. "Des made a comment in my presence to a case officer involved with National Chinese operations involving an airdrop of personnel onto the Chinese mainland in 1958; the comment was to the effect that anyone involved in the operation had better remember that those were not leaflets being dropped, but people and that there had better be as good a plan and preparation as possible. . . . He was indeed an honorable man, and no cowboy as some have painted him" (correspondence with McCarthy).

2. "Memorandum for the Record, subj.: Discussion with the President on Tibet, 4 February 1960," DDRS, #3577-1999.

3. Correspondence with Bhusang, 6 February 1998. In November 1959, fifteen Tibetans had arrived at Hale just days after the departure of the Pembar contingent. Athar interview.

4. Interview with Don Cesare, 20 July 1998.

5. Ibid.; Fosmire interview.

6. Interview with Willard Poss, 21 May 1999.

7. Ibid.

8. Poe interview; Poss interview.

9. McCarthy interview; Poss interview.

10. Cesare interview.

11. Although Eisenhower was reluctant to restart U.S. overflights, the ROC resumed aerial penetrations of mainland China (agent drops, not U-2 photo missions) within a month after the downing of Francis Gary Powers. See *Chung-kuo chih i*, p. 209.

12. Cesare interview. The Tibetans were prohibited from watching television because the CIA was afraid they would discover the location of Hale. Unknown to the agency, the students were already in the know. During 1960, some of the Tibetans had secretly watched a news telecast in the instructors' quarters and saw references to Denver. In addition, when

one of the interpreters accompanied a sick trainee to the clinic at Fort Carson, he saw a highway sign for Colorado Springs. Interview with Thinlay Paljor, 9 October 1998.

13. Poe was irritated with what he claims was a series of security breaches at Hale, including one incident when a Quonset hut burned down (apparently due to an exploding propane heater). Others suggest that Poe was irate because Zilaitis, rather than himself, was selected as Fosmire's deputy and eventual successor. Poe interview; Stark interview; Fosmire interview.

14. Most of the Hale case officers grew deeply attached to the Tibetans, leading to media reports that some even adopted Buddhism and chanted Buddhist mantras to seek solace (for the most recent such claim, see *Vail Trail*, 3 July 1998). Not true, says Fosmire, a devout Catholic. "The Tibetans held regular religious services at Hale, but there was never a case officer who converted" (Fosmire interview).

15. Greaney interview. On 23 July 1960, Dulles went to the Kennedy compound at Hyannis Port, Massachusetts, to give the candidate a briefing on sensitive matters. The next and last preelection briefing was held on 19 September at Kennedy's Georgetown town house. Tibet was not discussed at either.

16. Fosmire interview. Fosmire left the Tibet Task Force shortly thereafter; by March, he was in Laos as one of the first field advisers for the fast-expanding CIA paramilitary program there.

17. "Memorandum for the 303 Committee," 26 January 1968, in FRUS, 1964–1968, 30:741. In 1955, the National Security Council issued two directives (numbered 5412/1 and 5412/2) establishing a special committee to issue approval for all major CIA covert operations. Taking its name from the directives, the 5412 Committee initially consisted of representatives designated by the president, Department of State, and Pentagon. A representative chosen by the director of the CIA acted as the committee secretary. Decisions reached by the committee were forwarded to the president for final approval. During the Kennedy administration, the 5412 Committee was known as the Special Group. In June 1964, the name was changed again, this time to the 303 Committee.

18. Tibet was not the only place where the CIA was continuing its flawed concept of blind agent drops. In the spring of 1961, its Far East Division was just beginning a series of parachute infiltrations into North Vietnam. The program was to prove an embarrassing failure. For a detailed discussion, see Kenneth Conboy and Dale Andradé, *Spies and Commandos: How America Lost the Secret War in North Vietnam* (Lawrence: University Press of Kansas, 2000).

19. Knaus confuses two agents with similar names: Yeshi Wangyal (Tim) and Choni Yeshi, one of the Peary-trained members who first parachuted near Nam Tso and then again to augment the Amdo team (see Knaus, *Orphans*, p. 227). The former was the son of the Markham chieftain; the latter was a Lithang native and servant of Gompo Tashi.

20. Tim picked two teammates from among the group that had arrived at Hale in November 1959 and four from among his own group that had exfiltrated to Colorado in 1960. Athar interview.

21. Bhusang, making calculations from a Tibetan calendar, estimated the date of his parachute jump as 15 March, which would have been during a moonless period. Lobsang

Jamba, who jumped into Tibet with a different team on 2 April, distinctly remembers Tim's team departing Takhli forty-eight hours earlier on 31 March. Because it is during the full moon, 31 March is the more likely date. Interview with Lobsang Jamba, 10 October 1998.

22. Tashi Choedak interview. When the team passed through Kadena en route to Takhli, it encountered Temba Tileh, one of the two older agents who had parachuted near Nam Tso and exfiltrated via Nepal in 1960. Although the rest of the Nam Tso team had been dropped again to augment the agents near Amdo, Temba and the other older operative had remained behind at the safe house. Because he was still theoretically available for deployment, consideration was given to adding him to Tim's team, but given his age and unfit condition, the idea was quickly dropped. Lobsang Jamba interview.

23. Miles Johnson interview.

24. As the only surviving member of the Markham team, Bhusang is the sole source of information about its fate. Based on a 1998 interview with Bhusang, Knaus gives an account of the Markham mission in his book (see *Orphans*, pp. 228–232). For the account in this book, the authors relied on a detailed debriefing report for Indian officials dated 26 December 1980, just weeks after Bhusang arrived in Indian exile. The authors corroborated these details with information supplied by Bhusang in another Indian account entitled "Debriefing Report of Tseten Tashi, One of the Ten 'Spies' Released by the Chinese in November 1978," as well as a 6 February 1998 correspondence from Bhusang and extracts of an interview with Bhusang in a 1998 BBC documentary entitled "The Shadow Circus: The CIA in Tibet."

25. According to an official PLA history, the Chinese armed forces launched six major operations against rebel bases in Tibet during early 1960. Although sweeps continued through March 1962, Beijing declared that the backbone of the rebel movement was broken by July 1960. Siyi and Bian, *Zhong*, p. 1408.

11. Mustang

1. Bureau of the Dalai Lama, *Tibetans in Exile*, pp. 129, 171. Use of the Tibetans in this manner caused controversy. Boys as young as twelve were considered fair game for the gangs. In addition, the work, which included building dams and cutting roads along sheer mountainsides, was extremely hazardous. Deaths started to mount, and compensation was often not paid.

2. Hari Bansh Jha, *Tibetans in Nepal* (Delhi: Book Faith India, 1992), p. 25; Bureau of the Dalai Lama, *Tibetans in Exile*, p. 136.

3. Michel Peissel, *Mustang, a Lost Tibetan Kingdom* (Delhi: Book Faith India, 1967), p. 125.

4. Ibid., p. 203.

5. Interview with Gen Gyurme, 5 February 1998; Robert Ragis Smith, "The History of Baba Yeshi's Role in the Tibetan Resistance" (humanistic studies honors thesis, Johns Hopkins University, 1998), p. 26.

6. Mahendra's policy worked. For example, after a 1957 Chinese promise of assistance without strings, the United States saw no alternative but to boost its own aid. And after

Mahendra was feted in the Soviet Union in 1958, Eisenhower scrambled to match this with an invitation to visit Washington. Successive delays (some caused by the inability of palace astrologers to come up with an auspicious day) forced postponement of his U.S. tour to April 1960. Once in the United States, Mahendra spent the first seventeen days on official duties, followed by half a month of vacation stops, including a hunting trip in the Rockies. Nagendra Kr. Singh, *Foreign Aid, Economic Growth, and Politics in Nepal* (New Delhi: Anmol Publications, 1996), p. 14; interview with Ralph Redford, 4 December 1999.

7. Interview with John Cool, 12 January 1999. Even the CIA station at the U.S. embassy in Kathmandu suffered from poor communications. Redford was initially forced to rely on the British embassy to transmit coded cables to Washington, and a Jesuit missionary he had befriended, Father Marshall Moran, helped relay radio messages within the kingdom. Moran was later falsely accused of being a CIA agent. Redford interview; Donald Messerschmidt, *Moran of Kathmandu* (Bangkok: White Orchid Press, 1997), p. 215.

8. Redford interview.

9. Interview with Baba Yeshi, 11 October 1998.

10. Ibid.

11. Gen Gyurme interview.

12. Lobsang Jamba interview.

13. Ibid.; Gen Gyurme interview.

14. Lobsang Jamba interview.

15. The two radiomen had been trained on Saipan in early 1960 as part of a seven-man group; other members of that training contingent were used as Lhamo Tsering's staff at Darjeeling. Tashi Choedak interview.

16. Interview with Kenneth Cathey, 29 April 1998; Stark interview.

17. S. C. Bhatt, *The Triangle of India, Nepal, and China: A Study of Treaty Relations* (New Delhi: Gyan Publishing House, 1996), p. 147.

18. Baba Yeshi interview.

19. Gen Gyurme interview; Baba Yeshi interview; Knaus, *Orphans*, p. 242. As the Tibetans made their way to Nepal, New Delhi voluntarily turned a blind eye. Although news of the exodus appeared in Calcutta's *Statesman* newspaper, the Indian authorities convinced the editors of other leading dailies to spike the story. Cathey interview.

20. Peissel, *Mustang*, p. 264.

21. Baba Yeshi interview; Gen Gyurme interview.

22. Poss interview.

23. Lobsang Jamba interview.

24. Interview with Bista Temba, 21 October 1998.

25. Gen Gyurme interview; Baba Yeshi interview.

26. Datta, *Why Alliances Endure*, pp. 57, 78.

27. Critchfield's full title was head of the Near East and South Asia Division. "We handled everything from Greece, Turkey, and Cyprus, over to East Pakistan," recalls Critchfield. "There was even an ongoing debate over whether we had jurisdiction over Libya." Interview with James Critchfield, 27 February 2001.

28. Interview with James Critchfield, 9 November 1999; John Kenneth Galbraith, *A Life in Our Times* (Boston: Houghton Mifflin, 1981), p. 395. Galbraith claims not to have made

the "Rover Boy" comment during the CIA briefing. Correspondence with John Kenneth Galbraith, 6 July 1999.

29. "Memorandum from the Ambassador to India (Galbraith) to Under Secretary of State for Economic Affairs (Ball)," 30 November 1961, in FRUS, 1961–1963, 22:170.

30. In November 1960, the Indian government sent a protest to Beijing over airspace violations earlier that year by what New Delhi claimed were Chinese aircraft. Mullik, in fact, already knew that the planes had been flown by CIA pilots, following confidential discussions with agency officials. The Indian authorities at the time warned Ambassador Bunker that if the United States was planning more Tibetan airdrops in the future, it would be wise for the U.S. planes to avoid flying over Indian territory, because it would create a "tremendous furor if one was downed." Bunker correctly interpreted this to mean that the Indian government was not averse to covert aid for the Tibetans but was anxious to avoid turning public opinion against the United States. See "Telegram from the Embassy in India to the Department of State," 26 November 1960, in FRUS, 1958–1960, 19:814.

31. Critchfield interview; interview with Duane Clarridge, 12 November 1999. Galbraith himself makes negative light of the fact that the Tibetan operation began under Eisenhower's tenure. See "Memorandum from the Ambassador to India to Under Secretary of State for Economic Affairs," 20 November 1961, in FRUS, 1961–1963, 22:171.

32. Even within the Far East Division, support for the Tibet Task Force fluctuated. One who was less than steadfast was China Branch chief John Hart. According to Roger McCarthy, "Hart's support was more a reflection knowing Des [FitzGerald] was fully supportive, as was Dulles and [Deputy Director for Plans] Richard Bissell. Hart was not enthusiastic about paramilitary operations in general [as he] did not believe it was worth angering China and saw it as a no-win situation given political realities in India and China. Hart had served in Korea and was still impressed with Chinese streaming across the border along the Yalu, which he apparently read as Chinese military strength rather than the use of massed troops who were not well trained or led" (correspondence with Roger McCarthy, 12 October 2000).

33. Critchfield interview.

34. Cathey interview.

35. Ibid.

36. Hoskins interview.

37. Greaney interview; Cathey interview. In hindsight, Rositzke says that the Tibet project was "well run and run intelligently" (telephone conversation with Harry Rositzke, 20 June 1998).

38. The three radiomen had been part of a training contingent that arrived at Hale in November 1959. Athar interview.

39. Lobsang Jamba interview.

40. Gen Gyurme interview.

41. Galbraith, A Life in Our Times, p. 396.

42. Bista Temba interview.

43. Gen Gyurme interview.

44. Interview with Tashi Punzo, 14 October 1998. Punzo was one of the three guerrillas at Ross's side during the ambush.

45. One unit ate meat just twice between February and May Day 1961, read one report, and the shortages were starting to affect physical fitness.

46. J. Chester Cheng, "Problems of Chinese Communist Leadership as Seen in the Secret Military Papers," *Asia Survey* 4, no. 6 (June 1964): 862 n.

47. FRUS, 1961–1963, 22:170; Department of State *News Letter*, December 1961, p. 3.

12. Favored Son

1. Interview with Lyle Brown, 4 August 1998.

2. Ibid.

3. Lobsang Jamba interview.

4. Gen Gyurme interview.

5. *Colorado Springs Free Press*, 8 December 1961, p. 1.

6. Ibid.; *Colorado Springs Gazette Telegraph*, 8 December 1961, p. 1.

7. Wise, *Politics of Lying*, p. 191.

8. Cesare interview; Tashi Choedak interview.

9. James Critchfield, head of the Near East Division, had gone to New York in 1961 for a discreet meeting with Mullik, who was coming to the United States for an Interpol meeting. "We had decided to put our money on him," said Critchfield, "and invested a lot in a major briefing." It was on that occasion that Mullik restated his approval of the Tibet operation. Critchfield interview.

10. Apart from its dwindling role in providing paramilitary assistance, the Tibet Task Force was involved in some peripheral political action during the second half of 1961. For example, the CIA offered quiet support when the Dalai Lama announced plans in the summer of 1961 to begin scripting a new, more representative constitution. The agency also offered some discreet lobbying assistance when the topic of Tibet was again debated in the United Nations, resulting in a December 1961 resolution calling for an end to human rights abuses and supporting Tibetan self-determination.

11. Interview with William Grimsley, 21 April 2000.

12. "National Intelligence Estimate #13-4/1-62 (supplement to NIE 13-4-62), Annex B: Military," 29 June 1962, DDRS, #3010-1998. According to an official PLA history, clearing operations against the Tibet rebels concluded in March 1962. Over the previous three years, the Chinese armed forces claimed to have killed, wounded, or captured more than 93,000 traitors and taken 35,500 weapons, including over 70 cannons, 41 radios, and 25 parachutists. Siyi and Bian, *Zhong*, p. 1408.

13. During 1961, the companies were known as either Left Units or Right Units, depending on their location east or west of the Kali Gandaki. Beginning in 1962, they were given numerical designations between one and sixteen.

14. Brigadier J. P. Dalvi, *Himalayan Blunder* (Dehra Dun, India: Natraj Publishers, 1969), p. 166.

15. "Department of State Intelligence Report, subj: The Relations of Communist China and India: Problems and Prospects," 31 March 1960, DDRS, #353B-1981, p. 7.

[handwritten marginalia: ALL "FACTS", anyway I suppose — Not Believable!]

16. "CIA Special National Intelligence Estimate #13/31-62, subj: Short-term Outlook and Implications for the Sino-Indian Conflict, November 9, 1962."

17. Dennis Kux, *Estranged Democracies* (New Delhi: Sage Publications India, 1994), p. 202.

18. Major General S. S. Uban, *Phantoms of Chittagong* (New Delhi: Allied Publishers, 1985), p. 74.

19. The Tibetan guerrilla formation, later known as the Special Frontier Force, recognizes 26 October 1962 as its official date of establishment.

20. Gyalo Thondup interview.

21. Ibid.

22. Rowland, *History of Sino-Indian Relations*, pp. 168, 171.

23. *Aviation Week and Space Technology*, 19 November 1962, p. 39.

24. "Memorandum for the Record," in FRUS, 1961–1963, 19:396.

25. Editorial Note, in FRUS, 1961–1963, 22:324; "Letter from the Ambassador to India to President Kennedy," 13 November 1962, ibid., 19:381. In his recollection of the Harriman mission, Galbraith claims that he had serious reservations about the presence of Des FitzGerald, whom he described as one of the most irresponsible officers in the CIA. See Galbraith, *A Life in Our Times*, p. 436.

26. Interview with David Blee, 22 November 1999.

27. Ibid.

28. Hicks interview; interview with Cliff Costa, 3 February 1999; interview with John Condon, 3 February 1999; interview with Bill Lively, 3 February 1999.

29. "Fifteen DCIs' First 100 Days," *Studies in Intelligence* 38, no. 5 (1995): 4; *Aviation Week and Space Technology*, 26 November 1962, p. 30.

30. "Memorandum of the 303 Committee," 26 January 1968, in FRUS, 1964–1968, 30:741; Knaus interview.

13. Chakrata

1. Lieutenant Colonel Gautam Sharma, *Indian Army: A Reference Manual* (New Delhi: Reliance Publishing House, 2000), pp. 159, 166. The 4th Gorkha (Indian spelling of Gurkha) Rifles departed Chakrata in 1959; the 1st Gorkha Rifles departed in 1960.

2. Gita Mehta, *Snakes and Ladders* (London: Vintage, 1997), p. 9.

3. Biographic information on Biju Patnaik came from M. S. Kohli, 12 February 2001.

4. Mustakos interview. The Pentagon attempted to soft sell the number of advisers involved by saying that it would involve "35 of our people initially and perhaps more later." See "Memorandum from Robert W. Komer of the National Security Staff to President Kennedy," 16 February 1963, in FRUS, 1961–1963, 19:494.

5. Interview with Wayne Sanford, 21 November 1998.

6. Ibid.

7. Mustakos interview; interview with Thomas Thompson, 11 September 1997; interview with Charles Seifarth, 5 January 1997.

8. Sanford interview.

9. Mustakos interview.

10. Ibid.

11. Interview with Jamba Kalden, 13 March 1992.

12. Uban, *Phantoms*, p. 74.

13. Mustakos interview.

14. Thompson interview; Mustakos interview.

15. Uban, *Phantoms*, p. 79.

16. Interview with S. S. Uban, 5 February 1998; Seifarth interview; Thompson interview.

17. Uban interview; Seifarth interview.

18. Mustakos interview; Thompson interview. Uban recalls that one Tibetan hung himself because he could not parachute due to a malformed ankle (see Uban, *Phantoms*, p. 74). M. K. Anand, an airborne training officer who worked closely with Establishment 22, insists that there were never any suicides among the Tibetans. Interview with M. K. Anand, 15 February 2001.

19. Uban interview; Mustakos interview.

14. Oak Tree

1. Anand interview.

2. Prior to 1959, Thorsrud belonged to the Far East Division's aviation desk. In early 1959, however, the new deputy director of plans, Richard Bissell, decreed that all aviation-related units—particularly the U-2 project, which he had earlier managed—now be collected under a new Developmental Projects Division (DPD). The DPD answered directly to Bissell, enabling him to retain a close watch over the U-2. During the 1961 Bay of Pigs operation, however, the DPD's role was criticized due to its overly independent command structure. On 17 February 1962, Bissell resigned over the Bay of Pigs fiasco. Two days later, the DPD was disbanded. Strategic reconnaissance programs such as the U-2 subsequently went into a separate directorate, while covert air support units were grouped under the Air Branch of a new Special Operations Division (SOD). Both Marrero and Thorsrud now fell under the SOD.

3. Thompson interview. Plans for Intermountain to use the Fulton system in Indonesia are detailed in Conboy and Morrison, *Feet to the Fire*, pp. 162–165. Intermountain's involvement with a Fulton snatch from an arctic iceberg is recounted in William Leary and Leonard LeSchack, *Project Coldfeet* (Annapolis, Md.: Naval Institute Press, 1996).

4. Thorsrud interview.

5. *Aviation Week and Space Technology*, 3 June 1963, p. 21.

6. Sanford interview.

7. Thorsrud interview.

8. Anand interview. Mullik, who was aloof even in the best of times, may have felt pressure by mid-1963 to temper his cooperation with the United States. This was partly because Moscow, having weathered the Cuban missile crisis and no longer needing to appease Beijing, was looking to mend fences with New Delhi by again hinting at its willingness to

sell jet fighters. For its part, the United States was dragging its feet on cementing a major military aid package for India because the Kennedy administration did not want to completely burn its bridges with Pakistan and because the Indians were talking about arms assistance in unrealistic terms ($1.3 billion over five years was the excessive figure they proposed in May). Kux, *Estranged Democracies*, p. 213.

9. Interview with Angus Thuermer, 17 February 2000.

10. Once the Oak Tree parachute facilities were complete in early 1964, Establishment 22 no longer made use of Agra. The initial C-46 instructors under Welk included M. D. Johnson and Al Judkins—both veterans of the C-130 drops in Tibet—as well as Maurice Clough. They departed India after two months. Connie Siegrist and Tom Sailor provided additional C-46 training at Charbatia in early 1964. Interview with James Rhyne, 29 April 1998; interview with Connie Siegrist, 2 October 1993.

11. Rhyne interview; Thompson interview.

12. Interview with Bruce Walker, 9 June 1998.

13. Interview with Wangchuk Tsering, 13 October 1998.

14. Ibid.

15. Sanford interview. Indian fears about China's ability to resume an attack were probably overstated. The Intelligence Bureau believed that there were still 20,000 Chinese troops poised on the border as of mid-1963. Although the CIA put PLA strength in all of Tibet at 103,800 troops in May, overhead photography indicated only about 1,000 soldiers scattered along the Indo-Tibetan frontier. "National Intelligence Estimate #13-63, subj.: Problems and Prospects in Communist China," 1 May 1963, DDRS, #3012-1998.

16. Walker interview; interview with Cheme Namgyal, 30 January 1998; interview with Temba Wangyal, 30 January 1998.

17. Cheme Namgyal interview.

18. "Memorandum for the Special Group," 9 January 1964, in FRUS, 1964–1968, 30:731; Cheme Namgyal interview.

15. The Joelikote Boys

1. Sanford interview.

2. "Memorandum for the Special Group," 9 January 1964, in FRUS, 1964–1968, 30:731; Gen Gyurme interview.

3. With the CIA paying the hospital bill, Gompo Tashi was escorted to London by former Hale translator Rocky. He died in Darjeeling on 27 September 1964.

4. Interview with Pema Doka, 15 October 1998.

5. Gen Gyurme interview.

6. Bista Temba interview. Temba was a court official for the late king.

7. The Mustang leadership would claim that its lack of contact with the PLA was because the guerrillas had scared the Chinese out of their sector. More likely, the PLA saw little reason to devote assets against the placid guerrillas. Aside from unconfirmed reports of

PLA reconnaissance patrols near the northern boundary of Mustang, there were never any cross-border attacks against the guerrilla camps. Gen Gyurme interview.

8. Interview with Tendar, 30 October 1998.

9. Patterson later wrote a book about his trip to Tsum. See George N. Patterson, *A Fool at Forty* (Waco, Tex.: Word Books, 1970). The account in this book generally conforms to the recollections of Tendar.

10. Tendar interview.

11. Gen Gyurme interview.

12. The original villa was at F-20 Haus Khaz; within six months, the center shifted down the street to a slightly larger two-floor house at F-6/A Haus Khaz.

13. Walker interview. Even after the arrival of Knaus, Grimsley still retained responsibility for contact with the Tibetan refugee community in India; he also maintained close ties with Gyalo Thondup and channeled the CIA's stipend to the Dalai Lama's entourage at Dharamsala. Once Knaus began handling Tibet programs from India, the Tibet Task Force in Washington was downgraded to a desk function within the China Branch.

14. Colby's lament about agent operations in another communist country, North Vietnam, is recounted in chapter 9 of Conboy and Andradé, *Spies and Commandos*.

15. Once all the Tibetans had cleared out of Hale in mid-1964, the camp was declared "excess to U.S. Army needs" and officially closed by the end of that year. In 1966, the U.S. Forest Service assumed administration of the site. See "Hearings Before Sub-Committee of the Committee on Appropriations," House of Representatives, 89th Congress, 16 February 1965.

16. Within the CIA and Intelligence Bureau, Charbatia was code-named Station A, the Special Center was Station B, and Joelikote was Station C.

17. Gillian Wright, *Hill Stations of India* (Lincolnwood, Ill.: Passport Books, 1991), p. 94. Between 1960 and 1962, nearly 2,000 Tibetan refugees had assembled at Walung. Due to the scarcity of grazing land in that area and resultant disputes with Nepalese locals, most crossed into India. Bureau of the Dalai Lama, *Tibetans in Exile*, p. 158.

18. Lhamo Tsering interview. Team Q was intended as a "border watch communications team" that would primarily collect intelligence from refugees, traders, and herdsmen.

19. As the agent teams were preparing to cross into Tibet, the CIA had only anecdotal information on possible underground resistance. One clue came on 25 July 1964, when the Lhasa News Service announced rewards for turning in pistols, rifles, light machine guns, heavy machine guns, and even artillery pieces. See Ling Nai-min, ed., *Tibet 1950–1967* (Hong Kong: Union Research Institute, 1968), p. 528.

20. Team A, growing comfortable in Gangtok, did not budge. Team B in Shimla was equally unwilling to venture toward the border. Team T at Walung eventually crossed the frontier, only to sprint back to camp after three days.

21. Pemako's mystique among Tibetans derives from its frequent yeti sightings and a macabre cult in which travelers are killed by potions concocted by local women in order to gain merit and wealth.

22. Interview with Temba Wangyal, 1 February 1998. Temba was a member of Team D.

23. Cheme Namgyal interview. Cheme was a member of Team Z.

16. Omens

1. FBIS, East Asia edition, 16 October 1964, p. BBB1.

2. The CIA later admitted that its prediction of the first Chinese nuclear test was in large part a comedy of errors that resulted in an intelligence success. See H. Bradford Westerfield, ed., *Inside CIA's Private World* (New Haven, Conn.: Yale University Press, 1995), p. 244.

3. Interview with Lobsang Tsultrim, 10 October 1998.

4. Three other Tibet offices—in Kathmandu, London, and Tokyo—were not supported by CIA funds. The Kathmandu office, established in 1960, primarily handled refugee affairs.

5. In late 1964, the International Commission of Jurists conducted an interview of new refugees and concluded that there was systematic abuse of human rights in Tibet. Based on these findings, Gyalo wanted to push for a United Nations resolution calling for Tibetan independence. This met with resistance from India, which was willing to deplore Chinese violations of civil rights but considered anything more an unnecessary provocation of Beijing. In order to win New Delhi's approval, the resolution language was toned down for the October 1965 draft, which passed the General Assembly in December.

6. Sanford interview.

7. Interview with M. S. Kohli, 11 February 2001. Kohli led the Nanda Devi expedition.

8. Three out of four Helios had been destroyed by accidents before the end of 1964. In the first incident, which took place at the Charbatia polo field in November 1963, a plane slammed hard into the end of the runway in a downdraft, resulting in loss of the airframe but no casualties. In May 1964, a Helio dipped its wing into a river at night; the pilot died in the subsequent crash. In November 1964, an overloaded Helio clipped a fence line on takeoff. Rhyne interview; interview with S. K. Bajaj, 15 June 2000.

9. Interview with Harry Aderholt, 7 July 1992; Air America Captain William Andresevic, who had flown the Helio extensively in Laos, was ordered in the summer of 1964 to fly a Twin Helio to Bolivia for evaluation by the U.S. embassy. He gave the plane mixed reviews, in part because its extra weight placed too much stress on the rear wheel, and in part because it did not offer any additional cargo space over the regular Helio, despite the extra engine. The Indians, however, praised the Twin Helio for its enhanced stability on landing and the security offered by a second engine. Interview with William Andresevic, 21 February 1997; Bajaj interview.

10. Bajaj interview.

11. The Indians accused Pakistan of using U.S.-supplied tanks. A study by the State Department's Bureau of Intelligence and Research reported the use of infantry weapons, but not armor. Kux, *Estranged Democracies*, p. 270 n.

12. Ibid., p. 215.

13. During an end-of-tour briefing for CIA officials in 1963, Galbraith lavished praise on the agency. James Critchfield, the Near East Division chief, was in attendance and reminded Galbraith of his scathing 1961 criticism by rhetorically asking the ambassador, "Does this mean you're recanting the 'Rover Boys' comment?" Later, in March 1967, Galbraith wrote an article for the *Washington Post* in which he highlighted the CIA's India activ-

ities in a positive light. This created such a stir in the Indian parliament that both CIA director Richard Helms and Critchfield contacted Galbraith and implored him to be more discreet. "Telegram from the Embassy in India to the Department of State," 28 March 1967, in FRUS, 1964–1968, 25:827–828; Critchfield interview.

14. Sanford interview.

15. Condon interview; Costa interview. Both Condon and Costa flew on the 727 shuttles.

16. The director general of security also oversaw the Special Service Bureau (SSB). A brainchild of Mullik and Patnaik in late 1962, the SSB was an attempt to promote nation building among the tribal populations along India's frontiers with Tibet and Pakistan, in the event they were overrun by enemy forces. Through a combination of civic action and paramilitary training, an SSB border network was constructed with the assistance of British advisers. Mullik claimed that the SSB operated effectively during the 1965 war with Pakistan. See Mullik, *Chinese Betrayal*, p. 493.

17. In November 1964, Ken Knaus left the Special Center and returned to Washington. After more than half a decade of involvement with the Tibet project, Knaus shifted out of the Far East Division when Des FitzGerald, who would soon be promoted to deputy director of plans, invented for him the new slot of counterinsurgency officer for Latin America.

18. In several cases, teams infiltrating Tibet for a second season had their letter designators doubled. Team D, therefore, became Team DD during 1965. Temba Wangyal interview.

19. Cheme Namgyal interview; Tashi Choedak interview.

20. The case of singleton Ares, who was doubled for almost a decade, is detailed in Conboy and Andradé, *Spies and Commandos*.

21. Only one of the Establishment 22 guerrillas, who lost an arm in a firefight with the PLA, managed to reach India. Returning to Chakrata, he lobbied to undergo airborne training at Agra. Accommodating the resilient Tibetan, Indian instructors fashioned a special parachute harness that compensated for his missing limb. Anand interview.

22. The fate of Irving and the other agents captured by the Chinese was derived from details in a paper entitled "Debriefing Report of Tsenten Tashi, One of Ten 'Spies' Released by the Chinese in November 1978." An English copy of this report, which was prepared by Indian and Tibetan intelligence officials, was provided to the authors.

23. This was not the first time Beijing had treated infiltrators with surprising leniency. In November 1957, an ROC B-26 was downed on a covert mission over the mainland. Three crew members were captured and held for ten months before being unconditionally released back to Taiwan.

24. A censored 16 September 1965 State Department intelligence report gives details on PLA camps east of Tingri. Although the source of this information is deleted, the Tibetan agents at Tingri are likely suspects. "Department of State Research Memorandum, subj.: Summary of Chinese Communist Activities Related to India-Pakistan," 16 September 1965, DDRS, #1959-1998.

25. To improve the reliability and frequency of radio transmissions from Nepal, the Special Center began to deploy a large number of Hale-trained agents. At the Kaisang headquarters was Team K, consisting of two agents. This team, in turn, controlled five more two-man teams strung out along the Nepalese frontier. At the extreme northwest, in the Limi valley, was Team W; because Limi was populated by ethnic Tibetans who frequently

crossed to nearby sacred Mount Kailash, Team W spent its time debriefing these pilgrims. Two other teams went to Dolpo, the region just northwest of Mustang, and two more went to Tsum and Nashang, regions to the southeast.

26. "The Communist Chinese have made their presence felt in steadfastly neutral Nepal. They have built a road north to Tibet that everyone believes is a tank road" (*New York Times*, 15 September 1968, p. 112).

27. In July 1964, Air Ventures voluntarily flew a single covert mission at the behest of the CIA station chief in Kathmandu, Howard Stone. After a senior Chinese official secretly defected to the Nepalese capital (Beijing mistakenly assumed that he was dead), the CIA looked for ways to smuggle him out to Taiwan. Flying at low level, Air Ventures helicopter pilot Jerome McEntee took the defector to Charbatia without Indian complicity. On the pretext of servicing two ARC C-46 transports, a CIA-operated DC-6 arrived at Oak Tree, took aboard the ex-communist while the plane was taxiing at the end of the runway, and spirited him out of India. Interview with Robert Kay, 24 November 1999; interview with Howard Stone, 18 June 1998; interview with Henri Verbrugghen, 19 May 1999; interview with Jerome McEntee, 19 November 1999. Kay was the Air Ventures station manager; Verbrugghen was aboard the DC-6 flight that flew the defector out of Charbatia.

28. The CIA station in Kathmandu was extremely sensitive to charges of complicity with the guerrillas at Mustang. In September 1964, press statements from the Nepalese government claimed that four "huge" weapons caches had been uncovered in the countryside; it was later acknowledged that the weapons had come from China, apparently for communist sympathizers. The Soviet Union later attempted to link this discovery with Mustang and falsely claimed that CIA station chief Howard Stone had been declared persona non grata over the matter. In fact, the Nepalese government did lodge a protest against Stone, but for a different reason. Using what was then the latest recording technology, the Soviets had spliced together a tape of Stone supposedly making antiroyalist remarks, a copy of which was given to Nepal's foreign minister. U.S. Ambassador Henry Stebbins vigorously defended Stone against the forged tape, and the CIA chief remained in Nepal until his scheduled departure in late 1965. *New York Times*, 30 September 1964, p. 12; Stone interview; Rustem Galiullin, *The CIA in Asia* (Moscow: Progress Publishers, 1988), p. 79.

29. Verbrugghen interview.

30. Gen Gyurme interview.

31. Verbrugghen interview; interview with Franke Janke, 15 May 1999; interview with John Fogarty, 9 May 1999. Verbrugghen, Janke, and Fogarty were all kickers on the flight.

32. Baba Yeshi interview.

33. Gen Gyurme interview.

34. The Mustang guerrillas may have proved themselves of some value during the third quarter of 1965. During early September, a U.S. intelligence report detailed increased PLA truck and troop movement along the Lhasa-Xinjiang road north of Mustang. This coincided with the Indo-Pakistani conflict in Kashmir. Although the source of this information is censored, it was probably the Mustang guerrillas. "Department of State Research Memorandum, subj.: Summary of Chinese Communist Activities Related to India-Pakistan," 16 September 1965, DDRS, #1959-1998.

17. Revolution

1. Kux, *Estranged Democracies*, p. 250.

2. "Minutes of Meeting of the 303 Committee, 22 April 1966," 26 April 1966, DDRS, #2460-1999.

3. "Text of Cable from Ambassador Bowles," 28 April 1966, DDRS, #3302-1999.

4. Walker interview.

5. Tashi Choedak interview.

6. Gen Gyurme interview.

7. Ibid.; Tendar interview; Baba Yeshi interview; Lobsang Tsultrim interview.

8. "Memorandum for the 303 Committee," 26 January 1968, in FRUS, 1964–1968, 30:740.

9. During a July 1966 trip to Moscow, Mrs. Gandhi offered less than nonaligned remarks about the U.S. role in Vietnam. Although such words pleased her Soviet hosts, President Johnson was livid. Any further thought of linking Vietnam with India's willingness to open a second front in Tibet was quietly dropped.

10. Seifarth lived with his wife at a bungalow at Dehra Dun, a privilege only he enjoyed due to his close rapport with Brigadier Uban. Uban interview; Seifarth interview.

11. On his way back to San Diego, Gougelmann apparently unleashed some of his fury on captured Japanese. His official files include a letter of admonition dated 18 August for his conduct in the treatment of prisoners.

12. *New York Times*, 13 December 1947, p. 1.

13. Critchfield interview.

14. Interview with Don Stephens, 14 April 2000.

15. Interview with Alan Wolfe, 28 April 2000.

16. Gougelmann's maritime effort is detailed in Conboy and Andradé, *Spies and Commandos*.

17. Fosmire interview.

18. A sensor had been hurriedly left near the summit of Nanda Devi in October 1965, with the intention of assembling the device properly during the following climbing season. When a second expedition returned to the mountain in May 1966, it discovered that the nuclear generator had been swept away in an avalanche. Fearful that its contents would spill into the sacred Ganges River and poison millions of Hindu worshippers, U.S. and Indian mountaineers began combing Nanda Devi's lower slopes to locate the missing equipment. On 23 July, Gougelmann flew to the Nanda Devi Sanctuary aboard an ARC chopper to inspect this recovery effort.

19. Interview with Henry Booth, 11 April 2000.

20. Uban interview.

21. Sanford interview.

22. Jamba Kalden interview.

23. Although the Tibetans still occasionally made use of the large airborne training base at Oak Tree, Sarsawa's closer proximity to Chakrata made it the favored location for SFF parachute instruction.

24. Hale graduate Conrad, who sampled the special *tsampa* in 1965, remembers that it

had an oily residue but overall good taste. A 1997 letter to the author from Kellogg's Consumer Affairs Department stated that information on the *tsampa* was considered "proprietary and confidential." Cheme Namgyal interview; correspondence with Diane Backus, Kellogg's Consumer Affairs Department, 1 August 1997.

25. Anand interview.

26. Thuermer interview; Grimsley interview.

27. "Memo for Secretary from Acting Secretary," 21 March 1967, DDRS, #1524-1982.

28. Interview with Woodson Johnson, 27 November 1998.

29. Critchfield interview.

30. Victor Marchetti and John D. Marks, *The CIA and the Cult of Intelligence* (New York: Alfred A. Knopf, 1974), p. 50.

31. Lobsang Tsultrim interview; FRUS, 1964–1968, 30:741.

32. Interview with John Rickard, 15 November 1999.

33. Bajaj interview.

34. Grimsley interview.

18. Civil War

1. Gen Gyurme interview.

2. Gyalo Thondup interview.

3. Interview with Kesang Kunga, 6 February 1998.

4. Gen Gyurme interview.

5. Lhamo Tsering interview.

6. Tashi Choedak interview.

7. *A History of Sino-Indian Relations* and "American Diplomacy and the God King," *Foreign Service Journal* (February 1967): 36–37, were both published under the pen name John Rowland. *Tibet: A Chronicle of Exploration* (London: Routledge and Kegan Paul, 1970) was published under Waller's second pen name, John MacGregor.

8. As RAW director, Kao eventually came to wear a second hat as director general of security.

9. Targeting these sources was not new. Duane Clarridge, a CIA officer assigned to Kathmandu in the late 1950s, recruited a Nepalese trader who had good contacts at the Nepalese mission in Lhasa. See Duane R. Clarridge with Digby Diehl, *A Spy for All Seasons: My Life in the CIA* (New York: Scribner, 1997), p. 67.

10. Peissel, *Mustang*, p. 34.

11. "Memorandum prepared by the Central Intelligence Agency," 23 February 1968, in FRUS, 1964–1968, 30:660.

12. Wangchuk Tsering interview.

13. Arnold does not discount the possibility that his ROC competitors scored their own successes. "They might have had some of the same sources as us," he noted (ibid.).

14. Kesang Kunga interview.

15. Lhamo Tsering interview; Lobsang Tsultrim interview.

16. Gyalo Thondup interview. Gyalo kept the extent of his contact with Soviet officials a

secret from the CIA and Intelligence Bureau until after it ceased. During a December 1968 conversation with State Department officials, he admitted to having private meetings with Soviet officials, who had allegedly shown greater sympathy toward a potential Tibet resolution at the United Nations. "Memorandum of Conversation," 6 December 1968, in FRUS, 1964–1968, 30:743.

17. Interview with William Stites, 19 November 1998.

18. Tashi Choedak interview.

19. Blee interview.

20. Bajaj interview.

21. CIA airborne adviser Alexander MacPherson, a Scot by birth and a naturalized U.S. citizen, qualified the first Indian free-fall parachutist from an An-12 in May 1968.

22. Chutter, *Confidential Study*, p. 19.

23. In the summer of 1968, Tucker Gougelmann finished his tour and was replaced as the senior CIA paramilitary adviser by another former marine, Joseph "Dick" Johnson. In mid-1970, Johnson completed his posting and was not replaced by a successor.

24. Uban, *Phantoms*, p. 40.

25. P. P. Talwar, "Scruffy Guerrillas Are Full of Life," *Sainik Samachar*, 2 August 1987, p. 8.

26. Uban interview.

27. Ibid.

28. During the brief December 1971 war, there were fears in Washington that Beijing would intervene on behalf of Pakistan, which in turn would draw the Soviet Union into a wider South Asian conflict. If this had happened, Nixon would have warned Moscow that the United States would not accept Soviet intervention against China if Beijing took action against India. National security adviser Henry Kissinger claims that Nixon would have backed China in that scenario. If true, this is remarkable, given the CIA's nearly decade-long paramilitary program in India to guard against Chinese attack. "National Security Council Memorandum," 4 February 1977, DDRS, #3409-1999; Kux, *Estranged Democracies*, p. 323 n.

19. A Pass Too Far

1. Later guests included former secretary of defense Robert McNamara.

2. Interview with Gen Wongya, 27 October 1998; Bista Temba interview; Peissel, *Mustang*, p. 148.

3. Interview with Gyanu Babu Adhikari, 31 October 1998.

4. *The Rising Nepal*, 26 July 1974, p. 1; Gen Gyurme interview.

5. Tashi Choedak interview; Gyanu Babu Adhikari interview.

6. Gyanu Babu Adhikari interview; Gen Gyurme interview.

7. Gen Gyurme interview.

8. Interview with James Lys, 21 November 1998; Gyanu Babu Adhikari interview.

9. *The Rising Nepal*, 16 October 1974, p. 1. In January 1975, King Birendra handed out another 200 medals, certificates, and cash awards for the Mustang operation. *Far Eastern Economic Review*, 7 February 1975, p. 35; Gyanu Babu Adhikari interview.

10. *The Rising Nepal*, 15 October 1974, p. 1. Not wishing to point the finger at the United States, the Nepalese Home Ministry claimed that the captured gear could be purchased in "some markets."

11. *The Rising Nepal*, 12 September 1974, p. 1; 13 September 1974, p. 4.

12. Wangchuk Tsering interview.

Epilogue

1. Conversation with R. N. Kao, 14 February 1998.

2. Uban's son, Brigadier G. S. Uban, would later command the SFF until October 2000.

3. Anand interview; interview with Bruce Lehfeldt, 19 May 1999. One of the experimental chutes, with a twenty-eight-foot canopy made of nonporous cloth, was found unsuitable. A larger conical chute was used during successful high-altitude jumps at Ladakh during May 1977.

4. Lieutenant General K. S. Brar, *Operation Blue Star, the True Story* (New Delhi: UBS Publishers, 1993), p. 39.

5. *Far Eastern Economic Review*, 20 February 1976, p. 5; 20 May 1977, p. 33. Kathmandu's angst was somewhat understandable. Arms caches were still being uncovered several years after Kaisang was occupied (in 1976, Kaisang was converted into the Mountain Warfare School of the Royal Nepalese Army). Near Tangya, two boys herding yaks were killed by unexploded ordnance as late as 1991.

Index _____

See page 49 + Clipp NY Times Sept 15 – 2002

"Tim". BROugt by JST. v. H to USA. He had gone to Tibet from Outer - Mongolia as a youth. He has walked from there to The Dalai Lama's place in Tibet.

An Impressive man who Loved Ice-cream and scared son D. J. v. H in his play-pen. (NY-city)